SOVIET SCENE

SIX PLAYS OF RUSSIAN LIFE

TRANSLATED BY

ALEXANDER BAKSHY

IN COLLABORATION WITH
PAUL S. NATHAN

WITH AN INTRODUCTION BY ALEXANDER BAKSHY

NEW HAVEN

YALE UNIVERSITY PRESS

1946

THE OLIVER BATY CUNNINGHAM
MEMORIAL PUBLICATION FUND

The present volume is the twenty-second work published by the Yale University Press on the Oliver Baty Cunningham Memorial Publication Fund. This Foundation was established May 8, 1920, by a gift from Frank S. Cunningham, Esq., of Chicago, to Yale University, in memory of his son, Captain Oliver Baty Cunningham, 15th United States Field Artillery, who was born in Chicago, September 17, 1894, and was graduated from Yale College in the Class of 1917. As an undergraduate he was distinguished alike for high scholarship and for proved capacity in leadership among his fellows, as evidenced by his selection as Gordon Brown Prize Man from his class. He received his commission as Second Lieutenant, United States Field Artillery, at the First Officers' Training Camp at Fort Sheridan, and in December, 1917, was detailed abroad for service, receiving subsequently the Distinguished Service Medal. He was killed while on active duty near Thiaucourt, France, on September 17, 1918, the twenty-fourth anniversary of his birth.

CONTENTS

THE SOVIET DRAMA

BY ALEXANDER BAKSHY

DURING the entire century that preceded the revolution Russia produced only three dramatists of world standing—Gogol, Tolstoy (with some reservations), and Chekhov. Five other dramatists—Griboyedov, Sukhovo-Kobylin, Ostrovsky, Gorky, and Andreyev—hold honored places in the history of Russian drama. But the appeal of the first four of these is almost entirely confined to Russian audiences, and the world reputation of the last, Andreyev, has not proved enduring.

It is therefore no reflection on Soviet Russia to say that within the life-span of a single generation it has produced no plays to take rank with those that had already become part of the world repertory. On the other hand the pattern of Russian life has deviated so much from that of the Western world that even a good Soviet play often seems strange and alien to people who live under different conditions and have a different set of moral values.

In the early Soviet plays which denounce and ridicule the ways of capitalist society or glorify the Soviet heroes of the civil war this difference of outlook is not yet so marked as to present a barrier to their appreciation. The sufferings of the poor, the selfishness and lust for power of the privileged, the heroic loyalty to their cause of the revolutionary masses and their leaders—these all reflect moral values that are understood and largely accepted throughout the world. But Soviet society has gradually developed its own characteristically Soviet mental attitudes and ethics, and these, it has to be admitted, have proved much more foreign to the Western mind than mere revolutionary or proletarian sentiments. One such mental attitude which figures prominently in numerous Soviet plays—from the farcical "Squaring the Circle" by Katayev to the realistic "Far Taiga" by Afinogenov—is the ready acceptance of a paternalistic authority acting as supervisor, mentor, and arbiter in the private affairs of the citizens. Another, an expression of the new Soviet ethics, is the more recent emphasis on "positive" characters who are introduced into plays as models of Communist behavior. Confronted with these paragons of virtue, so thoroughly imbued with the ideal of public good that they are incapable of a single selfish act, the non-Russian playgoer or reader is apt to repeat the words of a character in Ilyenkov's "The Square of Flowers": "I don't like saints. It makes me nervous to be around them." Nor are these "positive" characters only honest, straightforward, considerate, and public spirited. They are also inexhaustibly resourceful and resolute—they always do the right thing at the right time. Unquestionably, as ideal types they are in line with the traditional concepts of the Russian intelligentsia. But the Western world is not accustomed to so much virtue in everyday life. Like Lenin in Pogodin's "The Chimes of the Kremlin," it believes in "imperfect, erring people." At least, being itself imperfect and erring, it feels it can understand them better.

All these important differences notwithstanding, the best of Soviet drama rises sufficiently above its local limitations to assume a significance that is universal. Certainly there can be no quarrel with social consciousness as such. Innumerable worthless plays with not a trace of civic spirit have been written and produced in America and Europe, just as innumerable worthless plays glorifying the revolution, industrial progress, or the defense of the Fatherland have been written and produced in Soviet Russia. It must also be remembered that Soviet playwrights, like other Soviet citizens, could neither retire into seclusion during the years of the civil war and the last World War, nor stand aloof from the political campaigns which marked the twelve frantic years of the Five Year Plans. Under those conditions it was inevitable that drama as art should suffer, however much immediate national or party interests may have gained through the playwrights' participation in the political life of the country.

A good illustration of what this meant in the fortunes of Soviet drama is provided by the first seven years that followed the revolution. During that period of political turmoil and physical privation the theaters continued to give performances and even managed to produce new plays. But Soviet drama was practically non-existent. The Moscow Art Theater did not produce a new play by a contemporary Russian writer until as late as 1925. Other "academic" theaters were equally backward. More significant still, the revolutionary and wildly experimental theaters, too, had very few original Soviet plays to offer to their public. The Meyerhold Theater produced one in 1921, but for the next four years was content to "stir the audience to political action" with the help of adaptations of foreign authors and Russian classics. The Theater of Revolution which was closely allied with Meyerhold and his school produced five unimportant plays by Soviet authors which dealt with historical or foreign themes, and only after 1924 was able to show some plays that reflected Soviet life and were, in a small way, contributions to Soviet drama.

An important cause of the dearth of plays was the reassessing of artistic values and rejection of the established forms of drama and the theater. As a Russian critic, P. A. Markov, put it:

"In those years 'beauty' seemed barren if it did not directly serve the cause of the revolution, while 'the life of the soul' carried no

meaning in the hours of struggle and armed uprisings. The theater
was condemned because its forms were no longer in harmony with
the demands of the time and because its content was foreign in
spirit. Intimate experiences, personal relationships, spiritual truth,
stories of love, partings, divorces, paled and vanished in the face
of hunger, wrath, and elemental calamities. Abstract beauty seemed
unimportant at a moment when all moral values were breaking down,
when the new life was crushing the old precepts and beliefs sternly
and relentlessly."

The reaction to the detached attitude toward the play took the
form of a dynamic stage spectacle in which the emphasis was on the
masses rather than on the heroes, and generalized, almost abstract
types replaced individual characters. To the theater this brought
striking and stirring productions (for the new stage technique was
extraordinarily resourceful and on occasions splendidly imaginative
in its effects), but to drama it contributed little of more than transient
interest.

There was one significant exception however, the play "Mystery-
Bouffe" * by Vladimir Mayakovsky. A fantastic story describing the
journey of a band of workers from the deluged Earth to Hell, Purga-
tory, Heaven, and back to the Earth, the play is a feast of sardonic
humor and daring imagery expressed in verse of savage vigor. One
of the first Soviet plays to be produced after the revolution (it was
staged by the author in 1918, and revived by Meyerhold in 1921),
it set the fashion for abstract characters and deliberate, unblushing
propaganda. But so unmistakably does it carry the stamp of authen-
ticity that distinguishes great talent that in spite of itself it survives
as a work of art and magnificent theater. Several years later Mayakovsky wrote two more plays, "The Bedbug" and "The Bathhouse."
Both of these viciously satirize the parasitic elements in Soviet life,
but compared with "Mystery-Bouffe" they are not nearly so felicitous
in invention nor daring in imagery.

Of all the other plays of this school, frankly propagandist in their
stories and antitheatrical ("constructivist") in stage presentation,
only "Roar China" † by S. Tretyakov (produced in 1926) can be
said to preserve some essential quality of genuine drama. Such popular successes of that era as the fantastically absurd "Party Ticket"
of N. Erdman (1925), the grotesque "Soufflé Cake" of B. Romashov
(1924), and the melodramatic "Man with a Brief Case" of A. Fayko
(1927), clever and marked by talent as they are, today have a hollow
sound as though they have been emptied of all substance—conflicts,
characters, sentiments—and only a literary shell remains.

The movement represented by these plays was already on the wane

* English version in *Masterpieces of Russian Drama,* by George Rapall Noyes (New
York, Appleton, 1933).
† London, Martin Lawrence Ltd., 1933.

when in the second half of the 'twenties an upsurge of new energy
raised Soviet drama from the doldrums and sped it on new courses.
Several trends became clearly marked. The most important one drew
its inspiration from the days of the revolutionary struggle for the
Soviets. The approach on the whole was realistic, but the emphasis
and treatment varied, some authors focusing their attention on the
life of a single family, usually of the middle or upper classes, others
attempting a broader picture of the struggle, with the revolutionary
workers holding the center of the stage.

Mikhail Bulgakov's "The Days of the Turbins," * based on his
novel of the same name and produced by the Moscow Art Theater
in 1926, is among the plays that stressed the effect of the revolution
on the personal fortunes of a number of closely related people. In
this case it is a family of White officers in the Ukraine who after the
withdrawal of the Germans are swept away by the onrush of revolutionary forces. The tenseness of action imparted to the play by the
master craftsmen of the Moscow Art Theater and the author's understanding attitude toward his characters, who are not held up to
scorn for being devoted to their counterrevolutionary cause, have
earned "The Days of the Turbins" the reputation of a minor masterpiece. This high rating is hardly merited. The play is essentially a
melodrama peopled with characters who have neither the solidity
nor the depth of fully visualized human beings.

The same lack of dramatic substance is felt in two other realistic
melodramas of the period, Boris Lavrenev's "Breakup" and Boris
Romashov's "The Bridge of Fire." With much less tolerance in their
treatment of the defenders of the old regime, these plays picture high-
placed families torn by the conflict of political sympathies among
their members. The best that can be said of this group of plays is
that they are definitely dated. Paradoxically enough, a play that out-
stripped them all in melodrama and realistic detail, "Lyubov Yarovaya" by Konstantin Trenyov, is the only one of their class that
caught the true spirit of the revolution and has retained its significance to this day.

"Lyubov Yarovaya" is a strange play. As far as its plot is concerned,
it stops at no consideration of realistic plausibility in working out
its central theme, the dramatic situation of a loving husband and a
loving wife fighting each other on opposite sides in the revolutionary
struggle. Nor is it above using cheap and hackneyed melodramatic
effects, as for example in a scene where a commissar, after shooting
his old friend and associate for looting, coolly resumes dictation of a
letter where he left off. All these obvious flaws, however, recede into
the background before the engrossing spectacle of a host of people
caught in the whirlwind of revolutionary events. Their comedy and
drama are brought to life with extraordinary vividness. The charac-

---

* English version in *Six Soviet Plays,* edited by Eugene Lyons (Boston and New York,
Houghton Mifflin, 1934).

ters are not abstract masks or mere types. The great majority of them are solid real people whose individual traits, observed with keenness and humor, make them intensely human. Its overflowing vitality explains the unflagging popularity of this play with Soviet audiences —from 1926, when it was first produced at the Maly Theater, to the present.

"Lyubov Yarovaya" forms a natural link with another and especially important group of plays which retell the saga of the revolutionary years. Equally, if not more, episodic and loose in their form and even broader in their approach, these plays throb with the passion and pathos of the revolutionary struggle. "Storm" by V. Bill-Belotserkovsky, "Armored Train 14–69" by Vsevolod Ivanov, "Prince Mstislav the Brave" by I. Prut, "The First Horse Army" and "An Optimistic Tragedy" by Vsevold Vishnevsky, "Intervention" by L. Slavin, and "The End of a Squadron" by A. Korneychuk are outstanding in this group.

"Armored Train 14–69" * (1927) and "An Optimistic Tragedy" † (1933) in particular are among the notable achievements of Soviet drama. There is little similarity between these two plays outside their revolutionary theme. The former tells the story of Siberian partisans rising against the White Russian allies of the Japanese invaders. The latter depicts the surging passions of an undisciplined and in part ruffianly force of sailors being tempered in the fire of the revolution into the fighting spirit of a disciplined body of men waging a life-and-death struggle for the revolutionary cause. (Incidentally they come to readily accept the leadership of a woman commissar whom in the beginning they threatened to rape.) There is realism and romanticism in both plays, but not the same kind nor in the same proportions. Ivanov's realism is that of characters, and his romanticism (a slightly theatrical brand) that of situations. Vishnevsky shows human passions in brutally realistic aspects, but the display of these passions is charged with such sweeping elemental power that the realism of "nature in the raw" assumes a decided romantic quality, and the entire play becomes a poem, a paean to revolution. In keeping with this romantic emotionalism "An Optimistic Tragedy" employs the device of narrators and commentators (in the original version, a Greek tragedy chorus) who supply the links between the loosely connected episodes. "Armored Train," on the other hand, though episodic, has a clearly outlined plot which follows the conventional rules of dramatic development.

Contemporaneously with the group of revolutionary plays just discussed two other trends appeared—one giving free play to fantasy and poetic imagination, the other attempting realistic portrayal of Soviet characters of the day.

* London, Martin Lawrence Ltd., 1933.
† English version in *Four Soviet Plays* (New York, International Publishers, 1937).

The poetic and fantastic trend found its most remarkable expression in a play which, though a great popular success on the stage, remained an isolated tour de force, leaving no influence on Soviet drama. It was Evgeny Zamyatin's "The Flea," produced in 1926. In the form of a folk tale it describes the discovery by an old Czar that the English have presented him with a mechanical flea that can dance; not to be outdone, the Czar orders Russian peasant mechanics to produce something even more wonderful; and this they finally accomplish by nailing microscopic horseshoes to the feet of the mechanical flea. The broad and often ribald humor of the play, the grotesque caricatures of its characters in the manner of popular prints, and the unsurpassed richness of the folk vernacular in which it is written make the play unique in the history of Russian drama. No matter that its author's claim to having followed the traditions of the Russian folk theater cannot be substantiated. Old Russia had puppet theaters (*vertep* and *Petrushka*) and picture theaters (*rayok*) in which the patter of the entertainer was the main attraction. It also had clowns and jesters who entertained in the streets (galled by their habit of joining funeral processions and turning them into riotous frolics Ivan the Terrible sought the assistance of a congress of churchmen to stop the nuisance). But except in the form of miracle plays which for a time were performed in a few churches, the popular stage as it was seen in the rest of Europe was unknown to the Russian masses. "The Flea" recaptures the waggish drollery of the Russian folk comedians, magnifying it by its own gusto and exuberant imagination. It is a matter of regret that its folk idiom defies translation into English and that one has to turn to the original to get the full flavor of this Soviet masterpiece.

A strain of fantasy, though of a different kind, is also marked in the plays of Yury Olesha. His "Conspiracy of Feelings," "A List of Benefits," and especially the delightful fairy tale, "Three Fat Men," show a poetic imagination that seeks to transcend the matter-of-fact implications of their revolutionary theme. Olesha is not always successful in blending realism with fancy, but more than any other young Soviet playwright he gave promise of great achievement—a promise unfortunately never fulfilled, since "A List of Benefits," produced in 1931, has proved to be the last of his plays to appear on the Soviet stage.

The whimsical trend found expression in one other interesting play, Ivan Kocherga's "The Watchmaker and the Hen" * (1934). Taking for his theme the emergence of Russia from the chaos of the early years of the revolution, Kocherga allows his imagination to play with two concepts of time, one as understood by a German businessman, which is measured by the clock and governs the usual sequence of events, and the other as seen and felt by the Russian characters of the play, which gallops here, slows down to a snail's pace there, and always makes fools of sensible people who judge a revolution by their "nor-

* English version under the title "Masters of Time" in *Four Soviet Plays*.

mal" standards. The play, which opens as a hilarious comedy involving the fortunes of a prize hen, grows more sober as it goes on, and ends on a note of complete seriousness. The failure to maintain the humorous mood of its first act is perhaps the chief defect of this otherwise highly imaginative and unusual play.

In the years that followed "The Watchmaker and the Hen," fantasy and poetic imagination have practically disappeared from adult Soviet drama. Their refuge, particularly in more recent years, has been the children's theater and to some extent plays in verse. Outstanding among children's plays are "The Golden Key" by Alexey Tolstoy, "A Tale" by Mikhail Svetlov, "Laughter and Tears" by Sergey Mikhalkov, and "Twelve Months," by Samuel Marshak, the latter a little masterpiece in its wit, fancy, and perfect craftsmanship that casts its spell on grownups perhaps even more than children. An ambitious attempt to break away from the realistic formula is Victor Gusev's war play in verse, "Sons of Three Rivers," which saw the footlights in 1944. But the talented young poet, author of several comedies in verse, who died on the eve of its opening, only succeeded in demonstrating how completely out of his element he was in dealing with a dramatic theme. His three rivers, the Volga, the Elbe, and the Seine, personified in images taking part in the action, are allegories lacking any significance of their own; his three couples representing Russia, Germany, and France are sketchily drawn and unconvincing; and his verse lacks distinction and is at times pompous.

Somewhere between fancy and realistic portrayal of contemporary Soviet life stands a group of early comedies which attain a great deal of freedom in the treatment of their material through the use of some old conventions of the theater. The particular source of these conventions in Russia is the dramatic form known as "vaudeville" in its original French meaning, signifying a light play interspersed with songs and dances. Borrowed from France in the early part of the last century, vaudeville dominated the Russian stage for several decades and brought forth a number of talented, if not particularly original, authors among whom D. Lensky has attained the status of a Russian classic. In its pure form of a full-length play with songs and dances vaudeville has been dead in Russia for nearly a century. But it has left its mark on the more serious Russian drama, and such characteristic vaudeville devices as free manipulation of the entrances and exits of characters without any regard to the realistic demands of the given situation, or handling of the plot as if it were a piece of music, with the theme or themes juxtaposed, contrasted, or repeated, are encountered in the work of some of the foremost Russian playwrights. Ostrovsky, with all his search for realistic character and motivation, was certainly much influenced by vaudeville in the form of his plays. Even Gorky makes use of the vaudeville convention by placing the action in an outdoor setting, a garden or a street, and bringing on his characters or sending them away on a stroll just as suits his convenience.

In Soviet drama Valentin Katayev's "Squaring the Circle" * (produced at the Moscow Art Theater in 1928) is vaudeville at its best. Starting with the comic situation of two young couples obliged to share a single room (a realistic enough predicament in Moscow of those days), Katayev embroiders it with inexhaustible wit and all the drollery that can be extracted from contrived juxtapositions and repetitions, both in dialogue and situations, as permitted by the vaudeville convention. The effect is often farcical, but it carries a substratum of truth and is more in the nature of a friendly and goodhearted caricature.

Still in the vaudeville tradition but to a lesser degree is Vassily Shkvarkin's "Father Unknown" (1933), one of the greatest popular successes of the Soviet stage. The comedy is built around a misunderstanding that is rather implausible. The characters too drift in and out at the bidding of the author just as they do in vaudeville. At the same time they are drawn from life, without much exaggeration and with enough individuality to make them appear real, and the plot, with the initial misunderstanding accepted, unrolls along logical lines, albeit in a crazy-quilt pattern.

Several other plays in the same flexible vaudeville convention have been written by Katayev and by Shkvarkin since their two great successes. It cannot be said that these have enhanced the reputations of their authors. Katayev has more and more come to rely on forced farcical situations, Shkvarkin on eccentricities of character. In neither case, even as pure entertainment, have the results been particularly happy.

Two less known but youthfully fresh plays with a marked imaginative touch, "The Railway Car and Marion" (*Vagon i Marion*) by Isidor Shtok and "Nonsense" by Konstantin Finn, belong to the same group of early Soviet comedies. Like Katayev and Shkvarkin, their authors have not fared so well during the lean years of Soviet drama that followed the early 'thirties. Both have turned to realism, Shtok in the field of children's plays, Finn in the comedy of manners. Some of Finn's plays, "Sashka" for example, have attained a considerable measure of success on the stage, not, however, due to the author's ability to tell an interesting story about interesting people (his plots are artificial and his characterization shallow) so much as to the fortuitous circumstance that they have provided "vehicles" for some of the best Soviet comedians.

The last trend to be noted, which had its beginning in the late 'twenties, is that of realistic drama and comedy. Much can be said of the different forms in which realism manifested itself in prerevolutionary Russian literature and drama. In Soviet drama realism has meant

* English version in *Six Soviet Plays*.

one of two things: either a portrayal of characters with the main accent on their psychology and the manner in which they react to the various problems that arise in their life; or a picture of the life of a group of people with the main accent on what these people actually do in solving the problems that confront them as a group. The psychological probers of character held the field in the late 'twenties. They were fewer in numbers than the others, but their plays were unquestionably richer and more convincing in the human experience they tried to picture. Lydia Seyfullina's "Virineya" (1926), one of the earliest plays in this group, though a poor adaptation of the author's novel, presents a fascinating study of a young peasant woman who could brush aside all conventions and yet retain an independence and integrity of character that ultimately brought her into the ranks of the revolutionists.

The same years witnessed the first dramatic efforts of Leonid Leonov, one of the most talented of Soviet playwrights, who is also a distinguished novelist. Of his two early plays, "Badgers" and "Untilovsk," the latter is especially interesting as revealing an unusual power of characterization coupled with searching insight into the psychology of morbidly twisted and complex personalities. Leonov has since written eight more plays, of uneven quality, some of them definitely feeble (such as his "Ordinary Man"), but including also one of the finest plays in modern Russian drama, "The Orchards of Polovchansk" (1938), and a war play that stands not far below it, "Invasion" (1942).

"The Orchards of Polovchansk" * has something of the poetically brooding atmosphere of Synge combined with an Ibsenesque interplay of emotional reactions and its own characteristically Soviet vigor and exuberance. The first act is particularly suggestive of Synge and Ibsen. An illicit love affair of the mistress of the house—a mistake long since acknowledged by the woman and redeemed by loyal love of her husband, whose second wife she is—is echoed in the husband's fear that their daughter is about to commit a similar mistake. The ghost of the old love affair rises from the grave with the sudden and unwelcome arrival of the former lover, a moral and physical wreck of a man harboring mysterious designs. The tense atmosphere is heightened by the anxiety of the father about his favorite son who, alone of all his children, fails to join the family reunion. But the arrival of the young people, buoyant, self-confident, and grimly patriotic, dispels the gathering clouds. With a touching understanding of their stepmother's trouble, they make her old swain virtually their prisoner, and discerning his anti-Soviet proclivities finally hand him over to the authorities. At the same time their boldness and firmness of purpose is a source of added strength to their father, enabling him to accept with resignation the heroic death of his absent son. And their sense of spiritual and social kinship with the young man who comes to woo

* English version in *Seven Soviet Plays* (New York, Macmillan, 1945).

their sister, after the early misunderstanding in which one of the brothers, a well-known athlete, gets the worst of a fight with the supposed intruder, resolves the problem of the girl's romance which at first aroused qualms in their father.

A comparison of "The Orchards of Polovchansk" with Chekhov's "The Cherry Orchard" is frequently made. The points of resemblance are actually few and superficial. They are confined in Leonov's play to the reversed symbolism of the orchard theme and a certain outward similarity of some of its minor comic characters to those in "The Cherry Orchard." On the other hand, so great are the differences in outlook upon life, general tone, and dramatic technique, that drawing any parallels between the two plays is largely arbitrary and futile.

There is certainly nothing even remotely Chekhovian in Leonov's "Invasion." * A play of strong contrasts and emotions, it has drawn thoroughly human and convincing portraits of Soviet men and women whose sense of decency and justice gave them the courage and spiritual power to face unflinchingly the horrors of Nazi rule.

As in several others of Leonov's plays, the central character of "Invasion" is a misfit in Soviet society, an embittered and egocentric young man who cares nothing for what happens to anybody. Unlike his father, mother, and sister, he does not burn with hatred of the brutal Germans. But even his callous heart rebels when he sees some of the ghastly things perpetrated by the invaders. Identifying himself with the cause of his people he opens a daring one-man war on the enemy, only to share the fate of many other brave spirits that took up arms against the Germans.

The play contains another unforgettable figure, a misfit like the first, but a sinister one, who could never forgive the revolution his loss of wealth and power. Emerging from obscurity and regaining the post of mayor of the city with the arrival of the Germans, this grasping, spider-like creature is cast off by his protectors in their flight before the advancing Russians. His pitiful attempts to save his skin prove futile, and he finally resigns himself to his fate.

These two characters with twisted minds dominate the play. But it has several "normal" Russians, among them the young man's father and mother, who are finely drawn and memorable. The play is not free of minor defects such as the rather mechanical construction of the last act and the overemphasis on physical horror.

"Lyonushka," Leonov's second war play, is marred by the piling up of horror, even more than "Invasion." Yet it is an absorbing play, intense to the point of incandescence, rich in the characterization of its peasant heroes, and profoundly moving in its story of the love of a young girl for a dying officer disfigured beyond recognition in a burning tank.

* English versions in *Four Soviet War Plays* (London, Hutchinson, 1944) and in *International Literature* (Moscow, 1943), No. 6.

Maxim Gorky enters the Soviet scene as a playwright, of the same school as Leonov, with his last two plays written after his return to Russia in 1928. Both "Yegor Bulychov and the Others" (1931) * and "Dostigayev and Others" (1933) † deal with the disintegration of Russian bourgeois society on the eve of the downfall of Czarism and during the early days of the revolution. Of the two plays, which are loosely connected in their plots, "Yegor Bulychov" is unquestionably the more colorful and dramatic. The crowning achievement of Gorky's career as a playwright, it reveals him not merely as a master of delineation of character (he was that in several of his earlier plays) but equally as a dramatist with a keen sense of theater. There are two scenes in "Yegor Bulychov" that display this latter quality to a supreme degree. In one Bulychov, whose fight against an incurable disease tempts him to probe the cure-all methods of quacks, questions a tuba player who treats his patients by making them play the tuba. Amused by the naïve dishonesty of the man, Bulychov, with sardonic contempt for those around him, orders him to "give it to them with all you've got," shouting to the blaring sounds of the tuba, "This is Archangel Gabriel trumpeting the end of the world." In the other scene Bulychov watches a fraudulent "holy man" rant and dance in simulated frenzy, only to realize his helplessness before a relentless fate and to shout his pained and awestruck protest as he goes down in an unequal fight. With "Yegor Bulychov" Gorky gave the Soviet stage a superb piece of realistic drama, instinct with the symbolism and eloquence of the pure art of the theater.

A figure of singular distinction in the Soviet literary scene, Alexey Tolstoy, who died last year, belongs to the same group of psychological realists. He gained literary fame before the revolution, was for some years an "emigré" in Western Europe, but returned to Russia in the early 'twenties to become an acknowledged leader in the Soviet literary world. His numerous plays represent a great variety of styles and genres. An early one, "Kasatka" (1917), has an elusive impressionistic poignancy reminiscent of Chekhov. In "Cuckoo's Tears" a comic anecdote is shot through with a warm sympathy for its heroes that borders on "tears through laughter." Among his other plays, which like these two deal with life in prerevolutionary Russia, several that are couched in satirical terms are far less successful: their satire somehow misses fire, and their characters tend toward conventional types. Soviet life supplied themes for "Patent No. 119" and "Road to Victory," and these, too, must be counted among his less successful efforts. It is a different Alexey Tolstoy, however, that emerges in his two historical plays, "Peter I" and "Ivan the Terrible" (the latter actually being two independent plays with the same central character). He rises to

* English versions in *Seven Plays of Maxim Gorky* (New Haven, Yale University Press, 1945), and in *The Last Plays of Maxim Gorki* (London, Lawrence and Wishart, 1937).
† English version in *The Last Plays of Maxim Gorki*.

exceptional heights especially in "Ivan the Terrible" (1944), a play of extraordinary grandeur of conception in which his psychological realism achieved its final fruition.

One of the most baffling personalities in Russian history, Ivan the Terrible has inspired many plays and novels, including "Death of Ivan the Terrible," a classic of the Russian stage by Count Alexey K. Tolstoy, highly talented poet, novelist, and playwright of the second half of the last century. Unquestionably the Soviet playwright's Ivan the Terrible" towers above all its predecessors. Whether the interpretation of its hero is correct or not (it runs counter to the traditional view of "the bloody Czar"), it is supremely convincing within its own terms and is unsurpassed in insight, vitality, the vigor and rich flavor of its Russian, and—especially in the first part—in sheer power of dramatic projection.

Few other Soviet dramatists have been as consistent in their psychological approach as Leonov, or as incisive and dramatic as Alexey Tolstoy in his historical plays. Alexander Afinogenov, whose first play appeared in 1924, wrote seven more before he began to probe the inner life of his characters instead of being satisfied with their political or social labels. His first attempt in this direction, "Portrait" (1934), describing the struggle of a former woman thief to retain the moral rectitude she won while a prisoner in a government labor camp, seems forced in its motivation, besides being overburdened with superfluous and far-fetched symbolism. But in his next play, "Dalyokoye" (entitled "Far Taiga" in this volume), he was far more successful. His portraits of the small folk living in the virgin forests of Siberia and yet feeling intimate ties with the rest of the nation, performing the tasks devolving upon them with a high sense of social responsibility, are warmly felt and sensitively and delicately drawn. There is little dramatic conflict in the play and what there is is stated more in terms of argument than of action, but the argument springs from the contrast of characters and has a psychological as well as political basis. As a picture of Soviet life in the early 'thirties, the play is both charming and informingly significant. Of other plays by Afinogenov "The Second Track," a sequel to "Far Taiga," has the same intimacy and charm but is even less dramatic. In his last two plays (he was killed in an air raid on Moscow), striving for a sharper dramatic collision, Afinogenov used means that defeated his purpose: in "Mashenka" * he resorted to artificially contrived situations; in "On the Eve" † he employed a conventional war plot with the violence of war as its dramatic theme.

A delightful play that has almost the same setting as "Far Taiga" and resembles it in general atmosphere is "Steep Bank" (1940) by A. Savelyev and E. Raimond, which has never been produced. It

---

* English acting version under the title *Listen Professor!* by Peggy Phillips (New York, S. French, 1944).

† English version in *Seven Soviet Plays*.

pictures an "erring" young woman who, after rising to a prominent position by sheer will power and energy, goes to pieces as a result of an unhappy marriage. With widening horizons of public work and the tactful help of her chief who is in love with her she afterward recovers. The play has quality, and the simplicity and earthiness of the characters make them blend with their country surroundings.

The realistic plays of psychological approach that have so far been discussed focus attention on the individual and the problems of life he has to face. The other and much larger group of Soviet plays, while realistic in material and treatment, has been primarily concerned with the social activity of the people as it has found expression in great industrial projects, the collectivization of farms, the exposure of so-called "wreckers," the fashioning of the patriotic spirit of the Red Army, and other similar phases of Soviet life. Although innumerable plays have been written on these subjects, in retrospect it is hard to point to more than a few that deserve any serious consideration.

Perhaps the most notable writer of this type of play is Nikolay Pogodin, who began his playwriting career with "Tempo" * (1930) and has since written over a dozen plays. A man with an observant eye and a keen sense of humor, Pogodin has supplied lively journalistic commentaries in dramatic form on a variety of social and political themes. He was one of the first to picture the chaotic conditions, the web of conflicting personal and group interests with deliberate sabotage thrown in for good measure, out of which rose the new industrial giants. His plots follow a pattern which has become a standard: initial difficulties, wise or inefficient leadership, growing enthusiasm of the workers, and triumph—a problem solved or a new record set. Typical of his and other similar industrial plots is his play, "A Poem of the Axe" (1931). An old steel plant is in difficulties due to the failure of experiments to produce rustless steel. There is talk of closing the plant, while a foreign concern supplying rustless steel to the government does all it can to stop the independent research of the Russians. One of the workers, Stepan, who once succeeded in producing steel of the required specifications, is distressed at his inability to repeat his success. With failure, the workers begin to lose interest in their work. But Anka, a woman worker, will not accept defeat. She rouses the wives of the workers and organizes them into an active unit. Their example spurs the men. With the help of the loyal engineers the experiments are resumed, and Stepan's faith and reputation are vindicated—he produces rustless steel.

Another of Pogodin's plays, "My Friend" (1932), has the distinction of having introduced to the Soviet stage the first "positive" Soviet character, Grigory Gay. An energetic and intelligent head of a construction project, Gay has to fight bureaucratic ineptitude, personal jealousies, and shortsighted policies of his assistants. Even his wife is

* English version in Six Soviet Plays,

against him. He breaks off with her, determined to go ahead with his plans. But the resistance is too strong for him. Disheartened, he takes to drink and even permits irregular handling of government funds. A high government official appears on the scene. He understands the cause of Gay's breakdown and instead of punishing him reminds him of his duty as a Communist. The stern but fatherly talk has an electrifying effect on Gay. He realizes his mistake, plunges into the fight again, and triumps over all obstacles.

Gay's ability to overcome his weakness and show how a good Communist can rise above all difficulties is apparently the quality that has made him a "positive" character in the eyes of Soviet critics. It is interesting to observe, though, that Gay finds strength for his recovery not in his inner Communist conscience but in the code of rules for good behavior binding the members of the Communist party. The credit for his success goes not to himself but to the party, an implication which until recently formed the main content of the term "positive character."

In "My Friend," as in the two earlier plays, Pogodin gives no evidence of attempting to probe below his characters' surface reactions. In "Aristocrats" * (1935) which deals with rehabilitation of criminals, he was faced with a psychological problem but he chose to treat it in the same manner as before. If it is true that in the prison camps in which former thieves, bandits, and prostitutes were forced to work on the construction of an important Soviet canal, the convicts were actually won back to honest life by appeals to their proletarian conscience and by the enthusiasm engendered by rivalry in work, we are still not given any insight into the inner processes which brought about this sweeping change in the deep-rooted habits of the criminal mind. Again the outside moral influence is all that matters. How far-reaching it is and how enduring its effects is left to conjecture.

Standing apart from Pogodin's plays on topical subjects are "The Man with a Rifle" (1937) and "The Chimes of the Kremlin" (1941), in which he goes back to the very beginnings of the Soviet regime. There is something in these two historical plays that seems to insure them a more permanent place in Soviet drama than can be said of Pogodin's other efforts. They are no less episodic in form or sketchy in characterization, and for all their historicity are just as politically pointed. But they have a human warmth, springing probably from nostalgic memories of the time they describe, that makes their characters real and believable. Their humor too is good-natured and appealing, though for the characters themselves some of the situations are anything but humorous (the spiriting away of Engineer Zabelin in "The Chimes of the Kremlin" without a word of explanation to himself or his family, only because Lenin wanted to consult him on a technical project, may seem amusing in the perspective of time but was hardly

* English version in Four Soviet Plays.

a joke for those whom it affected). But the plays are retrospective pictures of the past as seen by a Soviet writer of today, and allowing for the mellowing effect of time, they succeed in recapturing the atmosphere of those turbulent years.

Pogodin's plays on the problems of the day, like dozens of others of the same type that were cut to a more stereotyped pattern, with characters and situations taken out of stock and made to carry a politically colored message, were written largely under the slogan of "socialist realism," a concept put forward in the middle 'thirties principally in opposition to esthetic formalism, romanticism, and other "escapist" tendencies in literature and drama. Because realism alone was not considered enough and was to be qualified by the adjective "socialist," which called for a socialist outlook upon life, the term "socialist realism" was easily interpreted as a view of the Soviet scene revealing the social forces at work. Since the Communist party and its program were the most important social force in the Soviet Union, a shift of accent from the portrayal of life as it is to the declared objectives of governmental policies was inevitable. The result was disastrous for Soviet drama. After a decade of comparative resurgence, roughly from 1925 to 1935, there ensued a long period of dramatic sterility. As has been noted, plays were written and published in great numbers, but of so poor a quality that even the state-controlled theaters were reluctant to produce them, preferring to fill their repertoire with revivals of Russian and foreign classics. For the past seven or eight years not more than a quarter of the current productions in the Moscow theaters have been plays by Soviet authors. The more sensitive critics realized the danger of this development at its early stages. They accepted the Communist ideology but they wanted it to take on flesh and blood, the palpitant reality of life. Theoretically speaking, a synthesis of this nature is entirely conceivable, provided the ideology permeates the life of the people and is seen in its broader terms as distinct from the changing slogans of day-to-day politics. Apparently this condition has not been possible of fulfillment, since even the more talented writers, most of them sincere believers in Communism, have not been able to achieve the desired union of ideology and life. There was one period, the years of the war, when the official ideology was almost identical with the patriotic sentiment that swept the nation, and life itself provided innumerable examples of the unity of action with Communist or patriotic thought. Nevertheless the deluge of machine-made plays with stock characters now fitted into a war setting never stopped. Despite (or was it because of) the efforts of the governmental Committee of Art Affairs which went into the business of commissioning authors to write plays on set themes and "collaborating" with them in their work, with the declared object of raising the artistic level of Soviet drama and preventing "mistakes" in ideology, the average quality of Soviet plays remained as low as before. Complaints on that score were often voiced in the press and by the spokesmen of the Committee itself. The final verdict was passed by the Soviet Government which awarded Stalin prizes to three war plays (Leonov's "Invasion," Korneychuk's "Front," and Simonov's "The Russian People") produced in 1942, but in 1943 and 1944 gave the awards to Alexey Tolstoy's "Ivan the Terrible" and Marshak's "Twelve Months," neither of which had anything to do with contemporary Soviet life.

In so far as any attempts have been made to square "socialist realism" with the actual life of the Soviet people, they have found their most notable expression in the work of three playwrights, Alexander Korneychuk, Konstantin Simonov, and Alexander Kron.

"The End of a Squadron" (1934), Korneychuk's first play, was a promising beginning. Its story of a Russian naval squadron whose crew, after much factional strife, goes over to the Bolsheviks and torpedoes the ships rather than surrender them to the enemy, is a dramatic episode of the early days of the revolution told with considerable force and passion. His next play, "Platon Krechet" (1935), was a great popular success. There is an appealing quality in its central character, a brilliant young surgeon, addicted to playing the violin in order to keep his hands supple, whose romance with a girl nearly goes on the rocks because of his failure to save her father's life. The play however is often stagy in its effects, has a conventional and colorless villain in the surgeon's rival for the girl's affections, and resolves its conflict in a *deus ex machina* fashion with the inevitable intervention of a government commissar. A Ukrainian himself, Korneychuk is perhaps most successful in his warmly drawn portraits of Ukrainian peasants with their inexhaustible vein of native humor. They are the heroes of "On the Steppes of the Ukraine" and "Partisans on the Steppes of the Ukraine" * (the latter written in the first year of the war), whose threadbare plots are saved to some extent by the rich humanity of these peasant characters.

The play for which Korneychuk is best known today is "Front" † (1942). In it, with a daring never before attempted (or permitted) on the Soviet stage, he attacked the incompetence of some leaders of the Red Army. That the play had a sensational run in Russia and that the Soviet Government not only permitted its production but actually encouraged it throughout the country shows how important the play was considered at that critical stage of the war. But though in a political sense this success was fully deserved, there is little that can be said for it as a work of dramatic literature. The main and perhaps only virtue of "Front" is the author's fresh approach in choosing his principal characters. Here we have an old general, a bemedaled veteran of

* English version under the title "Guerillas of the Ukrainian Steppes" in *Four Soviet War Plays*.
† English version in *Seven Soviet Plays*.

the civil war, who is shown to have little technical knowledge of modern warfare; and contrasted with him, a young general who has this knowledge as well as the courage of his convictions, and who (an unprecedented example of Communist independence) defies the authority of his superior to carry out his own ideas in a critical operation. Korneychuk shows artistic sensitivity in not making the old general a fatuous curmudgeon, but a hearty and likable old fellow and not in the least stupid. The man's only fault is that he has been raised to a position for which he has no qualifications, and perhaps it is not quite fair to lay the blame for this on him. However, interesting as these two characters are, they are revealed more from the outside than the inside and never come fully to life. Nor are we given any dramatic evidence of the younger general's superior knowledge of military matters —we have to accept the author's word for it. This leaves the development of the plot entirely dependent on what the author wants to prove. Naturally, his hero is brilliantly successful in the operation he has planned and puts the old general to shame. Not content with this, Korneychuk even promotes him to the post of his opponent, for which purpose he has an influential government official on the spot who sees to it that talent receives due recognition.

Manipulation of the plot to point a moral is fortunately absent in the better plays of Konstantin Simonov. The lessons to be drawn from them are suggested by the life they picture and the particular moral and mental attitudes they choose to emphasize, rather than by the author's contrivances in handling the fate of his characters.

Little need be said of Simonov's first play "A Common Story," a demonstration of the ability of young Communists to rise above such a bourgeois prejudice as jealousy, in which the youthful author was obviously feeling his way as a playwright. He came into his own in his second play, "A Fellow from Our Town" (1941), whose action is set in the Far East at the time the Japanese attempted an undeclared war on Russia. It is a good example of an honest Communist approach to the realities of Soviet life, and at the same time a highly significant revelation of the scale of human values that has been evolving in Soviet Russia. To grasp the full significance of the play it is important to know in what light it appears to the Communist mind, and nothing can indicate this better than the review in *Izvestiya*, which it should be noted was written two months before the outbreak of war with Germany.

"A Fellow from Our Town," says the review, "is a play about the Soviet fatherland—about the fighters of the Red Army, masters of a terrifying war technique who crush the enemy wherever he dares to show himself—about love, friendship, loyalty, brotherhood. Finally, it is a play about the great international solidarity of the workers.

"Has this new Simonov play any defects? It has plenty of them. Its

construction lacks dramatic unity. It is broken up, often fragmentary.
The suspense sometimes falls off. The characters are not all live people.
Some are mere abstractions, human manikins.

"But the defects—and we make bold to assert this with the full sense
of responsibility for our statement—pale before the *political* resonance
of the play.

"The principal character of the play is Sergey Lukonin. . . . Picture to yourself a strapping young fellow from the Volga, with bris-
tling hair, stubborn in everything he does, who was the best athlete in
his college. His cocksureness borders on impertinence, but it springs
from his awareness of his power, from his indomitable will to achieve
his chosen goal, to command a tank in the Red Army. It is not without
reason that the audience takes such a liking to Sergey Lukonin. He is
a *type*. In various parts of our vast country, in thousands of towns and
villages Sergey Lukonins are growing up. . . . The Red Army has
forged a remarkable type of a resolute officer. We see his resourceful-
ness, bravery, ability to fire his men with enthusiasm. Taken prisoner,
Sergey exercises his self-control so well that not a single movement
betrays him to the White Russian who cross-examines him. He goes
into attack thirty-seven times, and remains alive. . . . In picturing
the life of the Red Army the author abstains from bright colors or
sugar-coating. The audience sees life at the front with all its customary
hardships. Yet the play inspires love of our fine army, educates one to
a sense of duty, to iron discipline, when personal interest, no matter how close to one's heart, gives way unquestioningly before the
interest of the state, of the people.

"Sergey is in love with Varya Burmina. Wherever he may be—
whether in school, in a garrison deep in the steppes, on a responsible
and dangerous mission abroad, or on the battlefield—everywhere
Varya is in his heart. . . . Unhappily, Simonov has not been very
successful with Varya. Varya has a great deal to say, but to tell the
truth little would be lost if she were taken completely out of the
play. Somehow Sergey would manage to do without her. She lacks
personality, character. Nor is she typical. . . . Simonov has been far
more successful with Varya's brother, Arkady. This tall, lanky man
shares popularity in the play with its tank crews. He is diffident—for
seven years he has not been able to muster enough courage to declare
his sentiments to the woman he loves. He is physically awkward. He
has a low voice. A gifted physician, an honest Soviet intellectual, he
does not parade his good points. Though a civilian (he is no more
than that in his own eyes) he finds himself, in the natural course of
events, in the advanced front-line positions. Arkady's tragic death
from a treacherous blow by an enemy prisoner is one of the most
poignant and memorable moments of the play."

Describing the final scene in which the tank column ready to launch an attack is addressed by Sergey calling his men to victory, the review concludes:

"There is no force in the world capable of resisting the blow of the Red Army when, ordered by the party, called upon by Stalin, it falls like an avalanche upon the enemy. The audience leaves the theater convinced of the boundless might of the Red Army. This is a moving play. It stirs up thoughts."

The cocksureness of Sergey Lukonin which the reviewer lauds and which he obviously shares must have received a severe shaking in the early stages of the war. It is precisely this attitude that was attacked by Korneychuk in "Front." But neither this overconfidence nor the patriotic fervor of the writer are the features that make this review significant. Its significance lies in the enthusiasm with which it greets the qualities of character developed in the young men of Russia by the Red Army. There can be no doubt that Simonov pictured the men as he saw them, and that he greatly admired them. And fine men they really are. But do they not already fall short of the "positive type" as it is seen today? Are they not already dated even for Russia, not to speak of the rest of the world which prizes initiative and intelligence no less than resoluteness and obedience to orders? The tendency of "socialist realism" not only to interpret life in the broader terms of Communist thought but to glorify the achievements of each passing year inevitably creates transient or false values, with the result that what is worshiped today is denounced tomorrow.

In "The Russian People" * (1942), celebrated in Russia and well known in other countries, Simonov comes closer to fundamental values. There is little indulgence in heroics and none at all in martial exuberance among the characters of this play, the army men and civilians engaged in the grim business of holding their bit of ground against the Germans or of going through mental tortures under the rule of the invaders. With a quiet courage and an unshakable will to resist to the end, these ordinary people, so little resembling the Sergey Lukonins of "A Fellow from Our Town," prove to be as invincible in spirit and a great deal more human. The play is enveloped in a lyrical mood that has endeared it to the Soviet public. It is this mood that holds the play together; for as a piece of dramatic craftsmanship "The Russian People" is palpably weak, being diffuse, episodic, and lacking in suspense, with characters not sharply enough outlined to stand forth from the background. It falls far short of being a great play, but it is a thoroughly honest and human one.

A highly popular war poem of his own, "Wait for Me," supplied Simonov with a theme for a play bearing the same title. It is a thesis play which tries to prove that wives should never give up hope for the return of their husbands fighting in the war. This faith, it argues, helps

* English version in *Seven Soviet Plays.*

their husbands, and those who keep it aflame live to see their husbands
return to them, while those who give up hope and seek consolation
in romantic adventures elsewhere find themselves cheated in the end.
A rationalization of an emotional attitude, "Wait for Me" buttresses
its case with implausible and laboriously contrived situations, and
fails to create the mood that was so well expressed in the author's
poem.

Simonov's characteristic lyrical strain comes to the fore in his next
play, "And So It Will Be" (1944), though this time it is not sufficient
in itself to overcome the triteness of his theme. As if in answer to the
question: What will it be like when the men come back from the war?
the play tells the story of a middle-aged colonel who on leave from the
front falls in love with a girl less than half his age. After much heart-
searching as to whether a man whose heart has been seared by bitter
suffering (the colonel's wife and daughter have been killed by the
Germans) and who is much older than the girl he loves, has any moral
right to marry her, the colonel, with the help of his friends and the
girl herself, is finally persuaded that he has that right. "And so it
will be," suggests the author; the old wounds will heal, and people will
again find happiness in life. There is no denying the warm sincerity
and charm of the play's characters. Some background details are interesting and entertaining. But the moral conflict described is bathetic—
a veritable storm in a teacup. The ghost of late-Victorian English gen-
tility seems to hover over the play. "Is it done?" is the big problem that
worries the hero, a Communist gentleman. After consulting the Communist Emily Post in the person of an old friend, a woman doctor, he is
assured that "it is done," whereupon with a clear conscience he embraces his happiness.

"Is it done?" This problem is the burden of several other Soviet
plays trying to formulate the code of good conduct for the new Soviet
society. It looms large in Alexander Kron's two plays, "Deep Prospecting" (1944) and "An Officer of the Navy" (1945). In "Deep Prospecting" a young Communist engineer in charge of an oil prospecting
project is faced with the dilemma: shall he go on drilling with a dubi-
ous chance of reaching oil and risk being accused of squandering government money, or shall he play safe by discontinuing the operation
and thus keep in the good graces of his superiors? He decides to play
safe. But one of his superiors has been on the spot waiting to see what
he will do, and when the engineer announces his decision tells him:
It is not done. A good Communist takes chances when necessary, even
at the risk of losing favor with the party, for sooner or later an honest
mistake will be recognized as such and forgiven. Placing one's own
interests before those of the people, however, is a crime, and a Communist who does that rules himself out of the party. The young engineer
is dismissed from his post and loses his wife into the bargain, since
she too has come to realize that he is not the kind of man she thought

he was. The Moscow Art Theater saw the play as "a deep prospecting" of the human soul and gave it a splendid production.

The same problem, only in a reversed situation, is tackled by Kron in his intensely earnest "An Officer of the Navy." A young naval officer engaged in war operations is a strict disciplinarian who holds an exalted view of his profession as an officer and a fighter. His unflattering comments on other officers and his occasional highhanded treatment of those who stand in his way leads to his being charged with criticizing his superiors, preaching professional militarism, and being needlessly strict in matters of discipline. The problem posed by the play is: Is it right for a Soviet officer to feel and behave as this naval officer does? The question is answered by the admiral who tries the case. Yes, the man is certainly too arrogant. But "Does he love the sea, the navy, his country? Is he loyal to the Communist party and to Stalin? Is he ready to sink the Fascists?" There is no doubt where the officer stands on these points. The case is dismissed. Going a step farther than Korneychuk in "Front," where the problem was one of superiority of judgment, Kron endows his hero with a moral superiority. As such the hero of his play, which has been staged by the Moscow Art Theater, has been acclaimed by the Soviet critics as a new "positive character," a man who takes pride in his military profession and is not afraid to stand by his convictions (which it so happens are also the convictions of the Soviet leaders).

It will be seen that the Soviet plays of the "socialist-realist" approach have largely been concerned with the growing pains of Communist consciousness. Where the theme came close to the more fundamental human values, as in Simonov's "The Russian People," the "socialist" point of view was hardly involved. In this respect the Simonov play and Leonov's "Invasion" meet on the common ground of human experience. The same experience however can be approached in yet another way. Psychology, character, and realistic plausibility of action are not the only means of communicating the emotional content of a play. There is also the theater itself with its time-honored conventions and its established nonrealistic genres of classical tragedy (both Greek and French) and high melodrama (which is "melodrama" because it does not rise to the "cathartic" power of tragedy, and "high" because it moves on the same emotional plane). "The Square of Flowers" by Vassily Ilyenkov is one of the few Soviet plays which boldly resort to the means of the theater itself to build up their emotional impact.

In a setting resembling that of "Invasion" a small Russian family consisting mainly of women suddenly finds itself confronted with the supreme test of saving their souls as honest people and loyal Soviet citizens rather than saving their lives by disloyalty and cowardice. The author takes this situation, which was common enough in the parts of Russia occupied by the Germans, and using not so much coincidence as accepted theatrical devices, shows step by step how the predicament of the family hiding a Soviet flier grows more and more menacing, how driven by their innate sense of decency the three women of the family rise to the moral ordeal of murdering a traitor, and how later, together with their old father, they bravely meet their doom at the hands of the Germans. There is splendid symbolism in the murder scene where the women, like the ancient goddesses of vengeance, slowly advance on the contemptible traitor to batter him to death, and similar symbolism in the emotional climax of the final scene, the burning alive of the old man and his only surviving daughter, much as this might savor of heroics in a more realistic treatment of the story. And this too has to be said of the play: besides being good theater it is sincerely and deeply felt.

A significant tendency in the Soviet drama, probably not unconnected with the desire to escape the narrow-minded pedestrianism of the "socialist-realist" school, has been the marked growth in the number of plays in verse. One of the best, after Mayakovsky's futuristic "Mystery-Bouffe," was "Vagram's Night" (1935) by Leonid Pervomaysky, a tragedy dealing with underground revolutionary activities during civil war. Others, of more recent date, include "Mazeppa" by Yakov Apushkin, "Jester Balakirev" by Anatoly Marienhoff, "Friendship," "A Moscow Girl," and the already-mentioned "Sons of Three Rivers" by Victor Gusev, "Long, Long Ago" by Alexander Gladkov, and "The Livonian War" by Ilya Selvinsky, the last being particularly notable for the quality of its verse and the richly colored picture it paints of the time of Ivan the Terrible.

It is worthy of note that most of these plays in verse deal with historical subjects. No similar trend toward a more imaginative view of drama has so far made itself felt in plays of contemporary Soviet life. It seems that a change in this direction is bound to come, if only because the still young but rapidly growing class of educated people in Soviet Russia is showing definite signs of nearing the end of its present stage of intellectual adolescence. There are signs, too, of a changing attitude in official circles. Some playwrights like Leonov and some theater directors like Alexander Tairov, who only a few years ago were constantly badgered by overzealous critics for either libeling Soviet life or indulging in hothouse estheticism, have lately been awarded the highest honors by the Soviet Government. Perhaps some day the present zeal for using the theater as a means for visual demonstration of copybook maxims (Soviet version) will pass too, and Soviet drama will gain that breadth of vision and imaginative power which inspire great thoughts and deep feelings and without which no nation's drama can flourish or survive.

LYUBOV YAROVAYA

BY KONSTANTIN TRENYOV

THE Russian civil war which forms the theme of this play covered a period of two and a half years (March, 1918, to December, 1920). At its height it was fought on three main fronts: in the east, on the Siberian border, where the anti-Bolshevik forces were led by Admiral Kolchak; in the west, on the approaches to Leningrad, where General Yudenich attempted a drive on the northern Russian capital; and in the south where the strong Volunteer Army under General Denikin, sweeping over the Ukraine, came to within a short distance of Moscow.

The action of "Lyubov Yarovaya" is laid in the south toward the end of the civil war when the White armies were finally forced to take to the boats and flee to Turkey. At the time France and England were supporting the Whites with supplies and munitions. A more active intervention with their own military forces had been attempted at the early stage of the civil war by the French, who occupied Odessa, and by the English, who invaded the southern Caucasus. The French intervention is recalled in the play by one of the characters, the sailor Shvandya, who refers to the famous episode when the crews of the French squadron mutinied and compelled withdrawal of their ships from Russian waters.

The author of "Lyubov Yarovaya," Konstantin Andreyevich Trenyov, was born in 1878, of peasant parents. Beginning his literary career at the age of twenty, he attracted attention by his short stories. As a dramatist he made his debut with the play "The Dorogins" published in 1912, but did not gain notice until after the revolution when his play "The Pugachov Time," which describes the peasant rebellion led by Pugachov in the reign of Catherine the Great, was produced by the Moscow Art Theater (1924). "Lyubov Yarovaya," his most outstanding success, followed two years later in the production staged by the Maly Theater of Moscow. He afterward wrote "A Wife," "Eperiment," "Gymnasium Students," "On the Banks of the Neva," and "War Leader," the latter play inspired by the leadership of General Kutuzov in the war against Napoleon. He died in 1945.

A. B.

LYUBOV YAROVAYA

CHARACTERS

TATYANA, works in KOSHKIN's office
HRUSTCH, her brother, one of KOSH-
  KIN's assistants
MAZUKHIN, another assistant to
  KOSHKIN
VIKHOR (MIKHAIL YAROVOY), an As-
  sistant Commissar
PAVLA PETROVNA PANOVA, a typist
FYODOR SHVANDYA, a sailor
GROZNOY, an assistant to KOSHKIN
PROFESSOR MAXIM IVANOVICH
  GORNOSTAYEV
ELENA IVANOVNA GORNOSTAYEVA
  (LYOLYA), his wife
ARKADY YELISATOV, an adviser to
  KOSHKIN
FIRST CITIZEN
SECOND CITIZEN
ROMAN KOSHKIN, a Commissar
FOLGIN, a city liberal
CHIR, a watchman
DUNKA (AVDOTYA FOMINISHNA
  KULESHOVA, DUNYA), a servant
MARYA, a peasant woman
LYUBOV YAROVAYA, a schoolteacher
IVAN KOLOSOV, an electrician
WORKMAN
MAKHORA, a girl
KUZMA ILYICH KOSTYUMOV, a Quar-
  termaster Sergeant
PIKALOV, a peasant drafted for the
  civil war
AN OFFICER
A HIGH-SCHOOL GIRL

THE GENERAL
FIRST SOLDIER
SECOND SOLDIER
THE DANCE DIRECTOR
COLONEL KUTOV
FATHER ZAKATOV, a priest
COLONEL MALININ
THE COMMANDER-IN-CHIEF OF THE
  WHITE ARMY
A REPRESENTATIVE OF THE LAND-
  LORDS
A REPRESENTATIVE OF THE MANU-
  FACTURERS
A NEWSBOY
A WOMAN CIGARETTE VENDOR
A LADY
A FLOWER VENDOR
A BOOTBLACK
FIRST GENTLEMAN
SECOND GENTLEMAN
FATHER ZAKATOV'S WIFE
THIRD GENTLEMAN
THE BARON
SEMYON SKOPTSOV, MARYA's son
THE BARONESS
AN ARMY CLERK
FIRST WORKER
SECOND WORKER
GRIGORY, MARYA's other son
AN ADJUTANT
FIRST LADY
SECOND LADY
COMMANDANT
A SENTRY

FIRST WOMAN	A SPECULATOR
SECOND WOMAN	SPECULATOR'S LADY
FOURTH GENTLEMAN	OLD WOMAN

WORKERS, BOURGEOIS CITIZENS, AND OTHER TOWNSPEOPLE, WHITE ARMY SOLDIERS AND OFFICERS, BAND, REPRESENTATIVES OF ENTENTE POWERS, CIVIC DELEGATIONS

ACT I

Office of the Revolutionary Committee and other revolutionary organizations in a private house formerly occupied by a wealthy family. The place is a-buzz with activity. The telephone rings.

TATYANA (*answering*). Yes. Comrade Hrustch? The Fifth? Hold the line. (*Shouts.*) Comrade Hrustch! The Fifth Division's calling you. (*Enter* HRUSTCH.) The Fifth Division, Andryusha.

HRUSTCH (*at the telephone*). Yes, this is Hrustch. Yes. A message? Read it to me. (*Prepares to copy it down.*) What's that? What's that? The Zheglov Bridge? Impossible! When? Five o'clock? Go on! Go on! Yes. I've got it. All right. (*Replaces the receiver. Excitedly, as he reads over the message.*) How the hell did it happen? Where's Mazukhin? Tanya dear, call comrade Mazukhin.

TATYANA. Comrade Mazukhin. Comrade Hrustch wants you. (*Enter* MAZUKHIN.)

MAZUKHIN. What's happened?

HRUSTCH. Here. Read it. (MAZUKHIN *reads. The telephone rings.*)

TATYANA. Yes. Comrade Koshkin? Just a moment. (*Goes into* KOSHKIN'S *office.*)

MAZUKHIN (*handing back the message*). H'm! (*Whistles.*)

HRUSTCH. Stop whistling.

MAZUKHIN. Who's whistling? I'm just humming. (VIKHOR *comes in from* KOSHKIN'S *office.*)

HRUSTCH. Comrade Vikhor, read this.

VIKHOR (*reads, trying to conceal his joy*). There, I knew it would happen!

HRUSTCH. What did you know?

VIKHOR. That those commanders should have been placed not at the Zheglov Bridge but against a wall. (MAZUKHIN *whistles.*)

HRUSTCH. You'd stand everybody against a wall.

VIKHOR. Yes, all those intellectuals.

HRUSTCH. We have to blow up the small bridges.

VIKHOR. You're a small one yourself, my boy! We have to blow up, but not the small bridges. Let's go see comrade Koshkin. The Zheglov Bridge is of great strategic importance. (*Goes off.* HRUSTCH *and* MA-ZUKHIN *follow.* TATYANA *returns.*)

TATYANA (*picking up the phone*). Comrade Koshkin will call you back in five minutes. (*She goes off. Enter* PANOVA *and* SHVANDYA.)

PANOVA. And you were actually there, comrade Shvandya?

SHVANDYA. Big as life. The Reds were on the shore, like where I'm standing now, and the French cruiser with the sailors was like where you're standing, comparatively speaking, that is. I could see and hear everything just as plain. Then one of the sailors steps right out to the middle and begins to lay into the rest of 'em—(*The telephone rings.*) He begins to lay into 'em, like I was saying. "Comrades," says he, "rise against the capitalists and the officers." (*The telephone rings.*) "We've shed our blood for 'em long enough," says he.

PANOVA. Answer the telephone.

SHVANDYA. What?

PANOVA. The phone.

SHVANDYA (*sauntering over to it*). "Long enough," says he. (*Lifts the receiver.*) Hello. Revolutionary Committee. "Long enough," says he. "We've shed our good blood for those dirty—" So what? You don't say. Well, the hell with you! It's bad enough trying to get anything done around here without you pestering me—I'm dizzy enough as it is, haven't even got time to blow my nose, like they say. How do you know—I might be busy making a report! I'm telling you, don't interrupt important business with that kind of tripe. (*Hangs up.*) "We've been shedding our blood for 'em long enough," he says. And on and on like that—

PANOVA. In French?

SHVANDYA. Perfect French.

PANOVA. But you don't understand French, comrade Shvandya.

SHVANDYA. What was there to understand? Did the capitalists drink their blood? They did. Anybody can understand that. Then pretty soon I see this same sailor coming up in a launch. A beard like this! Hair as long as a priest's. He comes up and opens his mouth—God, what a voice!

PANOVA. Who was it?

SHVANDYA. Marx, of course, who else could it have been?

PANOVA. Who?

SHVANDYA. Marx, I said.

PANOVA. I'm afraid you saw a little too much, comrade Shvandya.

SHVANDYA. Well, I did see a lot.

PANOVA. Marx has been dead for a long time.

SHVANDYA. Dead? Tell me another. If that's the case, who's supposed to be in command of the world proletariat? (*Enter* HRUSTCH.)

HRUSTCH. Comrade Shvandya.

SHVANDYA. Here. (SHVANDYA *follows* HRUSTCH *out. Enter* GROZNOY.)

GROZNOY. Please type this for me, comrade Panova.

PANOVA. Right away?

GROZNOY. Naturally. My handwriting's too scratchy—I'd better read it off to you.

PANOVA. That's all right. I can make it out. (*Takes the paper from* GROZNOY *and starts typing.* GROZNOY *stands watching her hungrily.*) Why are you staring at me like that? What I'm doing is just plain, ordinary work.

GROZNOY. You're a work of art yourself.

PANOVA. Oh, comrade Groznoy, you always make me blush.

GROZNOY. Do I? How?

PANOVA. By what you say, of course.

GROZNOY. And you, by your eyes—you don't just make me blush —you make me sweat.

PANOVA. That's frightful!

GROZNOY. You don't need to be frightened of me. But if I want to, you know, I can make a skunk pass out cold just by looking at him.

PANOVA. Really?

GROZNOY. An hour ago a doctor walked into my office. He was so tall he almost touched the ceiling—a beard down to here—spectacles. I gave him one of my looks—like this—and he turned white and began to shake all over.

PANOVA. It must have been quite a look. (GROZNOY *opens his leather coat to get a cigarette, revealing gold-braided trousers tucked into high boots just below the knees*.) My, don't you look impressive in that outfit!

GROZNOY. Does it suit me?

PANOVA. Very much—the gold braid is beautiful. But what's the idea of counterrevolutionary pants?

GROZNOY (*taken aback and closing his coat*). Just to dress up—let you see how I look. Now let me have your hand.

PANOVA. What for?

GROZNOY. You'll see. (*Pulls a fistful of jewelry out of his pocket.*) Not bad for trinkets, eh? (*Tries to put a necklace around* PANOVA'S *throat.*)

PANOVA. No, no, comrade Groznoy, don't do that.

GROZNOY. Why not?

PANOVA. There's no reason for it.

GROZNOY. Evidently you deserve it.

PANOVA. What will people think?

GROZNOY. They better not think anything!

PANOVA. And what if comrade Commissar sees it?

GROZNOY. Well, you can push the bracelet up your sleeve and let the pendant dangle down in there.

PANOVA. No, comrade Groznoy, you'd better keep these things yourself.

GROZNOY. All right. But remember, you can have them any time you want— I'll always carry them with me. As for you, I'll see that you never get away either.

PANOVA. But what if it's not in your power to decide?

GROZNOY. You don't seem to know my power. (*Hides the jewelry in an inside pocket. Enter* PROFESSOR GORNOSTAYEV *and his wife.*)

GORNOSTAYEV. Is there somebody here I can speak to?

PANOVA. This is comrade Groznoy.

GROZNOY. What do you want?

GORNOSTAYEV. Oh, it's you? Oh, yes, yes. Well, you see, some men with rifles came and locked up my library.

GORNOSTAYEVA. And Commissar Vikhor, the one with the shriveled arm—he's installed himself in our apartment, taken over all the furniture for himself, and got everything simply filthy. He uses foul language and he's killed three of my hens and written all over the place with their blood: "Finish off the unfinished bourgeois."

GROZNOY. Ho! Ho! Ho! What a head on his shoulders! Vikhor's a clever one all right! Even has hens working for the revolution. Hah!

GORNOSTAYEVA. I treasured the hens—

GORNOSTAYEV. The hens themselves don't matter. Let him eat them, but without the stupid symbols.

GROZNOY. Who the devil are you?

GORNOSTAYEV. I'm Professor Gornostayev.

GROZNOY. A professor? Ha! Ha! Ha! So what is it you want? We'll hand your books over to the reading room.

GORNOSTAYEV. That's just what you mustn't do.

GROZNOY. Now, see here. Don't you tell us what to do. I bet you've been having thousands of books all to yourself, while the rest of the country has one book to a thousand people. Is that a proper state of affairs?

GORNOSTAYEVA. But he has to work.

GROZNOY. What kind of work?

GORNOSTAYEVA. He writes.

GROZNOY. H'm, work. We'll have to look into what you write. Maybe it's counterrevolutionary propaganda.

GORNOSTAYEV (*studying* GROZNOY's *face keenly*). Yes, that's it all right.

GROZNOY. What do you mean, that's it?

GORNOSTAYEV. I'm asking, why such frightened eyes, my friend?

GROZNOY. My eyes—frightened? Just wait, I'll frighten you. Shvandya! (*Enter* SHVANDYA.) Bring this counterrevolutionary to my office. (*He goes off.*)

GORNOSTAYEVA. Max! Max! But it's useless!

GORNOSTAYEV. Somebody has to suffer for the hens too, it seems.

SHVANDYA (*walking up to* GORNOSTAYEV). Well, shove off. (*After staring fixedly at the* PROFESSOR *for a moment, walks aside in embarrassment.*) No, sir. I know my revolution. (*To* PANOVA.) Such a dead ringer, it's taken my breath away!

PANOVA. Dead ringer—for whom?

SHVANDYA. He's got the same face—same name—Marx! (*Enter* GROZNOY.)

GROZNOY. Shvandya! What's holding you up? I want the prisoner in my office.

SHVANDYA. Shove off! We've got a case here only Koshkin can decide. It's Marx himself! (*Enter* YELISATOV.)

YELISATOV. Greetings, comrades! Maxim Ivanovich! Elena Ivanovna! What fate has brought you here?

GORNOSTAYEV. Well, our hens have been killed, our library has been locked up, Commissar Vikhor has been—

YELISATOV. Just a minute. What have they done, comrade Groznoy?

GROZNOY. Ah, counterrevolutionaries! You should have heard them talk!

YELISATOV. But this is Professor Gornostayev. He's known all over Europe.

GROZNOY. We'll know him too. But here's the chief. (*He goes off. Enter* KOSHKIN, *surrounded by a group of* CITIZENS, *among whom is* FOLGIN.)

FIRST CITIZEN. What's the news from the front, comrade Koshkin?

SECOND CITIZEN. What with all the rumors, are we to go on with our work as usual?

KOSHKIN. At the front things couldn't be better. Comrade Panova, take down the business for today's meeting.

FOLGIN. Speaking as a representative of the intellectuals in public service, I wish to verify the rumors concerning the front. If the situation is immediately—

KOSHKIN. See that the intellectual in public service is immediately sent to dig trenches. Then he'll be able to verify the rumors concerning the front.

FOLGIN. But I represent people who work with their brains.

KOSHKIN. There's work for brains there, too. Take down the agenda, comrade Panova. (*Dictates.*) The question of a teachers' conference and of special courses for reëducating the teachers. The question of setting up a network of forty clubs in the city. The question of driving the entire bourgeois population without exception to dig trenches on Green Hill. The question of universal popular education without exception. The question of housing—eviction, moving, resettling, and sharing of quarters. The question of carrying out electrification by concentrated effort. What other questions are there, comrade Yelisatov?

YELISATOV. I think that's enough for one session.

KOSHKIN. All right. Also current business; that is, the question of counterrevolution. (*The* CITIZENS *scatter slowly.*)

YELISATOV (*to* KOSHKIN, *in a confidential manner*). The phone message is from the front?

KOSHKIN. No, from my grandmother's second cousin. Asks to be remembered to everybody.

YELISATOV. That's very nice of her. (*Loudly.*) Comrade Roman! Here's Professor Gornostayev—he wants to make a request.

KOSHKIN. Yes?

GORNOSTAYEV. That's right, I do. They've taken away my books.

GORNOSTAYEVA. They've killed my hens.

GORNOSTAYEV. That's right.

YELISATOV. Professor Gornostayev is the shining light of Russian science.

KOSHKIN (*shaking* GORNOSTAYEV's *hand*). Please sit down, comrade. We should have met long ago. (*To* SHVANDYA.) Shvandya, see that comrade Professor has his books returned immediately and— (*To* YELISATOV.) make out an immunity order for him. We need you, Professor, in the matter of popular education. Having temporarily taken over the duties of Commissar of Education, I've been hard at work writing down my project for universal education of everybody. Give it to me, comrade Yelisatov. (YELISATOV *hands him a paper.*)

GORNOSTAYEV (*reading*). "Concerning the universal functionizing of education of the working people." Comrade Commissar of Education, you're illiterate—

GORNOSTAYEVA (*frightened*). Oh, my God!

KOSHKIN. How can I be illiterate when I wrote it myself? Only I'm not too good at spelling. You know that knowledge is light, ignorance is darkness?

GORNOSTAYEV. I know.

KOSHKIN. No, comrade Professor, you don't know the whole of it. You only know that knowledge is light, you can see that right ahead of you. But about ignorance being darkness, that's something you only know from one side. Well, I learned it the hard way. Light shines right into your eyes. Darkness covers mine. So I hate darkness more than you do and I'll fight it to the last gasp. And anybody who doesn't want to help me and tries to sabotage me, he'll get light and dark both from me before he knows what hit him.

GORNOSTAYEV. Just so. I see the flame of faith in your eyes. The ones who came to me didn't have it—they only shook guns in my face.

KOSHKIN. You can't make a revolution without guns, comrade Professor.

YELISATOV. That's true.

KOSHKIN. Come back in an hour's time, comrade Gornostayev, with comrade Yelisatov. He's a big help to me. We'll work together. (*He goes off.*)

YELISATOV. That's right. We'll give the people all our powers, because in the past science was a white slave of capital, now it is a red comrade of the proletariat. Isn't that so, comrade Gornostayev?

GORNOSTAYEV. Eh? Oh, yes.

YELISATOV. We've met before, Maxim Ivanovich. You remember, in Odessa?

GORNOSTAYEV. Yes, of course, I remember. You're a dentist, I believe?

YELISATOV. Oh no, no! I'm a journalist and quite active in public affairs.

GORNOSTAYEV. Just as I was saying—a kind of dentist. (YELISATOV *and the* GORNOSTAYEVS *leave. Enter* CHIR.)

PANOVA. Well, whom have you informed on today, Chir?

CHIR. I believe in one God who judges the wealthy and the impious. For it is written: "In the morning the Lord destroyed all the sinful lands." (*Goes off.*)

PANOVA. The rat! (*Enter* YELISATOV.)

YELISATOV (*to* PANOVA). Koshkin holds a bad hand and he's trying to look pleased about it. But the game is lost. A report's just arrived—a crushing defeat. Our men have abandoned the Zheglov Bridge—

PANOVA. No, really?

YELISATOV. The Whites will be here in a couple of days.

PANOVA. I can't believe it!

YELISATOV. It's true. There'll be panic everywhere. (*Enter* SHVANDYA *carrying a paper.* YELISATOV *leaves.*)

SHVANDYA. Please copy this, comrade Panova.

PANOVA. Yes, comrade Shvandya. You look so fetching.

SHVANDYA. Who, me?

PANOVA. Yes, you. A perfect Cupid.

SHVANDYA. What makes you think so? (*Enter* DUNKA.) Oh, comrade Avdotya Fominishna. How are you? Now, here's real beauty.

PANOVA. What a gorgeous dress you have on!

SHVANDYA. You're just like a corsage or a little sprig of flowers in a pot. And the gloves too—

DUNKA. Don't touch them with your paws.

SHVANDYA. I only poked one finger. Are you going to the dance, Dunya?

DUNKA. That's got nothing to do with you.

SHVANDYA. You're wrong there, to put it mildly. I'm a conscious revolutionist, too.

DUNKA. I want to see comrade Commissar.

SHVANDYA. Easy as pie. What's it about?

DUNKA. None of your business. (*Walks toward* KOSHKIN'S *office.*)

SHVANDYA. Oh yes it is. Hey, you can't go in! (*Enter* KOSHKIN *holding paper which he hands to* SHVANDYA. *The latter and* PANOVA *go off.*)

DUNKA. I want to see you, comrade Koshkin.

KOSHKIN. What about?

DUNKA. I have to have two rooms because I have a lot of important friends and so far she's only given me her boodevahr and not even that till she took her spring chaise-lounge out. Make her give me her living room right away. I have ten times as many visitors as she has. Commissar Vikhor is coming for coffee tomorrow. What's he supposed to sit on? I ask you!

KOSHKIN. Who are you, comrade?

DUNKA. A housemaid, of course.

KOSHKIN. Then you should join the union and defend your interests in common with others. (*Goes off.*)

DUNKA. I don't need that sort of thing. I can defend myself by myself. (SHVANDYA *and* PANOVA *return with papers.* MARYA *enters from outside.*)

MARYA. Where is everybody?

SHVANDYA. Who do you want to see, citizen?

MARYA. Heaven knows who. Maybe you. You're a commissar?

SHVANDYA. No, not quite.

MARYA. Well, you look like one. It's three days now since I came here from my village but I can't get in to see the Commissar. The only one I do see is this painted scarecrow. (*To* DUNKA.) What's the idea of dolling yourself up in other people's dresses? Did you earn them? Were they made for you?

DUNKA. They were if I'm wearing 'em. Today everything belongs to everybody.

MARYA. What do you mean, "everybody," when it's split under the arms? Take it off, you sow!

DUNKA. Leave me alone, granny!

MARYA. Take it off, you slut. I'm warning you. Don't dirty those clothes. (*Starts tearing the blouse off* DUNKA.)

DUNKA (*defending herself*). What the hell are you trying to do, you counterrevolutionist? Let go!

MARYA. I'll show you who's a counterrevolutionist!

DUNKA. Help! Help! (*Runs off.*)

SHVANDYA. Are you off your trolley?

MARYA. Ah, the dirty pig! Look, such a nice blouse—and she's ruined it! (*Cries.*)

SHVANDYA. You're an old battle-ax.

MARYA. What do you mean, old? I'm only fifty—I'm going to live a long time yet. But my sons are gone. Now it's up to me to get along as best I can.

SHVANDYA. Where are your sons?

MARYA. How do I know? One of them never got back from fighting the Germans—he and my man both got lost. Then this war came along, and now the other two have disappeared.

SHVANDYA. Where were they fighting?

MARYA. First they were just fighting at home, between themselves. Then they left, each his own way. "Good-by, Ma," they said. "Good-by, you sons-of-bitches," says I, "don't you ever come back." And they haven't. Now, where can they be?

SHVANDYA. But which side were they fighting on?

MARYA. That's one thing I could never make out.

SHVANDYA. Simple. What did they say to each other?

MARYA. Grishka kept yelling at Syomka: "You, blankety-blank bandit!"

SHVANDYA. Bandit? Then Syomka must be a White.

MARYA. And Syomka yelled at Grishka: "You pogrom-maker!"

SHVANDYA. Pogrom-maker? Well, then, Grishka's a White. No, wait a minute, you're getting me all mixed up. Tell me again, which one's Syomka?

MARYA. Maybe some of these papers'll tell us who's who?

SHVANDYA. No, wait. I'll bet we find out without papers. What kind of business were they in?

MARYA. Business? Grishka didn't have any—not him—he was in service. And Syomka—well, that one had a business all right—he had a hundred sacks of wheat, of wheat alone, and he kept two farmhands during the summer.

SHVANDYA. Now you're talking. It's a cinch. Look for Syomka with the Whites, and Grishka—he ought to be around here some place.

MARYA. Here?

SHVANDYA. Come along with me, Ma. We'll go next door and ask some questions. They'll tell us everything we want to know.

MARYA. They will?

SHVANDYA. Revolution can explain everything, Ma.

MARYA. All right. Let's go. (SHVANDYA and MARYA go out. LYUBOV YAROVAYA enters, glancing about. A minute later PANOVA emerges from KOSHKIN's office, carrying some papers.)

PANOVA. Oh, welcome to our city, comrade Yarovaya.

LYUBOV. Is comrade Koshkin in?

PANOVA. He's awfully busy just now.

LYUBOV. Will you please tell him I want to see him?

PANOVA. He's given strict orders to keep all visitors out.

LYUBOV. But this is important—it can't wait.

PANOVA. You may not believe it, but comrade Koshkin's business can't wait either.

LYUBOV. Don't be flip. I haven't the time for it. (A pause.)

PANOVA. You've spent a whole day walking here from the village again?

LYUBOV. I'm used to that. I haven't been spoiled by express trains and automobiles. (Enter YELISATOV.)

YELISATOV. Hello, comrade Yarovaya! How've you been? Better, I hope. The country air does wonders after an attack of typhoid. But the schools aren't supposed to open for some time yet, are they? You ought to stay out there in the village.

LYUBOV. The Whites shelled and set the village on fire yesterday.

YELISATOV. The Whites? How did they get there?

LYUBOV. They were only an hour's march away yesterday.

YELISATOV. So close?

LYUBOV. By now they're probably in the village.

YELISATOV. It's impossible. Our troops are pressing them on all sides.

PANOVA. It must be awfully scary to get shelled. (YELISATOV *goes off*.)

LYUBOV. No, it's lots of fun.

PANOVA. Why do you always act this way toward me, comrade Yarovaya?

LYUBOV. I'd hardly call myself your comrade. And I'm not aware that I act in any way toward you. How soon will comrade Koshkin be free?

PANOVA. In a few minutes. We're both soldier's widows, both have to earn our living. So it looks as if maybe we are comrades.

LYUBOV. I don't think so. Just being widows doesn't make people comrades.

PANOVA. Your husband lost his life two years ago, mine two months ago.

LYUBOV. And what do you conclude from that?

PANOVA. Perhaps simply that my wound hurts more.

LYUBOV. Perhaps it does.

PANOVA. Care for a cigarette? Headquarters' stock.

LYUBOV. No, thanks. I'll smoke one of my own—schoolteachers' stock. (*Lights up.*)

PANOVA. Incidentally, has comrade teacher had much schooling herself?

LYUBOV. No, very little.

PANOVA. I can see that.

LYUBOV. No doubt. We had to go blind so that the likes of you could see more and better.

PANOVA. Yes, I have seen a lot. I've seen culture both in western Europe and in Russia and I can see what it means when an ignorant brute tramples down in a second what it took centuries to build.

LYUBOV. It couldn't have been too good, that product of the labor of centuries, if it could be trampled down so easily.

PANOVA. That's no criterion. Your husband and my husband were fine men. Mine was a wonderful architect—he built temples and palaces, and yet the bite of a single louse was enough to kill him. That was the end of a great creative artist—and the end of his temples and palaces too. They've gone to feed a louse.

LYUBOV. Others will be built.

PANOVA. Not in Russia, my dear. Here it's His Majesty the louse that reigns supreme—it will eat up everything.

LYUBOV. There are worse parasites than lice. Those are the ones that ate up my husband. While yours was building palaces, mine was seeing the inside of jails. You built palaces for yourselves; for us you built prisons. Did your husband fight the Germans in the war?

PANOVA. No!

LYUBOV. That's the spirit! Leave it to the dangerous enemies and ignorant brutes to defend their country. The noble and well-bred can hide behind their backs. My husband said to me as he was going off to fight: "Wait for me, Lyuba, I'll bring back a new life from the front. As for the past, we'll square accounts with them for that." So I'm submitting that account now.

PANOVA. For your husband?

LYUBOV. Not just for him—for all the ignorant brutes that built your palaces. (*Enter* KOLOSOV.)

KOLOSOV. Well, all set for the holiday, friends? Lyuba, I'm glad to see you. How do you do, Pavla Petrovna? (*To* LYUBOV.) Yelisatov told me you'd arrived—so I came right over!

PANOVA. Posthaste.

KOLOSOV. Posthaste.

PANOVA. Take a minute to catch your breath. Have a drink of water.

KOLOSOV. You must be hungry. (*Offers a roll.*)

LYUBOV. No, thank you.

KOLOSOV. Well, how goes it with you?

LYUBOV. All right. I'm back again, as you see. The Whites have burned our village to the ground.

KOLOSOV. Never mind, we'll build a new one.

LYUBOV. And how are things with you, Vanya?

KOLOSOV. I was thinking of looking you up tomorrow, and here you've come today.

PANOVA. Lucky man! Facts anticipate his every desire!

KOLOSOV. That's the way it always is with me. No sooner do I congratulate someone on a coming holiday than the holiday walks right in! (*As* PANOVA *exits.*) You don't look so good around the eyes.

LYUBOV. I know. I'm tired. (*The telephone bell rings.*) I just saw something in the Gornostayevs' window— (*Telephone rings again.*) It's very strange— (*Enter* TATYANA.)

TATYANA (*lifting the receiver*). Comrade Koshkin? Just a minute. Comrade Koshkin, you're wanted on the telephone. (KOLOSOV *goes off.* KOSHKIN *and* YELISATOV *enter from* KOSHKIN's *room.*)

KOSHKIN (*on the phone*). That's right. Put all the bourgeois to digging trenches right away! That's right!

YELISATOV. Please sign this, comrade Koshkin.

KOSHKIN (*still on the phone as he signs*). Yes. Yes. (*To* YELISATOV.) Who is it spelling in the old way?

YELISATOV. It's the secretary in the Department of Finance. He can't get out of the habit. (*Takes the paper and goes off.*)

KOSHKIN (*smiling*). A day locked up in a cellar would get him out of it all right. (*On the phone.*) Draft every available horse. That's all. (*Hangs up.*) Good morning, comrade Yarovaya.

LYUBOV. Good morning. The Whites burned Chugunovka yesterday.

KOSHKIN. I know. The bastards didn't even give you time to get over your typhoid.

LYUBOV. I'm not worrying about that.

KOSHKIN. Never mind. This is only a temporary evacuation. We retire without fighting. You won't have to wait long for our return.

LYUBOV. Comrad Koshkin, there are people waiting for you in the village, in the woods, in the quarries.

KOSHKIN. There are, eh? Thanks a lot, comrade Yarovaya. You always come with a little gift. But it's not a surprise. In fact, it's no more than I've been expecting. How many people are there altogether?

LYUBOV. More keep gathering all the time. They're waiting for some word from you—what to do. I'm going back to them right away.

KOSHKIN. Somebody else will have to carry my instructions to them. You're staying here.

LYUBOV. But I have important work to do there, comrade Roman.

KOSHKIN. You have more important work to do here.

LYUBOV. If you can trust it to a nonparty person like me—

KOSHKIN (*smiling*). I've done it before, my nonparty comrade Yarovaya. The last time the Whites occupied this place I trusted you with my own life and the life of my comrades.

LYUBOV. It's not worth talking about.

KOSHKIN (*in a low voice*). That cellar you hid us in then—we may need it for something else now.

LYUBOV. You can rely on me, comrade Roman.

KOSHKIN. Shvandya! (SHVANDYA *enters and he and* LYUBOV *shake hands*.) He'll instruct you. And he'll help us to keep in touch with each other.

SHVANDYA. I'll be right with you, comrade Yarovaya—just as soon as I deliver some packages.

KOSHKIN. There, now. He knows a lot, this fellow. He's seen Marx —not the true one, it appears, but then he's seen him twice.

SHVANDYA. What do you mean, not the true one, when he's just like his pictures and has the same name? (KOSHKIN *and* SHVANDYA *go out as* KOLOSOV *reappears*.)

KOLOSOV. I've been ordered to remove the strings—the music is over! (*Removes telegraph and telephone wires*.)

LYUBOV. Not for long—not our music. The Whites have sung their swan song.

KOLOSOV. Well, what *did* you see in the Gornostayevs' window?

LYUBOV. An embroidered face towel. I could have sworn it was the one I gave Misha when he left for the front—they were as alike as two peas.

KOLOSOV. There are lots of towels in the world that look like other towels.

LYUBOV. But it's exactly the same pattern I embroidered.

KOLOSOV. It's about time you were forgetting all that. After all, it's been two years. It must be fine out in the fields now.

LYUBOV. It is. Everything's green. (*Gunfire is heard.*)

KOLOSOV. And on that green earth men are embroidering with red silk, their brothers' blood.

LYUBOV. They're embroidering a new life—buying a new world with their blood.

KOLOSOV. It's a small price to pay, Lyuba, if it's somebody else's blood.

LYUBOV. Somebody else's? I've paid it with the blood that's dearest to me. And if necessary, I'll pay it with my own—I'm not worthy of his blood. I'm a narrow-minded, smug, cowardly woman. He was burning with a fierce flame, working undercover, and all the while I trembled with fear and whined, "Give it up! You can make yourself just as useful doing some safe public work out in the open." (*Covers her face.*) It makes me feel ashamed, it hurts me to remember. If he were alive I'd be marching by his side now, burning with the same fire. When I was delirious with typhoid I always saw him just as he was going to meet his death. I was walking through a wheat field heavy with ripe grain—

KOLOSOV. If I weren't me, Lyuba, but somebody else, somebody strong, I'd devote my whole life to drying your tears.

LYUBOV. If you weren't you, you'd certainly be somebody else. You're right there. You're a sad case, I must say.

KOLOSOV. Not really. I look ahead. I feel so happy it practically takes my breath away.

LYUBOV. It's because you look not ahead but at me.

KOLOSOV. What? Yes, of course—that too. (*Gunfire is heard.*)

LYUBOV. You hear? That's happiness. It's their day today but it's their last one. (*Enter* PANOVA.)

PANOVA. Did you hear it?

LYUBOV. Jolly, isn't it?

PANOVA. No, it scares the daylights out of you! (*Runs off. Enter* GORNOSTAYEVA.)

GORNOSTAYEVA. This is an outrage, ladies and gentlemen! He's a scoundrel! He killed my last hen, carried off a dozen of my best towels, and left this dirty one behind!

LYUBOV. Who did?

GORNOSTAYEVA. Why, that bandit, of course, that lodger of mine, Commissar Vikhor.

LYUBOV (*inspects the towel and turns pale*). Impossible—it's, it's— Here are his initials—I did them with my own hands—

KOLOSOV. What's the matter, Lyuba?

LYUBOV. I gave this towel to my husband just before he left. How did that man get it? Where is this Vikhor? I want to ask him.

GORNOSTAYEVA. He left early this morning.

LYUBOV. Give it to me, please.

GORNOSTAYEVA. You're welcome to it. (*Hands the towel to* LYUBOV, *who goes off with it at once.* KOLOSOV *follows her.*) But I'll expect something to make up for it. I can't go around giving away towels! (*Runs after* LYUBOV.)

The stage darkens; then the lights come up on KOSHKIN's *office.* KOSHKIN *is at his desk studying a map. Enter* SHVANDYA, HRUSTCH, MAZUKHIN, VIKHOR, *and* YELISATOV.

KOSHKIN. Are we all here? (*After a brief pause.*) Well, then, comrades. We're abandoning this town right away.

VIKHOR. What? Without a fight?

HRUSTCH. Surely we can hold it, comrade Roman.

VIKHOR. We can and will, Roman. It's clear as day.

KOSHKIN. It must be clearer than that to headquarters. We've received orders.

MAZUKHIN. If that's the case, of course we'll have to carry them out.

KOSHKIN. Naturally. The town will be temporarily abandoned. (*After a pause.*) All government institutions are to wind up their affairs. Comrade Yelisatov, I want you to list them for me in the order of their suspension.

YELISATOV. I'll take care of it, comrade Koshkin.

KOSHKIN. Right away.

YELISATOV. Yes, comrade Roman. (*Exits.*)

KOSHKIN. The plan is for all of us to stay on here and go underground. We'll organize guerrilla bands and keep harassing the enemy in the rear. Shvandya, you'll be in charge of hiding the arms. Everything is to be packed in cases and taken to the woods and quarries.

SHVANDYA. Yes, comrade Roman.

KOSHKIN. Go to it. (SHVANDYA *leaves.*) Announce to the citizens—those who want to can evacuate themselves. But it's got to be done without panic. Organize a few meetings and explain it. Is that clear?

HRUSTCH, MAZUKHIN, VIKHOR. Perfectly clear! Of course! It'll be attended to!

KOSHKIN. And now, comrades, one word more. (*To* VIKHOR.) Shut the door, Misha, will you? (*After a pause.*) Does everybody know that the Zheglov Bridge is in the hands of the Whites? (*Exclamations of surprise.*) Not everybody, it seems. Well, what are we to do, comrades?

HRUSTCH (*thoughtfully*). What to do? Blow it up and to hell with it! (MAZUKHIN *whistles.*) Do that again, will you?

MAZUKHIN. I'm not whistling.

HRUSTCH. You better not be.

KOSHKIN (*after a pause*). Well, comrades?

HRUSTCH. What's the good of saying "Well"? Just give someone the order and let him go ahead. We can't afford to waste time.

KOSHKIN (*as if to himself*). Nor the lives of our comrades.

MAZUKHIN. If it has to be done, let's not haggle over it.

VIKHOR. The Zheglov Bridge is of tremendous strategic importance—

KOSHKIN. Are you going to give us a lecture?

VIKHOR. And this crucial operation must be executed under your personal supervision, Roman.

KOSHKIN. All operations here are conducted under my supervision —those are the party's orders. The Zheglov Bridge is to be blown up under your supervision, Misha—those are my orders.

VIKHOR. Thank you, Roman. Consider it done. Just give me the men I know I can count on—Hrustch, Mazukhin, Shvandya—

KOSHKIN. No, Shvandya's staying with me. (*After a brief pause.*) Comrades Hrustch and Mazukhin, I place you under Vikhor's orders.

HRUSTCH, MAZUKHIN. Come on! Let's get going, Vikhor! (*All clasp hands in farewell.*)

KOSHKIN. Well, Misha, I don't have to tell you what an important job you've been entrusted with.

VIKHOR. You can depend on me, Roman. (*They embrace.*)

KOSHKIN (*turning to the others*). Boys, as soon as you're through, light out for the quarries. We'll all meet there. (*All except* KOSHKIN *go off, with* HRUSTCH *bringing up the rear, as* TATYANA *comes in carrying a package.*)

TATYANA. A package for you, comrade Koshkin—just came in the mail.

HRUSTCH. Good-by, little sister!

TATYANA. Where are you off to?

HRUSTCH (*momentarily at a loss*). I have to see to—a small job. (*Keeping his eyes on the tip of his high boot.*) This sole's a damn nuisance. I nail it back on every morning and by night it's loose again. (*Starts toward the door, then stops, returns, embraces his sister, kisses her, and hurries out.*)

TATYANA. What's the matter? Andrey! (*But* HRUSTCH *is already gone. She turns questioningly to* KOSHKIN.) What's got into him?

KOSHKIN (*reading, pretending not to have noticed anything*). Has anything happened?

TATYANA. He kissed me.

KOSHKIN. Who did?

TATYANA. My brother.

KOSHKIN. Oh, your brother. That's nothing. (*Enter* PANOVA. TATYANA *leaves.*)

PANOVA. Please sign this, comrade Koshkin.

KOSHKIN. Well, comrade Panova, what are your plans? Going with us or staying on with the Whites?

PANOVA. I don't like the Whites.

KOSHKIN. And the Reds?

PANOVA. I do like the Reds.

KOSHKIN. H'm! What is there about the Reds that you like? We don't seem to be birds of a feather at all.

PANOVA. I don't like all the Reds, just some of them.

KOSHKIN. For example?

PANOVA. That's a military secret.

KOSHKIN. Undoubtedly, to judge by appearances.

PANOVA. What do you mean?

KOSHKIN. Our military man is training his gun very carefully.

PANOVA. If he's training his gun, it's loaded with gold, not lead. His pockets are packed with gold. And it's all mine if I want it.

KOSHKIN (*raising his head*). Gold? What gold?

PANOVA. Rings, bracelets, watches. I've been told I can have it any time I say "yes."

KOSHKIN. Now, see here, citizen Panova.

PANOVA. Yes, comrade Koshkin?

KOSHKIN. You'd better not joke about these things. Groznoy and I are blood brothers. (*They stare at each other in silence.*)

The light shifts, coming up on the waiting room. Enter GROZNOY, *followed by* DUNKA. PANOVA *comes out of* KOSHKIN's *office.*

DUNKA. Comrade Groznoy, why did they take the truck away from me?

GROZNOY. What truck?

DUNKA. I'd just climbed on and he yells "Get off"! Who does he think he is, kicking me off a truck?

GROZNOY. Ah, go to the devil—you make me sick!

DUNKA. Don't you bark at me like a bull fiddle. I can blast right back at you.

GROZNOY. For Christ's sake! Clear out of here!

DUNKA. I'll carry this to comrade People's Commissariat! (*Enter* KOSHKIN.)

GROZNOY. Beat it! (DUNKA *takes herself off.*) Comrade Panova, get the papers ready for evacuation.

KOSHKIN. Slip me a cigarette, Groznoy, will you? (*To* PANOVA.) Take this down: Whereas, because of the demands of strategy I leave this city for a short time, I ask the citizens to maintain complete—

GROZNOY. We'll have to give orders to clear the jail during the night—get rid of everybody—

KOSHKIN. Is it necessary?

GROZNOY. We haven't been feeding them just to let them go scot free.

PANOVA. You are cruel, comrade Groznoy.

GROZNOY. A revolutionist must have a heart of steel and a breast of iron, comrade Panova.

KOSHKIN. Truer words were never spoken, Groznoy! You're right,

Yakov! (*Slaps* GROSNOY's *chest.*) Say, yours must be made of gold; it rings.

GROZNOY. Naturally.

KOSHKIN. Let's see it.

GROZNOY. Well, I'm off to look after things.

KOSHKIN. Come on, Groznoy, show us your chest, let's see it.

GROZNOY. Stop fooling, Roman.

KOSHKIN. Come, come. Don't be bashful. We're all friends.

GROZNOY. Go away, don't bother me. I have no time for nonsense.

KOSHKIN. Groznoy, unbutton your jacket.

GROZNOY. Now, what the hell—

KOSHKIN. I'm waiting, Groznoy.

GROZNOY (*drawing his revolver*). This joke's gone far enough!

KOSHKIN (*his own revolver in his hand*). In the name of the revolution! Drop that on the desk. (GROZNOY *puts his revolver down.*) And whatever's in your pockets—on the desk with it too! (GROZNOY *yanks various gold objects out of his pocket.*) You—bandit! Out into the hall with you! (KOSHKIN *follows him out.*)

GROZNOY (*off stage, choking up*). Roman, don't hold it against me!

KOSHKIN (*off stage*). Up against the wall! (*A shot. After a moment* KOSHKIN *reënters. He pauses, then resumes dictating.*) Where was I? Whereas I leave this city—I ask the citizens—to maintain complete order—

CURTAIN

ACT II

Scene 1

A street. On the corner the house occupied by the offices of the revolutionary authorities. All the doors and windows are open. The evacuation is in its final stage. Artillery fire in the distance is giving place to machine-gun and rifle fire. DUNKA is hastily loading the last of her possessions onto a cart. A PORTER comes up to her.

DUNKA. Wait, you stupid fool, I tell you, wait! There's room here for a sofa. Put the mirror on top and the trunk here on the side. Well, get going now—hurry up! Oh, for God's sake! (*She grabs up the remaining few things and runs off after the cart. Enter* CHIR.)

CHIR. Yes—yes—yes— "Let the women of sin run away from the face of our Lord." (*Goes off.* SHVANDYA *emerges from the house, glances around cautiously.*)

SHVANDYA. All right. (MEN *carrying boxes of ammunition come out of the house and go off down the street. Enter* KOSHKIN.)

KOSHKIN (*hiding his agitation*). Shvandya!

SHVANDYA. Yes, comrade Commissar.

KOSHKIN. Have you sent anybody after Lyubov Yarovaya?

SHVANDYA. I went myself. She'll be here in a minute. I don't know what to make of it, comrade Roman. There's fighting going on right outside the town. That means the Zheglov Bridge hasn't been blown up, doesn't it?

KOSHKIN. It does.

SHVANDYA. And Vikhor and the boys haven't got back either.

KOSHKIN. They haven't. We'll have to get them back.

SHVANDYA. Ah, you should have sent me with Vikhor.

KOSHKIN. Maybe I should have sent Vikhor with Groznoy—to the same place.

SHVANDYA. I'm going to help them. (*As though he is about to dash off.*)

KOSHKIN. Stay where you are! Don't you dare leave your post! Have you finished your job?

SHVANDYA. The boys are just taking the last cases.

KOSHKIN. Well, get it done quick and clear out of here as fast as you can or you'll be trapped like a rat.

SHVANDYA. Oh, no! Not on your life. You, comrade Commissar, had better get out of here quick yourself—every dog in town knows you— (*To the passing* WORKMEN.) Go ahead—it's all right. (*He disappears as* YELISATOV *comes on.*)

KOSHKIN. Comrade Yelisatov, take the car and go.

YELISATOV. No, you take it, my dear Koshkin, it's time you were going.

KOSHKIN. I'll leave last.

YELISATOV. No, better let me be last. The revolution needs you much more. I'll take care of the evacuation until the last minute.

KOSHKIN. How will you know when the last minute arrives? Do as you're told. Have this proclamation posted first and go straight to the railway station. (YELISATOV *leaves.* LYUBOV *hurries on.*)

LYUBOV. What are you doing here, comrade Roman? All the roads out of town are blocked.

KOSHKIN. Don't worry, I'll find a way out.

LYUBOV. But they might catch you.

KOSHKIN. Me? Not likely. But it seems they *have* caught Vikhor, Mazukhin, Hrustch, and the rest of the Zheglov party.

LYUBOV. Oh, God! What shall we do?

KOSHKIN. That's just the question—and that's why I called you here. We have to get the exact facts. If they've been caught, we must find out under what circumstances and where they are. I want you to do that.

LYUBOV. I will. Only please get out quickly.

KOSHKIN. No quicker than necessary. (*He shakes her hand firmly and walks off. She follows.* DUNKA *runs back.*)

DUNKA. Oh, my God! Oh, my soul and body! (*Enter* YELISATOV.)

YELISATOV. What brings you back, comrade Dunya?

DUNKA. Oh, my God! Where *is* comrade Commissar? They're not letting anybody out. The Whites are getting control of all the roads. I'll have to try another way. (*Goes off.*)

YELISATOV (*calling after her*). You'd better or your cheval glass may get damaged. (*He goes off. Enter* SHVANDYA, *glancing about.*)

SHVANDYA. All right now. (*Enter* WORKMEN *with more cases. They stop.*) What are you stopping for?

A WORKMAN. Look what the wind blew in, devil take her!

SHVANDYA. Where? (*Enter* MAKHORA.) Oh, that's as easy as pie! (*Rushes to* MAKHORA *and puts his arms around her. The* WORKMEN *carry off the cases behind her back.*) Well, good-by, Anyuta darling.

MAKHORA. Anyuta? My name's Makhora.

SHVANDYA. Is that so? And a sweet name it is too. Well, good-by. Don't feel lonesome.

MAKHORA. See here, this is the first time I've ever laid eyes on you.

SHVANDYA. Exactly. Just barely met and we have to part! Well, don't cry. Shvandya will come back. (MAKHORA *flounces off.* SHVANDYA *follows the* WORKMEN. *Farther upstage* VIKHOR *crosses hurriedly and disappears. Enter* GORNOSTAYEVA *and* LYUBOV.)

GORNOSTAYEVA (*calling after* VIKHOR). Ah, my good man! "Finish off the bourgeois like hens," is it?

LYUBOV (*following the direction of* GORNOSTAYEVA's *eyes*). Oh, who's that?

GORNOSTAYEVA. Why, it's that lodger of mine, Vikhor. He's been robbing people right and left. Now he has to run away empty handed. (*Sets off in pursuit of him.*)

LYUBOV. It's impossible. I must have imagined it. (*She is barely able to stand.* SHVANDYA *returns.*)

SHVANDYA. Lock them up and beat it! (*Noticing* LYUBOV.) What's the matter, comrade Lyuba?

LYUBOV (*recovering from the shock*). Oh, it's nothing. The Whites, it seems, have caught the Zheglov men, comrade Shvandya.

SHVANDYA. They've caught them all right—I told Koshkin we'll have to rescue them.

LYUBOV (*holding onto him as he starts to hurry away*). You mustn't —not like that. It requires caution.

SHVANDYA. To hell with caution! (*Runs off.*)

LYUBOV. Comrade Shvandya! (*She follows him. Enter* DUNKA, *then* MARYA.)

DUNKA. Oh, my God! Where is the Commissar? My furniture's lost.

MARYA. Well, those sons of bitches weren't with the Reds—let's see if they're with the Whites. (*To* DUNKA.) So you're all dressed up again? A regular haystack on your head! Oh, you dirty slut! (*She rushes at*

DUNKA, *who darts away.* MARYA *dashes out of sight as* DUNKA *runs into* QUARTERMASTER KOSTYUMOV.)

KOSTYUMOV. What's the trouble, mam'selle?

DUNKA. That crazy woman—she's been bothering me.

KOSTYUMOV. Why?

DUNKA. No reason—no reason at all! I haven't done a thing. But there's nobody to defend me.

KOSTYUMOV. Well, that *is* a pity! Permit me to be your defender. What's your name?

DUNKA. Avdotya Fominishna Kuleshova. And yours?

KOSTYUMOV. Kuzma Ilyich Kostyumov, Quartermaster Sergeant, Supply Service, Second Class. I'm looking for decent quarters.

DUNKA. Well, come along with me then. I'm all alone, you know. (*They go off.* MARYA *runs across the stage.*)

MARYA. No, they're not here. Somebody must have given them a good beating, the sons of bitches. (*She disappears.* SHVANDYA *comes in hurriedly, looking confused. He glances about and ducks around a corner, Machine-gun fire is heard. Enter* PIKALOV.)

SHVANDYA. The dirty dogs. Hello, there! Are you a comrade or the other kind?

PIKALOV. Both. I've been with the comrades and against the comrades.

SHVANDYA. Are you on our side or theirs?

PIKALOV. Ours. I've been a prisoner since fall. One day it's the Reds, the next day it's the Whites.

SHVANDYA. Have you any tobacco?

PIKALOV. I wish I did.

SHVANDYA. Oh—I think I've got some. (*They sit down and smoke.*) Are you from these parts?

PIKALOV. I come from around Tula. What about you?

SHVANDYA. My home's near Kursk. The village of Mitrevka. Shvandya's my name—maybe you've heard of me? Well, how is it out your way?

PIKALOV. Oh, so-so. First like this and then—well, it's nothing much. And your village?

SHVANDYA. Just the opposite. Are you class conscious?

PIKALOV. Who, me?

SHVANDYA. Yes, you.

PIKALOV. No, I haven't registered. How about you?

SHVANDYA. Me? Completely. Can't go any further. I'm as close to Marx as I am to you, so to speak.

PIKALOV. How's he? All right?

SHVANDYA. He's a nice old man.

PIKALOV. How soon will he let us go home?

SHVANDYA. After he's finished with the capitalists, he says.

PIKALOV. Holy Jesus!

SHVANDYA. First, he says, I'll smash the Russian capitalists, then I'll go gunning for the foreign ones.

PIKALOV. Well, I'll be—! My old woman's going to have to get in the crop all by herself again. (*An* OFFICER *strolls on.*)

OFFICER. Who are you?

SHVANDYA. It's us. I've got a prisoner here. (*A* HIGH-SCHOOL GIRL *runs on.*)

GIRL. Valya! Darling!

OFFICER. Lyalya! Darling! Am I glad!

GIRL. You're alive!

OFFICER. Surprised you, didn't I? (*To* SHVANDYA.) Don't loaf here. Take him to headquarters. (*Goes off with the* SCHOOLGIRL.)

PIKALOV (*puzzled—anxiously*). Which one of us is the prisoner here?

SHVANDYA. It seems you are.

PIKALOV. I've already been taken prisoner by other people. Now it's your turn.

SHVANDYA. All right. Lead me away.

PIKALOV. Lead you away. Where to, I'd like to know? I'm a stranger in this town.

SHVANDYA. Wait a minute, I'll look around. I think it must be that way. (*He walks around the corner; then both, without looking at each other, dash off in different directions. Choral singing has started up in the distance. Enter* CHIR *who proceeds to change the flags. Reënter* SHVANDYA, *in a great hurry.*) What shall I do, Grandpa? Is it the end? All the holes are plugged.

CHIR. My, my, dear brother in the Lord. How did you get stuck here?

SHVANDYA. I've been held up by business.

CHIR. What kind of business?

SHVANDYA. Important—on a world scale.

CHIR. Well, come along, Fyodor, servant of the Lord, I'll get you out. For it's written: "This day shall ye be with me in Heaven."

SHVANDYA. If it's written, I guess it's all right, then. (*A* PATROL OF WHITE SOLDIERS *comes on.*)

CHIR. Hey, brethren, this way. Here's one of the devils—the reddest of the Reds. (*The* PATROL *seizes* SHVANDYA.)

SHVANDYA. Wait, you striped Judas. I'll be back from hell to get you yet! (*The* PATROL *marches* SHVANDYA *off.*)

CHIR. You'd better pray—before your end. The thief repented on the cross. Lord in heaven, remember the warrior Fyodor. (*He goes off. Church bells begin pealing. A band plays. The* BOURGEOIS CITIZENS, *holding flowers, gather to welcome a column of* WHITE ARMY TROOPS.)

YELISATOV (*coming on with the* GENERAL *and* VIKHOR). Our worst trouble, Your Excellency, was trying to save the treasures of culture from those unspeakable vandals. We were in danger of our lives more than once. (*Pointing to* VIKHOR.) For example, here's Lieutenant Yarovoy—

GENERAL. Ladies and gentlemen! Rest assured that the anointed head of the Russian realm will not leave a single sacrifice you've made without a reward—in due time!

YELISATOV. Here's their last proclamation—it may interest you to read it. (*The* GENERAL *and the* CITIZENS *clustered about him read the proclamation. Enter* LYUBOV YAROVAYA. VIKHOR *is startled to see her and runs joyfully toward her.*)

VIKHOR. Lyuba!

LYUBOV (*stops as she catches sight of him*). What is this?

VIKHOR. Lyuba, it's you? (*For a moment* LYUBOV *leans against the wall; then, with a cry, falls into his arms.*) I've found you—at last. Lyuba, my darling!

LYUBOV. No, it can't be! Is it really you? I'm not dreaming? You—alive?

VIKHOR. Yes, alive.

LYUBOV. Misha—my dearest! I've cried over you for two years. The official notice said you were killed. Let me look at you. Are you sick? The way your arm hangs— (*Weeping, kisses his face and hands.*)

VIKHOR. Oh, it's nothing. Got it in the war. How are you? (GORNOSTAYEVA *rushes on.*)

GORNOSTAYEVA. Dear people! They've already been strung up, those rats! On Noblemen's Street there's a Bolshevik on every lamppost. That's the way to govern! Thank God, all our waiting wasn't in vain.

LYUBOV. Why have you stayed on?

VIKHOR. Good morning, Elena Ivanovna.

GORNOSTAYEVA (*noticing him*). Oh, you're here, my good man? You haven't left?

LYUBOV. Let's go, Misha, quick.

GORNOSTAYEVA. Please, officers, arrest this scoundrel. He's Commissar Vikhor.

GENERAL. What's the trouble, Lieutenant Yarovoy?

VIKHOR (YAROVOY). Just human ingratitude. The professor's wife is scolding me for not guarding her property well. She didn't know I was risking my life.

LYUBOV. What's that?

GENERAL. Yes, we nearly gave you up for dead.

GORNOSTAYEVA. Then you're—one of us? (*She shakes his hand happily and embraces him. Enter* HRUSTCH, MAZUKHIN, *and others of the Zheglov party under heavy guard.*)

YAROVOY (*reporting to the* GENERAL). The criminals who attempted to blow up the Zheglov Bridge.

LYUBOV. Misha? You? It can't be true! (*Faints.*)

CURTAIN

ACT II

SCENE 2

Night. A deserted spot outside the town near a ravine. No sound. Then
SHVANDYA's *voice can be heard singing, drawing close. Finally* SHVAN-
DYA *walks on between two* SOLDIERS. *They all stop.*

FIRST SOLDIER. Where the hell are we? The sky's bright but down
here you can't see where you're at. Halt! We'll take a rest. (*They sit
down.*)

SHVANDYA (*sings*).
            You're a cheat, my little doll—
            You didn't keep your word at all.

FIRST SOLDIER. Why the devil do we have to march you twenty versts
when you could have been hanged on the spot?

SHVANDYA (*lighting a cigarette*). Maybe that spot didn't appeal
to me.

FIRST SOLDIER. Well, right here, I think, is just the spot for you,
bandit—we'll finish you off and have done with it. You've been sentenced to die anyway.

SHVANDYA. That's fine, just fine. Thanks for your consideration.
Only first you have to deliver me to the central prison.

FIRST SOLDIER. It'll be dawn before we get there and then there won't
be time to hang you while it's dark.

SHVANDYA. I'm in no hurry. (*Sings.*)
            You're a cheat, my little doll—
            You didn't keep your word at all.

FIRST SOLDIER. Stop that ungodly dog howl!

SHVANDYA. Dog or frog, you have to clear your throat before you
croak. (*Sings.*)
            You said you'd love me rain or shine—
            Then you ran off with a pal of mine!

FIRST SOLDIER. Stop singing, do you hear? You're just one step from
being dead.

SHVANDYA. After I'm dead, I won't have enough voice left. Anyway,
it's not going to interfere with my dying.

FIRST SOLDIER. I'm glad you realize that much. You can't wave death
away. Besides, everything in this world is dust and ashes. Here, you're
a Bolshevik, you've sold yourself to the Germans, accepted money
from them, but you can't take it with you to the next world.

SHVANDYA. You bet. It's too heavy to carry.

FIRST SOLDIER. Ah! You must have raked in a lot?

SHVANDYA. Yes, quite a lot.

SECOND SOLDIER. How much, for instance? You might as well confess before you die.

FIRST SOLDIER. Maybe God will knock off a little from your sins.

SHVANDYA. It'd be easy to confess if I had a priest.

FIRST SOLDIER. Judases like you aren't supposed to have a priest. However, I'm a churchwarden.

SHVANDYA. Ah! Well, that might do.

FIRST SOLDIER. Well, tell me—make your confession—how much did you get from the Germans for selling our faith, our Czar, and our country?

SHVANDYA. They didn't treat us so bad. I've got to say that for them. A hundred guldens per head for the faith, two hundred for the Czar, and as for the country—we got a lump sum in sterling.

FIRST SOLDIER. How much is that in our money?

SHVANDYA. Well, I figure about forty thousand.

SECOND SOLDIER. Wow, the dirty capitalist!

FIRST SOLDIER. Where is the money?

SHVANDYA. On me—where do you think? I don't trust anybody with my capital.

FIRST SOLDIER. Let's see it.

SHVANDYA. If I show it to you, you'll take it away.

SECOND SOLDIER. We got every right, too. We ought to shoot you, you filthy parasite!

FIRST SOLDIER. So you want to take it with you to the next world?

SHVANDYA. No, what for? If I could leave it with a reliable man in this world—to pray for my soul when I go—that'd be all right with me.

FIRST SOLDIER. Give it to me. I'm a reliable man.

SHVANDYA. No, I better give it to him. He's more reliable.

FIRST SOLDIER. Why, he's only a farm hand. I had dozens just like him on my farm.

SECOND SOLDIER. Stop fooling around! Come on, let me have it. I'll have prayers said for you forty times.

SHVANDYA. That's too little, my friend.

FIRST SOLDIER. Hand it over, I'm telling you. Come on, or I'll flatten you. Hands up, you bandit! (SHVANDYA *raises his hands.*) Where is it? (*Searches and turns out* SHVANDYA's *pockets.*) All right now; I want the truth.

SHVANDYA. It was in my pockets. Maybe it's slipped through into the lining.

SECOND SOLDIER. There isn't any lining. Just holes.

SHVANDYA. Then it must have fallen out.

SECOND SOLDIER. These aren't the kind of pockets to hold capital.

FIRST SOLDIER. Are you making fun of us, you skunk? Where's the money?

SHVANDYA. You've got all the money, boss. I've just got my soul and a lot of hungry lice.

FIRST SOLDIER. Liar! If it weren't for German money you wouldn't be robbing and killing.

SHVANDYA. Looks like you're the one that's taking *me* to be killed. And for doing what you accuse me of, you demand German money, you pig.

FIRST SOLDIER. That's a lie. I'm not fighting for German money—I'm fighting for my land.

SHVANDYA. That's just what I'm fighting for.

FIRST SOLDIER. What's that?

SHVANDYA. Your land. To take it away from you and give it to this comrade here.

FIRST SOLDIER (*in a rage, raising his rifle*). So you're threatening me, bandit? Insulting me? Well, step back. Turn around, you filthy crow-bait!

SHVANDYA. No, thank you. I'm not used to turning my back.

FIRST SOLDIER (*to the* SECOND SOLDIER). You! Get ready to fire. Don't just stand there!

SECOND SOLDIER. Leave him alone!

FIRST SOLDIER. What? Fire, I tell you, or I'll shoot you too, like a dog.

SECOND SOLDIER (*jumping back and aiming his rifle*). I'll shoot you first, you dirty kulak—

SHVANDYA (*grasping the* FIRST SOLDIER *by the arms*). Halt, comrade. Don't waste a bullet. Don't make any noise.

FIRST SOLDIER. Help!

SHVANDYA (*clapping a hand over his mouth*). Let's pull him over to the gully. (*He and the* SECOND SOLDIER *drag their victim off into the darkness. A minute later a shot rings out. The pair return quickly.*)

SECOND SOLDIER. Where can we go now?

SHVANDYA. I know these parts. Like the inside of my own hand. What's your name?

SECOND SOLDIER. Yegor!

SHVANDYA. Ah, Yegor, the saint on a white horse fighting the dragon. Well, for the time being we'll walk back. This way, Yegor. This is the road to the quarries. (*They go off.*)

CURTAIN

ACT III

Late afternoon, turning to twilight during the second half of the act. The setting is the room of the first act. Posters on the walls, and a bill announcing a dance "For the benefit of the armed forces of southern Russia." PANOVA can be seen through an archway seated at a desk. KOLOSOV is repairing telephone wires.

LYUBOV (*appearing at the door*). Have you found out anything?

KOLOSOV. Not a thing. Everybody's saying the Zheglov men are sure to be executed. They're just waiting for the official papers confirming the death sentence.

LYUBOV. We know that much already. They won't pardon them. But when's the execution going to be? I just spoke to Shvandya—he's been with Koshkin and Koshkin's planning to attack the escort and free the Zheglov prisoners on their way to execution. But first we have to find out when and where it's going to be.

KOLOSOV. You can count on the execution's taking place as soon as the sentence gets confirmed.

LYUBOV. But the question is, when's that?

KOLOSOV. Maybe they've already had word.

LYUBOV. Just what I'm wondering. Panova ought to know—she knows everything. (*A young man, the* DANCE DIRECTOR, *bursts in.*)

YOUNG MAN. Ladies and gentlemen, the dancing tonight is to continue until dawn.

LYUBOV. What?

YOUNG MAN. I beg your pardon? There'll be a Cupid mail for the lovelorn. I'll be leading the dances myself. (*Straightens the bill on the wall and runs off.*)

LYUBOV. I'm going. I don't want to run into Mikhail.

KOLOSOV. Have you met since that day?

LYUBOV. No. I had it out with him then—and that was all. (*She goes off.* PANOVA *comes through the arch.*)

PANOVA. You have something in your pockets.

KOLOSOV. Could be. (*Pulls out two apples.*) Two things in fact. (*Hands her one.*)

PANOVA. We didn't have any light in those rooms back there last night.

KOLOSOV. Your strings keep snapping, O musicians to the Czar! (*He goes off. Enter* KUTOV *and* YELISATOV.)

YELISATOV. Welcome to our city, Colonel. Have you been here long?

KUTOV. I've just come—straight from the front. Good afternoon, Pavla Petrovna. I've made a report to His Excellency on the brilliant new victory near Seleznyovka. Have you heard what we bagged?

YELISATOV. Of course. Seventy prisoners and four machine guns.

KUTOV. Wrong. One hundred and seventy prisoners.

YELISATOV. But the telegram says—

KUTOV. Correct it. Fourteen machine guns and nine cannon besides.

YELISATOV. The telegram has already been published but we can add "according to supplementary reports."

KUTOV. While you're at it, mention that the spirit of the army is excellent and in many districts practically the whole population has been joining up as volunteers.

YELISATOV. And how goes it with the Reds?

KUTOV. Complete disintegration. Three quarters of their army have deserted and the rest have to be driven with bayonets and machine guns. The hydra of revolution is gasping its last and the moment is not far off when the entire Russian nation will rise in close order for the defense of one indivisible Russia, and shouting "The Lord is with us," will— (PANOVA *goes off*.)

YELISATOV. Have you brought anything with you?

KUTOV. Sugar.

YELISATOV. Much?

KUTOV. Three hundred pounds.

YELISATOV. How about the price?

KUTOV. Seven hundred thousand.

YELISATOV. Don't be greedy, Colonel.

KUTOV. Six hundred, not a kopek less.

YELISATOV. All right, I'll take it.

KUTOV. Immediate payment.

YELISATOV. Tomorrow.

KUTOV. In one hour, and not a minute later. (PANOVA *returns*.)

YELISATOV. Will you permit me, Colonel, to publish the interview in an extra edition?

KUTOV. Certainly. My dear Pavla Petrovna—what's the news with those blackguards, our noble allies?

PANOVA. New fashions, a new musical comedy. All Paris is a-twitter.

KUTOV. Never mind, my dear, don't let that upset you. When we get arms, we'll get the fashions too. Arkady Petrovich, you know His Excellency the Commander-in-Chief will be arriving soon.

YELISATOV. Of course I know.

KUTOV. By the way, last time His Excellency came here there was hardly any civil population in the streets. His Excellency noticed it—

YELISATOV. Did he? How extraordinarily observant of him.

KUTOV. He requests that the proper measures be taken this time.

YELISATOV. For the increase of the civil population? But who's to take the measures?

KUTOV. Well, all of us, of course, as far as possible.

YELISATOV. Hear that, Pavla Petrovna? Oh, you're so innocent. But Colonel, don't you think the time's much too short for such a serious assignment? With our present technique—

KUTOV. I see. You choose to make a joke of it. (*Enter* FATHER ZAKA-TOV.) Now our reverend father here could help too with a few inspired words—

YELISATOV. He might, but only with words.

ZAKATOV. Good health to you, ladies and gentlemen. Has his Excellency arrived yet?

PANOVA. No, not yet.

ZAKATOV. Is it true, the glad news that we've been blessed with a new victory?

KUTOV. Absolutely. We're waiting for His Excellency and expect an inspired speech from you.

ZAKATOV. I'll be very happy. All the more so since it is a double triumph. I just met Colonel Malinin in the square. He's straight from a punitive expedition—the rebellious villages have been made to realize their guilt and to repent. Mind my prophetic word—in another forty days you and I will be listening to the golden chimes of the Moscow bell towers. (*Enter* MALININ *and* YAROVOY.) And here is the author of the triumph—speak of the devil!

MALININ. Good afternoon, ladies and gentlemen. Reverend Father, may I ask a blessing? (*Holds out his hands to receive the benediction.*)

ZAKATOV. Blessings upon him who hath returned in peace.

MALININ (*kisses* ZAKATOV's *hand, then takes both* PANOVA's *hands and kisses them*). First one holy hand, then two divine ones.

ZAKATOV. The manner is decorous but the words bespeak the world's vanity.

PANOVA. Whew! What's the name of your perfume? I'll bet they call it "White Punishment"! You ought to smell what Colonel Kutov brought me from the front—it's lovely.

KUTOV. My congratulations on your success, Colonel.

MALININ. The same to you.

YELISATOV. Would you permit me to interview you now?

MALININ. Not till I've had a chance to report to His Excellency.

YELISATOV. Just the general outline.

MALININ. Well, if it's only an outline—

YELISATOV. What would you say prompted those villagers to harvest the landlords' crops and pillage their estates?

MALININ. Bolshevik propaganda, pure and simple.

YELISATOV. Were you able to apprehend the agitators?

MALININ. Every last one of them.

YELISATOV. What measures did you take to restore order?

MALININ. The most resolute and speedy measures. We operated according to the prescribed methods of burning down the villages and flogging the rebels. However, that's not for publication. Speaking on the record, I'd like you to point out that in a difficult campaign of two weeks' duration, the entire unit, from the commander down to the last soldier, was beyond praise. Every man was equally inspired and ready to suffer on the cross for the faith, go to the block for the Czar, or against the enemy's bayonets for his country. And for such beautiful hands as these—(*kisses* PANOVA's *hands*) through fire and water.

PANOVA. Who could have sent you to the block in those little villages? The peasant women?

KUTOV. The bayonets, too, would seem to be rather scarce in this area. (*Chuckles.*)

MALININ. I can assure you, my dear, that, to begin with, the Bolshevik plots in the rear are more dangerous than their bayonets at the front. And, in the second place, in our operations in the rear we didn't bayonet Jewish feather beds or fight to get perfume for ladies, as was done at the front by some people who are chortling now.

KUTOV. And in the third place, I believe, Reverend Father, it's more noble to exterminate Jews at the front than Russian peasant women in the rear.

MALININ. What's that?

ZAKATOV. On the one hand, yes, but on the other—and especially on the third—

YAROVOY. If you don't mind, gentlemen, I'd suggest you continue your arguments in the study and spare Father Zakatov from having to listen to them.

ZAKATOV. I'm vanishing—like smoke fleeing the face of fire. How about that summer place in the country, Arkady Petrovich? I'm anxious to buy one.

YELISATOV. I have just what you want, Father. (YELISATOV and FATHER ZAKATOV go off together.)

KUTOV. You put down peasant women, but the Zheglov Bridge was nearly blown up under your very nose.

MALININ. But it wasn't. And I've captured Mazukhin, Hrustch, and the whole gang of them.

KUTOV. You have?

MALININ. Yes, I.

KUTOV. That was all done by Lieutenant Yarovoy, and you have little ground to take credit for it yourself.

MALININ. You think so?

YAROVOY. Gentlemen, please. The moment is more serious than you imagine. So long as Roman Koshkin is not removed as a threat, our rear continues to be in great danger.

MALININ. We'll remove him. We've just had precise data—he's gone to the Orekhov woods. And that other one—what's his name?—the fellow who killed his guard on the way to his execution—

YAROVOY. Shvandya?

MALININ. That's it—Shvandya. He's in the Wolf gullies. We'll have to send detachments in both directions right away.

YAROVOY. I think you're mistaken, and while you and your detachments struggle through the woods and pick your way through gullies, the bridges and storehouses around here will be getting blown sky high.

MALININ. Don't worry about that. You have to understand—what we need here is moral pressure. The Zheglov gang should be hanged not in Zheglov village but right here, strung up along the boulevard.

KUTOV. Yes, that would make an impression.

MALININ. I'm going to ask His Excellency to give the order right away. (Lifts the telephone receiver.)

YAROVOY. I'm going to insist that you get no such order.

KUTOV. But think of the moral effect.

YAROVOY. I'd be glad, without any effects, to hang all of those brutes, and not only on the boulevard but all the way from here to Moscow. But just now the effect you're going to produce is to make this same Koshkin try and snatch them from their escort right outside the prison.

MALININ. Before that happens, Koshkin himself will be in our hands. But tomorrow morning when they see that garland strung up along the boulevard, you can bet it will be far more convincing than any Bolshevik handbills. Just trust an old campaigner.

KUTOV. We're playing a half-hearted game. If we've come out for terror, it's up to us to use terror—so people can see it.

MALININ. And generally speaking, we must be firmer with those who are really half Bolshevist at heart. Part of them should be sent to the front, the rest isolated here.

YAROVOY. You'll have nobody left but Yelisatov.

MALININ. Then you're for the semi-Bolsheviks?

YAROVOY. When it comes to fighting the Bolsheviks, I don't think my hands ever shake. And it's my opinion, gentlemen—

MALININ (*breaking in sharply*). Lieutenant Yarovoy, I advise you once and for all to keep your opinions to yourself and just pay attention to following the directions of His Excellency. (*Enter* GORNOSTA-YEVA; *then, a moment later,* FATHER ZAKATOV.)

GORNOSTAYEVA (*carrying a vendor's tray*). Now, I ask you, gentlemen! Lieutenant Yarovoy, Max has been arrested again. For the third time.

YAROVOY. When?

GORNOSTAYEVA. Just now. In the street. They handed me his tray and took him to the Secret Service Office.

YAROVOY (*to* MALININ). It seems your men have mistaken Gornostayev for Koshkin again. (*Smiling ironically,* KUTOV *goes off.*)

MALININ. All right. I'll call up and inquire. (YAROVOY *and* MALININ *go off.*)

GORNOSTAYEVA. For the third time. A sick man. And without the slightest reason.

ZAKATOV. Madam, the innocent and the guilty alike, they all say that. But the constituted authorities will sort the sheep from the goats.

GORNOSTAYEVA. But what's his crime? First they nabbed him because, they said, he worked with the Bolsheviks. Now, when the poor man tries to get along selling saccharin and acid crystals, they grab him because he's a speculator.

ZAKATOV. Don't worry, my beloved sister. If your husband is innocent, he will be set free with honor.

GORNOSTAYEVA. He's been set free twice already. I wish you such honor.

ZAKATOV. Well, Christ and his disciples suffered hunger, and beatings, and all kinds of passions, and if your husband is not guilty, it will all be credited to him, provided he takes it in a spirit of meekness. These are no Bolsheviks.

GORNOSTAYEVA. I'd rather see the Bolsheviks throw people in jail —they're supposed to be cutthroats, anyway. But these are our own authorities. We waited for them so impatiently and now we've got them. The entire intelligentsia are in prison.

ZAKATOV. Intelligentsia. The intelligentsia, madam, are being punished for their age-long disloyalty. Everything we see is the work of their hands. As you sow, so shall you reap. Take your husband—a professor. Ask him, what did he preach from his lofty chair? What did he teach the young people? Did he ever raise his voice in defense of the Czar and our faith?

GORNOSTAYEVA. Why do you jump on me? When the professor comes you can ask him what he taught. But I'll ask you, what did the people learn from you? Shepherds, indeed. Where's your flock? The professors were a mere handful and they were gagged and banished to Siberia, as my Max was, while you, you priests, were given crowns of gold, had the whole people entrusted to you for education. What did they learn from you?

ZAKATOV. Permit me, my beloved sister—

GORNOSTAYEVA. God put in your hands the safekeeping of the Czar. We relied on you. Have you kept him safe? You've been kicked out yourselves.

ZAKATOV. Allow me to reply to you on five specific grounds.

GORNOSTAYEVA. You have no ground at all. You've been chased out everywhere.

ZAKATOV. In that case, I'll begin with my fifth point. Why did your husband start a night school when the Reds were in power here? And why is he now in business peddling saccharin? What does this— (*Enter* MALININ.)

MALININ. The professor is free and will be here any minute.

ZAKATOV. You see how quickly justice is found. There was no need at all to get bitter and sow disorder. Intelli-gentsia! (*He goes off. Enter* PROFESSOR GORNOSTAYEV.)

GORNOSTAYEVA (*rushing to her husband*). Max! Max! What have they been doing to you?

GORNOSTAYEV. You see, this is freedom. (*To* MALININ.) May I go?

MALININ. Certainly, certainly, Professor. Please forgive the misunderstanding. By the way, you and I are old acquaintances. Do you recall?

GORNOSTAYEV. Oh, yes. I knew I'd seen your eyes somewhere. No, that was Dunka.

MALININ. What's that?

GORNOSTAYEVA. He's just absent-minded. He's always like that.

GORNOSTAYEV. Oh, yes. Now I remember. (*Stares at* MALININ.) Of course—of course. Captain Malinin, of the Secret Police. You searched my house, then packed me off to Vyatka—

MALININ. That's right. Now I have to come in and set you free. An old friend is worth two new ones.

GORNOSTAYEV. Yes. Exactly. Foul not the well that gives you water.

MALININ. What?

GORNOSTAYEVA. Come along, come along, for heaven's sake.

GORNOSTAYEV. Hand over my stock, Lyolya. (*Straps his tray around his neck and leaves with his wife.* MALININ, *too, withdraws.* PANOVA *comes in, on her way to the inner office with some papers. Enter* KOLOSOV. *He stops* PANOVA.)

KOLOSOV. Pavla Petrovna, what's that big envelope that's just come. Is it for Colonel Kutov?

PANOVA. Keep out of the way.

KOLOSOV. Is it about the Zheglov men? Please—for God's sake!

PANOVA. What business is it of yours?

KOLOSOV. Only two words from you: yes or no? and when?

PANOVA. You really have to know?

KOLOSOV. Yes. Their life depends on you.

PANOVA. How?

KOLOSOV. I can't tell you, but it's true. (CHIR *is heard off stage, singing.*)

PANOVA. Get out of here at once!

KOLOSOV. You're a good woman with a kind heart. I can't believe you're not sorry for them.

PANOVA. I'm sorry you're not going to be hanged with them. And if you don't get out of here—this minute, you'll make me feel so sorry I'll see that you're hanged too!

KOLOSOV. Go ahead. Only just tell me—has the confirmation of the sentence come through?

PANOVA. Chir! (*Enter* CHIR.) The electrician's finished his job here. Take him to the building manager. (CHIR *leads* KOLOSOV *off.* PANOVA *proceeds on into the inner office.* DUNKA *enters just as* YELISATOV *comes back through another door.*)

YELISATOV. Glad to see you, Avdotya Fominishna. How is everything?

DUNKA. I've come to get a pass to the front.

YELISATOV. What are you taking to our valiant fighters?

DUNKA. A little of this and that.

YELISATOV. I see you're doing your part.

DUNKA. Yes, of course. We all have to give our flesh and blood—for our faith and our country.

YELISATOV. We certainly do. By the way, I have three hundred pounds of sugar for you.

DUNKA. How much?

YELISATOV. A million two hundred thousand.

DUNKA. Land sakes! I only paid seven hundred thousand yesterday.

YELISATOV. That was yesterday. And today— You say you have to go to the front? I doubt that it'll be possible.

DUNKA. Mother of God! You want to do something good and you have to suffer for it.

YELISATOV. Serious operations are expected—so civilians are not allowed.

DUNKA. But I'm almost a military person myself. I have a medal, my husband is at the front.

YELISATOV. That's your husband. Your business is all in the rear— and it's big business too!

DUNKA. Well, one million.

YELISATOV. Solely out of respect for the valor of your husband at the front and your rear-guard virtues.

DUNKA. Of course. He's fighting there and I'm suffering here. But nobody gives any thought to me.

YELISATOV. I'm the only one who does. Remember when your mirror was so wantonly smashed?

DUNKA. If Kuzma Ilyich, my quartermaster sergeant, hadn't helped me calm down that time—

YELISATOV. That was later. After I'd already come along and said: "Here's a defenseless victim of revolution, a dove caught in the hurricane—"

DUNKA. As far as that goes, you were probably soft-soaping me, but I just can't resist educated talk. Or when anybody starts acting real nice and sweet.

YELISATOV. That's because you've got such a great capacity. The money, the sugar, and the pass to the front are all spot cash.

DUNKA. How about trusting me to pay half now and the other half in two days?

YELISATOV. Darling, I wouldn't trust myself for one second.

DUNKA. I give you my word of honor.

YELISATOV. Everybody knows there's nothing more honorable than my words, and I don't trust even them.

DUNKA. I hope you choke! (*Hands him the money.*)

YELISATOV (*at the door*). Here, Captain, is our patriotic citizen, Avdotya Fominishna. She's itching to go to the front.

COLONEL MALININ'S *office.* PANOVA *is on stage. Enter* LYUBOV YAROVAYA.

PANOVA. Who's that? Is it you, Chir?

LYUBOV. No, it's me.

PANOVA. Ah, comrade Yarovaya. Who do you want to see?

LYUBOV. You.

PANOVA. What about?

LYUBOV. I want to make an inquiry. Perhaps you'll help me.

PANOVA. What is it?

LYUBOV. Pavla Petrovna, it's about—the Zheglov men.

PANOVA. Now, listen—

LYUBOV. No, you listen.

PANOVA. Well?

LYUBOV. Help them. Tell me what you know. The lives of those men are in your hands.

PANOVA. If the lives of those men were in my hands, I'd have strangled them long ago.

LYUBOV. I don't believe you.

PANOVA. You'll have to believe. I'm being very sincere. If it were the other way round—the White murderers in the place of the Zheglov men, and you in my place—would you save them?

LYUBOV. We'll never be in each other's place. But you said yourself, we're both widows. Do you want to see more widows like us? (CHIR comes in.)

PANOVA. I do indeed. Please go now. What is it, Chir?

CHIR. This just came. (Hands her the mail and leaves.)

LYUBOV. What is it?

PANOVA. Mail.

LYUBOV. Could it be there?

PANOVA. Anything could be. (She goes off. LYUBOV steps quickly to the desk and searches the papers. CHIR returns.)

LYUBOV (glances about, her eyes meeting CHIR's). I'm here to see the Colonel. But he's not in.

CHIR. No, he isn't.

LYUBOV. I'll have to wait.

CHIR. Yes, you'll have to. (A pause.)

LYUBOV. May I have some water?

CHIR. Slake your thirsty soul with the waters of piety.

LYUBOV. So you won't give me any? Oh, you Judas! (Starts to leave.)

CHIR (barring her way). Not Judas but Job—that's my holy name.

LYUBOV. Let me go.

CHIR. You'll have to wait.

LYUBOV. All right. So you're with the Whites now?

CHIR. He's become transfigured—and his vestments are as white as snow.

LYUBOV. Oh, you've become transfigured into Christ!

CHIR. It was the red devils who almost transfigured me into an antichrist. (Enter MALININ.)

MALININ. What is it? What do you want?

LYUBOV. I've come—to inquire about something.

CHIR. She wants to inquire into the letters.

MALININ. The letters? (To CHIR.) Leave us. (To LYUBOV.) Who are you?

Lyubov. I'm a schoolteacher. I have to make an inquiry.

Malinin. What about?

Lyubov. Some of my pupils have been arrested. The boys are of good, noble families, fine upbringing. It's an obvious mistake.

Malinin. Those things do happen. Will you sit down, please? Well?

Lyubov. So I've come to inquire—about their release.

Malinin. Are you just inquiring, or pleading for them?

Lyubov. Yes, I do plead for them—please release them.

Malinin. What's your name?

Lyubov. Ya—Yarovaya.

Malinin. Any relation to Lieutenant Yarovoy?

Lyubov. Yes, a distant one. As a student he once came as a guest to our estate. But he turned out to be a Red and we asked him to leave.

Malinin. Where's your estate?

Lyubov. My God, where are all the estates today? When, dear Colonel, when are you going to return them to us?

Malinin. Patience, madam, patience. With God's help, we'll return everything.

Lyubov. Our only hope is God and you.

Malinin. Thank you. We're doing our best. Well, I'll find out about your case right away. Please wait a minute.

Lyubov. Certainly. (Malinin *goes off, leaving the door slightly ajar.* Lyubov *goes to the desk and again begins searching through the letters. The door flies open, as* Malinin *appears on the threshold.*)

Malinin. Well! What do you want to find out? Out with it.

Lyubov. I won't tell you.

Malinin. So you ask for the return of your estate? (Lyubov *makes no answer.*) Very well. (*Picks up the phone.*) Twelve. Lieutenant Yarovoy? Please come to my office immediately. (*Hanging up.*) So you refuse to answer? But in that case, how are we ever going to find your estate? (*Enter* Yarovoy.)

Yarovoy. What's the matter, Colonel?

Malinin. There—

Yorovoy. Lyuba!

Malinin. A relation of yours?

Yarovoy. My wife.

Malinin. Is that so? I had no idea.

Yarovoy. What's happened?

Malinin. Your wife has shown a strange interest in our papers.

Yarovoy. Ah! I thought so! (*Laughs.*) I ask your forgiveness, Colonel. This is a little family drama. (*In a low voice.*) My wife is morbidly jealous. It's awful. She keeps expecting to find letters to me from some other woman and she suspects that my amorous correspondence is carried on through this office. Lyuba, come with me.

The waiting room in the same house. PANOVA *at desk. Enter* KOSHKIN, *dressed in peasant clothes and carrying a basket.*

KOSHKIN. Comrade Panova.

PANOVA. Who is it? Roman—what do you want?

KOSHKIN. I've brought you some berries straight from the woods.

PANOVA. You're mad, Roman. They'll catch you the first thing!

KOSHKIN. Has the confirmation of the verdict arrived? When's the hanging? Where?

PANOVA. Whose hanging?

KOSHKIN. Tell me, quick.

PANOVA. I don't know.

KOSHKIN. Yes, you do.

PANOVA. Go away!

KOSHKIN (*pointing a revolver at her*). Well? We've played long enough. You know me. The lives of my Zheglov comrades are dearer to me than my own. (*Off stage* CHIR *is heard, singing.*)

PANOVA. Go away! Somebody's coming!

KOSHKIN. I don't joke about these things. I'll be waiting. Send exact information through Yarovaya.

PANOVA. For God's sake, go away! (*He disappears.* CHIR *comes in singing.* "Reign thou glorious—") What is it, Chir?

CHIR. Did you call me?

PANOVA. No.

CHIR. An old man is given to imagining things.

PANOVA. Cross yourself when it comes over you.

CHIR (*crosses himself*). Fine smell, these berries. They must be from the woods. Yes, sir, some people aren't afraid to pick them right under the noses of the partisans. (*Enter* YAROVOY.)

YAROVOY. What do you want, Chir?

CHIR. I was just saying these berries have a fine woodsy smell.

YAROVOY. Who could have given them to you?

PANOVA. An admirer—of my divine beauty.

CHIR. Only the Lord God has divinity.

YAROVOY. Get the hell out of here. (CHIR *leaves.*) May I know who your admirer is?

PANOVA. No.

YAROVOY. He got the berries from a locality swarming with partisans. He's a brave man.

PANOVA. He's not a coward.

YAROVOY. Apparently this is a real romance.

PANOVA. In a small way.

YAROVOY. Does this romance business by any chance read "Roman's business"—capital R-o-m-a-n apostrophe s? (*They stare each other full in the face.*)

PANOVA. Are you a reader of other people's romances? (KUTOV

appears at the door. He pauses briefly, listens, then disappears.)

YAROVOY. I'm a jealous man.

PANOVA. In that case, you'd better be jealous of your wife.

YAROVOY. My wife? And who is the other party?

PANOVA. You'll pardon me but I'm not an informer.

YAROVOY. You'll have to pardon me, too—if you are informed on.

PANOVA. Dear me, you seem to be confusing me with your wife.

YAROVOY. No. I'm not confusing you. She doesn't work at headquarters and won't have to answer with her head for knowing the Reds and the partisans—the Greens. (*He goes off. Enter* KUTOV.)

KUTOV (*holding himself in check*). Pavla Petrovna, I'm jealous too. You and somebody else are leading me around by the nose. Tell me, I beg of you, who is the gentleman?

PANOVA. Yours must be a pretty poor nose not to smell out the right person.

KUTOV. Pavla Petrovna, don't torture me. I say again, I'm ready to throw my honor and everything I have at your feet.

PANOVA. Do you really have anything besides your honor?

KUTOV. Besides my honor, I have forty thousand dollars in a London bank—and all this is yours—yours.

PANOVA. Colonel, I'm not for sale. And please don't interrupt my work. Saviors of the country! (YELISATOV *appears at the threshold.*)

YELISATOV. Shall I be in your way?

KUTOV (*irritably*). Not at all. (*Goes off.*)

YELISATOV. Now, what other good news is there about our scurrilous noble allies? (*Opens a newspaper.*) Ah! Monte Carlo— You know, dear, last night I won a hundred dollars again. But Captain Kulkov lost even his engagement ring. Wanted to shoot himself, but I persuaded him to go to the front. He'll either get shot there or he'll find the dollars.

PANOVA. Where do you get all your luck?

YELISATOV. It comes from betting just on sure things. The Kulkovs stick to the white—they're determined to win Russia "the one and indivisible."

PANOVA. And what do you play?

YELISATOV. All colors. Of the two indivisibles I'm sure to win at least one.

PANOVA. How do you mean?

YELISATOV. I mean either Russia or you.

PANOVA. I'm afraid I don't—

YELISATOV. Either Russia in Moscow or you, my one and indivisible, in Paris.

PANOVA. I don't know what you'll get in Moscow or Paris but right here you've got a good chance of getting a slap in the face, and not just one either.

YELISATOV. Ah, how your eyes flash! I'd better take cover or I'll be struck by lightning. (*An automobile horn is heard.*) His Excellency the

Commander-in-Chief. (*The formal welcome to the* Commander-in-Chief *gets under way. A* Band *plays. A* Guard of Honor *lines up.* Representatives of the Entente Powers, Father Zakatov, *various* Civic Delegations *take their places. Enter the* Commander-in-Chief, *followed by his suite, including* Malinin *and* Kutov.)

Zakatov. Permit me, Your Excellency—our eagle commander soaring over Russia—to offer you our congratulations on the victory at Seleznyovka. Those thousands of prisoners, of guns and machine guns, are a pledge of the imminence of the hour when the Russian people will drive the thieves and highwaymen from our country, will enter our Mother Moscow, and to the golden pealing of its forty-times-forty bells will return the throne and the country to its anointed master.

Commander-in-Chief. Thank you.

A Representative of the Landlords. We men of the land, Your Excellency, live by the faith that at the hour when the Russian land, as a whole, is returned to its sovereign lord, it will be returned in its parts to us, its local landlords, since the whole can be formed only of parts, and Holy Russia can be alive only so long as our sacred property is kept alive.

Commander-in-Chief. Thank you.

A Representative of the Manufacturers. We, too, Your Excellency, we men of industry, believe that the wrecked industries can be restored only by the hand of our lawful master whose return is impatiently awaited by the Russian working man and his elder brother, the manufacturer.

Commander-in-Chief. Thank you.

Folgin. Speaking in the name of the intelligentsia, allow me, Your Excellency, to ask a question—just what kind of monarchy is being referred to here?

Commander-in-Chief. Thank— What's that?

Folgin. If it is a constitutional monarchy, we welcome it. But if it is an autocracy— (*The* Commander-in-Chief *stares at* Folgin *angrily, eyes bulging. His neck grows crimson. He turns and walks out of the room.* Father Zakatov *and a number of others follow him. The* Crowd *begins to whisper. Soon the whispers turn into an indignant clamor.*)

Malinin. What a tactless thing to say, Mr. Folgin.

Folgin. But I've been dreaming of a constitution all my life.

Malinin. And I've been fighting a constitution all my life. Do you understand?—Fighting. (*All leave, except* Panova *and* Malinin.) So tonight we're dancing till dawn, my dear?

Panova. Till the sun rises.

Malinin. You're my sun. (*He kisses her hand. Enter* Kutov.)

Kutov. Well, Colonel, have you forgotten? His Excellency is waiting for you. I'm not your orderly.

Malinin. All right. I'll try to remember that. (*Goes off, humming to himself.*)

KUTOV (*irately*). Good. I'll remember it too. Pavla Petrovna, it's either him or me.

PANOVA. Is it? And suppose it's neither you nor him?

KUTOV. Stop your dangerous game, Pavla Petrovna.

PANOVA. Instead of stopping, why don't we try some other combinations?

KUTOV. For example?

PANOVA. For example—if it isn't you and it is him?

KUTOV. Then I'll kill him.

PANOVA. And if it's you and him both?

KUTOV. Then I'll kill both of you.

PANOVA. My! That's a lot of killing for one day. A little too much, in fact.

KUTOV. Pavla Petrovna, it would pay you to be more careful over a powder keg. Remember, I know of your connections not only with the Reds but also with the partisan Greens.

PANOVA. You can't scare me. Everybody knows why I worked with the Reds.

KUTOV. Well, then. (*Quietly.*) You come to my place tonight, or tomorrow the Secret Service will be looking into that question. Eight o'clock.

PANOVA. Ah! (*Between her teeth.*) Very well. (KUTOV *kisses her hand and goes off. Enter* LYUBOV.)

LYUBOV. For the last time—I'm here because Roman sent me.

PANOVA. Is it really the last?

LYUBOV. Has it arrived?

PANOVA. It has.

LYUBOV. Where is it?

PANOVA (*animatedly*). In Colonel Kutov's brief case.

LYUBOV. Is that—true?

PANOVA. It is. Only hurry up or he'll be going and taking the brief case with him. (LYUBOV *leaves.* DUNKA *rushes in.*)

DUNKA. Hey, lady, Yelisatov isn't here, is he?

PANOVA. No, lady.

DUNKA. *I'm* no lady, to be perfectly frank.

PANOVA. Then don't be frank.

DUNKA. Well, you can't hide that kind of thing under a kerchief. Ah, isn't he a crook, that son-of-a-bitch Yelisatov? The sugar he sold me is half sand. You pay your good money and you take a beating from a filthy skunk. Ah, God! God! The dirty son-of-a-bitch! (*She runs off. Enter* YELISATOV *and* KUTOV.)

YELISATOV. I said to him, Your Excellency, we are men of honor, of duty, and we sacrifice our personal interests for our country.

PANOVA. A minute ago Dunka expressed her interest in you—said you were a crook and somebody's son.

YELISATOV. We all are sons of Russia, Pavla Petrovna.

PANOVA. No, she traces your genealogy somewhat differently.

YELISATOV. I'll trace her. Which way did she go? (PANOVA *points to a door.*) I'll find her. (*Walks out through the opposite door.*)

KUTOV. Finish up your work quick. I'm going home.

PANOVA. All right. You go wait for me in the square. I won't be long.

KUTOV. Thanks. I'll be waiting. (*He goes off, coming face to face with* LYUBOV *as she enters.* LYUBOV *stops and follows him with her eyes. Enter* YAROVOY.)

YAROVOY. Pavla Petrovna, the General wants you to bring him the foreign newspapers. (PANOVA *leaves.*) What are you doing here? (LYUBOV *starts to go but* YAROVOY *bars her way.*) Wait.

LYUBOV. Are you going to arrest me?

YAROVOY. Lyuba— My God!— Stop this torture. We no sooner met than we parted again. Don't you want to see me? Every night for a month I've been pacing up and down under your window—

LYUBOV. Two nights you didn't.

YAROVOY. When?

LYUBOV. When you were on the tribunal. The next morning there were bodies hanging from the lampposts.

YAROVOY. Where's that Lyuba who had such unbounded faith in me?

LYUBOV. Where are you?

YAROVOY. I'm here, with you, with the same truth.

LYUBOV. That truth is with me now.

YAROVOY. They've taken it away and put in something else. Those sealed-car tricksters! But I'm the same as I was, I swear to you.

LYUBOV. I swore by your memory long ago to hate what you are now —to hate it to the death!

YAROVOY. What's brought this curse on us?

LYUBOV. Yes, what?

YAROVOY. Listen to me as you used to in the old days.

LYUBOV. I wasn't listening then to the same man.

YAROVOY. Then you didn't listen well. You're not listening now either. You're excited by something else.

LYUBOV. No, I'm listening—I am. I know all your sorry words: we are greedy pigs disguised as revolutionists. We've betrayed our noble allies. We are the outcast Cains of the world, slayers of our brothers, pogrom-makers, political hoodlums of the Black Hundred stamp.

YAROVOY. No, worse. They at least fight for religion and their country, and your kind think only of their pockets and their bellies.

LYUBOV. Good-by. (*Starts to go off.*)

YAROVOY. Wait. How little you know, Lyuba!

LYUBOV. And do you know so much?

YAROVOY. Too much. (*Off stage shouts: "Health to His Excellency —Hurrah!"*) Near Zamostye, we went over to attack the Germans. Suddenly a bunch of self-seeking traitors shouted, "Down with war!" One of them plunged a bayonet into my back, another sent a bullet through my arm, and then they turned and ran. I was picked up by the Germans, who restored me to health and showed how a people that had won true freedom, such as we've never even seen in our dreams—how this people is now carrying out a genuine revolution and defending culture. For that freedom, as you remember, I didn't spare either myself or you. Nor am I going to spare those who spat on that freedom and drowned it in the people's blood. This is a war to the end.

LYUBOV. Under the command of the same old Secret Police officers who for ages have been drowning that freedom in the people's blood.

YAROVOY. They're no more than a bunch of doomed men—dry leaves spinning in a whirlwind. We'll manage with our own men.

LYUBOV. Hangmen?

YAROVOY. The hangmen are on the other side.

LYUBOV. On your lampposts.

YAROVOY. This is a battle front. And I won't let you cross the lines to the other side, Lyuba. It wasn't for that that I've found you. Why, it would be going against nature, if you and I went different roads. .

LYUBOV. It's worse than that. The roads are not different. We've run into each other on the same road, and one of us will go over the precipice.

YAROVOY. Lyuba, I won't permit this to happen. (*An* OFFICER *runs in.*)

OFFICER. My God, what a calamity! A terrible thing, Your Excellency. (YELISATOV *rushes in. The* COMMANDER-IN-CHIEF, *the* GENERAL, MALININ, PANOVA, *and several* OFFICERS *come in from the other rooms.*)

YELISATOV. A terrible accident! Colonel Kutov has been killed.

VOICES. How did it happen? When? Where?

YELISATOV. Just a minute ago, around the corner, in the square. Apparently he was hit over the head.

VOICE. Was he robbed?

YELISATOV. No, only his brief case was taken. (YAROVOY *glances at* LYUBOV *and* PANOVA.)

CURTAIN

ACT IV

SCENE 1

Evening. A small park in the center of town. A dining pavilion with a terrace. A BAND. PEOPLE *coming and going.* NEWSBOYS, CIGARETTE VENDORS, *etc.*

NEWSBOY. Extra! Extra! Read all about it! Sensational victory!

CIGARETTE VENDOR. First quality cigarettes. Lowest price in town!

NEWSBOY. Extra! Extra! Sensational victory of the White Army! End of the Bolsheviks!

CIGARETTE VENDOR. Highest quality cigarettes. Save money—get them here—ten cigarettes for ten thousand!

NEWSBOY (*furtively, to the* CIGARETTE VENDOR). One o'clock at the bridge.

CIGARETTE VENDOR. Right. Finest quality cigarettes. (*A well-dressed* LADY *is having her shoes shined. An* OFFICER *stands by*.)

LADY (*singing in a low voice*).

> All we had
> Has had its day
> And down the river
> Passed away.

FLOWER VENDOR. Fresh chrysanthemums—sweet-scented pinks.

GORNOSTAYEVA. Saccharin, soda, peppercorn, acid crystals!

NEWSBOY. Extra! Extra!

CIGARETTE VENDOR. First quality cigarettes! Lowest price! (*Furtively, to the* BOOTBLACK.) One o'clock at the bridge.

BOOTBLACK (*as though not hearing*). Right. Shoe polish, rubber heels, laces! Real bargains! Here's shoe polish for you— (YELISATOV *is sitting at one of the café tables with a map spread before him*.)

FIRST VOICE. Mr. Yelisatov, please reserve me another lot in the first street.

SECOND VOICE. Don't be so greedy! Mr. Yelisatov, I'd like to put in my order for a lot in the first street.

YELISATOV. Gentlemen, the sale of vacant lots in the health resort of tomorrow, beautiful "Arcadia," is drawing to a close. I've only got a very few left.

FIRST GENTLEMAN. May I see on the map just where my lot is?

YELISATOV. Certainly. Have you been out to look it over? Here's the huge recreation hall.

FIRST GENTLEMAN. Is that where all those thick weeds are now?

YELISATOV. No, it's a garbage dump. Excellent fertilizer for the soil.

FIRST GENTLEMAN. All right. I'll take it. Here's a deposit.

ZAKATOV. I'd like one more lot in the first street.

YELISATOV. I'm sorry, that was the last one.

ZAKATOV'S WIFE. Oh, my God! You can't do that!

YELISATOV. You can have one in the second. It's an excellent lot. Here it is. Next to the future Fountain of Dreams. And here's the deed for your first lot.

ZAKATOV. Well, Mother, you make the settlement. (ZAKATOV'S WIFE *hands* YELISATOV *the purchase price and receives the deed of sale. The* SECOND GENTLEMAN *runs up*.)

SECOND GENTLEMAN. Mr. Yelisatov, have you kept two lots for me?

YELISATOV. I haven't a single one left, gentlemen. The sale of lots for the health resort of tomorrow, beautiful "Arcadia," is now over. (*Rolls up the map and puts the money away.*)

SECOND GENTLEMAN. But I'm giving my life for our country.

YELISATOV. We're all giving our lives. However, if you must get rid of your money, I can still let you have some Astrakhan pelts and some groats, but only in wholesale lots.

THIRD GENTLEMAN. It's a deal, Baron. For your house in St. Petersburg you get my villa in the Crimea and five pounds of sugar.

BARON. But how about a suit? Incidentally, it's got to be sugar and not fruit drops. (PANOVA *comes out of the pavilion, followed by* MALININ, *who is visibly tipsy.*)

PANOVA. The moon's rising. But I'm through with dreaming. The Russian moon—it looks just as dirty and fouled as the Russian land.

MALININ. Never mind. We'll shine it up for you and it will look just perfect.

PANOVA. Thank you. And you're a perfect fool. Is it because you're drunk or are you always that way? Don't be offended. I'm really thinking about myself. Here I'm drunk and acting like a fool. Yet I used to be clever. That's because of the way I'm dressed. A badly dressed woman can't be clever.

MALININ. Restore me to life, Pavla Petrovna, and I'll dress you like a queen.

PANOVA. Restore me to life and I'll dress myself—like Panova.

MALININ. Like sweet little Pava, Pavochka—

PANOVA. Colonel, you're forgetting yourself.

MALININ. No, I don't forget even in my dreams that I'm a colonel and in the Secret Service at that. (*The* DANCE DIRECTOR *rushes on.*)

DANCE DIRECTOR. Ladies and gentlemen, on with the dance! Les cavaliers, engagez les dames! (*Runs off in the opposite direction. An* OFFICER *steps up smartly before* PANOVA.)

OFFICER. Pavla Petrovna, if you please. (*He leads her off to the dance.* MALININ, *about to follow, is stopped by* YAROVOY.)

YAROVOY. Colonel Malinin.

MALININ. Yes?

YAROVOY (*in a low voice*). Go right on enjoying yourself but please be on your guard.

MALININ. Why, have you tracked down the murderers?

YAROVOY. Well, it's hard to say just yet.

MALININ. But why did they specially choose Colonel Kutov?

YAROVOY. It's a mystery. They were looking for something in his brief case.

MALININ. But they sneaked the brief case back—with all the papers intact.

YAROVOY. For the present I can say nothing definite.

MALININ. They're getting so damned insolent! We've got to answer back right away—the confirmation of the verdict has arrived and now there's nothing to keep us from stringing up the Zheglov gang along the boulevard the first thing in the morning—at sunrise.

YAROVOY. Yes, that's exactly what Koshkin's waiting for.

MALININ. Koshkin's far away.

YAROVOY. Koshkin is right here.

MALININ. What do you mean, here?

YAROVOY. Here, in town. And I have an idea that the Kutov affair is his doing.

MALININ. I see.

YAROVOY. Koshkin's got something up his sleeve. Some kind of plot's afoot but I can't figure it out yet. We're chasing each other around in a circle. However, I've set a trap for him.

MALININ. What kind of a trap?

YAROVOY. A kind in which all of them'll be caught tonight. But you'll have to give me all the men you can spare right away.

MALININ. Yes, of course. For a prize like that!

YAROVOY. What's the news from the front?

MALININ. Nothing since those disturbing reports earlier in the day.

YAROVOY. Disturbing? But we've encircled Globa's army.

MALININ. A printer's error. Read: Globa has encircled us.

YAROVOY. Is that so? Well, watch your step. (*He goes off.* MARYA *comes dashing on, pushing aside anyone who happens to be in her way. She jostles* MALININ.)

MALININ. Look where you're going, you old fool!

MARYA. To hell with that! I hear Syomka's been around. (*Enthusiastic shouts from the diners on the café terrace.*)

A VOICE. I propose a toast to the august imperial family!

MARYA. I hope you choke on it.

VOICES. Hurray!

MALININ. What did you say, woman?

MARYA. What did I say? I didn't say nothing.

MALININ. Hey! Soldier!

MARYA. What did I say? Just a word, that's all: "I hope you like it."

MALININ. Like what?

MARYA. How do I know what they're eating over there?

MALININ. I'll give you a taste of the ramrod. (*To* SEMYON, *who has come in response to his outcry.*) Take her away.

SEMYON. Ma—Mama!

MARYA. Hey, who's that?

SEMYON. It's me, Semyon Skoptsov. How are you, Mama dear? (*Kisses her.*)

MARYA. You? Where's your eye? You sons-of-bitches! May you have as easy a time breathing as I've had looking for you! May you get yours in the next world!

MALININ. You may consider yourself lucky that your son is an invalid. (*Goes up the stairs to the pavilion.*)

MARYA. I wish you such luck. Where's Grischka?

SEMYON. I'm looking for him myself, Mama dear. But I'll find him, even if he's six feet under. I'll get back what he owes me—the pair of horses he drove away, the thirty-six bags of wheat he dug up, everything else I lost on my farm. I'll track him down, even if he's pushing up daisies. I'll drag those horses out of him nerve by nerve. I'll draw my wheat out of him with his blood, drop by drop.

MARYA. He must be in his grave, I'm thinking.

SEMYON. I'll find him even there. I'll search the country from end to end but I'll get back what belongs to me. Where was he, that bandit, when I was slaving my guts out, saving every kopek? He went out and learned to read and write and found himself a nice soft spot working for a merchant. Then put that same merchant up against the wall. Robbed his own brother. I struggled for twenty years and he made off with it in one night.

MARYA. A couple of devils, both of you. Only one eye left.

SEMYON. Never mind. I'll close both of his for him.

MARYA. Regular roughnecks, damn your hides! Come on, I'll make you some cakes.

SEMYON. I can't. I'm on duty.

MARYA. Then I'll bring them here. One eye. How am I ever going to get you a wife now? (*She goes off.* LYUBOV *and* KOLOSOV *appear, keeping to the shadows.*)

LYUBOV. Why wait?

KOLOSOV. I think it's tonight. There are signs they're making ready for the execution.

LYUBOV. What kind of signs?

KOLOSOV. A detachment of soldiers has been brought into the prison since sunset. Also Chir is cooking a memorial dish and singing funeral hymns. He always does that before an execution.

LYUBOV. Go tell Roman about it. I'll be waiting for directions behind the school. (*They go off in different directions.* FOLGIN *and* YELISATOV *come out onto the terrace.*)

FOLGIN. Good God, man! The only salvation lies in humane laws.

YELISATOV. Why do you have to shout?

FOLGIN. Only the law can stop reaction.

YELISATOV. You're wrong. It's unlawful to stop reaction. Reaction is a counteraction equal to the action and it must stop only when the law of nature commands it.

FOLGIN. The people will stop it.

YELISATOV. The people themselves are now in a state of violent reaction. (*He pays the* WAITER *and comes down from the terrace. Walking toward him are* GORNOSTAYEV *and* ZAKATOV.)

ZAKATOV. Blessed are the poor, for they will inherit the earth.

YELISATOV. Let others inherit. My business was selling. What's happened to your business?

GORNOSTAYEV. It's all over. My wife has taken it upon herself to run the shop. I work for Dunka as a watchman, for a piece of bread. Gentlemen, what a wonderful time this is for the language! It's regaining its primary literalness. My wife has taken the business upon herself—it's literally so. There she is. The piece of bread is also literally so. Here it is.

FOLGIN. What do you know? It's really true. Today I was driven out into the street—in the literal sense of the words. I've been put in a room occupied by two men laid up with typhus. The doctor said if I get the infection, with my weak heart, it's certain death. And the two men are delirious, dirty, overrun with lice—

ZAKATOV. Ye-es, the Russian people is a great holy mendicant. It lives in stenches and sores, wallows in foul deeds, yet it proclaims the pure and holy truth to the world. Yes, Russia, in bloody travail, is giving birth to the new truth.

YELISATOV. You're not being literal there—the symbol is questionable. It's quite possible that this isn't travail but dysentery.

GORNOSTAYEV. What's the dysentery from?

YELISATOV. From many things. From the immoderate use of freedom, for example.

FOLGIN. To live in Russia with such convictions— (*Goes off.*)

YELISATOV. Is there any Russia left? Or convictions either?

ZAKATOV. Not convictions, but faith. The God-seeking people is eagerly searching for God's truth.

GORNOSTAYEV. Ye-es . . . ye-es. For the signs of truth.

YELISATOV. They searched my house seven times. Tore up the floors. Took everything for the God they're after. Even bore away my furniture, those bearers of God's truth.

ZAKATOV. God will repay you a hundredfold.

GORNOSTAYEV. H'm . . . yes. (*Looking closely at* YELISATOV.) Are you the builder of villas?

YELISATOV. In what sense?

GORNOSTAYEV. A swindler—selling—nonexistent land.

YELISATOV. Professor, how can you? Now you're being much too literal.

GORNOSTAYEV. Ah? I'm sorry. Perhaps it's somebody else. (YELISATOV *leaves. Enter* KOLOSOV.) But it's clearly the sign of moral degeneration: brilliant dialectics over an extinguished ethics. (FOLGIN *returns hurriedly.*)

FOLGIN. Professor, I need your advice—

GORNOSTAYEV. Advice? (*In the distance, the voice of* GORNOSTAYEVA: "*Saccharin, peppercorn, acid crystals!*") Tell me, who is that calling?

KOLOSOV. Your wife.

GORNOSTAYEV. What an unpleasant voice!

FOLGIN. Professor, I have some important business to—

GORNOSTAYEV. You have? At your service. What is it? Diamonds or flour?

FOLGIN. Neither. I'm an honest man. (*In a hurt tone of voice.*) I'm merely a member of the local land commission.

GORNOSTAYEV. What's the trouble?

FOLGIN. You see, every human being has his own clock in the infinite. The clock ticks, counting off his time on the blue dial. The gold hand of my clock has moved up to the black numeral.

GORNOSTAYEV. Cut it short, and speak prose.

FOLGIN. I've been bitten by a louse.

GORNOSTAYEV. You mean literally or figuratively?

FOLGIN. Figuratively, my eye! I just pulled the damn thing off. What shall I do?

GORNOSTAYEV. Scratch yourself—change your linen—

FOLGIN. But it's a typhus one. In two weeks it'll be the end of me!

GORNOSTAYEV. That's not so sure.

FOLGIN. But it is! This is so new and so great. Two weeks of life and then dust, nothing. But the two weeks are mine. I'm my own master, free of any restraints, of any fear of the future. I can do anything—a magnificent act of heroism, an act of unheard-of baseness, a terroristic act. I can blow up the earth! And all that is nothing as against eternity, which I've now entered since the bite. Well, your advice?

GORNOSTAYEV. What did you do before you were bitten?

FOLGIN. I worked in a government department and always dreamed of a constitution, although I kept it to myself. (GORNOSTAYEV *goes off, shaking his watchman's clapper.*)

KOLOSOV (*who has been listening*). Listen, there's a job cut out for you. An act of magnificent heroism.

FOLGIN. What is it?

KOLOSOV. Saving the lives of five men. They're to be executed today.

FOLGIN. You mean the Bolsheviks?

KOLOSOV. Yes, five human lives!

FOLGIN. There's a collision of two principles here—saving a man and helping a Bolshevik. I'll have to think it over.

KOLOSOV. There's no time to think.

FOLGIN. One must always find time for thinking. (*Both of them go off.* PANOVA *and* LYUBOV *enter, coming face to face.*)

PANOVA. Ah, Lyuba dear. Going to the dance too? Wait a minute. I have an indiscreet question—did you get the papers?

LYUBOV. I have nothing to say to you.

PANOVA. But I have. Murderers! What did you do? (*Bars* LYUBOV's *way.*) I wanted to help you save some men from death and you answered my help with blood, with murder!

LYUBOV. It was your answer to him, apparently, this murder.

PANOVA. What? Oh, you scoundrels! You made use of me for your vile ends and then you turn the blame on me! Well, you won't get away with it. I'll see to it you all hang from the lampposts tomorrow.

LYUBOV. Just be careful you don't get caught up with us.

PANOVA. You're threatening me? I was clean and guiltless until you came along, and you've spattered me with Kutov's blood. Now you're going to have to answer for it.

LYUBOV. All right. Let's go to headquarters. You should have taken up this work long ago.

PANOVA. Oh, I know—death holds no terror for you. But I'd find something for you—something more terrible than death.

LYUBOV. You've already found it for yourself. What are all of you but dancing corpses? (*Sails past her.*)

PANOVA (*after her, gnashing her teeth*). I'll make you dance, too. (*Enter* YELISATOV.)

YELISATOV. Pavla Petrovna, you owe me the last waltz. (*Leads her off.*)

LYUBOV (*discovering* CHIR *behind a tree*). You here, too, you toad? (*Goes off.*)

CHIR. Our Lord the avenger has bidden us to cleanse the earth of the rich who've devoured the homes of the widows, and of the poor who've driven God out of their homes. (*Slowly following* LYUBOV.) Remember, O Lord, the well-being of the possessed Lyubov, the harlot Pavla, the lickspittle Arkady. (*To* YAROVOY *as he comes on.*) Your Honor.

YAROVOY. Yes.

CHIR. A word with you about our Lord.

YAROVOY. What's that? (*Continues on his way, without stopping.*)

CHIR (*stepping in front of him and whispering*). A minute ago here two daughters of Babylon held secret converse.

YAROVOY. What about?

CHIR. The harlot Pavla says, "I was pure and innocent, almost like a virgin," she says, "and you," she says, "you deprived me of all my innocence through a dead body and by shedding blood," she says.

YAROVOY. What are you blathering about, you fool?

CHIR. I heard it with my own ears. "I wanted to help you," she says, "and because of that I've been robbed—" (*Continuing to whisper, follows* YAROVOY *out.*)

GORNOSTAYEVA (*at the entrance to the pavilion*). Saccharin—finest crystal saccharin— (KOLOSOV *approaches.*)

KOLOSOV. Let me have a small bag. (GORNOSTAYEVA *hands it over. A* BARONESS *comes up, wiping her eyes.*)

BARONESS. Oh, my God! Oh, my God!

GORNOSTAYEVA. What's the trouble, Baroness?

BARONESS. Haven't you heard? He's traded our St. Petersburg house —for a suit and some sugar! I can't bear it! With our noble blood!

GORNOSTAYEVA. My dear, your husband's at least got something. Mine has traded away his stock like a fool. Somebody buys soda from him and he throws in some saccharin. He's paid a thousand and he gives five thousand change. He's done so well we don't see bread for days at a time.

BARONESS. Neither do we. I've had nothing but tea since morning. Now when we return to St. Petersburg, we'll have to stop at a hotel. (*Weeps.*)

KOLOSOV. Allow me. (*Takes some white bread out of his satchel and offers it to her.*)

BARONESS. What are you—?

KOLOSOV. Please take it.

BARONESS. But I don't even know who you are.

KOLOSOV. Never mind. It's fresh bread.

BARONESS. Really, I don't know if I should.

KOLOSOV. Let me cut it. (*Gives a piece to* GORNOSTAYEVA.) If you please.

GORNOSTAYEVA. No, really. Although now that I think of it, it seems to me I've met you somewhere. But what about yourself?

KOLOSOV. Oh, I've had plenty to eat and couldn't touch a thing except cake.

GORNOSTAYEVA. You have a sweet tooth.

BARONESS. And you, Elena Ivanovna, do you like Brunswick cake? It's perfectly delicious! You mix yolk of egg with nutmeg—

GORNOSTAYEVA. No, what can be better than puff pastry with fruit? (*They both race on rapturously.*)

BARONESS. And orange peel, remember? You make holes in the peel, pour in butter mixed with white of egg, sprinkle rose water over it, and then glaze it. It has such an aroma—I remember, Countess—

GORNOSTAYEVA. You cut the puffed dough into rounds, brush the edges with whipped egg, and put glacéed fruit in the center. Oh, I used to make such good ones! I remember—

BARONESS. Just to think of it—I return, and the dining room and refectory are no longer mine. (*Weeps.*)

KOLOSOV. There, there—calm yourself. Here's a pear.

BARONESS. Father Zakatov says we'll be there in six weeks.

KOLOSOV. Your Zakatov is lying. Calm yourself.

BARONESS. How dare you?

GORNOSTAYEVA. Who then, according to you, isn't lying?

KOLOSOV. I'm not.

BARONESS. Well, then, suppose you tell me when we will be in St. Petersburg.

KOLOSOV. Well—not so soon.

GORNOSTAYEVA. Would you say in a year's time?

KOLOSOV. No, I wouldn't say that either.

BARONESS (*raising her voice*). So that's the sort of man you are!

GORNOSTAYEVA. What insolence!

BARONESS. I'm going to call for someone to arrest you!

KOLOSOV. First you'd better eat.

BARONESS. You can't bribe me with food. (TWO GENTLEMEN *rush up, attracted by the commotion.*)

FIRST GENTLEMAN. What's the trouble, Baroness?

SECOND GENTLEMAN. Has something happened?

BARONESS. Why, here's a Bolshevik who is openly spreading propaganda.

GORNOSTAYEVA. What are the authorities doing?

SECOND GENTLEMAN. What's that?

FIRST GENTLEMAN. Who? This one? I'll call the Secret Police right away.

KOLOSOV. Oho! Good appetite, ladies! (*Runs off.*)

FIRST GENTLEMAN. Hold him! Hold him! He's a Bolshevik! (*General confusion and shouting.* CHIR *runs across the stage, presently followed by* DUNKA.)

CHIR. Come on, brothers! Let's get our hands on Shem, Ham, and Japheth!

DUNKA. Oh, my God! What are we going to do? Mobilize yourselves!

VOICES. Where's the Bolshevik? Which one's the Bolshevik? My God, it's awful! The Bolsheviks are outside the town! (*A* CROWD *has collected in the shadow of the houses. We see* LYUBOV *and* PANOVA, *among others. Murmurs of pleasure and relief mingle with exclamations of alarm.*)

VOICES IN THE CROWD.

Our men are coming up!

Comrades, they're taking the Zheglov men out of jail!

Comrades, let's rescue them!

Coachman, to the station!

A hundred thousand!

They're at Dogtown already!

Koshkin's finished off the Baroness!

They all ought to be finished off, every last one of them!

DUNKA. Oh, my God! What are we going to do now, good comrades? People, mobilize yourselves! (*Enter* MALININ, YAROVOY, *and several other* OFFICERS. *The* CITIZENRY *calm down.*)

VOICES.

Calm down, folks!

There aren't any Bolsheviks!

Everything's all right in town!

The situation at the front couldn't be better!

MALININ. Band! The national anthem! (*The anthem is played, restoring order.*)

DUNKA. Those God-damn comrades! Look at all the stink they've kicked up! Turned my bowels to water, that's what! (GORNOSTAYEVA *and the* BARONESS *walk by, the center of an excited group.*)

VOICES. Congratulations on your miraculous escape! Was it really Koshkin himself?

GORNOSTAYEVA. Nobody but Koshkin! I swear!

BARONESS. Koshkin! Koshkin!

GORNOSTAYEVA. I remember him only too well. When they arrested my husband. How could I possibly fail to recognize him? (*Enter* YELISATOV.)

BARONESS. He tried to bribe us with bread at first. "I'm far too noble," I said. Then suddenly he flashed his knife! Oh!

YELISATOV. You're the Russian Charlotte Corday! Only more so! She did in a revolutionist with her knife, but when a revolutionist raised a knife to you, you did him in with words!

FLOWER VENDOR. Immortelles! Sweet-scented pinks! (*The little park gradually falls quiet. People stroll past. One can hear single sentences like the following.*)

PASSERS-BY.

Do you want two tons of paper?

I'll buy diamonds—

Corn-meal flour—

Two hundred dollars, f.o.b.

Gentlemen, enroll in the officers' and workers' detachment!

We have to be backed up by the masses.

Nonsense! Not by the masses but by religion.

Gentlemen, enlist in the detachment of His Grace the Archbishop.

I assure you in Paris today they're wearing only very, very short skirts.

Musya dear, you're wrong.

I swear to you. And also very low necklines. (*In the darkness the* WORKERS *are gathering.*)

VOICES.

Comrades, quiet. Our men from the factory will be here any minute and then we'll go to the bridge—as Koshkin has ordered.

Will Koshkin be there?

Koshkin's waiting there now. (*Quiet sets in. Other* WORKERS *arrive. Suddenly* KOSHKIN *appears in the crowd, calling forth ejaculations of surprise.*)

Comrade Koshkin! You? Why are you here? You mustn't stay.

KOSHKIN. Never mind that. What's the news?

VOICES.

We have the exact facts, we've checked them.

It's coming out just as you said.

They're taking the Zheglov men out at one o'clock. The route is across the Old Bridge to the Dog's Ditch.

The gallows are set up there already.

KOSHKIN. Already?

A VOICE. I saw them with my own eyes.

KOSHKIN. They are in a hurry.

A VOICE. We'll set the boys free. Our men are closing in on the bridge in three detachments, just as you ordered.

KOSHKIN. That order is cancelled. (*Exclamations of bewilderment.*) You're to scatter right away. Nobody's to go near the bridge.

A VOICE. And who's going to free the Zheglov boys, comrade Koshkin?

KOSHKIN. Nobody.

A VOICE. Are you joking, Koshkin?

KOSHKIN. Everybody is to be out in the vacant lot behind the school at one o'clock. You'll wait there for my orders.

A VOICE. And that's just when they'll be hanging the boys! (*General excitement.* TATYANA *cries.*)

KOSHKIN (*to* TATYANA). How did you get here? (*To a* WOMAN WORKER.) Comrade Krasnova, take her home. Comrades, quiet!

VOICES.

How can we be quiet?

Shall we be quiet while they quiet the Zheglov boys?

Comrade Koshkin, speak out.

KOSHKIN. You can't always speak frankly, comrades. And what's done will speak for itself in due time. Why isn't Shvandya here?

A VOICE. He's due any minute.

KOSHKIN. Well then, comrades. Scatter now and assemble, one by one, in the vacant lot. (*The* WORKERS *disperse.* KOSHKIN *is alone when* KOLOSOV *rushes on.*)

KOLOSOV. Comrades! (*Glances about.*) Where are— Comrade Roman, what are you doing here? Yarovoy is hunting you.

KOSHKIN. Well, we'll see yet who's the wolf and who's the hunter. And why are you running around like a hare?

KOLOSOV. Why! They're to be executed tonight. More blood—

KOSHKIN. Are you scared?

KOLOSOV. No, I've never known fear. But I'm afraid of other men's blood.

KOSHKIN. Then why do you push yourself into other men's blood?

KOLOSOV. I want to prevent it being shed.

KOSHKIN. What are you up to? Going to try to interfere?

KOLOSOV. No, only to help men stop this blood letting. I've been in this war for six years now. I've come to see—that men will bleed each other white if they're not stopped by love.

KOSHKIN. Well, go ahead and stop it. I've seen plenty of blood too, and I've grown to realize that blood can be of different kinds. There's pure blood, and there's putrid blood—which must be let out.

KOLOSOV. That's not true.

KOSHKIN. Have *you* found the truth?

KOLOSOV. I'm seeking it.

KOSHKIN. And I've found it. Ever since I was a boy I followed its trail—until finally I tracked it down—it's hiding in the homes of the rich and powerful. And the doors are barred to our kind. I'm going to smoke it out of there. I'll drag it out by the tail into the sunlight. I'll mop up the floor with that truth of yours!

KOLOSOV. What you found wasn't the truth,

KOSHKIN. You're right there—I found a vile perversion of truth. Go take my message to Lyubov. Tell her we'll meet at her place at one o'clock.

KOLOSOV. All right. Only you'd better get away from here too. It's not healthy for you.

KOSHKIN. Is there any place that *is* healthy for me? You're a funny one. Go along now. I have to wait for Shvandya. (KOLOSOV *leaves. For a while* KOSHKIN *is alone. Then* SHVANDYA *appears, moving furtively in the shadows.*) Is that you, Shvandya?

SHVANDYA. Yes, comrade Roman.

KOSHKIN. You're late. I began to think you'd lost your way.

SHVANDYA. As if I didn't know this neighborhood like my own mother! As if they didn't try to hang me on those lampposts! The factory people haven't showed up yet?

KOSHKIN. They came but I sent them away.

SHVANDYA. To the bridge?

KOSHKIN. No, in the other direction—to the vacant lot.

SHVANDYA. Why not the bridge?

KOSHKIN. Because the bridge would be playing right into Yarovoy's hands.

SHVANDYA. A-ah! What do you mean?

KOSHKIN. You'll find out soon enough. Now, another thing. The Whites are just about licked. They've been pushed back all along the line today. Near Usonya they're in a pocket, everywhere else they're on the run.

SHVANDYA (*joyfully*). A-ha! On the run, are they? Then they must be tripping all over themselves!

KOSHKIN. By tomorrow they'll be here. Our object now is to act before they come and not only save the Zheglov men but keep the whole prison out of their hands.

SHVANDYA. It's easy to say. The whole garrison's on its toes.

KOSHKIN. We'll see about that.

SHVANDYA (*after a pause*). We've got to go right out and get the people to fight!

KOSHKIN. That's pretty big talk. You'll have a nice little job on your hands.

SHVANDYA. Easy as pie! (*A* PATROL *goes by.*)

KOSHKIN. Sh-h-h—

SHVANDYA (*in a confidential tone*). Comrade Roman, can you tell me why this is? Where I come from the new moon looks white, and here it's the other way around! Then if you screw up your eyes, and then, like they say, you unscrew them—

KOSHKIN. Quiet.

SHVANDYA. What I want to say is, if you take the moon on a world scale—

KOSHKIN (*grabbing him and giving him a shake*). Now, then.

(*Listens. After a pause.*) It's quarter to, now. At one o'clock on the dot all the boys will be in the vacant lot behind the school, in the weeds. You wait here for any remaining comrades and lead them straight out to the lot. (*He goes off. An* ARMY CLERK *and* MAKHORA *come around a corner singing in low voices.*)

SHVANDYA (*to himself*). Who the hell's barging in now?

MAKHORA. Real lovely weather, isn't it?

ARMY CLERK. Couldn't be better.

SHVANDYA. There's that baggage again.

ARMY CLERK. Please sit down, little one.

SHVANDYA. Damn it! How can I scare them away?

ARMY CLERK. If to this weather one could add, say, love—

MAKHORA. Let's just leave love out of it.

ARMY CLERK (*moving up to her*). Not on your life! Say, what's the idea moving so close to the edge?

MAKHORA. But you're positively squeezing me!

ARMY CLERK. Quite the contrary. But if you keep moving, you'll fall right off on the ground. You're already only half on. Here, let me support you. (*He puts his arm around her waist.* SHVANDYA *pinches* MAKHORA. *She screams.*)

MAKHORA (*jumping to her feet*). Hey! What do you mean, pinching me, you ignorant baboon?

ARMY CLERK. Who? Me?

MAKHORA. Who else, I'd like to know?

ARMY CLERK. Why, let me bust open right here on this spot if I pinched you prematurely, so to speak.

MAKHORA. I'll bust you open for sure! Why, even Sublieutenant Stameskin never so much as pinched me. Not once! You lousy ignoramus! (*She goes off. The* ARMY CLERK, *stunned, follows her. A group of* PEOPLE *walk by, talking quietly.*)

FIRST VOICE. They've all gone crazy. Since sunset nothing but "God Save the Czar."

SECOND VOICE. A lot of good it'll do them. Today it's "God save the Czar"—tomorrow it'll probably be "Save the people, O Lord!"

THIRD VOICE. Well, they'll be singing their last pretty soon.

SHVANDYA (*emerging from his hiding place*). I see from your conversation, comrades, you're completely conscious people. But, incidentally, when those White rats start running away tomorrow, they'll hang all your comrades. Are you just going to stand by and watch? (*The men regard him suspiciously.*)

FOURTH VOICE. Well, if they show us, we'll watch.

SHVANDYA. Then you'll permit the White hangmen to kill people?

FIFTH VOICE. We've seen hangmen of all colors.

SHVANDYA. Then you're not conscious people.

FIRST VOICE. And who are you?

SECOND VOICE. A Bolshevik or a police stooge?

SHVANDYA. Who? Me?

THIRD VOICE. Yes, you.

FIRST VOICE. Of course, that's what he is—he's a police stooge.

FOURTH VOICE. Surround him, boys.

FIFTH VOICE. Let's see what he's got on him. (*They encircle* SHVANDYA.)

SHVANDYA. Comrades, citizens—I'm not a woman, or a hen to be plucked!

FIRST VOICE. You can see he's a slick article.

SHVANDYA. It's a pity, you see, I haven't the time, or I'd explain it to you. (*Tries to get away.*)

SECOND VOICE. No, you're staying right here.

SHVANDYA. I swear I don't have time. But, incidentally, I want to call something to your attention—a little devil's been born to a woman over in Dogtown—everybody ought to see it. And in the next block here there's a wachmaker's store with gold watches and the doors wide open, and anybody who wants to can get—

THIRD VOICE. Don't you try to pull the wool over our eyes.

FOURTH VOICE. You'll get your own blacked!

SHVANDYA. Never entered my mind! You, com-bro-citizens, are you Whites or the other way?

FOURTH VOICE. And who are you?

SHVANDYA. Who? Me? I'm on your side, of course. Haven't you recognized me?

FIRST VOICE. Let's recognize him with a quick one to the jaw! (GORNOSTAYEV *passes by*.)

SHVANDYA. And here's the teacher Marx himself—he'll explain it to you.

FIRST VOICE. Which Marx?

SECOND VOICE. Crazy, lying son-of-a-bitch!

THIRD VOICE. Big mouth!

SHVANDYA. You got me wrong. He really is Marx. Maybe not Karl himself, but his younger brother. Com— Mr. Marx!

GORNOSTAYEV. Ah? What is it?

SHVANDYA. Would you step over here, brother Marx.

GORNOSTAYEV. Max? I don't believe I've had the pleasure—what is it you want?

SHVANDYA. It's they who want some explaining—how to become conscious people. As proletarians of all countries, we must unite. But, on the other hand, Russia is indivisible. Please.

GORNOSTAYEV. Please what? Who are you, gentlemen?

FIRST VOICE. And who are you? (*The men now surround* GORNOSTAYEV. SHVANDYA *slips out unobserved.*)

SECOND VOICE. Are you really Marx's brother?

GORNOSTAYEV. Brother? Whose brother?

THIRD VOICE. That fellow says you are. (*Glances around.*) Where is he?

FOURTH VOICE. Beat it, the dirty rat!

FIFTH VOICE. He's a stooge, you can count on that.

FIRST VOICE. Then you're not a relative of Karl Marx?

GORNOSTAYEV. No, I'm not a relative of Karl Marx.

SECOND VOICE. If he were, he'd be strung up by now.

THIRD VOICE. Say, this is Dunka's professor!

GORNOSTAYEV. So far I'm only Dunka's watchman. Well, what's happened?

FOURTH VOICE. Nothing's happened. The Whites are going to hang the Zheglov men. It seems that's not enough for them.

FIFTH VOICE. Their stooges try to catch more people in the streets.

GORNOSTAYEV. Another execution. Something has to be done to stop it.

FIRST VOICE. What can be done?

GORNOSTAYEV. We have to fight against it.

SECOND VOICE. With what?

GORNOSTAYEV. With words. Words are the most powerful, and the only irresistible, weapon against evil. Come on, gentlemen. (*He starts off. The men follow him a short distance, then, unnoticed by him, vanish around a corner.*) You know, gentlemen, words tame even the elements. We'll persuade them. (*A* PATROL *marches on, with* YAROVOY *and* SEMYON *at the head of the* SOLDIERS. GORNOSTAYEV *turns to them.*) Gentlemen, I hear you're going to stain our land with more blood of its defenseless sons?

YAROVOY. What do you want, Professor?

GORNOSTAYEV. I and these honest citizens— (*Glances about, in embarrassment.*) There must be some citizens here.

YAROVOY. What citizens?

GORNOSTAYEV. Honest ones. Well, it doesn't alter— Gentlemen, don't do it.

YAROVOY. Out of the way, Professor.

GORNOSTAYEV. Man has been working for tens of thousands of years. From a half-beast he has grown into a half-god. Out of his cave he came crawling on all fours—now he's soared to the sky. His voice is heard for thousands of miles. Is he a man or a god? It turns out this is all an illusion. We are the same half-beasts, and before we get out of here in express trains and automobiles, let's scalp our enemies even if they are our brothers—

YAROVOY. Professor, cross the front line and explain all this to the Bolsheviks. They'll understand you and stop scalping.

GORNOSTAYEV. If you, the flower of culture, are unable to understand—

SEMYON. What the hell do you mean wagging your tongue here? Why, I'd shoot my Bolshevik brother like a dog.

YAROVOY. Silence, Sergeant!

SEMYON. Let me arrest him, sir.

YAROVOY. Shut up!

GORNOSTAYEV. I appeal to you all, don't let's have the people's blood on our hands!

YAROVOY. Professor, hold your tongue! Go your way. (*To the* SOLDIERS.) Now you—keep your eyes peeled! This is a dangerous night. Everybody is to be on the alert. The patrols are to keep in touch with one another. (YAROVOY *and the* SOLDIERS *go off.* GORNOSTAYEV *proceeds on his way, beating his clappers furiously.* DUNKA *comes on from the opposite direction.*)

DUNKA. You *are* watching my property well.

GORNOSTAYEV. Very well.

DUNKA. The house is way down there, and where the hell are you? What do you eat my bread and salt for, parasite? (GORNOSTAYEV *moves on, shaking his clapper.*) You pay out your good money and all you get for it is aggravation. (*She leaves. The place is deserted. Reënter* YAROVOY, *followed by* SEMYON.)

YAROVOY. Call Colonel Malinin.

SEMYON. Yes. sir, (*Goes off into the pavilion. Enter* MALININ.)

MALININ. Well, what is it?

YAROVOY. Dance your last dance, Colonel.

MALININ. What's that?

YAROVOY. It's all over with us. They've made a break-through at the front.

MALININ. Impossible!

YAROVOY. Our forces are retreating in all haste.

MALININ. Well, it might have been expected.

YAROVOY. We're under orders from headquarters to keep this a secret until tomorrow.

MALININ. So tomorrow we evacuate the town?

YAROVOY. That's right, tomorrow. But if we don't get rid of Koshkin right away, in the morning, when the situation becomes known, he'll get rid of us. (*Enter* PANOVA.)

PANOVA. Colonel, the cotillion.

YAROVOY. The Colonel has a headache. He's going home.

MALININ. Yes, excuse me. Not feeling well—a little too much to drink. Good night. (*Kisses her hand and leaves.*)

PANOVA. What's happened?

YAROVOY. Not a thing.

PANOVA. There was something he didn't say.

YAROVOY. He's left that to me. Come over here, please.

PANOVA. I'm listening.

YAROVOY. No, I'll be listening to you. What were you talking about with my wife here?

PANOVA. When?

YAROVOY. Five minutes ago.

PANOVA. Oh, about dances. However, you should ask your wife— she's closer to you.

YAROVOY. Maybe, but I'm asking you.

PANOVA. Is this an interrogation?

YAROVOY. You might call it that.

PANOVA. It won't get you anywhere.

YAROVOY. I'll try.

PANOVA. Try then.

YAROVOY. What was the confirmation you were talking about?

PANOVA. Confirmation? That's hardly the word. Except mutual negation, there's nothing between me and your wife.

YAROVOY. Which side are you on?

PANOVA. Neither.

YAROVOY. And whom are you trying to harm?

PANOVA. Everybody I consider harmful.

YAROVOY. I consider you harmful, too, and I'm going to arrest you right away.

PANOVA. That will be harmful to you.

YAROVOY. Listen, you Delphic Oracle! Without your magic fumes I can foretell a future that will be extremely harmful to you. You'd better drop your ballroom quips. The ball is over.

PANOVA. Give me a cigarette. Here's something in exchange. (*Pins a pink to his coat.*)

YAROVOY (*gives her a cigarette*). Well?

PANOVA (*singing in a low voice*).

> Well, well, well—
> Now school is done
> Into the yard
> Our darlings run!

You'd better run over to the schoolyard—teacher's pet! (*Points in the direction of the school.*)

YAROVOY. What are you driving at?

PANOVA. It's just that I'm so frightened I'm ready to tell you everything. But first of all hurry over to the schoolyard. Somebody's waiting for you there.

YAROVOY. There's nobody waiting for me.

PANOVA. And I say there is. You can believe a woman who's sincere only with you. Poor, dear lieutenant of the revolution. You're rushing about, risking everything—when the game is already lost.

YAROVOY. And what's your game?

PANOVA. I'm your partner—in the same tight corner. But you have a way out—down there—the schoolyard. For me, so far—it's still a blind alley. Hurry up now. I'll wait for you here.

YAROVOY. You'll tell me everything then?

PANOVA. Everything. Now I'll go finish my chartreuse. Hurry up, or I'll go home. (*Goes off.*)

YAROVOY. No, you won't! Skoptsov! (SEMYON *steps out of the darkness.*)

SEMYON. Yes, sir.

YAROVOY. Keep that lady under observation. Don't take your eyes off her!

SEMYON. Yes, sir. (*Goes off.*)

CURTAIN

ACT IV

SCENE 2

Later the same night. The schoolyard. LYUBOV *is peering out toward the vacant lot. Enter* YAROVOY.

LYUBOV. Who is it? Comrade—

YAROVOY. It's I.

LYUBOV. What—what do you want?

YAROVOY. I've come to you for the last time, Lyuba. Tomorrow you won't see me.

LYUBOV. I know. But I don't want to see you tonight either.

YAROVOY. I still want to talk to you tonight.

LYUBOV. What is there to talk about? Please go.

YAROVOY. I want to ask you—

LYUBOV. I won't answer you. Go away.

YAROVOY. I won't go without that. Cursed be everything that's come between us. I have nothing now besides you. Can't you understand?

LYUBOV. No, I'm afraid I can't.

YAROVOY. Lyuba, there was a time when I took all my cares only to you.

LYUBOV. I've forgotten that time.

YAROVOY. Now I have nobody to tell how agonizing it is to be in this impossible situation.

LYUBOV. Who's keeping you in it?

YAROVOY. You're the only one who can help me. Only let those eyes of yours look deep into my heart.

LYUBOV. Look into it yourself. What's brought you here?

YAROVOY. My aching heart—ah, yes, it's suffered as much as my body.

LYUBOV. I know. And where will you go when you leave me?

YAROVOY. I want to be with you forever.

LYUBOV. Forever? That's too far off. What about tomorrow morning?

YAROVOY. If you turn me away, I won't be alive by morning. But if you still have any trace of love for me—no, a trace of pity, you'll understand me, you'll raise me from this grave—only you can do it, if you but wish it.

LYUBOV. If I but wish it— Has there ever been an hour, or a minute, when my heart wasn't bleeding with longing, with pity for you. If you only knew my unutterable sorrow! Twice I buried you—

YAROVOY. But I've come to life again.

LYUBOV. To make me suffer more. I used to go out into the fields to cry over your unknown grave. I lamented to the wind, to the grass—

YAROVOY. And my heart was listening to you—

LYUBOV. I always heard your voice—the thing one usually forgets first. Your dreams have become my work. But to hear you pronounce somebody else's hateful words—

YAROVOY. We'll find the words—

LYUBOV. To see you with those—

YAROVOY. I'm only with you—

LYUBOV. Is that the truth?

YAROVOY. It is, it is, Lyuba my life—

LYUBOV. To be with you again— Do you realize what you're doing to me, what you mean to me?

YAROVOY. I know, Lyuba.

LYUBOV. Your hair's turning gray. You've grown thin, Misha.

YAROVOY. And you too—only your eyes are the way they were—just the eyes. We'll find those words again.

LYUBOV. Don't speak. We need no words. There's only one thing we need—you know it—we have to save the men. When it's done, come back—I'll wait for you. (SHVANDYA *appears on the fence.* YAROVOY *sees him and starts toward him.* SHVANDYA *instantly disappears.*) What is it, Misha?

YAROVOY. Yes, I'll go.

LYUBOV. Go. Hurry up. There's no time to lose.

YAROVOY. No, there isn't. (*He leaves. Enter* SHVANDYA.)

SHVANDYA. Who was that, comrade Lyuba?

LYUBOV. That was a friend, a friend, Shvandya.

SHVANDYA. Why did he leave just then?

LYUBOV. He'll come back with wonderful news. Look, Shvandya, what a gorgeous night.

SHVANDYA. Yes, sir—some night.

LYUBOV. In three years this is the first time I've noticed those shadows. Look—on the ground under the trees—as though the moonlight were weaving lace! (*A number of* WORKERS *file in.*)

FIRST WORKER. Comrade Yarovaya.

SECOND WORKER. Isn't comrade Roman here yet?

SHVANDYA. He's coming soon. (*Enter* KOSHKIN *and* GRIGORY.)

KOSHKIN. Hello, comrade Yarovaya. (*To* SHVANDYA.) Well?

SHVANDYA. I went out to stir up the people. Well, it was a tough job to make any headway—

KOSHKIN. Did you stir them up?

SHVANDYA. No, I had to beat it. They have no class consciousness, those people. They began playing games with me. If it hadn't been for Marx popping up out of the deck and if I hadn't trumped with him, it would have been curtains for me.

KOSHKIN. Well, boys, this is a serious night. Tomorrow maybe we'll be the masters here. But tonight our place is only on the lampposts. They were laying a trap for us on the bridge. It didn't work. Now our first business is to seize and hold the prison. We're not going to give up our comrades to be strung on the lampposts.

LYUBOV. It will never happen, comrade Roman.

KOSHKIN. All we need is to hold them off tonight. Tomorrow will be our day. Where are the arms?

FIRST WORKER. I know the place, comrade Roman.

KOSHKIN. All right, lead the way. Shvandya and comrade Yarovaya are to keep watch and maintain contact. (KOSHKIN, *the* WORKERS, *and* GRIGORY *climb over the fence.*)

LYUBOV. Go stand over in that corner, Shvandya.

SHVANDYA. Yes, ma'am. (*He leaves. Coming into sight as they move cautiously along the street are a group of* WHITE SOLDIERS, *with* YARO-VOY *and* SEMYON *among them.*)

YAROVOY (*in a low voice*). Close in on them. Skoptsov, surround the vacant lot.

SEMYON (*in a low voice*). Yes, sir. (*His mother,* MARYA, *runs up to him.*)

MARYA. I barely caught up with you. Here are the cakes.

LYUBOV. It's like a dream— (*She glances about, sees the* SOLDIERS, *dashes off in the direction of the vacant lot. But before she can get very far the* SOLDIERS *have seized her.*)

YAROVOY. Lock her up in the school and guard her.

LYUBOV. Misha! You unspeakable—! (*They lock her into the school.* KOSHKIN, GRIGORY, *and others of the* WORKERS *run across the school-yard. They clash with the* SOLDIERS, *force them aside, and make for the fence. Some get over it and disappear.* KOSHKIN, *with* GRIGORY *close behind him, is astride the fence and is about to jump over.*)

YAROVOY. Get Koshkin—Koshkin!

KOSHKIN. Ah! A familiar voice!

GRIGORY (*on the fence*). Comrade Roman! (*He tries to pull him over.*)

KOSHKIN. Let go! All I want is just one look in his eyes. (*Jumps down and rushes toward* YAROVOY.)

YAROVOY. Yes, look before you die. (SEMYON *and several other* SOL-DIERS *seize* KOSHKIN. GRIGORY *dashes to his side.*)

SEMYON. Aha! Grigory!

MARYA. Grisha!

GRIGORY. Hello, brother Semyon!

SEMYON. And good-by, bandit! (*Both draw their revolvers.*)

MARYA (*thrusting herself between them*). Shoot your own mother then! (*The* SOLDIERS *seize* GRIGORY *and march him off with* KOSHKIN.)

SEMYON. Don't worry, Mother. I told you I'd find him in his grave. I've found him even sooner than that—right outside his grave.

MARYA. I hope you'll lie in it first!

YAROVOY. Take the old woman away. Let the schoolteacher go free.

MARYA (*to* SEMYON). Why did I ever bear a devil like you?

LYUBOV (*emerging from the school, horror stricken*). Why was I ever born into this world?

CURTAIN

ACT V

Courtyard at White Army headquarters. The end of the day. A sudden and panicky evacuation of the Whites. Whistling locomotives, tooting automobiles, rattling supply wagons are heard in the distance. OFFICERS *are rushing about. On the veranda* YAROVOY *is studying some papers. The telephone keeps ringing. Enter* MALININ.

MALININ. Here's an order. His Excellency has left and put me in charge of the evacuation and you in charge of the defense of the town.

YAROVOY. Very good, Colonel.

MALININ. We're falling back to our allies for reinforcements.

YAROVOY. You can fall back. We'll go on fighting here.

MALININ. And who is "we"?

YAROVOY. "We" means "not you."

MALININ. Ah? H'm. Well, fight on. Oh, by the way, His Excellency ordered that now that Koshkin has been captured, he and the Zheglov men be liquidated in the prison immediately.

YAROVOY. The General must have thought I caught Koshkin just to let him go free. (*Enter the* BARON *and the* BARONESS, *carrying their luggage.*)

BARON. Hurry up, my dear.

BARONESS. But I feel giddy again.

BARON. In God's name, Colonel, give us an automobile.

MALININ. I cannot, Baron. Hurry and you'll catch the train. (*Enter an* ADJUTANT.)

ADJUTANT (*to* MALININ). Colonel. (*Hands him a paper.*)

BARONESS. The train! But they'll smother me to death! (*Enter the* GORNOSTAYEVS.)

GORNOSTAYEV. Who is it they're going to smother?

BARON. The Baroness.

GORNOSTAYEV. That's nothing. Right here they're going to strangle half a dozen men. (*Going toward* MALININ.) You can't do it, my friends.

BARON. What men do you mean?

GORNOSTAYEVA. The Zheglov gang. Imagine worrying about them!

BARONESS. I'm just a weak woman but I'd strangle them with my own two hands.

MALININ. Well, ladies and gentlemen, you really should hurry up. (*He goes off, the* BARON *and* BARONESS *following.*)

BARON. What about an automobile? (*Enter* YELISATOV, *heading toward them.*)

BARONESS. Mr. Yelisatov, what about the title deed?

YELISATOV. I'll mail it to you abroad.

BARONESS. I'll be waiting for it. I want to return straight to my estate.

YELISATOV. Don't worry. Good-by. (*Goes inside.*)

GORNOSTAYEVA. Max, let's go away, I implore you.

GORNOSTAYEV. Lyolya, you know yourself—I make trips abroad only for scientific purposes.

GORNOSTAYEVA. Well, let's go for scientific purposes. (*They leave. Enter, in a rush, the* FIRST *and* SECOND GENTLEMAN, *acompanied by several* LADIES.)

FIRST GENTLEMAN. Ladies and gentlemen! The allies have made a miraculous landing. A sentry down at the port was the first to see it.

FIRST LADY. All of a sudden out at sea—great big clouds of smoke—and oh, so many smokestacks!

SECOND GENTLEMAN. But why doesn't headquarters know anything about it?

FIRST LADY. Because—it's a miracle! (FATHER ZAKATOV *and his* WIFE *bustle in carrying traveling bags.*)

SECOND GENTLEMAN. If it's a miracle, the Father here must know about it.

SECOND LADY. Reverend Father, do you know about the miraculous landing?

ZAKATOV. Where?

FIRST LADY. Out on the water— Smoke, and smokestacks blazing away—

ZAKATOV. It's possible, everything's possible, beloved children. (*The* COMMANDANT *dashes by.*) Sir, my wife and I have been promised a four-passenger car.

COMMANDANT (*to* ZAKATOV'S WIFE). Of course, of course, ma'am, number thirteen.

ZAKATOV'S WIFE. Oh, but that's unlucky! Give us number fourteen.

YELISATOV (*who has stepped out again*). On to Moscow, Father?

ZAKATOV. I've been urging you on to Moscow but you doubting Thomases wouldn't listen to me.

SECOND LADY. But now we have the miraculous landing, Father.

ZAKATOV. Then, beloved children, let's turn our steps in that direction. But—let your shepherd precede you. Well, where's my car, Commandant? (*He goes off, accompanied by his* WIFE. DUNKA *runs in, followed by men carrying her belongings.*)

YELISATOV. Going to Paris, Avdotya Fominishna?

DUNKA. You expect me to stay here with those ignorant brutes? (*She continues on her way.* YELISATOV *goes in once more. A loud argument breaks out off stage.*)

ZAKATOV (*off stage*). My beloved child! You shouldn't have got into this car—it's occupied.

DUNKA (*off stage*). The hell it is!

ZAKATOV. Beloved child, prayers would be more fitting from your lips. But you have to get out on three grounds—firstly—

DUNKA. Cut it out, Father. Me get out? Not on your life!

ZAKATOV'S WIFE. You get right out this minute! A priest's automobile is no place for your fat behind!

GORNOSTAYEV (*running over toward the car*). Let Dunka go abroad, please let her! (YELISATOV *comes out of the house, carrying baggage.*)

YELISATOV (*shouting*). Pavla Petrovna! I'm here. I've got space for us in a car—just a few details to be taken care of. I'll be right back! (*He goes into the house again as* PANOVA *enters.*)

PANOVA (*after him*). Hurry up! (*To* LYUBOV, *who comes on.*) My dear! Going to join your husband? Good luck to you. What's brought you together? Koshkin, it seems?

LYUBOV. What's that you say?

PANOVA. It's simple enough: you betrayed him.

LYUBOV. It's you who betrayed him, you dirty tramp!

PANOVA. You're wrong, my dear. One betrays his friends. I caught enemies. But thank you for your help.

LYUBOV (*making a movement to draw a revolver*). No, I don't want to waste a bullet on you—I need every one.

PANOVA. In that case we can have a heart-to-heart talk. (*Her face close to* LYUBOV'S, *speaks in a quiet voice, with deep feeling.*) You're worse than a snake. I loathe those eyes of yours—green with age-old spite—the scaly wrinkles on your forehead that clamps your sorry, poisoned little mind like a vise! Your lips that twist like slimy worms. A million-headed hydra! I hate you—and I'll go on hating you till the end of my life!

LYUBOV. That's all you've got in your life, you viper with drawn fangs. Crawl away—out of our country!

PANOVA. Crawl over it, you typhoid lice! (*Enter* YELISATOV.)

YELISATOV. Everything's ready, Pavla Petrovna. Come, get into the car. In a week you and I will be in Paris. (YELISATOV *and* PANOVA *go off.* YAROVOY *steps out onto the veranda, glancing through some papers.* LYUBOV *walks up to him.*)

YAROVOY (*lifting his head*). Lyuba!

LYUBOV. Set Koshkin and the Zheglov men free.

YAROVOY. Your request can't be granted, Lyuba.

LYUBOV. This is not a request, it's a demand.

YAROVOY. By whom?

LYUBOV. By me. I betrayed Koshkin to you last night, so now I'm demanding.

YAROVOY. Then it's only a question of Koshkin?

LYUBOV. All right. We'll start with Koshkin. Give him back to us!

YAROVOY. You think I've rented him for a day?

LYUBOV. You think it's funny? Look into my eyes. Perhaps it will be the last time. Why did you come to me last night?

YAROVOY. Lyuba! I swear by my soul which—belongs to you, I went only to see you. I didn't know I'd meet them.

LYUBOV. Then make good your oath—release them. Save them; it's in your power!

YAROVOY. If it were only in my power to save you from them! That's enough, Lyuba. This is a fight to the death. Hands are raised to cut off heads. The first head to fall will be the one that glances back. And you demand that I glance back?

LYUBOV. It was you who made me glance back by trickery last night. Like a snake you crept into my heart only to sting it mortally.

YAROVOY. That was an accident for which you're not to blame.

LYUBOV. I'm not to blame? For the happiness of pressing my head against your breast, look how many heads I've laid at your feet! (*The telephone rings.*)

YAROVOY (*answering*). Yes. What? I'll be right with you. Well, Lyuba, good-by. Bury me for the third time.

LYUBOV. You—you're not going to save them?

YAROVOY. Run along—I'm busy.

LYUBOV (*drawing a revolver from her pocket*). All right, then!

YAROVOY. Ah! That's a good idea! You're a clever girl. (*Steps forward, pulling open his jacket.*) Bury me in fact!

LYUBOV. No, it's not your life I want. (*She turns the revolver on herself.* YAROVOY *springs toward her, wrests the revolver from 'her hand, and puts it in his pocket.*) Well, that only puts it off—if you execute Roman, I'll kill myself. (YAROVOY *presses the bell button. A* SENTRY *comes in.*)

YAROVOY. Lock up the prisoner in that room—and see that she stays there! (*The* SENTRY *takes* LYUBOV *off.* KOLOSOV *bursts in.*) What do you want?

KOLOSOV. I wanted to speak to her.

YAROVOY. Ah! See here. I know where you stand, and that's why you're still free. Can you take her out of town right away?

KOLOSOV. No.

YAROVOY. Why not?

KOLOSOV. She won't go.

YAROVOY. And why won't she?

KOLOSOV. Release Koshkin.

YAROVOY. That will be all.

KOLOSOV. It would be such a big thing if you would!

YAROVOY. Go. Or you'll find yourself in the same place Koshkin is.

KOLOSOV. That's exactly what I'm asking for. If you have to have somebody, take me instead of Koshkin. You'll kill her otherwise—she won't want to go on living.

YAROVOY. Who wants you?

KOLOSOV. I'm harmful to you, anyway.

YAROVOY. No, you're harmless. Go. But come back for Lyuba in an hour's time. I can hand her over only to you. (*He goes off. There is the sound of an auto horn and of a car arriving.* KOLOSOV *walks down the street, soon coming up against* SHVANDYA *in an officer's coat.*)

SHVANDYA. Comrade Kolosov.

KOLOSOV. Who are you?

SHVANDYA. Don't you recanize me?

KOLOSOV. Shvandya!

SHVANDYA. That's the one.

KOLOSOV. You've crawled out a little too early.

SHVANDYA. Or maybe we're too late? We have to get the comrades out.

KOLOSOV. They've just arrested Lyuba Yarovaya.

SHVANDYA. Where?

KOLOSOV. Right here. Yarovoy did it. He posted a guard and drove away.

SHVANDYA. Then we'll have to spring her. Any officers there?

KOLOSOV. Nobody, just the guard.

SHVANDYA. Then it's easy as pie. Let's get going.

KOLOSOV. What do you mean? Free her by force?

SHVANDYA. No, sir. Just nice and easy like. (*Shouts at* KOLOSOV.) All right, you! Shut up! (*Steps up onto the veranda.*) 'Shun! I'll knock the Bolshevik stuffing out of you! You think you've crushed us? That's a lie, you Red devils! We've counter-attacked all along the front. The generals have returned. Everybody is being sent back. . . . Now, where's that dispatch? (*Pulls out an envelope.*) Lay a second wire and be quick about it! Well? Are you on strike, eh? (*To the* SENTRY.) Where's Lieutenant Yarovoy?

SENTRY. He just drove off in a car.

SHVANDYA. Where to?

SENTRY. I don't know, sir.

SHVANDYA. It's your duty to know. Or are you thinking of joining the Reds? I'll join you! (*Picks up the telephone.*) Give me one thousand two hundred. Hello! Lieutenant Yarovoy? Sublieutenant Prince Kurnosovsky speaking. That's the one; I have a rush dispatch for you. Hand it over to the sentry? Yes, sir. What Bolshevik woman? Just been arrested? I'll inquire. Sentry, is there a woman prisoner here?

SENTRY. Yes, sir.

SHVANDYA (*into the phone*). Yes, sir. There is a woman prisoner here. What do you say is to be done with her? I'm to conduct her personally to the prison? Yes, com—Lieutenant, I'll take her right away. Have no fears. She won't slip away from me. And the sentry is to remain to guard the dispatch? Yes, com—Lieutenant Yarovoy. Well, so long. Bonjour. (*To the* SENTRY.) Bring the prisoner here. I'll drive her to the jail. And you—here, take this dispatch and wait with it for the Lieutenant.

SENTRY. But I can't do that without an order, sir.

SHVANDYA. Wha-at? Didn't you hear me on the phone? I'll clean out your ears for you! Well, open the door—hurry up! Prisoner, come out. Forward march! And you guard the dispatch.

SENTRY. What am I to report to the Lieutenant, sir?

SHVANDYA. Are you deaf? Tell him Sublieutenant Prince Kurnosovsky gave you the orders. Are you through, electrician? You can go. (*The* SENTRY *goes off.*) Well, comrades, scat! (*He disappears.* LYUBOV *and* KOLOSOV *walk down the street. In a recess a group of* WORKERS *are standing.* TATYANA *is with them. Half-whispered phrases can be heard.*)

VOICES.

I suppose they've all cleared out.

The last columns have marched off.

Only some left at the jail and the station.

Comrades, are the Zheglov boys done for?

How can we help them?

What would *you* do?

Such is fate.

We ought to try.

With bare hands again?

But they have Koshkin, Hrustch, Mazukhin there. Are we just going to hand them over?

Are we? We've already handed them over.

TATYANA. You have, you have. You're all masters at handing over. So long as Hrustch risked his life for you, you said "Let Hrustch do it," and when Hrustch is to be hanged, you say "Let Hrustch hang." (*She cries.*)

A WOMAN (*mimicking*). "With bare hands, with bare hands"— Well, wait until they tie your hands and string you up on a lamppost the way they did my man. The father hangs on the lamppost and under the lamppost his three kids—stretching their arms to their father. And I'm—here. Yes, wait.

VOICES.

Our troops are already this side of Gromovaya.

They'll be here by morning.

Earlier than that. Ought to be here at dawn.

Can't we rescue the men? (LYUBOV *walks up.*)

LYUBOV. Comrades! Our men will be here at sunrise. And tonight the comrades who fought in the rear of the enemy will be hanged here.

A WORKER. That's just what we're talking about.

LYUBOV. Are you going to stand by and wait, doing nothing? How do you think you'll look tomorrow in the eyes of your comrades from the front?

A WORKER. Better to gouge out our own eyes.

LYUBOV. What will you welcome them with? With the dead bodies of our fighters? They'll ask you, "And what did you do, comrades, to snatch our heroic brothers from the White Guard's nooses?" What will you answer them?

VOICES.

That's right, comrades!

We'll get them out!

We ought to be ashamed, worrying about our own skins!

Let's go set them free!

LYUBOV. Comrades, go to the vacant lot behind the school. You'll find arms there.

VOICES.

Hurrah!

Sh— Quiet— Scatter— Phone the factory. Everybody meet on the square, and from there on to the jail. (*The* CROWD *moves off. A gradually rising din is heard. The* BOURGEOIS CITIZENS *are fleeing in panic. With them are the retreating* WHITE TROOPS, *with their wounded, sick, etc.*)

FIRST GENTLEMAN (*to the* SECOND). What are you selling?

SECOND GENTLEMAN. Nothing.

FIRST GENTLEMAN. Maybe you have something. I don't mind the price. Do you sell boots? I need some.

SECOND GENTLEMAN. I need them myself. (*Goes off.*)

FIRST GENTLEMAN (*following him*). Will you take a hundred thousand? Here it is.

THIRD GENTLEMAN (*rushing on*). All the White money has been voided. They've just announced it at the bank.

FOURTH GENTLEMAN. Well, I have nothing except Kerensky and Czarist money, thank God. I foresaw all this.

THIRD GENTLEMAN. The Kerensky and Czarist money have also been voided! (*They go off. Enter* YAROVOY.)

YAROVOY. Is everything all right?

SENTRY. Yes, sir.

YAROVOY. How's the woman prisoner?

SENTRY. As you ordered—I handed her over to Sublieutenant—

YAROVOY. What? What sublieutenant?

SENTRY. Prince Kurnosovsky, who spoke to you on the phone—

YAROVOY (*after glancing into the empty room*). What are you supposed to be doing here?

SENTRY. Guarding the dispatch.

YAROVOY (*opens the envelope, finds it empty, tears it to pieces, and throws them into the soldier's face*). I'll have you shot for this! (*The telephone rings. He strides over to answer.*) Yes. A crowd? Moving on the prison? Get your companies out in the square and set up machine guns. Stand by for further orders. (SEMYON *darts in.*)

SEMYON. The crowd's right smack up against the prison, sir—throwing rocks.

YAROVOY. Open fire—on those in front!

SEMYON. Naturally. That witch of a schoolmarm—do we bump her off too?

YAROVOY. Schoolmarm? You don't mean—?"

SEMYON. The one who hid Koshkin in the school last night. I'll give it to her myself.

YAROVOY. I forbid you—without an order. She's to be taken alive.

SEMYON. Well, they won't give her up without a fight.

YAROVOY. Go. Wait for my orders over the telephone.

SEMYON. We can't wait.

YAROVOY. Go, I tell you. (SEMYON *leaves.* YAROVOY *paces, agitated, near the telephone, picks up the receiver, replaces it. A* CROWD *is heard shouting. The telephone rings. He answers.*) I know. Stand by for my orders. Fall back to the gate. (MALININ *hurries in, followed by* CHIR.)

MALININ. Lieutenant Yarovoy! What's the meaning of this inaction? Why don't you give the orders to open fire?

YAROVOY. There's time enough for that.

MALININ. What do you mean? I hear some Bolshevik woman has come right up to the soldiers and is trying to win them over.

CHIR. The same one who was searching through your papers.

MALININ. Ah, that one. Now I understand. Lieutenant, give the order to fire, at once.

YAROVOY. I'll ask you not to interfere with my orders.

MALININ. I'm a colonel.

YAROVOY. I've been given full authority here.

MALININ. Give the order or I'll arrest you as a traitor.

YAROVOY (*draws his revolver*). Well?

MALININ. Going over to the Bolsheviks?

YAROVOY. If it weren't for your kind, there wouldn't be any Bolsheviks left.

MALININ. Lieutenant Yarovoy, I'll ask you to follow me.

YAROVOY. Colonel Malinin, I'll ask you to go pick up your traveling bags.

MALININ. Are you giving me orders?

YAROVOY. You'll be only too glad to carry out this order.

MALININ. We'll have a talk another time. Bolshevik! (*He goes off.* SEMYON *runs in.*)

SEMYON. What does it mean, sir? Are we leaving the Zheglov men alive?

YAROVOY. The Zheglov men? Shoot them right away. Go.

SEMYON. They won't hand them over to me.

YAROVOY. I'll telephone orders. (*Rings the telephone.*) Give me the prison. (*Rings again. There is no answer.*) Oh, the devil! (*Triumphant shouting is heard in the distance. An* OFFICER *rushes in.*) What's going on out there?

OFFICER. The people have taken the prison.

YAROVOY. Have they? What were the troops doing?

OFFICER. The troops withdrew into town without a shot. Some have gone to the station.

YAROVOY. Fine. Let them choke on their prison. Lieutenant, the power is still in our hands until tonight. At night we'll set out for the woods. The war is continuing.

OFFICER. But who's going to fight?

YAROVOY. The loyal sons of the country with the fresh help of the allies.

OFFICER. Sons? Of the country? The allies? (*Whistles and tears off his epaulets.*) No, thank you, I've had my fill. (*Runs off.*)

SEMYON. The Bolsheviks are already running things, sir. They're pouring out of all the houses and hoisting red flags everywhere—it beats me where they get them— They're arresting everybody—

YAROVOY. Surround and shoot them. (*Enter* SHVANDYA *with a few* WORKERS.)

SHVANDYA (*pointing at* YAROVOY). Ah, there's our man. Take him, comrades.

YAROVOY (*whipping out his revolver*). Stay where you are! (*He runs off, firing. The* WORKERS' PATROL *runs after him. Enter* PIKALOV *with* GORNOSTAYEV *as prisoner.*)

GORNOSTAYEV. My good friend! How many truths do you think the people have thought up?

PIKALOV. I wouldn't know.

GORNOSTAYEV (*grasping* PIKALOV's *coat and shaking him*). Thousands. And when people try to make a thousand little truths into one big truth, it's the same thing as—taking a thousand rats and making them into an elephant.

PIKALOV. Stop shaking me. I'm not a fruit tree. A prisoner's just supposed to keep on walking, not shake his guard.

GORNOSTAYEV. We're walking all right but we can't seem to find anybody.

PIKALOV. Can I help it if there aren't any good officers left?

GORNOSTAYEV. Hand me over to a bad one.

PIKALOV. A bad one won't do. Two men have tried to figure it out already. One says, "Take the envelope to him." The other one shouts, "It says 'important' on the envelope—you better take him along with it." All I can figure out, old man, is you're on the spot—when a man is taken along with an important envelope that means you might just as well kiss him good-by. Say your prayers, old man. (*They go off. In the distance* YAROVOY *can be glimpsed, on the run. A* WORKERS' PATROL *comes on.* CHIR *strolls on from the opposite direction.*)

CHIR. And he commanded them to throw in a net, and a great multitude of fish were caught.

A WORKER. What are you jabbering about, grandpa?

CHIR. Cast your net in this block, comrades, and you'll catch a huge fish.

A WORKER. Go your way, old man. (*The* PATROL *marches off. Enter* SHVANDYA. *A* SPECULATOR *and his* LADY *loaded with baggage run across his path.*)

SHVANDYA (*singing after them*).

When my mother gave me a send-off,
All the kinfolks came to say good-by.

(*Enter* MAKHORA. *He bumps into her.*) Ah, Makhora darling! You look worn out. What's eating you?

MAKHORA. What else but love—for you!

SHVANDYA. Have you been keeping in touch with the White Guards, dearie?

MAKHORA. Me? I wouldn't let them touch me with a ten-foot pole.

SHVANDYA. And who was it the night before last who politely pinched you on this here spot?

MAKHORA. Why, was it you?

SHVANDYA. Positively. With my own hand.

MAKHORA. I guessed it right away.

SHVANDYA. Then you're a completely conscious woman. (*Glances keenly at* CHIR *and walks up to him.*) Hello, Chir. Don't you recanize me?

CHIR. Glory to God! Fyodor, the strangled servant of the Lord! I said prayers for you forty times asking God to receive you into his mansion—

SHVANDYA. And he refused me. "How dare you show yourself before my eyes?" says he. "Chir sent me up, my Lord," says I. "Ah, the ignorant fool," says he, "go send him to me—I'll explain it to him in short order." "Yes, comrade," says I. So here I am, come back to fetch you. Forward march!

CHIR. It's angels, Fedya, that are sent for one's soul.

SHVANDYA. That's just what I told God myself. "No," he says, "a sailor is more to be trusted." Take him, boys.

CHIR. He's lying, comrades. There's no such thing as God.

SHVANDYA. Then why did you send me to him?

CHIR. That was just to be agreeable. Let me go, comrades. There's no God, or may I drop dead right on this spot.

SHVANDYA. You got it all wrong, Chir. Now's the time to be talking Bible talk. (*They all leave. Enter* PIKALOV, *with* GORNOSTAYEV, *hatless, walking close behind him.*)

GORNOSTAYEV. Somebody is passionately denying the existence of God—that means he's recognized the existence of his neighbors. Well, friend, where are we to go now?

PIKALOV. Damned if I know.

GORNOSTAYEV. If there's nowhere to go, let's sit down. Perhaps that will make our brains work better.

PIKALOV. Not likely, seeing you've lost your hat.

GORNOSTAYEV. Doesn't it seem to you, my friend, that we're looking for truth by moving away from it? Since it's known that when truth is sought at a crossroad, it is sure to be found at one's own side.

PIKALOV. God, you're driving me crazy! How am I going to get rid of you?

GORNOSTAYEV. I don't know. I would be glad to bribe you but I've nothing to give.

PIKALOV. I've never taken a bribe in my life.

GORNOSTAYEV. Have you ever been offered one?

PIKALOV. No.

GORNOSTAYEV. Neither have I.

PIKALOV. What class do you belong to?

GORNOSTAYEV. I'm a professor.

PIKALOV. You mean like in the circus?

GORNOSTAYEV. Why the circus?

PIKALOV. The other night one was explaining about rats and elephants. He was a smooth talker, too.

GORNOSTAYEV (*regarding him keenly*). Listen, you citizen of the new life—

PIKALOV. Well?

GORNOSTAYEV. What if you liquidate me?

PIKALOV. You're a fool. How about the envelope? Who'll sign the receipt?

GORNOSTAYEV. I'll give you a receipt for my death.

PIKALOV. No, I'm not used to that sort of thing.

GORNOSTAYEV. What are you used to?

PIKALOV. Well, there's my wife—she still has to work my bit of land all by herself. The gelding must have died by now. Last spring I borrowed a sack of grain from a neighbor. Now I not only have to pay that back, but— See here, don't you try to talk your way around me! (SHVANDYA *strolls on.*)

SHVANDYA. Ah, comrade Marx! And you too, friend! What's the trouble?

PIKALOV. Ah, what a hell of a mess!

SHVANDYA. Holy smoke! Are you a prisoner again?

PIKALOV. I wish I was. It's worse. I have to escort a man, and with an envelope at that—damn it. It's enough to drive you crazy.

SHVANDYA. Who's the envelope for?

GORNOSTAYEV. Apparently for me. But there's no one here with authority to open it.

SHVANDYA. Well, that's easy as pie. (*Opens the envelope, turns the paper this way and that, and after a not-too-successful attempt at reading it, hands it to* GORNOSTAYEV.) Read it, papa, I'm hoarse.

GORNOSTAYEV (*reads*). "Safe conduct. Bearer of this, Professor Gornostayev, is under special protection of the Soviet authorities—is not subject to arrest—is to receive every assistance—"

SHVANDYA. Why, this was written when I was still in the office, only we didn't have time to mail it.

PIKALOV. So that's what's given me all this trouble!

GORNOSTAYEV. You see, my friend, everything in the end has its reasonable cause.

PIKALOV. What am I supposed to do with him now? Put him up against the wall?

SHVANDYA. You're an unconscious wall yourself.

PIKALOV. I just didn't have the time to join the party.

SHVANDYA. Comrade Marx has a head, you might say, on a world scale, and you want to put him up against a wall! Come along, Papa Marx, I'll explain everything to you. It's easy as pie. (*They go off.* LYUBOV *comes on, finishing bandaging her wounded arm.* KOLOSOV *appears, hastening toward her.*)

KOLOSOV. Lyuba, you have to save him. He's surrounded.

LYUBOV. Who is?

KOLOSOV. He, Mikhail, of course.

LYUBOV. Then he hasn't left? He's stayed on for another hunt?

KOLOSOV. It's he who's being hunted. He's there, in the alley, darting around like a squirrel. They've surrounded him. Where can we hide him?

LYUBOV. On my breast, next to my heart. Last night he warmed and lulled me to sleep next to his heart. This time I'll sting him.

KOLOSOV. No, Lyuba. Don't bring destruction on yourself. Hide him in the school.

LYUBOV. Run along, you innocent. (YAROVOY *runs in.*)

YAROVOY (*taking a step toward* LYUBOV). Lyuba! (*She turns away from him abruptly.*)

KOLOSOV (*reaching the door, to* YAROVOY). This way.

YAROVOY (*after a few seconds of hesitation*). Ah, it makes no difference. (*He and* KOLOSOV *disappear through the door. A* PATROL OF WORKERS *rushes on. They run into an* OLD WOMAN *just approaching.*)

A WORKER. Have you seen an officer running this way, auntie?

OLD WOMAN. He didn't run away, my boy. He's gone through that door. (*The* PATROL *starts through the door, as* YAROVOY *comes out, wearing* KOLOSOV's *blouse.*)

A WORKER. Where is officer Yarovoy?

YAROVOY. I don't know. (*He walks on.* KOLOSOV *appears, dressed in* YAROVOY's *uniform.*)

KOLOSOV. Here I am.

A WORKER. Let's go.

YAROVOY (*as he runs past* LYUBOV). Good-by, Lyuba.

LYUBOV. Oh, you accept such sacrifices? (*To the* PATROL.) Just a minute, comrades! That man isn't Yarovoy. This holy innocent is masquerading. Yarovoy just ran out that way. (*The* PATROL *run after* YAROVOY.)

KOLOSOV. Lyuba, what have you done to yourself? (*A mounting noise of people rejoicing drifts in from a distance. Men and women* WORKERS, *shouting happily, gather from all parts of town to mingle with the throng surrounding* KOSHKIN *and the liberated* ZHEGLOV MEN. *Here and there frightened* BOURGEOIS *stand quietly in nooks and corners.*)

VOICES. Boys, there's Koshkin and the Zheglov men! Hurrah!

TATYANA. Where's Hrustch? My brother? Has anyone seen my brother? (*Led by* KOSHKIN *and the* ZHEGLOV MEN, *the* CROWD *pours into the square singing and shouting "Hurrah!"* TATYANA *rushes to* KOSHKIN.) Where's Hrustch? My brother? Have they hanged him?

KOSHKIN (*smiling*). Hang him, indeed. You wouldn't find a lamp-post big enough for him. (HRUSTCH *comes forward.*) Look at the height he's put on! (TATYANA *throws herself into* HRUSTCH's *arms.*)

HRUSTCH. Hello, comrade Yarovaya! Were you the first one to get it? Did it take a big nip out of you?

LYUBOV. That's nothing. Nobody was seriously wounded. We broke them up before they could shoot.

KOSHKIN. And we sat behind bars and took it all in at our leisure. (*Smiling.*) However, comrades, it's too early to sit back and relax. The enemy is sitting quiet biding his time till he can leap at our throats. Everybody must be on his guard! (SHVANDYA *comes on with a group of armed* WORKERS)

SHVANDYA. Comrade Roman! (*Throws his arms around him.*) So— so—

KOSHKIN (*tenderly*). So what, Fedya?

SHVANDYA (*brushing away a tear*). We got knocked out but then we came to and now it's the other way around. (*Enter* GORNOSTAYEV *and* PIKALOV. SHVANDYA *shouts to them.*) Did you find the hat?

PIKALOV. We did. But damn it, it's somebody else's.

KOSHKIN. Comrade Gornostayev, I'm glad to see you. Now we're going to wage war against ignorance, aren't we?

GORNOSTAYEV. Certainly. Certainly. That's just what I've come for —to talk about my friend here. (MARYA *bursts in, rushes to* GRIGORY.)

MARYA. You here? Where's Semyon?

GRIGORY. Digging a grave for me.

MARYA. Where?

GRIGORY. Either in other lands or right here, Mother. (YAROVOY *darts out from somewhere behind, pursued by a* PATROL. *He runs into* KOSHKIN.)

KOSHKIN. Ah! Commissar Vikhor. Here we meet again, and we've nothing to talk about. So—good-by.

YAROVOY. Good-by, Lyuba. (LYUBOV *turns away from* YAROVOY, *who is immediately led off.*)

LYUBOV (*she glances after him, closing her eyes with a groan, but quietly recovers her self-control*). Comrade Roman, the arms hidden under the logs have been handed out to the proper parties.

KOSHKIN. Thank you. I've always regarded you as a loyal comrade.

LYUBOV. No, only from today am I a loyal comrade. (*Music draws near. High up,* SHVANDYA *is hanging a red flag.*)

KOSHKIN. Fasten it tight, Shvandya!

SHVANDYA. Just what I'm doing! On a world scale!

CURTAIN

THE CHIMES OF THE KREMLIN

BY NIKOLAY POGODIN

THE years of the civil war in Russia were marked by a complete breakdown of economic life and by widespread privation. In 1920, while fighting was still going on on various fronts, Lenin appointed a committee of experts to work out plans for the electrification of Russia. The report submitted by this committee ushered in the Soviets' "planned economy" of the following years and laid the foundation for the subsequent Five Year Plans initiated by Stalin. Since Lenin formulated his slogan, "Soviets plus electrification is communism," electrification has made great strides in Russia. But the slogan itself has lost much of its original meaning. The gasoline engine has proved to be much more important than electricity in mechanizing agriculture (one of the primary objects of Lenin's plan), and furthermore machine-building and other heavy industries had to be developed before electrification could be carried out on the vast scale that was planned by Lenin.

"The Chimes of the Kremlin" pictures the setting and the first steps of Lenin's plan. In doing this the author introduces a number of historical figures, such as Lenin, Stalin, and Dzerzhinsky (head of the Cheka), and presumably draws on authentic facts in telling the story of Engineer Zabelin, though Zabelin himself is a fictional figure. The English Writer who figures in the play is obviously a take-off on H. G. Wells, who visited Russia at that time.

Nikolay Fyodorovich Pogodin, author of the play, was born in 1900, the son of a peasant. As a newspaper reporter and columnist he traveled widely in Russia observing and describing the growth of the great industrial projects and the changing social scene. This work supplied him with material which he used for his plays, sometimes, particularly in his early plays, dramatizing the actual conflicts he had observed. His first play, "Tempo," appeared in 1930. It was followed by "A Poem of the Axe," after which in quick succession came "My Friend," "Snow," "After the Ball," "Aristocrats," "The Man with a Rifle," "Gioconda," "Silver Valley," "The Chimes of the Kremlin" (1941), "The Boatwoman," and "Creation of the World."

A. B.

THE CHIMES OF THE KREMLIN

CHARACTERS

HOMELESS CHILDREN
WOMAN DOLL VENDOR and other VENDORS
AN OLD WOMAN
PASSERS-BY
MONK
ZABELIN, ANTON IVANOVICH, engineer
MILITARY CADETS
SOLDIER
A MAN IN HIGH BOOTS
SPECULATOR
ZABELINA, LYDIA MIKHAILOVNA, wife of engineer ZABELIN
MASHA, her daughter
RYBAKOV, ALEXANDER MIKHAILOVICH, a former sailor
CHUDNOV, hunter
KAZANOK, bell ringer
ANNA, CHUDNOV's wife
LIZA, her daughter-in-law
STYOPKA ⎱ LIZA's children
MARUSYA ⎰
LENIN, VLADIMIR ILYICH (ILYICH)
ROMAN, CHUDNOV's son and LIZA's husband
A BEGGAR WOMAN
ASSISTANT REPAIRMAN
BEARDED REPAIRMAN
HEAD REPAIRMAN
AN OLD WOMAN
SKEPTIC
FRIGHTENED LADY, wife of the SKEPTIC
OPTIMIST
KNITTING LADY, wife of the OPTIMIST

COOK (PRASKOVYA)
CHAIRMAN OF THE HOUSE TENANTS' COMMITTEE
MILITARY MAN
SECRETARY TO LENIN
WATCHMAKER
STALIN
DZERZHINSKY, head of the Cheka
ENGLISHMAN, a famous writer
MILITARY MEN
CIVILIANS

ACT I

SCENE 1

The Iversky Gate in Moscow. A shrine with oil lamps burning before the icons. An April evening. A stout, red-faced woman is selling dolls. Nearby, a man in a winter coat, a SPECULATOR, is pacing up and down looking for customers. Moscow citizens stroll by. They are poorly and oddly dressed. They live on the "hunger ration."

HOMELESS BOY (*sings*).
> Oh, I'll die, I'll die,
> And they'll bury me.
> And no one will know
> Where my grave may be.

WOMAN DOLL VENDOR. Satin dolls, silk dolls, brocade dolls. All the same price—seven hundred fifty rubles. No better gift for children.

VOICES OF DIFFERENT VENDORS. Imported groats—of finest oats. Delicious to eat. Better than meat. Goods only—no cash. Goods only.

Army boots, deserters' prewar leather boots—

Anybody want Poltava lard? Brought it from Poltava myself, hard, fresh lard. I'll trade for gold rings—engagement rings.

Saccharin, scientific tablets, as good as sugar. Aromatic sensation—dirt cheap.

Belt, belts, belts!

Hygienic satin girdles and brassieres. The last word in fashion and medicine! Latest style—straight from Paris.

AN OLD WOMAN. Lace—Brussels, Paris, Chantilly.

VOICES OF HOMELESS CHILDREN (*playing cards*).
Hey, you pulled this ace out of another pack! (*There is a fight.*)
I swear by the Revolution!
Put the money back where it belongs.
Stop fighting. I'll put it back.
No more of your cheating if you want to play.
I swear by the Revolution! (*The game is resumed.*)
I bet half a million smackers.
It sounds fine but where is it? Lay it out.
Here it is.
Watch your step! Take it easy!

PASSERS-BY. Have you heard about the comet? They say it's bigger than the moon and has a red tail.

The comet's a lot of nonsense. But England will get the Bolsheviks by hook or by crook. (*A MONK walks slowly through the crowd, eyes lowered.*)

MONK (*in a low but clear voice*). Old crosses of cast gold exchanged for flour.

PASSER-BY. Do you have bells too?

MONK. Why, have you a buyer?

PASSER-BY. You Judas! You'd sell the Iversky Virgin Mary if you had a chance.

HOMELESS BOY. Hey, fellows, look! The engineer that sells matches is coming. Let's take all the money and cigarettes out of his pockets— he'll just blubber, "You bad boys!" (ZABELIN *comes on. He has a clean- shaven face, with neatly trimmed gray hair and mustache. On his head is an engineer's peak-cap, and the jacket of an engineer's uniform can be seen under his old coat. He wears a stiff white collar and an ex- pensive tie.*)

ZABELIN (*taking his place by the wall*). Prewar safety matches manu- factured by Lapshin. (*After a long pause.*) Prewar safety matches manu- factured by Lapshin.

HOMELESS BOY. Hello, engineer.

ZABELIN. Hello, young fellow.

HOMELESS BOY. How're things with you?

ZABELIN. As bad as with you.

HOMELESS BOY. Go on. You live in a house and I live in an empty tank.

ZABELIN. I'll soon be moving into a tank too.

HOMELESS BOY. Move first, and then complain. How much did you make today?

ZABELIN. I don't know.

HOMELESS BOY. We'll count it up for you.

ZABELIN. How?

HOMELESS BOY. I used to be at the head of the class in arithmetic. (*The boys search* ZABELIN's *pockets and take all the money they can lay their hands on.*) All right, get on with your business, engineer. We'll be back and see you again. How about running over to Tverskaya Street, boys? We'll get free kasha there. (*Sings.*)

> Oh, we sank their boat
> In the old Don River.
> Now the fish are eating
> White Army liver!

A VENDOR. Belts! Belts! (*The* BOYS *snatch the belts and run away.* MILITARY CADETS *are heard singing offstage.*)

A WOMAN'S VOICE. Oh, my God! Please hide me, I've got strips of lard under my skirt—tied all around me! (*The* CADETS *walk past.*)

DOLL VENDOR. The best gift for the kiddies. Satin dolls, silk dolls, brocade dolls. (*A Red Army* SOLDIER *pauses beside her.*)

SOLDIER. How much are these?

DOLL VENDOR. Seven hundred fifty each.

SOLDIER. That's robbery! What do you take money for? It's just a doll. What good is it?

DOLL VENDOR. You don't need it, you can keep moving.

SOLDIER. Don't need it? I certainly do. Come on, let's talk business —how much?

DOLL VENDOR. Seven hundred fifty.

SOLDIER. Slice it in half, hey?

DOLL VENDOR. If you want to joke, go somewhere else.

SOLDIER. Come on, take five hundred. After all, you understand yourself—this isn't a horse. It's only a doll—a toy.

DOLL VENDOR. If you don't understand anything yourself, don't talk. What are you pawing them for?

SOLDIER. All right. Then you pick out the biggest one.

ZABELIN. Are you buying them by weight?

SOLDIER. Damn it—you can't even see what you pay your money for. (*Watches the woman.*) Don't you give me that squint-eyed one, auntie.

DOLL VENDOR. Stupid! That's not a squint—she's got an expression on her face.

SOLDIER. If you won't knock anything off your price, the least you can do is give me first-class merchandise. (*To* ZABELIN.) Isn't that right?

ZABELIN. What do you want a doll for?

SOLDIER. Asking *me* such a question! I'm taking it to a little girl, my daughter. I'm going home from the front—I've been discharged. Want to buy a gift. How much are the matches?

ZABELIN. I don't overcharge people.

SOLDIER. Do they strike?

ZABELIN. I've never deceived people.

SOLDIER. I don't know. I bought a chunk of bread yesterday. I bit off a piece, and it was bitter. I threw it to a dog, and he wouldn't touch it either. If they're guaranteed to work, I'll give you a strip of these money stamps and stock up. There's a famine in matches in all the villages. Oh, there's a famine in everything these days. (*Unrolls a long strip of money stamps.*) We're rolling in hundreds of thousands—living on velvet.

ZABELIN. Did you fight long, soldier?

SOLDIER. Since it turned from an imperialist war into a civil one.

ZABELIN. I see. You haven't won much, soldier—only a doll and a pack of matches.

SOLDIER. Whatever it is, it's a gift. Well, I'll miss my train if I go on talking to you. What time is it?

ZABELIN. I don't know. The clock in the Kremlin doesn't strike any more.

SOLDIER. What's the matter with it? On the blink?

ZABELIN. Yes, my friend, the principal clock of the state is on the blink. The chimes of the Kremlin ring no more. Happy journey with your doll, soldier.

SOLDIER. You can't mix me up with that kind of talk— I've knocked around too much. But you may find yourself up against a wall if you're not careful.

ZABELIN. Do you think that'll make things better? No, it won't.

SOLDIER. I don't know if it will or not, but it would be a good thing to put you up against a wall anyway. Well, good-by. I'm in a hurry. (*Goes off.*)

A MAN IN HIGH BOOTS. Step this way, all interested in antireligious literature. "What the wife does when her husband is away," written by Dostoyevsky. "One hundred jokes and anecdotes from the life of Count Sologub." (*Passes out of sight.*)

ZABELIN (*to the* DOLL VENDOR). The chimes of the Kremlin are silent. What's your opinion about it?

DOLL VENDOR. My alarm clock fell off the bureau and stopped too. I don't know where I can get it fixed.

ZABELIN. Forgive me, but what you just said is stupid.

DOLL VENDOR. If you're so damn clever, why waste your breath on stupid people?

SPECULATOR. Imported groats of finest oats. Delicious to eat. Better than meat. Barter only. Barter only.

A VENDOR. Will you take a scarf?

SPECULATOR. It depends.

A VENDOR. Pure Orenburg wool. Never worn.

SPECULATOR. Where is your scarf?

A VENDOR. Where are your groats?

SPECULATOR. Not far from here. I'm an honest tradesman. Don't be afraid.

ZABELIN. Listen, salesman of groats—

SPECULATOR. Yes, Your Excellency.

ZABELIN. If the chimes in London, on Westminster Abbey, had fallen silent, what would an Englishman have said?

SPECULATOR. I really couldn't say, Your Excellency.

ZABELIN. The Englishman would have said that England was done for.

SPECULATOR. Quite possible. Quite possible.

ZABELIN. It would mean the heart had stopped beating, groats salesman.

SPECULATOR. You should discuss this with your wife, at home, Your Excellency, not with us.

DOLL VENDOR. If you want the Cheka to get you, you're welcome to it. We don't.

SPECULATOR. For such talk, Your Excellency, they can set you to work cleaning outhouses—that'll be the abbey for you.

DOLL VENDOR. What do you mean, anyway, going around acting like an anti-Soviet liberal? You've got your nerve—talking to my customers and slipping in propaganda against the Kremlin! If you

don't like the Reds, why don't you light out for the Crimea and General Wrangel? You're no Soviet speculator. Here I'm bawling you
out and you don't even answer, just turn up your nose at me. A fine
Jesus you are—Jesus without disciples!

MONK (*he has been listening to this argument from a distance*). I
exchange gold for flour. Pure old gold from monasteries exchanged
for flour. (*Walks up to* ZABELIN.) I've been looking at you and thinking—you carry a great fire in your heart!

ZABELIN. Pardon me, I've never had anything to do with priests.

MONK. That comes from mistaken notions, my friend. Now the
priests have been trampled underfoot, and what's the result?

ZABELIN. And I suspect talking to you especially would be most
objectionable.

MONK. You've cut loose from the shore—you'll drown, my dear sir!

ZABELIN. I repeat, I don't have anything to do with priests or crooks.

MONK. You're a devil—that's what you are!

ZABELIN. Get away from me, you old swindler.

MONK. Swindler yourself!

ZABELIN. I'll punch you in the nose!

MONK. I swear you're possessed! You're raving mad! (*As the* MONK
walks off, ZABELINA, *the engineer's wife, comes on. She is about forty
but looks and acts much younger, with no trace of passing years or
dowdiness. She wears good winter clothes and has a warm woolen scarf
over her head.*)

ZABELINA. Anton Ivanovich! Have you been quarreling again?

ZABELIN. I live in the streets.

ZABELINA. Who forces you to live in the streets? Who drives you into
them? Nobody that I know of.

ZABELIN. The government.

ZABELINA. I just can't understand you.

ZABELIN. We'll talk about it when your understanding gets a little
broader. And generally speaking, I'd advise you to pay more attention
to looking after your daughter. I don't need to be watched over and
protected.

ZABELINA. But Masha isn't a child either. She's beginning to live her
own life.

ZABELIN. That's just it. I won't be surprised if she turns into a street
girl tomorrow.

ZABELINA. Anton Ivanovich, think what you're saying! Good God
—Masha, our own daughter!

ZABELIN. An hour ago your daughter went into the Hotel Metropole
with a man.

ZABELINA. The Metropole is no longer a hotel. The Second House
of the Soviets is there now.

ZABELIN. I don't know what a House of the Soviets is. The Metropole is a hotel. Our daughter went into a room occupied by a man. I saw it myself.

ZABELINA. I'm fed up with your fancy didos. You're my husband. You can divorce me. But I won't stand for such talk.

ZABELIN. If that man doesn't call on us in the next three days, I'll take my own measures.

ZABELINA. Why don't you go home? Your hands are frozen. Ah, it's a hard, a bitter life we're living today.

ZABELIN. All Russia's living a hard and bitter life today. (ZABELINA *goes off. A man in patent-leather high boots comes on.*)

MAN IN HIGH BOOTS (*to* ZABELIN). Count Cagliostro! I have half a cask of home-made liquor. Would you care to join in as a partner?

ZABELIN (*stepping away*). Prewar matches manufactured by Lapshin!

AN OLD WOMAN. Lace—Brussels—Chantilly—

CURTAIN

ACT I

SCENE 2

A room in the Hotel Metropole. The room has long since lost its hotel look. One sees great quantities of newspapers and books lying all around in disorder. On the table are a spirit lamp, black bread, a tea-pot, glasses, and packs of cartridges. On the wall over the bed hang a carbine, a sword, and a revolver in a holster. MASHA ZABELINA, *wearing a coat and cap, is standing just inside the door, which is closed. At the end of the room, upstage,* RYBAKOV *is looking through a book.* MASHA *watches him for a long time with a smile on her face.*

MASHA. Why did you lock the door?

RYBAKOV. So nobody would get in.

MASHA. That's not true. (RYBAKOV *does not answer.*) Open the door. I want to go.

RYBAKOV. I won't.

MASHA. Do you have the slightest idea what you're doing? (RYBA-KOV *is silent.*) It's a low-down trick to lock the door and hide the key, like a crook. You smile. It's a loathsome smile, I assure you. I want to go, do you hear me?

RYBAKOV. I hear you.

MASHA. Well?

RYBAKOV. I'm not going to open the door.

MASHA. I'll jump out the window.

RYBAKOV. Go ahead.

MASHA. What a cheap stunt! It certainly shows you in your true colors. Is it your idea that when a girl comes to see you, the first thing to do is lock the door?

RYBAKOV. This is not a cheap stunt.

MASHA. It's disgusting.

RYBAKOV. Quite the opposite.

MASHA. It's vile.

RYBAKOV. I must have a talk with you—that's all.

MASHA. Behind a locked door?

RYBAKOV. What else can I do?

MASHA. And you write me letters saying you love me?

RYBAKOV. Well, what else can I do, if you please? Many a time I wanted to talk to you, but you bowed to me with a grin and walked out. Try and bow this time. It won't work.

MASHA. So this is a trap.

RYBAKOV. Perfectly correct. It is a trap. Sit down.

MASHA. What right do you have to take this tone? Are you trying to give orders to me?

RYBAKOV. Sit down.

MASHA. I won't sit down.

RYBAKOV. Well, it's all the same to me. You can stand on your feet until morning.

MASHA. What do you mean, until morning?

RYBAKOV. Until morning means until morning.

MASHA. Rybakov, are you drunk?

RYBAKOV. I've had enough of your tricks, Mariya Antonovna. I'm not a plaything for you—but a human being like yourself. You've had a better education than me and your background's nothing like mine. But for some reason or other, every time you're with me, you're extremely rude. Very well, then. I'll behave like you. Until I get an answer from you this door won't open and you won't leave this room.

MASHA. All right. Say what you have to say.

RYBAKOV. What is there to say? You already know everything.

MASHA. But you wanted to speak to me. Speak then; I'm listening.

RYBAKOV. It's all wrong, Mariya Antonovna.

MASHA. For the hundredth time I ask you not to call me Mariya Antonovna. I gave you permission to call me Masha a long time ago.

RYBAKOV. I have nothing to say. Everything's been said ages ago.

MASHA. My dear Rybakov, I will not be your wife.

RYBAKOV. Why not?

MASHA. I don't know. Calm yourself. Good-by. Open the door.

RYBAKOV. That's no answer. That's not the way to speak.

MASHA. That's my exact and final answer.

RYBAKOV (*suddenly with despair*). Then why isn't your face the face of a stranger? When a girl turns a man down, she can't have such kind and merry eyes. Or are there really girls whose tenderness and beauty don't mean anything? "Lovely like an angel from heaven; like a demon, evil and sly?"

MASHA. My goodness! Didn't you know that? Of course I'm a demon— I'm evil and sly!

RYBAKOV. Why are you so gay?

MASHA. You're a hero of the civil war—it's ridiculous—shameful—

RYBAKOV. So you think a hero of the civil war isn't a human being?

MASHA. I didn't say it right. Think of the time we're living in! You visit Lenin's home—

RYBAKOV. You're all wrong, Mariya—you're all wrong, Masha. We're not Puritans.

MASHA. How do you know about the Puritans?

RYBAKOV. Why do I spend all my nights reading? Just for nothing? I'm working to join the Communist University.

MASHA. What did you read last night?

RYBAKOV. Lermontov's novel, "The Hero of Our Time."

MASHA. And before that?

RYBAKOV. "Letters from Afar."

MASHA. Would you like me to guide you in your reading?

RYBAKOV. Masha, do sit down a minute.

MASHA. Open the door.

RYBAKOV. I won't.

MASHA. This is indecent. You're humiliating me.

RYBAKOV. Is it decent to make fun of a man?

MASHA. I'm not making fun of you.

RYBAKOV. You'll stay here three days and three nights, and I won't let you go till you give me a really serious and sincere answer.

MASHA. I gave you my answer.

RYBAKOV. That was no answer.

MASHA. Because you don't happen to like it?

RYBAKOV. No, not for that reason.

MASHA. It's all the answer you'll get.

RYBAKOV. Then you'll have to stay.

MASHA. All right— I will.

RYBAKOV. That's fine.

MASHA. Please don't smoke so much, and open the window.

RYBAKOV. I'm sorry (*Opens a small hinged pane in the window.*)

MASHA. Why don't you make use of some weapon? Take the revolver —frighten me.

RYBAKOV. I have no desire to frighten anybody.

MASHA. A girl friend of mine was ordered by her boss to marry him within three days. If she refused, he said, he would have her and her parents sent to Siberia as former bourgeois.

RYBAKOV. A dirty skunk like that ought to be shot.

MASHA. What's the difference between him and you?

RYBAKOV. There is a difference.

MASHA. What is it?

RYBAKOV. I love you— You know it.

MASHA. Don't you dare to talk to me about your love. It makes me sick to hear you.

RYBAKOV. It makes you sick?

MASHA. It does. (RYBAKOV *unlocks the door and throws it wide*.)

RYBAKOV. There's a real answer—sincere and honest.

MASHA. Do you take it as an offence?

RYBAKOV. At least it's genuinely human. Please go.

MASHA. Do you mean just go?

RYBAKOV. This is the end. And really it should have been over long before this. Please go. (MASHA *starts off, running into her mother*, ZABELINA, *just outside the door*.)

ZABELINA. May I come in?

MASHA. Mama! How did you get here?

ZABELINA. I got the number of citizen Rybakov's room downstairs.

MASHA. Why have you come? What's happened?

ZABELINA. Please let me in first. (*Enters and addresses* RYBAKOV.) How are you, young man? Now you can see what sort of a mother-in-law you're going to have.

MASHA. Mama, whatever gave you that idea?

ZABELINA. What you told me.

MASHA. But you don't know anything about it.

ZABELINA. I know everything. How else could I have come here? Oh, it's not at all nice in here, young man. So much rubbish around! Besides, why so many newspapers? After you've read them you should throw them away. You don't live well, Alexander. I know your first name is Alexander. What's your father's name?

RYBAKOV. Mikhail.

ZABELINA. Mine too. Lydia Mikhailovna. I know everything, Alexander Mikhailovich.

RYBAKOV. But I know nothing.

MASHA. I implore you, Mama, don't say anything more.

ZABELINA. I won't say a word. It's about time you came to see us, young man.

RYBAKOV. I've never been invited.

ZABELINA. I don't know about that. But you should have insisted and called on us a long time ago. (*To* MASHA.) Your father saw you with Alexander Mikhailovich today and knows you're here.

MASHA. Oh, no— That can't be true.

ZABELINA. How did I get to know about it?

MASHA. What did he say?

ZABELINA. We must hurry home, Masha dear. I'll tell you on the way. As for you, young man, you're invited to our house this Saturday evening—around seven. (*Glances about again.*) It's a good room but, my, how you've neglected it! Good-by.

RYBAKOV. Masha, what am I to do now?

MASHA. Do whatever you please. (ZABELINA *and* MASHA *leave*.)

RYBAKOV. I never felt so dead beat. Maybe I ought to get the hell out of Moscow!

CURTAIN

ACT I

SCENE 3

The edge of a forest by a lake. A hunters' tent. Early spring. Shortly before dawn but still dark. A lighted lamp is hanging near the tent flap. Close by, over a campfire, a teakettle is heating. A peasant hunter, CHUDNOV, is puttering about the fire. KAZANOK, a village bell ringer, stands leaning on an old rifle.

CHUDNOV. Dear God, give us a fine sunrise! I'll pray to you every day, O Lord, I swear I will.

KAZANOK. It's going to be a foggy sunrise, Chudnov. I can read the signs.

CHUDNOV. But there's not a cloud in the sky, the weather's clear. I don't see where any fog can come from. Now comrade Lenin and I won't be able to hunt again.

KAZANOK. What time is it? It must be after four.

CHUDNOV. That's right. Well, I'll go get some brushwood. You stay here, keep your eyes open, and watch the lake.

KAZANOK. I'm no kid, I know. (CHUDNOV *goes off*.) I remember once in the winter, when Ilyich came for a fox hunt, it all came to nothing too because of a snowstorm. Who's there? (RYBAKOV *appears*.)

RYBAKOV. Friend.

KAZANOK. No, you're not.

RYBAKOV. I'm telling you a friend. That means a friend.

KAZANOK. Stay where you are.

RYBAKOV. All right.

KAZANOK. You're no friend.

RYBAKOV. Who am I?

KAZANOK. A stranger.

RYBAKOV. Old man, turn your weapon away; it can probably shoot.

KAZANOK. It can.

RYBAKOV. Then what's the idea of aiming at me?

KAZANOK. Who are you?

RYBAKOV. A sailor.

KAZANOK. Where do you come from?

RYBAKOV. Moscow.

KAZANOK. You're under arrest.

RYBAKOV. What's next?

KAZANOK. Hands up. (CHUDNOV *returns.*)

CHUDNOV. Hold on; that's a friend. That's comrade Rybakov, take it from me. Why, he's a sailor, he's come with Ilyich, and you put him under arrest. Now, how could you make such a fool of yourself?

RYBAKOV. And that's not all. I carry a Mauser, and his is just an old blunderbuss. But a guard is a guard and he's not the timid type either. It's a good thing you're guarding Lenin.

KAZANOK. He's a friend— All right, then. It's my job to find out. Don't feel sore.

RYBAKOV. I'm not sore at you.

KAZANOK. You're not sore but you keep snorting at me.

RYBAKOV. Naturally I did, when you made a grab at me.

KAZANOK. That's my job. Grab and hang on. I'm a guard, a government man now. (*In a normal, friendly tone.*) Well, so long. (*Goes off.*)

RYBAKOV. Where's Ilyich?

CHUDNOV. Gone to the lake.

RYBAKOV. Alone?

CHUDNOV. Don't worry. We've posted guards all around. Sit down. Tea'll be ready in a minute. The only thing is I have to make it out of carrots and they stink so— I can't figure out why. Oh, Lord, not a thing to be had—no tea, no sugar, no kerosene.

RYBAKOV. Don't complain to me. Don't I know?

CHUDNOV. Rybakov, has anything happened down in Moscow?

RYBAKOV. How do you mean?

CHUDNOV. Anything special?

RYBAKOV. I don't know. I don't think there's been anything special. Why?

CHUDNOV. Well, comrade Lenin arrived looking as if he had something on his mind. We came here today— He didn't say a word. I lit the lamp. He fiddled around with some cartridges for a while. Then he dropped that and got up and walked up and down, and finally he said: "I'm going to the lake. Don't look for me. I'll call you myself." And left.

RYBAKOV. All the same, you'd better go and remind him very gently that tea is ready.

CHUDNOV. No, I don't think that's necessary.

RYBAKOV. And I think it is. He's forgotten about it—he'll miss his tea and get chilled to the bone. It was hours ago when we got here.

CHUDNOV. Here's a spoon. Stir the tea so the carrots won't all lump together. Maybe you're right; I'll go. (*Goes off.*)

RYBAKOV (*sings a snatch of song in a low voice, then recites haltingly*).

> There water nymphs sit on the boughs—
> And footprints of fantastic beasts
> Are seen on secret forest trails.
> A hut stands there—

Tea with carrots— (CHUDNOV *enters*.) Well?

CHUDNOV. Go call him yourself. I haven't the nerve. I could see him in the distance—there's more light by the lake than here. He's sitting there leaning against something and gazing across at the other shore. For all we know he may be working out plans this minute, and we, like fools, don't understand and want to drag him up to have tea.

RYBAKOV. All right. Let's wait. We'll heat up the tea later on, comrade Chudnov. Ah, what a night! Do you hear the rustling and whispering on the lake? Chudnov, do you have water nymphs here?

CHUDNOV. Water nymphs? At this time of night the nymphs are all in their huts, snoring their lungs out.

RYBAKOV. I'm asking you about the water nymphs that sit on the boughs.

CHUDNOV. We don't have that kind in our county.

RYBAKOV. That's a pity.

CHUDNOV. Sorry. We can offer you only what we have.

RYBAKOV. You know, Tikhon Ivanovich, we've done all sorts of wild things during the revolution but the stars are just the same as they've always been. Eternity—that beats me!

CHUDNOV. If you ask me, Alexander, I think it's time for you to get married.

RYBAKOV. Sure, it's time.

CHUDNOV. One minute you ask about nymphs and the next you're star-gazing. Come back here after Easter; we'll pick you out a little nymph for a bride.

RYBAKOV. I have one.

CHUDNOV. You say you have but you act restless.

RYBAKOV. I'm sort of in love, Tikhon Ivanovich.

CHUDNOV. Well, I'm sorry for you. Such a brave sailor, and now he's been caught. Look out. I know those Moscow girls. You've got to know how to handle them. But I'll say this much—you don't have to be afraid of them either. In this business, the same as in war, if you get scared you're lost. Let her be afraid of you, but you strut before her like a cock of the walk.

RYBAKOV. No, comrade Chudnov, I'm serious. But mind, not a word about this to Ilyich.

CHUDNOV. Afraid? Quiet, Rybakov. I hear his footsteps. He's coming up. Put on the kettle.

CURTAIN

ACT I

Scene 4

The peasant home of the Chudnov family. The living room has three windows. A Russian stove can be seen in the entranceway. In the room proper are benches, a table, several icons hanging in a corner, and on the wall, surrounded by crude prints and family photographs, a cheap lithographic portrait of Lenin. CHUDNOV's *old wife* ANNA *and their daughter-in-law* LIZA *are cleaning up the room.* LIZA's *children, the girl* MARUSYA *and the boy* STYOPKA, *are whispering together rapturously.*

ANNA (*to* LIZA). Take the high boots out. What are they doing on the bench, stinking up the place with tar? The hunters will be back any minute and the room's a mess. (*To the children.*) Whispering again! I'll whisper you. Get up on the stove where you belong. (LIZA *takes the boots out. Enter* KAZANOK.)

KAZANOK. Wishing you a happy holiday, Anna Vlasyevna.

ANNA. Same to you.

KAZANOK. I've come to tell you Vladimir Ilyich will be here in a minute.

ANNA. Oh, good heavens! What a memory I've got! Kazanok, run over to the bell tower.

KAZANOK. God in heaven! What's the idea?

ANNA. My head's reeling. I don't know. (*Reënter* LIZA.) Liza, tell me, why is Kazanok supposed to be over at the bell tower?

LIZA. Roman left orders to ring the big bell in case of a meeting.

KAZANOK. I'll do that all right. (*Goes off.*)

LIZA. Wait! He'll make a terrible din, I'm certain.

ANNA. Wait, Kazanok! (KAZANOK *returns.*)

KAZANOK. What's the matter?

ANNA. You've got to be careful how you ring that bell. Look—you keep an eye on the alley. We'll send Styopka—he'll wave a stick at you from the alley—that's when you strike the big bell. But just strike it every now and then, Kazanok. Slowly, like you'd do for morning service.

KAZANOK. You can't teach me. Kazanok knows how to strike the bell for comrade Lenin. (*Goes off.*)

ANNA (*to the children*). Up on the stove, you there!

LIZA. Why are you hiding the children?

ANNA. How can we show these little Arabs to such a guest? Here are the keys; get a table cloth out of the chest—take mine, the one with the fringe.

LIZA. Don't get nervous, for heaven's sake. What's there to be nervous about?

ANNA. Run along, get the cloth. The table's bare. (LIZA *leaves*. ANNA *turns to the children*.) Get up on the stove, I tell you!

STYOPKA. We know, Granny—

ANNA. And don't you peek out, or laugh, or make any noise.

STYOPKA. May we look at him when he's looking the other way, Granny? (*Reënter* LIZA.)

ANNA. I'll look you with a belt on your behind!

LIZA. Oh, Lord! I wanted to change their linen—then I looked and the shirts aren't ironed.

ANNA. Don't stand there doing nothing, Liza. (LIZA *goes off*.) I wonder if we shouldn't cover the icons? Oh, let them be. No use making believe we're something we're not. (LIZA *rushes in*.)

LIZA. They're coming.

ANNA. Who is it?

LIZA. Lenin and Father.

ANNA. Just the two of them?

LIZA. Yes, just them.

ANNA. Our village folks didn't recognize them, then. Well, God be with us! You stand at the door—watch when to serve, when to take away. Here, take this kerchief, cover your head—it's not nice like that. (*Enter* LENIN *and* CHUDNOV. LENIN *is wearing a fur coat and a cap with ear flaps*.)

CHUDNOV. This is my old woman, Anna Vlasyevna.

LENIN. How are you?

CHUDNOV. And this is my daughter-in-law, Liza.

LENIN. Good morning.

ANNA. What have you brought back from your hunting trip?

LENIN. Not a thing, believe it or not. We're such wonderful hunters that for every pound of game we need a pound of powder.

CHUDNOV. Why blame yourself over nothing? You couldn't see a thing through the fog. I never saw such a fog in all my life. It covered the lake like a blanket.

LENIN (*taking off his coat near the door*). Whose heel is this?

ANNA. Oh, dear! That does it!

LENIN. Who's there? Come on, comrades, come down here. Oh, two of you, eh? Come down, both of you.

STYOPKA. Shall we come down, Granny?

ANNA. All right. (*To* LENIN.) They never stay clean a minute, those little devils.

LENIN (*to* STYOPKA). What's your name?

STYOPKA. Styopka.

LENIN. Styopka. Why not Stepan?

STYOPKA. I'm both, Stepan and Styopka.

LENIN (*to* MARUSYA). And what's your name?

STYOPKA. Hers is Marusya.

LENIN. Why do you answer for her?

STYOPKA. She's a scaredy-cat.

LENIN (*to* MARUSYA). Are you afraid of me?

MARUSYA (*blithely*). No.

LENIN. Then why hide on top of the stove?

STYOPKA. We're supposed to be hiding from Lenin.

LENIN. And Lenin came all the same.

STYOPKA. Where is he?

LENIN. Right here.

STYOPKA. Go on. You're not Lenin.

LENIN. No, really? Then who am I?

MARUSYA. You're just a peasant from another village—here on a visit.

STYOPKA. Lenin's not a bit like you.

LENIN. What is he like?

STYOPKA. There's his picture; see for yourself.

LENIN. That grand, stiff-looking man is not the least little bit like Lenin.

STYOPKA. Maybe you're like him?

LENIN. I am. (ANNA *attempts to intervene*.) No, no. Please, let's thresh this thing out. (*To* STYOPKA.) I insist I resemble Lenin.

STYOPKA. You're not a bit like him. There's the real one, because he was printed by machine.

LENIN. No, I'm the real one—he's not.

STYOPKA. Yes, he is.

LENIN. No, I am.

STYOPKA. Let's bet.

LENIN. Let's.

STYOPKA. What's the bet?

LENIN. I don't know.

STYOPKA. A lump of sugar.

LENIN. All right. (*Takes off his fur cap*.) Well, who's the real one now? (STYOPKA *glances at* LENIN, *then at the portrait, and retreats to the grownups*. LENIN *puts on his cap*.) And now?

MARUSYA. Now you're not the real one again.

LENIN (*taking off his cap*). And now?

STYOPKA. The real Lenin.

MARUSYA. Styopka, where are you going to get the sugar?

STYOPKA (*with sudden resolution*). Granny, shall I run over to the bell tower?

LENIN. Why to the bell tower?

ANNA. He's just talking. Go get the samovar, Liza.

CHUDNOV. Sit down, Vladimir Ilyich.

LENIN. Thank you.

ANNA. Tea will be ready in a minute.

LENIN. Thank you. A lively boy.

CHUDNOV. Always up to some mischief—simply terrible.

LENIN. When I was his age I was lively and mischievous too. Boys are a mysterious race, and we don't treat them right. We don't know how. We'll have to learn many things. If we don't, we'll be gobbled up. (*Walks over to the bench by the stove.*) What's this? A splinter lamp? A real old splinter lamp?

CHUDNOV. Do you really know about people lighting splinters in the villages?

LENIN. Do you use this thing?

CHUDNOV. Yes, we light it when there's no kerosene given out.

ANNA. It crackles—more cheerful than being in the dark.

LENIN. Yes, of course, it's more cheerful. (*Enter* ROMAN *carrying a half-filled bag. He has not expected to find* LENIN *in the house so early.*)

CHUDNOV. This is my son, Roman—the chairman and what have you.

LENIN. Good morning, chairman. What's that you have in your bag?

ROMAN. Stage props.

LENIN. That's interesting. May I see them?

ROMAN. Of course. (*Looking embarrassed, he pulls out a tall silk hat.*)

LENIN. A silk hat. (*Takes it, turns it over, and flicks it with his finger.*) Silk. A marvelous thing. So you have your own theater?

ROMAN. The Proletcult.

LENIN. What is the Proletcult?

ROMAN. I'm not too sure myself. In a manner of speaking it means proletarian culture.

LENIN. Where did you get this silk hat?

ROMAN. I bought it in the Sukharev market in Moscow.

LENIN. And who's going to play in it?

ROMAN. I am.

LENIN. As what?

ROMAN. A banker.

LENIN. A banker, eh? Is it very difficult to act a banker?

ROMAN. No.

LENIN. I'd never attempt it.

CHUDNOV. It's simply terrible, Vladimir Ilyich.

LENIN. What's terrible?

CHUDNOV. Well, he comes home from the army just an ordinary human being and suddenly he's a banker. The children are growing up and the father's an actor.

LENIN. It's all to the good that he's an actor. Take me, for example. I could never play a banker, and he can. You and I, comrade Chudnov, are old-fashioned folk.

CHUDNOV. Yes, Vladimir Ilyich, we are old fashioned. (*The bell ringer* KAZANOK *rushes in.*)

KAZANOK (*from the threshold*). In the name of the Father, the Son, and the Holy Ghost—

LENIN. What's that?

KAZANOK. Listen to me—blithering like a fool! This is me, Panteley Kazanok, village bell ringer and public fireman. (*To the others.*) Excuse me. I'm running right back to my post! I'll be in my place, don't worry. (*To* LENIN.) We're glad, all of us. I ring the bells not by any rules but from my heart. I just ring! There's Kazanok for you—just as you see him—nothing to hide! Good-by! (*Runs off.*)

LENIN. Why is he running away?

ANNA. He's just a simple, honest soul.

ROMAN (*coming forward to the center of the room and standing up straight*). Permit me, Vladimir Ilyich—permit me, comrade Lenin, to invite you to the Proletcult to have tea with us. And also to ask you to address us at a meeting.

ANNA. No, Vladimir Ilyich, don't go to the Proletcult for tea. They haven't even got a decent samovar.

LENIN. Well? Perhaps it's not worth going to the Proletcult. We can have tea here, can't we? Allow me to stay here. And it might be a good thing to skip the meeting. (RYBAKOV *rushes in.*)

RYBAKOV. I've shot them! Four birds! (*Holds up ducks.*) I waited for a breeze from the field—and I was right. The wind cleared it up over the water. (*To* CHUDNOV.) There's the fog for you!

LENIN (*disappointedly*). Tikhon Ivanovich—

CHUDNOV. It's my fault, Valdimir Ilyich—

LENIN. Ducks—real wild ducks. You and I philosophized about the causes of fog, inclement weather, and other whims of nature, and he shot them.

ANNA. How could you have disgraced yourself like that, hunter?

CHUDNOV. Don't rub it in, Mother! (*To* LENIN.) But as near as I could figure it out, Vladimir Ilyich, your mind wasn't on hunting at all today.

LENIN (*with surprise*). Wasn't it?

CHUDNOV. Well, that's how it looked to me.

LENIN. Really? Well, maybe you're right. I was a bad hunter today, comrade Rybakov, but then— (*As if changing the subject.*) then you're splendid. And you're not a hunter, only a sailor.

RYBAKOV. It looks as if I've upset everybody. Have I?

LENIN. Of course you've upset us. What hunter wouldn't feel upset? You waited for a breeze from the fields and outsmarted the old hunters. That's a valuable gift for you, Tikhon Ivanovich, fine ducks. Hide them away or the cats will be after them. (*At this moment there is a sudden pealing of bells outside. Listening.*) An alarm? Yes, that's what it is.

ANNA. Kazanok just couldn't hold back.

CHUDNOV. Blast his hide! What a devil!

ROMAN (*at the window*). You can't do anything now. The whole village is up.

LENIN. In that case, let's all go. Oh, that bell ringer—he's sounded off about me to the whole village. Well, being a bell ringer I suppose he couldn't do anything else. Comrade Chudnov—

CHUDNOV. Yes?

LENIN (*putting on his coat*). It's a troublesome business to live with the Bolsheviks, isn't it?

CHUDNOV. It certainly is, Vladimir Ilyich.

LENIN. You never can tell what they may think up tomorrow.

CHUDNOV. You're right about that, Vladimir Ilyich.

LENIN (*as if speaking to himself*). We have to think, comrade Chudnov—think and think again. Let's go out, comrades, or his enthusiasm will bring the whole bell tower crashing down. (LENIN, CHUDNOV, *and* RYBAKOV *go off.*)

ANNA. I look at him and can't stop wondering. Why, he's a czar.

LIZA. What?

ANNA. A czar!

LIZA. Whatever are you saying, Mother? Lenin is the chairman of the Soviet government.

ANNA. That's what you call him. To us he's the czar.

LIZA. You're hopeless. I'd better run along and see what's doing.

ANNA. Run along, dear, run along. (LIZA *goes off.* ANNA *turns to the icons.*) Lord, bless him with good health, happiness, and joy and make all his wishes come true. Forgive me, O Lord, praying for an unbeliever.

CURTAIN

ACT I

SCENE 5

The Kremlin embankment and boulevard. Night. Dim light from a few lampposts. Seated on a bench under a tree is RYBAKOV. *For a few seconds he whistles a tune softly, then begins to sing.*

RYBAKOV (*singing*).
              No, not for me can ever be
              Another spring nor golden summer—
(*An old* BEGGAR WOMAN *comes on.*) If I can spot Mars with my naked eye, that means yes; if not, no.

BEGGAR WOMAN. Young man! Can you spare a poor old woman a cigarette?

RYBAKOV. Here you are.

BEGGAR WOMAN. Thank you, young man. (*Goes off.*)

RYBAKOV (*singing again*).

> Oh, not for me can ever be
> Another spring, nor sweetly sing
> The nightingale, nor heart take wing—
> No, not for me—no, not for me.

(*Pauses, wrapt in thought, gets up, gazes at the sky a long time. Enter* LENIN. *He glances at* RYBAKOV *and recognizes him.* RYBAKOV *rouses himself.*) Vladimir Ilyich!

LENIN. Sasha Rybakov, what are you doing here?

RYBAKOV. Why are you alone, without guards?

LENIN. I've slipped away from them.

RYBAKOV. How do you do that?

LENIN. I won't tell you. That's the secret of an old revolutionist. You see, I had a very long conference and now I'm out for a secret stroll. My reason for being here is legitimate, so to speak. And yours? Why are you alone, counting stars at midnight?

RYBAKOV. I am counting—I won't deny it.

LENIN. Are you in love, comrade Rybakov?

RYBAKOV. Yes.

LENIN. Ours is a cruel, terrible time—there seems to be no room left for love. But you needn't be afraid. Go on loving, and more power to you, as long as you feel that way. Only I want to give you a little advice. Don't follow the new fashion in love. Stick to the old one, comrade Rybakov. I've heard about these new relations. So far they're just loose and ugly.

RYBAKOV. I've seen some pretty ugly things too.

LENIN. Have you ever read how the writer Chernyshevsky loved? Read it. (*Stops suddenly, takes* RYBAKOV *by the elbow, and asks in an intimate tone, quietly.*) It's a fine thing to be in love, isn't it? A wonderful feeling, eh?

RYBAKOV (*with embarrassment*). Yes, it is.

LENIN. One more bit of advice—don't believe Kollantay and her theories of love. (*They go off. Three streetcar* REPAIRMEN *come on, pushing a handcart with tools.*)

ASSISTANT REPAIRMAN. Did you see? Lenin.

BEARDED REPAIRMAN. Sh-h-h! We're not blind. You spotted him— all right, keep it to yourself. You have to be careful.

HEAD REPAIRMAN. Light the lamp. Let's see what we have here. (*They light a lamp and test the car-tracks by tapping them.*) Let's move on. And put the light out or we'll run out of candles. (LENIN *and* RYBAKOV *return.*)

LENIN. What's the time, comrades?

HEAD REPAIRMAN (*to his assistant*). Some light. (*Draws out a pocket watch on a chain.*) Quarter past two. You used to be able to tell the time by the Kremlin chimes. Now the big clock's silent,

LENIN. It's very bad. The Kremlin clock should never be silent. Sasha, you must find a man to repair it. But he must understand old mechanisms.

RYBAKOV. We'll find one, Vladimir Ilyich. There must be someone around who can do it.

LENIN. Well, plenty of people have tried to make the chimes work but had to give it up.

BEARDED REPAIRMAN. Stay awhile with the working class, comrade Lenin.

LENIN. I never go away from the working class.

BEARDED REPAIRMAN. Have a chat with us.

HEAD REPAIRMAN. He likes to wag his tongue, this one—crack jokes.

LENIN. You find you can joke?

BEARDED REPAIRMAN. What's there to worry about? We've smashed capitalism good and proper.

LENIN. Smashed capitalism isn't going to fill your belly.

BEARDED REPAIRMAN. Now we'll start building socialism.

LENIN. Do you know how to build it?

BEARDED REPAIRMAN. There are lots of kind people in the world. Somebody will tell us.

LENIN. True, there are lots of kind people. But you can't believe all of them. It's far easier to destroy capitalism than to build socialism.

BEARDED REPAIRMAN. Is that right?

LENIN. We're the first to begin. There's nobody we can learn from. Furthermore, we're wretchedly poor.

BEARDED REPAIRMAN. You hit the nail on the head that time. We've gotten as poor as mice.

LENIN. All the same, we'll have to build—and with no one to help us either. The poor and hungry will be the ones to start building.

BEARDED REPAIRMAN. Well, there's nothing the Soviet system can't do. The Bible folk wanted to build a tower to reach the sky—that was in Babel—and not a damn thing came of it. And why? The Bible says because of the confusion of tongues. And I say to you it was because they had no Soviet system. Joking apart, Vladimir Ilyich, whatever the Soviets want they can do.

LENIN. What makes you so confident of the power of the Soviet system?

BEARDED REPAIRMAN. Let me tell you a parable. Are you in a hurry?

LENIN. No, go ahead.

BEARDED REPAIRMAN. Here you have three men—Moscow streetcar repairmen, night workers, the proletariat—neither saints nor sinners —just people. Under what other system would these men work all night for a miserable chunk of bread? (*Pulls out a piece of bread.*) Not under any. Now look at us—we work till we drop, we rest, get up, and go on welding again. That's why I believe in the power of the Soviet system.

HEAD REPAIRMAN. Well, we've taken enough of comrade Lenin's time. Come along, boys, we have a lot to do.

BEARDED REPAIRMAN. Excuse us if we haven't talked very straight— we've done our best.

HEAD REPAIRMAN. Good night, comrade Lenin.

LENIN. Good night. (*The* REPAIR CREW *go off.*) Do you love the Russian people, comrade Rybakov?

RYBAKOV. Yes, of course.

LENIN. You will very much when you've lived as long as I have. If Tolstoy hadn't thought up his Tolstoyanism, nobody could have given us a better picture of the Russian character. But the old fellow could never understand the workers— Well, I don't feel like going home. It's all right for you, you're in love. But why should I be losing sleep? You don't know? Well, I'll tell you in strict confidence—I like to dream sometimes. I stroll along by myself and build castles in the air. Of course, we're not going to raise a tower up to heaven, but with the people we have one can dare—one can dream.

RYBAKOV. Somebody's coming. (*The* BEGGAR WOMAN *reappears.*)

BEGGAR WOMAN. I'm coming.

LENIN. Who are you?

BEGGAR WOMAN. I'm a beggar. Give an unhappy old woman something for a meal, sir.

LENIN. Have you got anything on you, Sasha?

RYBAKOV. No, nothing.

LENIN. Neither have I. (*To the* WOMAN.) I'm sorry.

BEGGAR WOMAN. And you wear an Astrakhan hat! You're worse than beggars yourselves.

RYBAKOV. You'd better go to sleep, old woman.

BEGGAR WOMAN. I don't sleep nights—that's when I work. I beg in taverns, railway stations.

LENIN. You call that work?

BEGGAR WOMAN. My work's as good as any. Today we're all in the same boat—every last one of us walking around like starving animals. You look like a man who lives by his brains. But how much did you bite off today?

LENIN. How do you mean, bite off?

BEGGAR WOMAN. I mean eat.

RYBAKOV. Shall we move on, Vladimir Ilyich?

LENIN (*to* RYBAKOV). Wait. (*To the* WOMAN.) And before the revolution, what were you?

BEGGAR WOMAN. The same as now—a beggar.

LENIN. Then what are you kicking about? You haven't lost anything.

BEGGAR WOMAN. No, my dear man, our beggar class has lost more than anybody.

LENIN. What has your class lost?

BEGGAR WOMAN. Before the revolution I lived like a queen. In those days I worked as a holy innocent—had thirty-five hundred gold rubles in the bank.

LENIN. Where did you get them?

BEGGAR WOMAN. I had my regular customers. I never stooped below merchant families of the first rank. What kind of money do I make nowadays? Who gives us anything? Lenin's run the whole country into the ground and people say he's not far from being a beggar himself. He doesn't live like a human being himself and he won't let anybody else. Well, sail along. I'll be going about my business. (*Goes off.*)

LENIN. What do you say, young man?

RYBAKOV. An insolent old woman, that's all.

LENIN. But it's terrible. Even beggars live worse than before the war. In the villages people sit at night with splinter lights. Have you seen it?

RYBAKOV. Pretty often.

LENIN. Splinter light—that's what we had before the kerosene lamp, young man! Do you realize what these things mean? Yesterday I got a letter from the Urals. There, in the armament plant at Zlatousk, men have to use their hands to keep the machines turning. (*Pauses.*) For a long time I've been thinking about the electrification of Russia. What's your opinion, are we ready now, today, to start introducing electricity?

RYBAKOV. Comrade Lenin, you can see a thousand miles ahead. And I—my mind could never have conceived of such a thing.

LENIN. Don't mention this to anybody for the present or they'll say I'm mad. It's still a dream so far—

CURTAIN

ACT II

SCENE 1

A boulevard in Moscow. The Gogol Monument. An OLD WOMAN *is sitting on a bench, a wicker baby carriage in front of her.*

OLD WOMAN. There now. He's gone to sleep, my prince. Sleep, my darling, sleep, my prince. (*With nothing to worry her, she dozes off.* RYBAKOV *dashes on. He glances around and instantly looks distressed.*)

RYBAKOV. There's Gogol for you! (*Pulls out his watch.*) Gogol doesn't have to worry, but I'm at least fifteen minutes late. With her temper, this is a catastrophe. (*Turning quickly to the* Old Woman.) Comrade nurse!

Old Woman (*offended*). Young man, how do you know I'm a nurse?

Rybakov. I'm sorry, it doesn't really matter.

Old Woman. Maybe not to you but it does to me.

Rybakov. Well, here's a baby carriage, a baby— Don't be cross, I want to ask you something.

Old Woman. Don't make so much noise. Can't you see he's asleep?

Rybakov (*in a whisper*). I'm sorry, I won't. I wanted to ask if you'd seen a young woman walking around here before I came?

Old Woman. Go along, don't bother me. I can't make head or tail out of your mumbling.

Rybakov (*taking her by the arm*). I beg of you to answer my question.

Old Woman. Where are you dragging me? I'll scream!

Rybakov (*pulling the* Old Woman *away from the baby carriage*). It won't help you. I'm a detective. I repeat: have you seen a young woman near this monument any time during the last few minutes?

Old Woman. A young woman? Yes—a girl sat next to me and admired my grandson.

Rybakov. For God's sake, what was she like? Very charming, wasn't she? In fact, beautiful. Did she have black gloves?

Old Woman. Yes, she did have, I'm sure of it. Black gloves.

Rybakov. Did she leave very long ago?

Old Woman. Just this minute.

Rybakov. Which way did she go?

Old Woman. That way.

Rybakov. If I find her, I'll remember you for the rest of my life. Thank you. (*He goes off. The* Old Woman *tries to compose herself.*)

Old Woman. Detective—the fellow's mad! And I'm none too strong —why, I might have died of fright. What a terrible man! (*Recovering her breath, she prays silently, crosses herself, and resumes her seat on the bench, gazing in the direction in which* Rybakov *ran off.*) Now he's caught up with her—bringing her back here. I'd better make myself scarce. Save us, O Lord, and have mercy on our souls. (*She goes off, pushing the carriage.* Masha *and* Rybakov *enter,* Masha *keeping her distance.*)

Rybakov. I know it's my fault but you don't have to ignore me— I can hardly keep on my feet. I frightened a woman here almost to death.

Masha. That'll do, Rybakov. I know all your maneuvers. A person gets tired of this caveman stuff.

Rybakov. Caveman, is it? Let it be caveman then. And what are you?

Masha. What I am, as I must look to you, I really don't know. But

I've thought a lot about it. Ever since the day my parents found out about us, I've lost all sense of direction or purpose—I just feel frazzled. I don't know whether you'll understand me, but whether you do or not, I may as well tell you anyway—I've gone from hope to despair— I've been waiting for your help—last night I didn't so much as close my eyes—and you—you don't give a damn, do you? A date with a young lady—how important! And the young lady seems to have gone soft, too—even asks you for a date herself. God, I've got so I hate this monument! It must have been put here just to enjoy my misery.

RYBAKOV. Masha, you don't let me get a word in edgewise.

MASHA. I'm talking to you and you don't understand a thing.

RYBAKOV. If I'm such a blockhead, maybe you'd do better not to talk to me at all.

MASHA. How could you have failed to come today of all days?

RYBAKOV. What do you mean, fail to come, when I'm here?

MASHA. Don't you understand, this isn't just an ordinary date! My father's at home waiting. You're supposed to call, introduce yourself, talk to him. You don't seem to realize what it means. He's a terrible man—why, he might even order you out of the house!

RYBAKOV. I'll refuse to leave.

MASHA. What are you saying?

RYBAKOV. Just that I won't leave, that's all.

MASHA. Well, I must say! You do have a way of easing a person's mind. Nothing worries you. Everything, to you, is simple and pleasant. There's nobody to hold you down. But I haven't told you everything about Father. Just for spite, he sells matches in the streets. Engineer Zabelin walks through Moscow selling matches!

RYBAKOV. A queer fish.

MASHA. But he's dear to me, he's my father, I love him. If you knew him as well as I do, you'd love him too.

RYBAKOV. What's the matter with him? Let's try and convert him to Christianity.

MASHA. That's just the trouble—it's almost impossible to change him. Why, he'll only laugh at you in the most insulting way. Really, I don't know what's going to happen. When you didn't come, I thought, "Well, that's fate."

RYBAKOV. I've been on the go for three days looking for someone to repair a clock.

MASHA. I see. A simply staggering reason. You should have thought up something a little better. You had only one thing on your mind— to repair a clock.

RYBAKOV. Exactly—just one.

MASHA. Thank you.

RYBAKOV. Stop it, Masha. I had to break through terrific obstacles to get here. I get on a streetcar—it stops. Why? The current is cut off. I jump on a truck—it's headed for a place miles away. I hop into a cab, drive one block—a police whistle: the driver has no license, hasn't registered.

MASHA. What's it all about? Streetcars, cabs, licenses—

RYBAKOV. I've been given the job of finding a man to repair the chimes of the Kremlin.

MASHA. Rybakov, you're so simple minded. You imagine everybody must know all about that. *I* don't know a thing.

RYBAKOV. You don't know a thing and still you feel offended. Why?

MASHA. But have you found the man?

RYBAKOV. I have. But if you knew what it cost me. As soon as you mention what clock they have to repair, they all get frightened. One miserable Jew in a skullcap squatted on the floor, covered his head with his hands, and said: "You can shoot me but I won't go." I scoured old Moscow from end to end and finally found a man. He's coming to the Kremlin today. But I'm afraid, worried—

MASHA. Why?

RYBAKOV. I didn't tell him which clock it is that needs repairing. If you only knew, Masha, what I've been carrying around with me in my mind. The other night, walking around deserted streets, I ran into Ilyich. It's a mystery to me where that man finds his ideas. I even wonder at myself—it's as though I've flown, too, far ahead where nobody's ever been before. It embarrasses me—because it isn't me but Lenin. Now I'll know to the end of my days that some people exist to whom nothing is far, nothing is frightening, nothing is impossible.

MASHA. Sasha dear—I feel so relaxed with you now. I don't know why, but everything I was so wrought up about seems to have simply vanished. Have you remembered that today is Saturday? They're expecting you at home. Will you come?

RYBAKOV. I will.

MASHA. And if Father jumps on you, will you be ready for him?

RYBAKOV. Leave it to me.

MASHA. But you weren't ready when I jumped on you.

RYBAKOV. With you—with you I'm tame.

MASHA. Is that so?

RYBAKOV. I love you. I write letters to you every night—and tear them up in the morning.

MASHA. Why do you do that? Mail them to my address.

RYBAKOV. I can't get the right words. I think about love, I feel it, I read about it— I know my love is the real thing— You understand? True love, without a single outside thought. But I can't find the right words to express it.

MASHA. You've just found them. I believe you, and that's enough. I don't know why, today I believe you more than ever. But I have to go home now.

RYBAKOV. May I walk with you?

MASHA. I wish you could but we might bump into my father.

RYBAKOV. What kind of a father is he, anyway? You make him sound like an impregnable fortress!

MASHA. Wait and see. Well, I'll take a chance. Take my arm, please.

RYBAKOV. *Merci.*

MASHA (*laughing*). Don't, Rybakov. Just be yourself, without *merci.*

RYBAKOV. I second the motion. (*They go off.*)

CURTAIN

ACT II

SCENE 2

The ZABELIN *home.* ANTON IVANOVICH'S *workroom, in which nobody works any more. It is evening. Present are* ZABELINA *and her guests: a* LADY *busily knitting and her husband, an* OPTIMIST; *a* FRIGHTENED LADY *and her husband, a* SKEPTIC.

ZABELINA (*continuing a conversation*). Anton Ivanovich is getting more and more impossible. The other day I saw him getting into a row with some monk. Yesterday, I'm ashamed to say, he had a fight with an acquaintance of ours.

SKEPTIC. At home or out in public?

ZABELINA. Outside the Maly Theater, at seven o'clock in the evening.

SKEPTIC. Who won?

ZABELINA. Anton Ivanovich, of course. You should hear what caused the rumpus. The man used to work under Anton Ivanovich. Now, as he was going into the theater, he forgot himself a little—tapped Anton Ivanovich on the shoulder and spoke to him in a patronizing tone.

FRIGHTENED LADY. Was he a Bolshevik?

ZABELINA. No, not a Bolshevik, but I'd say rather advanced in his ideas.

FRIGHTENED LADY. Anton Ivanovich is in a dangerous position—he may be thrown into the Cheka.

SKEPTIC. Who hasn't been thrown into a jail nowadays? Everybody has.

FRIGHTENED LADY. You haven't.

SKEPTIC. Not yet, but never fear.

FRIGHTENED LADY. For God's sake, don't say such things! You might at least stop frightening me when we go visiting.

ZABELINA. For my part, having to stand by and watch Anton Ivanovich, I keep a bundle of his linen always ready. I begin to believe that he's bound to be jailed.

OPTIMIST. Anton Ivanovich expresses himself emotionally, and people aren't jailed for their emotions.

FRIGHTENED LADY. But he beat up a man with Bolshevik ideas. That's a terroristic action.

OPTIMIST. People punch noses when necessary under any regime.

SKEPTIC. They'll jail Anton Ivanovich all the same. You'll see.

FRIGHTENED LADY. This man can drive you to tears!

SKEPTIC. Half the population of Moscow is talking about Zabelin selling matches in the streets. Do you think the Bolsheviks are idiots, that they don't understand anything?

FRIGHTENED LADY. Now, our Volodka has turned a Futurist. All day long he does nothing but read that poem called "A Cloud in Pants"— a dreadful thing.

ZABELINA. Perfectly horrifying. Do people really write such verse?

KNITTING LADY. They call it a poem. Volodka tells everybody it's the greatest work in all literature. I can't tell you how indecent it is. The author, speaking in the first person singular, mind you, proposes some positively unspeakable things to a woman!

OPTIMIST. Didn't Pushkin do the same?

KNITTING LADY. Pushkin made his proposals within the limits of decorum, and Mayakovsky comes right out and says it.

OPTIMIST. They're all tarred with the same brush. Volodka might just as well be a Futurist. It's bread.

ZABELINA. No, really? Do the Bolsheviks give you a food ration for verses?

KNITTING LADY. I didn't believe it myself but it's true—they really do.

SKEPTIC. Wait till they put Anton in jail—you'll see everything.

FRIGHTENED LADY. He's driving me to tears. Morally he's worse than the Inquisition. You promise everybody jails and shootings.

ZABELINA. Dmitry Dmitriyevich, even if you are a relative, that croaking of yours is neither pleasant nor polite! (*Enter* MASHA.) Have you been working all this time?

MASHA. Yes.

ZABELINA. You'd better hurry and have something to eat.

MASHA. I don't want anything.

ZABELINA. You don't look well. You need some nourishment.

MASHA. No, I don't. I'll eat later. (*Shakes hands with the guests.*)

OPTIMIST. Where do you work, Masha?

MASHA. At the Famaid.

OPTIMIST. What *is* the Famaid?

MASHA. We give relief to the starving.

OPTIMIST. Are things really as bad as they're said to be?

MASHA. Very bad. Famine is spreading like the Deluge.

SKEPTIC. That flooded the world; now it's Russia going under. The Americans are feeding their cattle on white rolls, while in Russia famine is cutting our population in half. (*To his wife.*) Show me where I exaggerate. (*Enter* ZABELIN.)

ZABELINA. Forgive us—we've taken over your workroom, Anton Ivanovich. It's warmer here.

ZABELIN. I see you have. (*Shakes hands.*) It used to be a workroom, now it's a crypt. What have you been talking about?

SKEPTIC. What do people talk about today? Famine, death, arrests— our native themes.

ZABELIN. The savages have seized a civilized ship, tossed the crew overboard, and gobbled up all the food. What's next? They have to navigate the ship but they don't know how. They've promised socialism but nobody knows where to begin. (*To the* SKEPTIC.) Dmitry Dmitriyevich, do you know?

SKEPTIC. I don't and I don't want to.

ZABELIN. When I was young I used to fly to the moon—in theory, of course. But here my daughter is ready to go through fire and water for the Bolsheviks. All her sympathies are on the other side. We are counterrevolutionists, Bourbons. (*Enter the* COOK.)

COOK. There's a sailor asking for the Zabelins.

FRIGHTENED LADY. A sailor? Why a sailor?

SKEPTIC. Don't you know why sailors come?

ZABELINA. Oh, please don't get upset. I'm sure it's not a sailor.

COOK. I'm not blind. You can see he's a sailor—and all het up, too.

SKEPTIC. I've no papers on me. Perhaps my wife and I had better just slip out through the back door?

FRIGHTENED LADY. I'm afraid to go. The sailors may catch us and think we've been running away.

ZABELINA. Don't get upset, please. He's not a sailor in the usual sense. (*To* MASHA.) Well? Why don't you go and show him in? (MASHA *leaves. The guests look puzzled.*)

ZABELIN. Most likely it's an admirer of our daughter. He dresses like a hero of the cruiser *Aurora*. I've seen him.

SKEPTIC. Why do you permit heroes off the *Aurora* to become your daughter's admirers?

ZABELIN. And why, this very minute, my dear cousin, did you want to run away from my house? Only a short time ago you'd never have permitted yourself such an idiotic notion as running away from the Zabelin house. We have cause for weeping and you indulge in irony. (*Enter* MASHA *and* RYBAKOV.)

MASHA. Ladies and gentlemen— (*She breaks off awkwardly.*)

ZABELIN. Why do you stop? Are you frightened at having called us ladies and gentlemen in front of your visitor? I'll teach you how to speak. Say "citizens," and your visitor will not be shocked.

MASHA (*to* RYBAKOV). I told you—Papa always makes fun of me.

(*To the company.*) This is my friend, Alexander Mikhailovich Ryba-kov. He was in the war—and had many interesting experiences.

SKEPTIC (*shaking hands with* RYBAKOV). Indeed a great pleasure—

FRIGHTENED LADY. I can't make out—are you a sailor or a civilian?

RYBAKOV. I was a sailor but I fought on land. Now I've been discharged.

FRIGHTENED LADY. Then why do you wear sailor pants? We thought it was a raid; instead you've just come on a visit.

RYBAKOV. Why a raid? I'd never have thought my place was being raided.

SKEPTIC. That's natural. You are the conquerors—you've won almost a continent.

RYBAKOV. Well, we're still pretty far from that.

ZABELIN. When will that happen?

RYBAKOV. Under socialism.

ZABELIN. What year?

RYBAKOV. I'm sorry I can't answer you on that point.

ZABELIN. You can't disclose your secret?

RYBAKOV. It's not that. I just don't know.

ZABELINA. *Sit* down, Alexander Mikhailovich. Here's an ash tray. Would you like to see our family album? Here—have a look.

FRIGHTENED LADY. Why give him the family album? They're all dull, uninteresting people. (*To* RYBAKOV.) Better look at these—views of Italy—Rome, the Colosseum—Vesuvius—

ZABELINA. Masha dear, why don't you go see about tea?

MASHA (*going off*). All right, Mama.

ZABELIN. Have you been in Italian waters, sir?

RYBAKOV. No, I've seen nothing except the Baltic.

ZABELIN. Are you, sir, a member of the Communist party?

RYBAKOV. Yes. Why?

ZABELIN. It might be interesting to know what a Communist thinks when he finds himself among us.

RYBAKOV. What is there to think? It's plain enough.

ZABELIN. Of course, it's plain enough for you. As far as you are concerned, we are just bourgeois scoundrels. But these scoundrels worked all their lives like galley slaves. In return for our labor capitalism gave us a measure of prosperity and comfort—what's left of that you can see in this room. And what can Communism offer me? Very well, I'm ready to receive the food allowance you grant today, but I'm denied that. The new society has no need of me because I know how to build power plants and today such plants are shut down. I'm unemployed. We're not interested in electricity today. Electric energy has been replaced by the steaming ox. And like Prometheus I now give people fire—from morning till night I stand at the Iversky shrine and sell matches.

SKEPTIC. And for doing this, you, like Prometheus, will be put in chains.

ZABELIN (*to* RYBAKOV). And what do you say, sir?

RYBAKOV. Frankly, I can't understand why you're still at large.

SKEPTIC (*rapturously*). Did you hear that? Listen!

ZABELIN. Go to the telephone and report me.

RYBAKOV. They don't need any reports from me. And anyway, it's beside the point. You're annoyed with us—but for no reason. In your place, I'd have been working a long time already. Between us, you know you're not a Prometheus, you're just a plain saboteur.

ZABELIN. Well, how do you like that? A man calling at my house for the first time is surprised I haven't been thrown in jail, calls me all sorts of names, and doesn't care a damn. He's pleased with himself. Good God, the people that come into our homes!

OPTIMIST. Our Volodka talks just like that. Every day he calls me an unliquidated bourgeois. I put up with it.

ZABELIN. Volodka is your son. And who is this? (*To* RYBAKOV.) Do you have the slightest idea of civility?

RYBAKOV. It's extraordinary. You've been talking about the Soviets not very politely, and I risked my life for them time and again. I didn't shout or lose my temper. I merely stated you are a saboteur.

ZABELIN. I told you the truth.

RYBAKOV. Tripe, not truth. It's I who told you the truth.

ZABELIN. Just a minute. Is it untrue that I'm unemployed?

RYBAKOV. It is.

ZABELIN. Is it untrue that you've cast me off like an old shoe?

RYBAKOV. It is.

ZABELIN. In that case, sir—in that case, please leave this house. I've got along this far without knowing you and I have no wish to now.

RYBAKOV. I'm not going to leave.

ZABELIN. Oh, I see—I've forgotten you can requisition my apartment.

RYBAKOV. I haven't come to requisition.

ZABELIN. Stay, then. I'll go.

RYBAKOV. But I won't let you. It amuses me to see you rave. You act like a wild man.

ZABELIN. A savage?

RYBAKOV. That's right, a savage.

ZABELIN. And you've come to enlighten me?

RYBAKOV. What do you think? Of course.

ZABELIN (*laughing*). Well, I like that! Now I can't fight back—he's so disarmingly simple and sure of himself, this young blusterer! He wants to enlighten me. Very well, comrade missionary, go ahead, enlighten. (*Enter the* COOK.)

COOK. The chairman of the House Tenants' Committee is here.

ZABELINA. Alone?

COOK. No, ma'am.

ZABELINA. Not alone?

COOK. There's a military man with him, quite stern looking. (*The* CHAIRMAN OF THE HOUSE TENANTS' COMMITTEE *raps on the half-opened door and inquires, off: "May I come in?"*)

ZABELINA. Come in, come in. (*Enter the* CHAIRMAN, *followed by a man in uniform.*)

CHAIRMAN. Citizen Zabelin, it's requested that you go with this— comrade.

ZABELIN. I've been expecting this right along.

MILITARY MAN. No unnecessary delay, please.

ZABELIN. I've been ready for a long time.

MILITARY MAN. Let's go, then.

ZABELIN. Just a moment. (*With a bow that takes in everyone.*) Forgive me—I've called you at the wrong time. (*To his wife.*) Good-by.

ZABELINA (*giving her husband a small bundle*). God be with you—

ZABELIN. Masha's in the dining room? Never mind. Now I'm off.

MILITARY MAN. You'll find a car waiting outside.

ZABELIN. I understand.

ZABELINA. Anton, they can't do this to you! (*The* MILITARY MAN, ZABELIN, *and the* CHAIRMAN *go off.*) Anton! I won't let them take you! Take all of us! March me off too! And where's the order? Call the chairman back! Comrade chairman! (*The* CHAIRMAN *returns.*) Did they give you an order?

CHAIRMAN. Don't worry about that—they've crossed all the t's and dotted all the i's. (*He goes off. Enter* MASHA.)

ZABELINA. Well, Masha dear, we have no father.

MASHA. But why, in heaven's name? He didn't belong to any party.

RYBAKOV. Excuse me, but I have a different impression. I don't believe Anton Ivanovich has been arrested.

SKEPTIC. Why was he taken away then, and where, if I may ask?

RYBAKOV. I don't know, citizen, why, or where. There's no sense in guessing. If you like, Masha, let's go and find out—it's near here. If they've arrested him, they'll tell us.

MASHA. Mama, I'll go. Don't cry, Mama.

RYBAKOV. Good-by. Good-by, Lydia Mikhailovna. Believe me, it isn't the way it looks.

CURTAIN

ACT II

SCENE 3

LENIN's *private office in the Kremlin.* LENIN, STALIN, DZERZHINSKY *are seated. Enter a* SECRETARY.

SECRETARY. There's a watchmaker outside. He's been sent by Ryba-kov.

LENIN. Show him in.

SECRETARY. Right away. (*Goes off.*)

LENIN. I can't stop thinking nights of the chimes—not ringing. We have to start them again. (*Enter the* WATCHMAKER. *An old Jew, he is dressed in a well-worn but neat black suit; a starched white dickey, yellowed with age, shows under his vest, and cuffs in a similar condition extend from under his sleeves. A black bow tie tops off his stiff collar. He is trim, brisk, and rather like a Frenchman in general appearance. As he comes in, he bows and sets his old satchel on a chair.*) Good afternoon, comrade. Are you a watchmaker?

WATCHMAKER (*after a pause*). A single homecraftsman.

LENIN. Excuse me, I don't understand—why single?

WATCHMAKER. Today skilled artisans like myself have the honor of being classed as "single homecraftsmen without a motor."

LENIN. A single craftsman without a motor?

STALIN. Evidently the watchmaking artisan has been wronged. Who has wronged you?

WATCHMAKER. I'm not going to take advantage of this opportunity to make complaints to comrade Lenin. I never make complaints. I've been asked here to do a job.

DZERZHINSKY (*nodding sympathetically to the* WATCHMAKER). Go ahead, make your complaints, don't hide anything.

LENIN. And I'll ask them to give us some tea. (*Rings the bell.*) Tell them we'd like some tea. (*To the* WATCHMAKER.) It's a hard life, isn't it? Hunger, ruin, chaos? You're worn out? Starving?

WATCHMAKER. Like everybody else. (*Tea is brought in, with a saucer filled with tiny pieces of sugar.*)

LENIN (*pointing at* STALIN). And this comrade says you've been wronged. Perhaps he's mistaken?

WATCHMAKER (*with a trace of despair*). I didn't expect these questions. I was happy I was remembered. There was a time, you know, when I repaired clocks for Count Lev Nikolayevich Tolstoy.

STALIN. Oho! That's no joke. Tolstoy wouldn't go to a bad watchmaker.

LENIN. And what was Tolstoy like? What did he talk to you about?

WATCHMAKER. He wore high boots—a very strong-looking man. His portraits don't give you any idea. I can't remember now what he talked about. He liked to ask questions. He could tell a good watch.

DZERZHINSKY. And, of course, he paid well?

WATCHMAKER. No. Because he was Lev Tolstoy I charged him much less.

LENIN. Did he realize?

WATCHMAKER. I don't think so.

LENIN. And what is it you feel wronged about now? We too have that weakness—asking questions.

WATCHMAKER. I hadn't planned anything—I don't know what to tell you. Of course, I understand "the times are out of joint," as Hamlet says.

LENIN. To be or not to be?

WATCHMAKER. You're right. A thousand times over. I don't get enough work.

DZERZHINSKY. We have state workshops. I suppose they're very bad?

WATCHMAKER. I was ordered to work in one. So I went and took a job that nobody else could handle. I came across a remarkable English clock, a real Norton, unique. It was made before railways were invented—it's at least three hundred years old. I worked on it a month. And all the thanks I got was that they held a meeting on my account and told me I wasn't earning my keep. When it came to answering them, I was unwise enough to tell them a fable by Æsop.

LENIN. Æsop? Which one?

WATCHMAKER. I told them about the fox who taunted a lioness for bearing only one cub in her life. The lioness replied to the fox: "But then I bear a lion." Æsop says what matters is not quantity but quality.

LENIN. And what did they say to that?

WATCHMAKER. The chairman of the meeting said Æsop was a counterrevolutionary and an agent of the Entente Powers, and I was an agent of Æsop's. They threw me out.

STALIN (*suppressing his amusement*). As an agent of Æsop's? (*Bending over his desk,* LENIN *begins to laugh.* DZERZHINSKY *and* STALIN *laugh too, and so does the* WATCHMAKER.)

LENIN. And you say you haven't been wronged. Of course, you have. What can you do? They never read Æsop. It's more important to them to repair alarm clocks than rare English chronometers. But we have a job for you.

WATCHMAKER. Just a minute. (*Opens his satchel and hastily puts a magnifying glass to his eye.*) I'm ready.

LENIN. I'm afraid your tools won't do here.

WATCHMAKER. My tools?

LENIN. You'll need something different.

STALIN. You'll need tools of a different size. (*Indicates the size.*)

DZERZHINSKY. I think this mechanism weighs several tons.

WATCHMAKER. But I'm a watchmaker.

LENIN. That's why we're asking you to set the chimes of the Kremlin going.

WATCHMAKER. What? The clock on the Spassky Tower?

LENIN. Yes, my friend. Will you take it on?

WATCHMAKER. Man made it, man broke it, it's up to man to make it go again.

LENIN. But when men were making it there was no such hymn as the "International." Today we want to teach the chimes of the Kremlin how to play the "International." Can you teach them?

WATCHMAKER. I'll try.

LENIN. Good. You can start work tomorrow.

WATCHMAKER. Could I go there right away? I'd rather not wait.

LENIN. By all means.

STALIN. Our friend's had good schooling. He may be an agent of Æsop but he loves his work.

DZERZHINSKY. Should anybody interfere with you or any difficulties arise, phone this number. (*Gives the man a note.*)

WATCHMAKER. Who am I to ask for?

DZERZHINSKY. Dzerzhinsky.

WATCHMAKER. And he will help me himself?

LENIN. Yes, we'll ask him. As for terms, you arrange that with our Kremlin commandant.

WATCHMAKER. There can be no terms. I'm the first watchmaker in the world who's going to tune the chimes of the Kremlin to play the "International."

LENIN. But a food ration wouldn't hurt you?

WATCHMAKER. Oh, of course, a food ration wouldn't hurt. Thank you for the order, for your confidence. Excuse my being a bit upset. I'd better go to the tower. (*Goes off.*)

STALIN. Humanity—every imaginable type— (*Enter the SECRETARY.*)

SECRETARY. Engineer Zabelin has arrived.

LENIN. Send him in. (*The SECRETARY leaves. ZABELIN comes in.*) Engineer Zabelin?

ZABELIN. Yes.

LENIN. Anton Ivanovich?

ZABELIN. Yes.

LENIN. How do you do? Please sit down. (*LENIN sits down. A pause.*) Well, what is it going to be, sabotage or work?

ZABELIN. I didn't think you could be interested in my personal problems.

LENIN. Believe it or not, we are. As a matter of fact, we want to consult you about a very important question.

ZABELIN. I don't know— Can my advice be of any value?

LENIN. Who is it you're doubting—yourself or us?

ZABELIN. For some time, now, nobody has been interested in my advice.

LENIN. Evidently people were interested in other things. Don't you think so?

ZABELIN. Yes, that's true. They had other interests.

LENIN. And now it's your advice that's needed. So what's bothering you?

ZABELIN. I'm a little—befuddled, so to speak.

DZERZHINSKY. Your little bundle seems to be in your way. Put it down somewhere and have a seat.

LENIN. You must have been going to the baths? Today is Saturday, bath day.

ZABELIN. Yes, of course—I was thinking of going to the baths.

LENIN. We won't keep you long. Sit down. (*To* STALIN.) Tell him about your conversation with the scientist.

STALIN (*to* LENIN). We haven't told citizen Zabelin what it's all about. Let me state the facts.

LENIN. Yes, of course.

STALIN (*to* ZABELIN). We Bolsheviks have always been interested in the fundamental problems of rebuilding Russia. Amateurs' interest, pipe dreams—are pleasant but futile. We've always opposed them. Right now the Soviet Government is interested in the question of how we can start in on the electrification of Russia, today, by ourselves, without outside help, with our own hands. So, on the instructions of comrade Lenin, I had a talk with a certain scientist about a program of building hydroelectric power plants. That scientist—before the revolution he owned stock in an electric company—carried on our conversation rather reluctantly. However, despite this reluctance, he very energetically maintained that in Russia electric power had no future. As you know, our country is flat, and its rivers flow slowly, whereas to produce electric power you need something like Niagara Falls.

ZABELIN. Only an ignorant man could say that.

STALIN. Excuse me, he's a scientist of authority.

ZABELIN. Or a swindler.

STALIN. That's different.

LENIN. But why a swindler? You have to prove that.

ZABELIN. May I ask you to come look at the map?

LENIN. Let's go. (*They all walk over to the map.*)

ZABELIN. I'm ready to show you a dozen places where we can build hydroelectric plants right now, in the natural conditions that exist there. Here and here— And can't we have one here?

LENIN. What's that?

ZABELIN. The Dnieper rapids.

LENIN. Where can you build there?

ZABELIN. Somewhere in the lower reaches, in my opinion, but not down by the sea, of course.

LENIN. Wouldn't it be fine, though, if we could build a great electric tower right on the seashore! Look out—here we come!

ZABELIN. This is of course the peat region. But there's the Angara River in the East, Mount Elbrus in the Caucasus—

LENIN. Could you prepare me a general memorandum on this subject?

ZABELIN. I hesitate to say definitely. I haven't done any work on these questions for a long time.

LENIN. What kind of work have you been doing?

ZABELIN. Nothing.

DZERZHINSKY. You're not telling the truth. Engineer Zabelin sells matches.

LENIN. Who do you mean?

DZERZHINSKY. The engineer stands in the streets and sells matches.

LENIN. Do you sell wholesale or retail, by the box? Listen, this is terrible. Disgraceful, my dear man. Sell matches at a time like this! You ought to be shot for such a stunt, believe me.

ZABELIN. I've been ready for that a long time.

LENIN. Ready for what? To die a martyr? Who forces you to sell matches?

ZABELIN. I have nothing else to turn my hand to.

LENIN. How's that—nothing else? Such nonsense!

ZABELIN. Nobody's called for my services.

LENIN. Why must we call you? Before we came, did you sit and wait until you were called? However, if the idea of the electrification of Russia fails to inspire you, you can go on selling matches.

ZABELIN. I don't know—if there's much I can do— (LENIN *moves off angrily without answering.*)

STALIN. That, of course, we don't know.

ZABELIN. I'll never make a Bolshevik.

STALIN. That's possible.

ZABELIN. You're planning to build socialism in Russia, and I don't believe in socialism.

LENIN (*with a sudden flash, cheerfully*). But I do. Who's right? You think you are, and I think I am. Who can decide between us? Well, let's ask Dzerzhinsky. Most likely he'll say I'm right and you're wrong. Will that satisfy you?

ZABELIN. I realize what I say is like child's prattle to you.

STALIN. But you're not an expert on socialism?

ZABELIN. No, of course not. I can't say I know much about it.

STALIN. Why, then, do you pass judgment on something that's not in your field? Do you know comrade Krzhizhanovsky?

ZABELIN. No, I don't.

LENIN. Well, he told me you've had vast experience as an electrical engineer—that you've built plants—and here you are selling matches! It's monstrous!

ZABELIN. I'll give that up.

DZERZHINSKY (*to himself*). Thank God!

LENIN (*to* DZERZHINSKY). What did you say?

DZERZHINSKY. I said "Thank God."

ZABELIN. As I understand it, it's being proposed that I take up serious work.

STALIN. Speaking for myself, I'd advise you to—very strongly.

ZABELIN. But you hardly know me.

LENIN. We know a little.

ZABELIN. There's nobody in the Communist party who could recommend me.

LENIN. Believe it or not, there is.

ZABELIN. I don't know who it can be.

DZERZHINSKY. Me.

ZABELIN. But how do you know me?

DZERZHINSKY. It's my official duty.

ZABELIN. Oh, yes—I'd forgotten that.

DZERZHINSKY. And since I'm recommending you to the government, allow me a word of advice. At the moment you're all mixed up, aren't you?

ZABELIN. Completely.

DZERZHINSKY. And a little excited too. You need to calm down. Go home, think the matter over, and then give us your answer.

LENIN. Will you let us know tomorrow?

ZABELIN. I'll do that.

LENIN. Good-by. (ZABELIN *bows and walks to the door.*)

DZERZHINSKY. You've forgotten your bundle.

ZABELIN. Oh, confound it!

LENIN. The baths! You still have time.

ZABELIN. No, I wasn't going to the baths. Everybody decided I was being taken to the Cheka—so my wife handed me this little bundle.

LENIN. Oh, I see. That's different. Just a minute. (*Rings the bell.*) These are harsh times. There must be tears and distress at your place. (*Enter the* SECRETARY.) Send the engineer home in an automobile. Right away. (ZABELIN *and the* SECRETARY *go off.*) Well, what do you think? Will he go to work?

DZERZHINSKY. I'm sure he will.

STALIN. He didn't keep much back. Came right out in the open with what he thought.

LENIN. If we could only rouse all these old bears in a hurry—hundreds of them have gone into hiding.

STALIN. We'll rouse them, Vladimir Ilyich.

LENIN. Well then, comrades, it's time we opened the meeting of the Council of Labor and Defense.

CURTAIN

ACT II

SCENE 4

ZABELIN's *workroom. The same evening. Characters as in* SCENE 2, *except that* ZABELIN, MASHA, *and* RYBAKOV *are absent.*

SKEPTIC. But I tell you we ought to check up on that order for his arrest.

ZABELINA. Check up or not, it won't help me any. The results will be the same.

FRIGHTENED LADY. Never, not even on my deathbed, will I forget this nightmare. If I'd seen it in my dreams I'd have jumped out of bed screaming. And here, in real life, they came and took him away without a word.

SKEPTIC. Let's go home. You're shaking all over. Now she'll have insomnia for a month. Even American sleeping pills won't do any good.

ZABELINA. Wait awhile. Masha will be back soon. (*The* COOK *comes in.*)

COOK. Lydia Mikhailovna, the house must be surrounded! I looked out those windows—soldiers; then out the others—more soldiers.

FRIGHTENED LADY. Put the lights out!

OPTIMIST (*looking out the window*). Soldiers—just ordinary soldiers.

SKEPTIC. Do you expect them to send extraordinary soldiers after you?

OPTIMIST. They're just standing and waiting for something.

FRIGHTENED LADY. I implore you, put out the lights.

SKEPTIC. But you'll be even more frightened in the dark.

KNITTING LADY. I'm not afraid of anything but I think, too, it might be better to put the lights out and light an oil lamp. Do you have a lotto set, Lydia Mikhailovna?

ZABELINA. Lotto? Whatever for?

KNITTING LADY. In case they come in and start looking us over, we can just be playing lotto.

OPTIMIST. The main thing is not to lose heart. You want to play lotto—all right, bring the lotto.

FRIGHTENED LADY. But do put out the light.

ZABELINA (*to the* COOK). Praskovya, bring the jar with the wick. (*Puts out the lights.*) I'll go get the lotto. (*She goes off. There is a pause.*)

KNITTING LADY. While we're at it, let's play for money.

FRIGHTENED LADY. Money? Oh, no, never. Why, that's gambling!

KNITTING LADY. Nuts will do just as well.

SKEPTIC. Where shall we get nuts?

KNITTING LADY. Lydia Mikhailovna is bound to have some. (ZABE-LINA *returns with the oil lamp and lotto game.*)

ZABELINA. Pass out the cards. Who'll call the numbers?

KNITTING LADY. Do you have any nuts, Lydia Mikhailovna?

ZABELINA. I have other things to think about, my dear.

FRIGHTENED LADY. Give me the bag. I'll call them.

ZABELINA. Masha ought to be back any minute. I expect she'll have found out something.

FRIGHTENED LADY. Twenty-two—six—ninety-one. (*The* COOK *returns.*)

SKEPTIC. Well, how goes it?

COOK. They're standing out in front now. They look angry—keep staring up at our windows.

ZABELINA (*to the* COOK). Go look out the dining-room window, Praskovya. If they come in, tell them we have guests.

THE OTHERS. No, don't. Don't do that.

ZABELINA. No, you'd better not say anything. (*The* COOK *goes off.*)

FRIGHTENED LADY. Forty-four—twenty-six—

OPTIMIST. One more and I'll have a row!

FRIGHTENED LADY. Thirteen—sixty-one—eighty-one— (*The* COOK *comes back again.*)

ZABELINA. Now what?

COOK. They seem to have gone away. (*Crosses to the window.*) No, they're over at this corner, all in a bunch.

SKEPTIC. With rifles?

COOK. Yes, rifles.

FRIGHTENED LADY. Two—one—I can't go on! I hear footsteps. Somebody's coming. Turn the lights on! (*The light is turned on. At the door stands* ZABELIN.)

ZABELINA. Anton Ivanovich—you?

ZABELIN. I.

ZABELINA. Anton—why are you standing there? Please, darling, sit down. (*Calls out.*) Masha! Where is she? Oh, I'm all mixed up. Why did Masha go? Why do you stand there, Anton, looking so bewildered? Come here, let me kiss you. (*Embraces him, tears running down her cheeks.*)

ZABELIN. Don't cry.

ZABELINA. Forgive me. We decided you were done for—I felt utterly helpless. There was only one good man who didn't lose his head—

ZABELIN. Who was that?

ZABELINA. That fellow that came to see us. I forget his name.

ZABELIN. The sailor! No, he's not the kind to lose his head.

ZABELINA. Such a cloud has passed over us, O Lord! Well, what was it? A mistake?

ZABELIN (*with his own meaning*). That's something I shall have to answer tomorrow.

ZABELINA (*scrutinizing him*). Your face looks so strange. You're all worked up, Anton. What's happened? Where were you?

ZABELIN. I don't remember.

ZABELINA. He's all excited, yet he sounds cheerful, and he talks just the way he always does. "I don't remember," he says. Don't you remember anything at all, didn't you see anything?

ZABELIN. I saw the ground slip from under my feet. (*To the* SKEPTIC.) Who's been tearing at my soul the whole year? Well? Did they throw me in jail? They know Zabelin! They thought of shooting me but didn't, because there's no other Anton Zabelin. Why are you staring at me? Don't I look like myself any more? And what is it to look like oneself?

ZABELINA. Anton, but nobody can understand your allegories.

ZABELIN. Never mind, he understands me perfectly. Where's Masha? I've had nothing to eat since morning. Look, Lydia Mikhailovna, we have guests, and the table isn't laid. We could have an old-fashioned Moscow supper out of your supplies. Get out the student wine—you know—the kind we used to buy for fifty kopecks a bottle.

ZABELINA. I'll do everything, but tell me—where were you?

SKEPTIC. Where did they take you to?

OPTIMIST. You've been gone exactly three hours.

ZABELIN. Not three hours but three years.

ZABELINA. Again—allegories, riddles?

ZABELIN. I've been made a Field Marshal and ordered to conquer India! (MASHA *rushes in.*)

MASHA. I've been running my legs off. They couldn't tell us anything but Rybakov kept insisting— I stood at the door, afraid to come in. I thought— Oh, Papa darling!

ZABELIN. Don't cry. Look how your poor heart's beating! Do you love your foolish father?

MASHA. Oh, yes!

SKEPTIC. Where were you?

ZABELIN. In the Kremlin.

SKEPTIC. Is that all?

ZABELIN. That's all.

ZABELINA. But tell us the details.

ZABELIN. There were no details.

KNITTING LADY. I understand Anton Ivanovich— I'm the only one who does. It's so romantic, the way he's come back. Anton Ivanovich, you're in a romantic mood. You have an air of mystery. I adore you.

Don't ask him questions. You want to be alone? Yes? I'm right, I do understand you, don't I?

ZABELIN. I want to talk to Masha.

ZABELINA. Well, that's a good sign. The last few months he's done nothing but quarrel with Masha.

SKEPTIC. But why did he jump on me? As if I were to blame for what's happened!

OPTIMIST. If the matter ends with a glass of student wine, how can you be indignant, my esteemed friend? (*All, except* ZABELIN *and* MASHA, *go out.*)

ZABELIN. What's this dress you have on? All dolled up for your admirer?

MASHA. This is what I wear to work every day. And I've never lured admirers with dresses. That was a stupid thing to say.

ZABELIN. I'm a stupid old man, then?

MASHA. How can you be interested in talking about admirers at a time like this?

ZABELIN. Where's Romeo?

MASHA. What Romeo?

ZABELIN. The modern Soviet version. Where's the sailor?

MASHA. But we went together to find out about you.

ZABELIN. Because you were so happy?

MASHA. How can you? You ought to be ashamed!

ZABELIN. I'm not talking about you—but about him.

MASHA. You don't know him and you'd better not say any more.

ZABELIN. You were a fool not to have married Captain Aleysky. You'd be living in Paris now.

MASHA. I've been told Captain Aleysky is playing the balalaika in Paris.

ZABELIN. It's better to play the balalaika in Paris than sell matches in Moscow.

MASHA. Then why didn't you go to Paris? They were after you to.

ZABELIN. Because I'm a Russian.

MASHA. And what am I?

ZABELIN. You women are chameleons. Helen of Troy lived pretty comfortably with her Paris. Salammbo fell in love with a barbarian. You, with a sailor. I can't live without turnips—in Paris they feed you on frogs. (*Suddenly sings a snatch of a frivolous French song, does a turn around the room, and stops before* MASHA.) Is my life all in the past? Masha, my little daughter, look at me—is my life in the past?

MASHA. Papa dear, tell me what's on your mind. You must. Why should your life be in the past?

ZABELIN. Never mind that. Where's the sailor?

MASHA. What do you want him for?

ZABELIN. I'd like to have a talk with him. Sit down. You're not going anywhere. (*Picks a book from a shelf.*) *Electrical Engineering*, by Anton Zabelin. You were a tot, Masha, when I was writing this book. You'd come in sometimes and say: "Papa, are you writing? I'll sit over here." You'd sit for a while, then climb up on my back, and we'd romp all over the room. Now you're big and clever, and your father's a little afraid of you. Everything I've been saying here is nonsense. You've realized that, I'm sure. You see, I was in the Kremlin, talking to them— Why don't you say something? You should be beside yourself with joy, bubbling over with comments—

MASHA. Are you annoyed that they sent for you?

ZABELIN. Are you happy?

MASHA. I'd be very happy, if you had a different attitude.

ZABELIN. Do you know what's happened? I thought I was a man of learning, a builder, a creator, and suddenly that's all gone up in smoke!

MASHA. Papa, what happened? Tell me so I can understand.

ZABELIN. All my life I slaved away, went through mental torture seeking answers to my little problems—now all that's gone up in smoke. Mere trifles, hack work, childish puttering. They've killed your Zabelin, done him in. At first I didn't get their idea, then it came to me on the way home—struck me full force.

MASHA. Please try to explain it calmly. I don't know a thing—I can't follow you.

ZABELIN. Don't hurry me, Masha. We'll thresh it all out together before tomorrow. You see, tomorrow I have to give them my answer.

MASHA (*rapturously*). They're asking you to work?

ZABELIN (*in a whisper*). They're telling me to—it's an order. I can't sell matches any more. I gave my word.

MASHA. Thank God.

ZABELIN. Just what they said. Now look, dear. I have to ask you something—and you're the only one I *can* ask, because you understand me thoroughly and know their ways. What I have to find out from you—in strict confidence—is this: Can I hold my own in these times or am I washed up?

MASHA. You're asking that, you? Of course you can. I give you my word.

ZABELIN. Wait, this isn't something to be answered on impulse.

MASHA. Would they have asked you to the Kremlin if it weren't so?

ZABELIN. That's something else again. They know Zabelin; you know your father.

MASHA. But don't you remember what nearly drove us to a break?

ZABELIN. You were after me to start working. Again you don't understand my question. Put me side by side with the sailor and answer: Will I be able to get along with him? I'm serious—this is no time for sarcasm. The sailor and I, spokes in the same wheel—is that possible? (*He waits for her answer. She is silent.*) Eh? You can't picture such a combination either.

MASHA (*suddenly*). I can! You have to get a job you love. Tell me what they offered you.

ZABELIN. I'll tell you later. Wait—look at me. Can I really hold my own?

MASHA. I can't find words. But what I wouldn't give to make you believe me!

ZABELIN. Masha! You realize—they want to do away with the slothful, samovar Russia, Russia sitting on its haunches like the priest's wife. Just think!

MASHA. Then why are you hesitating? If you feel sorry to lose that—go, sell your matches. (*Mimicking him.*) "Prewar—safety matches—"

ZABELIN. Don't you dare make fun of me!

MASHA. Tell me, dear, what are you thinking about?

ZABELIN. I'm thinking of my workroom—it's terribly run down. Aren't you ashamed? Your father's an engineer and his workroom is a grocery store. (*Calls out.*) Praskovya! (*The* COOK *comes in.*) Bring the broom, quick! (*The* COOK *leaves.*) Come on, Masha, let's clear the table. Out with all this garbage! Wait, sit down a minute. I'll tell you something.

MASHA. I'm listening, Papa.

ZABELIN (*in a low voice*). I've just seen a man of genius.

CURTAIN

ACT III

SCENE 1

Inside the Spassky Tower where the clock mechanism is located. Night. The WATCHMAKER *is working on the chimes.*

WATCHMAKER. "Arise, ye prisoners of starvation . . ." Major or minor, who knows what key I'm singing in? When a man's mind is going around in circles, his head is no earthly help to him. (*Taps on his forehead.*) Hey, there! Will you tell me what's major and what's minor? What? I don't hear you. My brain is silent. Maybe I'm asleep. Here's the water—the bread—myself. (*Drinks water.*) Why blame the brain when it's the ear that's missing—the musical talent? Now, my daughter—she's a pianist—she says to me: "Papa, you're in a minor mood," and I understand that—it means a bad mood. But mood isn't music, although music makes mood— (*Losing his temper.*) The Conservatory ought to be in my place trying all night to figure out which key to tune the chimes. This isn't an alarm clock, you musical gentry. This is the chimes of the Kremlin. Where are you, musicians? You're asleep in your homes as befits normal beings, and I, like a madman, am tuning up the chimes at three o'clock in the morning. My job is mechanisms; I'm a watchmaker, but chimes are music, and I'm no Rimsky-Korsakov. (*The chimes ring, the* WATCHMAKER *listening intently.*) Maybe if I call one of the guards? If I'm lucky, the man may have a good ear. I need a living soul here. I'm not a philosopher who likes being alone; I'm a craftsman and I have to show my work to people. (*He goes off. The clock mechanism slowly continues to operate. The chimes ring twice. The* WATCHMAKER *returns.*) They can't help me. They're guarding the Kremlin. But let's agree once and for all, comrade watchmaker, there's the saying: "A job to do means see it through." (*Listens.*) You begin to hear things in this tower— No, I have to start all over—twenty times all over—a hundred times— (*Resumes work. Enter* RYBAKOV.)

RYBAKOV. Excuse me—it's rather late, isn't it?

WATCHMAKER. Who's that?

RYBAKOV. A representative of insomnia, science, and inspiration.

WATCHMAKER. Oh, it's you—that fellow? Where do you come from?

RYBAKOV. From Theater Square. I popped out of my porthole and right up here. I was sitting, studying, and, having the fresh air habit, I opened the window. Just as I reached the destruction of Carthage, I suddenly heard a strange ringing of bells. I realized what it was, left Carthage, and rushed over here. So I can congratulate you. Speak, my friend. I heard it myself—they're ringing.

WATCHMAKER. If you came to congratulate me, you shouldn't have left Carthage.

RYBAKOV. But I just heard it again, this minute, down in the square —they were playing.

WATCHMAKER. Playing what?

RYBAKOV. They strike, ring, live.

WATCHMAKER. Do you ever go mad?

RYBAKOV. Under certain conditions.

WATCHMAKER. I'm under such conditions now.

RYBAKOV. I get it. Well, in a nutshell, what has to be done?

WATCHMAKER. You've got to listen.

RYBAKOV. Is that all?

WATCHMAKER. Have you a talent for music?

RYBAKOV. I doubt it. I used to harmonize with the boys on the ship.

WATCHMAKER. That'll do. Now stand and listen.

RYBAKOV. Yes, sir, stand and listen. (*The* WATCHMAKER *releases the chimes. They ring discordantly.*)

WATCHMAKER. What does that remind you of?

RYBAKOV. Nothing.

WATCHMAKER. And you're yelling at me—they're playing! I want the "International," and what do I get? Chaos, without rhyme or reason. I tell you a Conservatory should be right here to help me with the music.

RYBAKOV. I can bring anybody you want.

WATCHMAKER. But you have to find them, wake them up.

RYBAKOV. What is it you're doubting, father? I can wake up the whole Conservatory. I undertake to arrange any consultation you want. It's up to you—do you want it or not?

WATCHMAKER. Look. Know what I think? You'd better not. It'll start such a business, we'll lose our heads. You see, they're used to working with little hooks, and the bells here weigh two tons each. They're used to dealing with the key of C and such like, and what's needed here is a key like this— (*Shows a monkey wrench.*) I need a man with a soul. Will you have the patience to stay here till morning?

RYBAKOV. As long as you want. I'm ready to turn the wheels by hand, I'll swing in place of the pendulum—but we mustn't retreat.

WATCHMAKER. You're the man I need. We have to find the first bell, then the second. I thought I was getting the tune, but I don't trust my ear.

RYBAKOV. Well, just suppose you try what you thought was right.

WATCHMAKER. I'll give you the first bell. (*Strikes a bell.*) How's that?

RYBAKOV. That's a problem.

WATCHMAKER. I know it's a problem. I want to know how it sounds to you.

RYBAKOV. Hold your temper. I've had no experience.

WATCHMAKER. Have I?

RYBAKOV. I'm not saying anything. You can't figure it out with one stroke. I'd like to hear—what d'you call it—the scale.

WATCHMAKER. But I don't know where to begin.

RYBAKOV. Just go back to the tune you had before.

WATCHMAKER. All right, I'll get it. (*Tinkers with the works.*)

RYBAKOV (*looking around for the first time*). An old machine. It must have been built by Germans.

WATCHMAKER. English, I'd say.

RYBAKOV. Everything you pick up, it's Germans, Englishmen, Swedes. Have you read today's *Pravda?*

WATCHMAKER. I haven't slept at home for two nights. What's happened?

RYBAKOV. Electrification of Russia is about to begin.

WATCHMAKER. I'm a little man. My chief job for the moment is to make the chimes play. Listen! (*The chimes play something resembling the "International."*)

RYBAKOV. Hold on there! Just a minute! (*The* WATCHMAKER *stops the mechanism.*) I've got it. It's remarkable. Do it again. No, don't. What we need is to change some bells.

WATCHMAKER. I agree with you. Three or two?

RYBAKOV. Three.

WATCHMAKER. That's what I thought but I didn't trust my ear. I know—only I have to figure it out. (*He almost disappears inside the works.*) Electrification of Russia— That's not likely to come off.

RYBAKOV. Think about your bells.

WATCHMAKER. Don't worry—I'm thinking. And what do you think about electrification?

RYBAKOV. It'll come off.

WATCHMAKER. Do you know the difference between you Bolsheviks and the rest of us?

RYBAKOV. What is it?

WATCHMAKER. When we think it won't come off, you think it will, and the other way around.

RYBAKOV. Well, I think if it doesn't come off here, you'll have to jump off this tower and I'll follow you.

WATCHMAKER. You jump first and I'll follow.

RYBAKOV. We'll jump together.

WATCHMAKER (*in a serious tone*). You think I won't? I certainly will. Or I'll smash my head against this wall. In thirty years of work I've never had a single complaint from my customers. If I muff this job, I'm finished as far as I'm concerned. (*Throws down his tools.*)

RYBAKOV. What's the matter? It's been going fine.

WATCHMAKER. What's been going fine? Where? I've mixed up all the bells. See for yourself—the beginning is all wrong again. I've mixed it up a hundred times.

RYBAKOV. I've got an idea. What if we got a grand piano up here? (*Looks around.*) No, not enough room. Not even for an upright. What can we think up?

WATCHMAKER. Wait—I've got it. I'll make the third bell go fifth, and the fifth go second. Now let's be quiet—very quiet. (*Works.*) I'm switching on the chimes.

RYBAKOV. Fine. No, wait. There's an echo up here. We can't hear what anything sounds like. Look, father—one of us will have to go downstairs and listen, out in the open air. I'll call up to you from there. Just a minute. Wait. (RYBAKOV *disappears.*)

WATCHMAKER. All right, but hurry up! Quick! Now let me see— I hope this is it (RYBAKOV's *voice from below: "I'm listening!" The* WATCHMAKER *switches on the mechanism. The chimes play the opening bars of the "International" correctly—then stop. The* WATCHMAKER *stands motionless beside the mechanism.* RYBAKOV *rushes in.*)

RYBAKOV. Go down, listen for yourself.

WATCHMAKER. There's nothing more I can do.

RYBAKOV. It worked! The right tune!

WATCHMAKER (*indifferently*). The tune— (*Suddenly.*) It worked?

RYBAKOV. It did. That was the tune all right!

WATCHMAKER. No false notes?

RYBAKOV. You've done a perfect job.

WATCHMAKER. Not so fast. The job's far from done yet. Now you've got to stay with me—I won't let you go. Only it'll be hard on you walking up and down all those stairs.

RYBAKOV. I'll manage. But you ought to have a rest. You must be worn out.

WATCHMAKER. No, not any more. But I'm not going to let you go—you have to act for the whole Conservatory. Damned if I don't feel like a real hero!

RYBAKOV. Yes, sir, it's turning out to be mighty interesting! All Moscow's asleep—but not a soul can even dream what the two of us are creating up here in the tower!

CURTAIN

ACT III

SCENE 2

A conference hall in the Kremlin.

LENIN (*glancing at his watch*). Has the English writer come?

SECRETARY. Yes, just now. (*Smiles.*)

LENIN. What are you smiling at?

SECRETARY. It's strange how he scrutinizes and feels everything.

LENIN. Naturally; he's just arrived from London and besides he's a writer. Haven't you read about him?

SECRETARY. Yes, I have.

LENIN. Ask him to come in, please. After my talk with him, I'm having a conference here. Just a minute. What did the watchmaker tell you?

SECRETARY. Says today, without fail.

LENIN. We must tell Rybakov about it. Call him immediately. And call up engineer Zabelin, please—remind him that he'll have to speak at a state conference of decisive importance. Now you may ask the English writer to come in. (*The SECRETARY goes off.*) They say he's an interesting person, a friend of Edison, a man of searching intelligence. (*The ENGLISHMAN enters.*) Have I kept you waiting?

ENGLISHMAN. No, not at all.

LENIN (*shaking his hand*). Ulyanov—Lenin. Please be seated. (*The ENGLISHMAN sits.*) Are you staying long in Soviet Russia? What are you working on?

ENGLISHMAN. I'm going to write a book attacking Marx.

LENIN (*smiling*). That ought to be very interesting.

ENGLISHMAN. I'm tired of him.

LENIN. Of whom?

ENGLISHMAN. Marx.

LENIN. Have you been giving so much time to the study of his works?

ENGLISHMAN. To be frank with you, I could never finish reading them. But I know his dogmas—all his tricks.

LENIN. In that case, of course, you're the very man for the job.

ENGLISHMAN (*sincerely, with feeling*). Please don't think I believe the stories in the foreign press that you're a Mason.

LENIN. I know a lot of nonsense is written about me.

ENGLISHMAN. But in one respect I think they're right.

LENIN. And what would that be?

ENGLISHMAN. That you're cut off from Russian life.

LENIN. Why do you think so?

ENGLISHMAN. It's so difficult to get to you—there are so many guards about. How can you keep in touch with your people?

LENIN. Keeping in touch with the people isn't a question of guards.

ENGLISHMAN. But let's get back to Marx.

LENIN. I'm listening.

ENGLISHMAN. I can't understand, Mr. Lenin, how you can divide the world into the poor and the rich. It's primitive, crude, and shallow. There are honest people among the rich, just as there are among the poor. Well, it's for the forward-looking honest people among the rich *and* the poor to join forces and build a sensible socialism. I can see by your eyes you don't believe in this idea.

LENIN. I don't believe it for a single minute.

ENGLISHMAN. Oh, it's sheer fanaticism to believe only in the Bolshevik concept of socialism.

LENIN. Your government spent a lot of money to prove, with the help of guns, that our concepts were wrong.

ENGLISHMAN. I was one of those who protested against that.

LENIN. Oh, yes, I know. You are one of those honest ones. But it didn't help, did it?

ENGLISHMAN. Well, no.

LENIN. And why?

ENGLISHMAN. Because they had the power, not we.

LENIN. They have the banks, they have the guns—and you have honesty. What's your honesty worth as compared with even a single rusty gun? You've no sooner started in on your sensible socialism than they set up their miserable gun and begin banging away. You must admit that's entirely possible. What are you going to do then? Fire back? But that's Bolshevism. Run away? But what about socialism?

ENGLISHMAN. Mr. Lenin, you're giving me typical Red propaganda.

LENIN. But I happen to be the most deep dyed of the Reds.

ENGLISHMAN. Why, Mr. Lenin, you surprise me— (*The sound of the chimes breaks in—the first two or three bars of the "International."*)

LENIN (*listening*). How's that?

ENGLISHMAN. You're capable of being humorous, whereas every impartial observer coming from the West can easily see that you're on the brink of disaster.

LENIN (*in a serious tone*). Please tell me what you've seen here in Russia.

ENGLISHMAN. I've noticed that the Russian men don't shave very regularly.

LENIN. That's true, they're not too clean shaven.

ENGLISHMAN. Furthermore, they walk about in rags. Perhaps you find this subject unpleasant?

LENIN. Please go ahead. I'm very much interested in knowing what else you've seen here.

ENGLISHMAN. Everybody goes about carrying rolled-up packages. At first I couldn't make it out—then it was explained to me—it's their food, their dinner. They take porridge home from the office, wrapped in newspaper.

LENIN. That's kasha.

ENGLISHMAN. Here nobody walks in the streets. Everybody runs. Maxim Gorky has only one suit of clothes.

LENIN. Is that true? Did he tell you that?

ENGLISHMAN. His friends told me.

LENIN (*reflectively, as if to himself*). It's a hard life for everybody. For Gorky too. (*Suddenly narrowing his eyes, fires point blank at the* ENGLISHMAN.) How many suits have you?

ENGLISHMAN. I don't remember—perhaps ten or twelve.

LENIN. You have twelve and Gorky only one. You see what a difference! But please continue.

ENGLISHMAN. When I caught cold I couldn't get any drugs at the chemist's.

LENIN (*sadly*). It's terrible—I know it's terrible.

ENGLISHMAN. I've been shown bread that's no bread at all. And I've heard that somewhere in the Volga region people are dying of famine. Is that true?

LENIN. It is.

ENGLISHMAN. Human efforts can't stop this catastrophe. In no time there'll be nothing left in Russia except village muzhiks. With your cities out of existence, the railroads will rust away. I see Russia in darkness—the terrible darkness of her end, catastrophe, destruction—

LENIN (*simply, reflectively*). I suppose we do make a ghastly sight. In darkness—I'm sure there's darkness too. No, no, I'm not arguing. I can see that's how it must look to others—

ENGLISHMAN. I've heard you're proposing a plan for the electrification of Russia?

LENIN. We're going to present this plan to the people.

ENGLISHMAN. You're a dreamer, Mr. Lenin. You have a vast, flat country, slowly freezing to death, with a population that is more

Asiatic than European, a country gasping its last breath—and you dream of giving it electricity! You're a strange dreamer, Mr. Lenin!

LENIN. Come to see us in ten years' time.

ENGLISHMAN. But in ten years will you be here to see?

LENIN. We will be. You don't believe it? Come and you'll see for yourself. I'm a dreamer. It seems to me we are here for good, forever.

ENGLISHMAN. I realize, Mr. Lenin, that every word you speak is meant to be taken seriously. If you believe as you do, you must have secrets that are not known in the West.

LENIN. Oh, quite the contrary! We're very frank—too frank.

ENGLISHMAN. What, then, sustains your faith and dreams?

LENIN. If I tell you, you'll only be annoyed! You'll say, typical Red propaganda again. I believe in the working class—you don't. I believe in the Russian people—that horrifies you. You believe in honest capitalism—I don't. You've thought up a clean, sweet Christmas socialism —I advocate the dictatorship of the proletariat. Dictatorship is a harsh word—heavy, sanguinary, cruel. One doesn't toss off such words lightly. But there's no other way of dreaming about electrification, socialism, Communism. Forgive me, but I'm saying very ordinary things. I have no secrets.

ENGLISHMAN. Your faith staggers a person—or it can drive him mad! It's beyond comprehension. Here you're facing misery, horror—yet, standing on the edge of a precipice, you talk about electrification. I refuse to understand. (*The chimes ring out two or three bars of the "International."*)

LENIN. Come to see us in ten years' time.

ENGLISHMAN. No, you're hiding something. You know something that we in the West don't. You're holding back.

LENIN. I give you my word of honor that we tell the truth, openly, from beginning to end.

ENGLISHMAN. You're tired. I noticed it when I came in. Good-by, Mr. Lenin. Thank you for the talk. Possibly you're right and I'm wrong. The future will show. Good-by.

LENIN. Good-by. But mind you come and see us in ten years.

ENGLISHMAN. Very well. (*Goes off.*)

LENIN (*pauses to think, then bursts out laughing*). Have you ever seen such a Philistine—such a petty, hopeless Philistine! (*The* SECRETARY *comes in.*) Everybody here? We can begin?

SECRETARY. Everybody.

LENIN. Have you found Rybakov?

SECRETARY. Yes, he's come.

LENIN. Call him in. (*The* SECRETARY *leaves.* RYBAKOV *enters.*) Hello, comrade Rybakov. How's your romance—still blooming?

RYBAKOV. Fresh as a daisy.

LENIN. Do you remember what I told you in secret?

RYBAKOV. I do.

LENIN. Glad to hear it. How about the university—are they letting you in?

RYBAKOV. They have to. I work day and night.

LENIN. Did they tell you why I wanted to see you?

RYBAKOV. No.

LENIN. Your watchmaker is finishing today.

RYBAKOV. I know.

LENIN. I can't believe it—I find I'm quite excited.

RYBAKOV. Wait a minute, please. I'll check on it. (*Moves toward the door.*)

LENIN. Stay right here. We have universities here too, you know. You can learn something.

CURTAIN

ACT III

SCENE 3

The same hall. An important conference is in progress. Figures of the era of War Communism catch the eye. One notices men wearing blouses under ordinary jackets, or under leather jackets—the dominant fashion of the time. Some men who only a short time before were fighting at the front retain a distinct military bearing. Among them are several CIVILIANS *with the characteristic appearance of the revolutionists of 1917.*

Upstage, sitting at the table, is LENIN. *Some of those present are obviously seeing him for the first time—to them everything here is a new, unusual, and stirring experience. Nobody smokes. All are silent, reserved, and deeply serious. Several men are jotting down notes in their notebooks.* LENIN *reads questions passed up to him, writes something on them, and puts them to one side.*

Engineer ZABELIN *has been speaking for some time and is now concluding his report.*

ZABELIN. In concluding my report, I ask to be forgiven for having been somewhat confused and agitated, since this is the first time I've ever spoken at such an important state conference and spoken of things which are the sum and substance of my life. Yes, comrades— (*Pauses and repeats.*) Yes, comrades, every expert in energetics, if he loves Russia, must honestly admit that since the time of Peter the Great there hasn't been another mind possessed of such daring, such majestic ideas. We of today cannot even grasp the magnitude of the foundation now being laid in the history of our country. (LENIN *is instantly on his feet.*)

LENIN. I've received a few notes. Allow me to answer them right away. The men from the Kursk district write that their horses are dying, that there isn't enough chaff to hold out until spring. Wouldn't it be more fitting to solve this urgent problem first and then take up such a huge business as electrification? A comrade from the Putilov plant expresses grave doubts about the people. (*Reads from a note.*) "The proletariat has gone into petty trade. Men make cigarette lighters— Our technicians are either Whites or anti-Soviet liberals—" (*Lays the note aside.*) Don't we know all that? I had a talk with a famous English writer today. He calls himself a socialist but he belongs to that strange class of people who see revolution as a kind of Christmas Eve party. They believe in the brotherhood of neat and clean people who, according to them, will embrace and kiss each other and then build socialism. These are the dreams of romantic young ladies which we've always laughed at. You see, comrades, the point is that I believe in erring, imperfect people. I want to say that we'll build socialism with the bricks left us by capitalism and not wait for the arrival of the new Communist race. Take a man who at any minute is ready to give his life for the revolution—isn't he poisoned by the great multitude of sins of capitalism? What do you think? I mean the downtrodden, worn-out man who has been mutilated by serfdom, the Czarist regime, army discipline. We have no other kind of man. With him we carried out the epoch-making enterprise of the November revolution, with him we destroyed three huge White armies, with him we drove the English ignominiously out of Russia. Just think what this erring man has performed! Why, it's counterrevolution not to love our man, not to believe in him, not to prize him above all the blessings of the world. On our road there will be chaff and dead horses; even now we have people dying by the thousands— It's a horror which the human mind refuses to comprehend. But we have no right to yield the revolution to the chaff. To make a revolution, great as this revolution may be, is only half the job—one tenth of the job. When the days of the barricades are over, there come the workdays, the hard, grimy trivialities of everyday life. A true revolutionary, as we see him, is the man who's ready to make new, unheard-of sacrifices, the incommensurable, unprecedented, terrible sacrifices of everyday life, since there is no other way, never can be, never was in the history of mankind. We must, at all cost, try and save horses, fight the famine, sow in the ancient way, handful after handful. But if, in doing this, we forget the things for which our people have shed so much blood, borne such trials, shown such superhuman heroism, then, I say to you frankly, it's all as good as lost. We have to look ahead and dream—yes, dream. And at once, today, we have to give the people a slogan that is simple and that captures the imagination—the Soviet regime plus electrification. I think this will be Communism in the true sense of the word. I think this will be the beginning of an unprecedented, revolutionary change in the entire way of life of this vast, still medieval, poverty-stricken, ruined, and yet most majestic country in the world. We can afford to wait for nothing and nobody. We must create socialism here and now, build the future this very minute! Forgive me, I've let my thoughts run away with me. I meant to answer each of these questions in turn but I see I've answered them all at once. (*The chimes on the Spassky Tower begin to ring.* LENIN *makes an involuntary gesture calling for silence. Hurrying over to the window, he throws it wide and listens. Then turns to the gathering and speaks with profound joy.*) You hear? They're playing. This is a great thing, comrades; this is for ever and ever. When everything we're dreaming and arguing about has come to pass, this clock on the tower will be ticking off new time—time which will show the world new advances in electrification, new dreams, new and more daring efforts. And I'm sure those men of the future will understand and appreciate our toil and sacrifices that are breaking the ground for them today.

CURTAIN

FATHER UNKNOWN

BY VASSILY SHKVARKIN

VASSILY SHKVARKIN's play, which was produced by the Theater of Satire in 1933, pictures the Soviet life of those days. The rebellion against the "bourgeois prejudices" in matters of sex and family relations had already passed its peak, and the new-won freedom was honored more in word than in deed. Still stricter morals came to prevail during the next decade, when marriage and family ties became the cornerstone of the Soviet society.

The setting of the little tragicomedy played out in "Father Unknown" is a summer countryhouse, a "dacha," within a commuting distance of Moscow. The custom of moving to a countryhouse for the summer is an old established one in Russia, particularly among the residents of big cities. The plains and woods around Moscow and Leningrad are dotted with innumerable "dachas," which in summer harbor a large proportion of the population of these cities, and in winter are deserted and shuttered up.

Vassily Vassilyevich Shkvarkin was born in 1893. His first play, "In the Dark Reign," dealt with the revolutionary struggle under the Czarist regime. He subsequently wrote "Around the World," "The Harmful Element," "Swindler," "Who Goes There?" "Father Unknown," "A Simple Girl," "Spring Review," and "The Day of Judgement."

The English version of "Father Unknown" published in this volume was made in collaboration, at different stages of the work, with Mr. Julian Leigh and Miss Dorothy Joseph, whose assistance is here gratefully acknowledged.

A. B.

FATHER UNKNOWN

CHARACTERS

YAKOV, a technical student taking a practical course in road construction in the summer; a Mohammedan from the Caucasus

KOSTYA, a fellow student

MANYA, a young actress preparing to make her first appearance on the stage, age 20

OLGA PAVLOVNA KARAULOVA, MANYA's mother, who was graduated from high school 35 years ago and has since done nothing but keep house

SERGEY PETROVICH KARAULOV, MANYA's father and OLGA PAVLOVNA's husband; an old musician who plays the cello in an orchestra

SENYA PERCHATKIN, a young dental technician

FYODOR FYODOROVICH PRIBYLEV, a civil engineer, age about 40

ZINA, MANYA's friend

AGRIPPINA SEMYONOVNA, a midwife

RAYA, a technical student

YOUNG MAN, SENYA's friend

RYVKIND, a dentist

ALEXANDER MIRONOVICH, RAYA's father, a Jew

POSTMAN

ACT I

SCENE 1

A wooded spot. Two old birch trees. A small country house with a porch and balcony. In the open space in front of the house is a flower bed. Table and benches.
KOSTYA *comes out on the balcony and looks about him musingly. He is followed by* YAKOV.

YAKOV. Are you here to enjoy the country, Kostya, or to work? Tell me what you've come for. You're here to survey a road. Right?

KOSTYA. Yes, of course.

YAKOV. All you can survey in those fine white pants is the landscape. (*Hands* KOSTYA *a book.*) Read it aloud.

KOSTYA. There's something wrong with my throat. I'm hoarse or something.

YAKOV. Hoarse? All right. Sit down. (*Takes the book, turns the pages.*) Here we are. Paved roads. Will your delicate health permit you to listen?

KOSTYA. All right. Go ahead.

YAKOV. Transverse profile. (KOSTYA *looks about him and sees* MANYA *leaving the house with a play script in her hand.* YAKOV *reads.*) "The longitudinal cross section of the road is designated by the term 'transverse profile.' "

KOSTYA (*gazing at* MANYA). That's right.

YAKOV (*reads further*). "The profile indicates the relative position of the road with reference to the surface of the ground."

KOSTYA. That's right.

YAKOV (*raises his head and continues in the same tone*). Here I am, reading away as if to a child, and the dope won't even listen.

KOSTYA. That's right. (YAKOV *stops reading.*) Well? Go on. The profile of the road—

YAKOV (*rises and sees* MANYA). You're a liar. You mean the profile on the road. Now I understand the white pants and the sore throat.

KOSTYA. Quiet, please!

YAKOV. You should have warned me.

KOSTYA. What about?

YAKOV. Your critical condition. People with typhoid fever or the grippe should give warning to others.

KOSTYA. But I have no typhoid fever.

YAKOV. It's all the same. You're in love, and that means you're sick.

KOSTYA. Yakov! She'll hear you! Can't you yell at me in a low voice?

YAKOV. Oh, Lord! Now I must share the room with a lovesick swain!

KOSTYA. That's not contagious.

YAKOV. Very unpleasant, just the same. You'll be shaving every day now. First it's white pants, tomorrow you'll be wearing a white collar. And before you know it you'll fall so low as to put on a necktie. Tell me the truth, now—did you bring a necktie with you?

KOSTYA. Suppose I did.

YAKOV. How can one live with you?

KOSTYA (loudly, after seeing MANYA walk off). Shut up, you blue-nosed governess!

YAKOV. I'd make you take that back if I didn't think you'd lost your senses.

KOSTYA. Don't be angry, Yakov. Can't you understand? I am—I have—I feel —Oh, Yakov, old pal! (Throws his arms about YAKOV.)

YAKOV. Just look at him. Now he jumps on you like a madman. (MANYA appears again in front of the house.) I'll tell her to knock some sense into you. Ma— (KOSTYA pushes YAKOV into the house.)

MANYA (holds a play script in her hand). I am alone on the stage. Here are the footlights—and the people in the audience are out there. Oh, dear! I'm so nervous I'm afraid to look at them. They frighten me. They don't know that this is my first appearance. No, I'd better not look that way. I mustn't get excited. So. Silence. But suppose they begin to cough like a consumptives' home? I won't be able to bring out a word. I may be a flop. I once heard of an actress who failed so horribly that her wig turned white with grief. Anything can happen on the stage. But I mustn't fail. No, I'll be so good they'll all talk about me. But how can I play the part when I don't understand it? It all happens before the revolution. A girl lives with the man she loves. That's nothing to get excited about. He leaves her. What of it? She is going to have a child. Well, what could be more natural? Her parents discover it and throw her out. What a tragedy! As if there were no other place to go. All her friends forget they ever knew her. I would tell such friends where to go. Finally, the heroine meets a young student. He attracts her. She attracts him. But when he learns about the child he stops coming around. Good riddance, say I. But she suffers, the poor thing—suffers through four acts and eight scenes. What for, is what I'd like to know. Why should all this make anyone suffer? People used to be so stupid about life. Oh, if I could only meet such a girl—talk to her, observe her. It's all so absolutely beyond my comprehension. The author might have explained it to me but it seems he's dead—he died naturally, of lack of royalties. Well, that's all very well for him but I have to play in the darn thing next month. Here are the footlights, the audience—I come in—and I haven't the slightest idea of what it's all about. (OLGA PAVLOVNA comes out on the porch.) Mother!

OLGA PAVLOVNA. What is it?

MANYA. Did you ever have any lovers?

OLGA PAVLOVNA (*drops a cup*). Heavens! What a question to ask your mother! Look at my cup! That's what always happens when you ask me things.

MANYA. But tell me—did your friends turn against you?

OLGA PAVLOVNA. Summer always makes you silly. (*Someone in the house is heard playing the cello.*)

MANYA. *Please* listen, Mother. Didn't you really have any adventures when you were young?

OLGA PAVLOVNA. I'm not Baron Munchausen. He had adventures.

MANYA. Then what did you want to live for?

OLGA PAVLOVNA. Thank you. That's a nice thing to say.

MANYA. What I mean is, what did you do with your life?

OLGA PAVLOVNA. I gave it to you, my dear. Gave it all to you.

MANYA. Then you wasted it.

OLGA PAVLOVNA. I realize that now.

MANYA. You know, I could make you over, you and Father. Would you like me to make new people out of you?

OLGA PAVLOVNA (*drops another cup*). Stop talking when I'm handling china. Sergey! Sergey! (KARAULOV *enters, a cello bow in his hand.*)

KARAULOV. What's the matter, Olga? You've broken into my Tchaikovsky.

OLGA PAVLOVNA. Tchaikovsky, nothing. I've broken my china. Just listen to your daughter here.

MANYA. Tell me, Father, did you ever ruin a woman?

OLGA PAVLOVNA. There! See what I mean?

KARAULOV. A woman? Why, certainly. There were two women that I nearly ruined.

MANYA. What did they do? Shoot themselves? Jump into the river?

KARAULOV. They took poison. Almost died.

MANYA. Go on, Father. Tell me everything. Where did it happen?

KARAULOV. In our house.

MANYA. How? Tell me how!

KARAULOV. I caught fish for dinner. It poisoned them.

MANYA. Oh, Father, I don't mean stuff like that! I mean—hasn't any woman suffered because she loved you? You're a musician, an artist—you must have been romantic—

OLGA PAVLOVNA. Never.

KARAULOV. Certainly I was.

MANYA. Stop it, you two. Father—go on—did you drive any of your admirers to suicide?

KARAULOV. Look here, young woman. Nearly all my life I've been merely a member of an orchestra, and you should know women ruin themselves only for soloists. Even then they don't die for them.

MANYA. Oh, you're so colorless.

KARAULOV. Colorless, are we? Well, what do you think of that?

MANYA. Oh, if you could just throw me out of the house. At night. When it's freezing. I have no coat, I wrap a shawl about me. The frozen tears fill my eyes and the moaning wind pursues me through the deserted streets. (*Exit, playing the part.*)

OLGA PAVLOVNA. Goodness gracious! What's come over her?

KARAULOV. Love causes that—or indigestion.

OLGA PAVLOVNA. Without a coat—at night—it's love.

KARAULOV. Who can it be?

OLGA PAVLOVNA. I think I can guess. It's a man.

KARAULOV. Never mind the guessing. Better tell me who comes to the house.

OLGA PAVLOVNA. Nowadays the young men don't go to any houses. They know their place—on the porch, but no farther.

KARAULOV. On the porch! Well, who's courting Manya on the porch?

OLGA PAVLOVNA. Nobody, nor anywhere else. People no longer do any courting.

KARAULOV. Then how do they—? Don't they meet, come together somehow—?

OLGA PAVLOVNA. How they do it I don't know and I'm afraid to guess. Most Romeos today are no good. I try to keep them away from here. There's one coming along now to make his morning call. (*Pushes her husband toward the door.*) We must let him think we're out. (*They go. Enter* SENYA, *holding a guitar. He looks up at the windows and takes a seat at the side of the open space opposite the house and facing it.*)

SENYA (*sings*).
> Tell it not to the whole generation,
> This is just between you and me,
> That my spirit is sick with frustration
> And my health not all it should be.

(*He looks up at the windows. Somebody closes one of them.* SENYA *sings in a lower voice.*)
> I know my chances to win her are small
> And as soon as my hopes are dashed to the ground
> On the rocks I'll smash my guitar and all—
> Or perhaps to the junk heap I'll banish its sound.

(*Another window is shut with a bang.* SENYA *sings in a tragic whisper.*)
> My prospects are horribly cheerless,
> Yet I'll fix them up in a while—
> 'Neath a train I will throw myself, fearless,
> And from under the wheels I will smile.

(*One of the windows is flung open and* KARAULOV *sticks his head out.*)

KARAULOV. If you're exerting yourself for Manya's benefit you're only wasting your breath. She's out. You'd better do your singing in that direction. (*Angrily shuts the window.*)

SENYA. Now I've gone and made a mess of it again. (*He walks over*

and taps gently on a window. Both windows are flung open and
KARAULOV *appears in one,* OLGA PAVLOVNA *in the other.* SENYA *speaks
to each in turn.*)

OLGA PAVLOVNA. What do you want?

SENYA. I beg your pardon for disturbing you.

KARAULOV. Anything else?

SENYA (*to* OLGA PAVLOVNA). It did not show much culture on my
part. (OLGA PAVLOVNA *shuts the window.* SENYA *addresses* KARAULOV.)
I mean I want to apologize for the unorganized singing within a resi-
dential zone.

KARAULOV. Is that all?

SENYA. That's all.

KARAULOV (*shuts the window*). Caruso.

SENYA (*withdrawing*). Caruso. What have I done to be called names?
It seems you have to be a born ruffian to get along in this country. (*He
bows to the house with diffident politeness and walks off. The* KARAU-
LOVS *appear on the porch.*)

KARAULOV. I steered him in the wrong direction. Look, what's that?

OLGA PAVLOVNA. Where?

KARAULOV. There, on the path, walking up to Manya.

OLGA PAVLOVNA. Oh, that's engineer Pribylev. I don't mind him.
He's constructing a road here. You know him—Pribylev, Fyodor
Fyodorovich Pribylev—a man of substance, not like those two students—Kostya and that Mohammedan Yakov. Look, he's kissing her
hand.

KARAULOV. You mustn't stare as if it were a house on fire. Just look
indifferent. Breathe the fresh air. But wait a minute, it's no longer
done—is it?—to kiss hands in public?

OLGA PAVLOVNA. That's not in public, it's in the woods.

KARAULOV. There he goes again, he's kissed her palm this time. Even
in the woods there's a limit, you know.

OLGA PAVLOVNA. Oh, well, in his case it's excusable. He has his own
summer house, a good job, and the manners of a gentleman. God grant
it, God grant it!—

KARAULOV. Grant what, to whom?

OLGA PAVLOVNA. Happiness—to Manya. They're coming here.
(*Pushes* KARAULOV *into the house.*)

KARAULOV. Where are you pushing me?

OLGA PAVLOVNA. Get off the porch. Don't be in the way. (*They leave.
Enter* MANYA *and* PRIBYLEV.)

PRIBYLEV. Manya, little Manya. You are an actress. You have no
right to go on the stage until you have known passion. (*He reaches out
his hand to her. She steps aside.*) You think you're running away from
me? No. You're running away from art. Remember, all the great
actresses loved.

MANYA. They didn't love you, did they?

PRIBYLEV. Manya, little Manya. You don't want to understand. Let me explain. (*Takes her hand.*) Let's go to your room.

MANYA. No. I won't understand it in my room either. (*Takes her hand away.*)

PRIBYLEV. Well, now, how is one to get closer to the younger generation? Very well, then. Rebuff me. Drive me away. I'll shut myself up, live only in myself. You don't know the tragedy of a life spent in solitude. (*Rests his head in his hands.*) Would you like to go for a drive in a car with me?

MANYA. No.

PRIBYLEV. Yes, it's bitter to be lonely. How about a motorboat?

MANYA. No, thank you.

PRIBYLEV. Then what is the difference between you and the old-fashioned misses who were swept away by the revolution?

MANYA. They would have believed in this great love of yours. I don't.

PRIBYLEV. Very well. I'll convince you. I will. Meantime, won't you just take a look at my heart, if only out of artistic curiosity?

MANYA. I may some day. Just now I must get on with my work. (*Enter* SENYA.)

PRIBYLEV (*walks out backward*). Manya, little Manya. (*Collides with* SENYA.) What's this, a post? Oh, I beg your pardon, my error. (*Exit.*)

SENYA. I know, he was suggesting something. The nerve of him! I should parry the thrust and strike back— But there you are. I haven't enough arrogance. (*Shouts after* PRIBYLEV.) You're a post yourself! Manya, what is it that your father holds against me?

MANYA (*studying her part*). What makes you think there's anything?

SENYA. There is, I tell you. I asked for you and he sent me in the wrong direction, to the ravine. No, I was born under an unlucky star.

MANYA. What do you mean?

SENYA. They say there are certain sinister constellations—the Crab, Aquarius, and others— Do you believe that? I'm sure I was born under one of the foul things. May I sit down?

MANYA. You may, but you can't stay long. (*Reads her part.*)

SENYA. Of course, with my luck, the only place I could stay for long would be in prison. I'm worried about a certain purely theoretical question. Manya, is my profession a very disgusting one?

MANYA. Why? There's a need for men like you today. You're a technician—

SENYA. Yes, but what kind of technician? A dental technician. My field of activity—pardon the expression—is the oral cavity. I've been wanting to get out of that cavern somehow. I want a life of wide horizons, and what horizons are there in the oral cavity?

MANYA. Well, you should study, try to improve your mind.

SENYA. Don't I do just that? Between you and me, I'm reading the *Complete Encyclopedia*. It's hard, though, damn it!

MANYA. Have you read much of it?

SENYA. I've reached "absurdity," in volume one. Then too, I live according to plan. (*Pulls out a notebook.*) Here is my program. For June—to try to get a second-hand suit. July—to improve my psychology. Manya— (*Makes a movement as if to embrace her but checks himself, his hand still in mid-air.*) Manya, I've decided to be bold. (*Springs to his feet.*) My biography is in your hands!

MANYA. What's the matter with you? (*Lowers the play script.*)

SENYA. I feel just as if I were making a parachute jump from an airplane. The wind is blowing, the earth is five miles below, they're pushing me from behind, but I haven't the nerve to jump. What if the parachute should fail to open? What would be left of me? Only a shapeless mess and memorial services.

MANYA. What's come over you, Senya?

SENYA (*covers his eyes with his hand*). Here goes! I'm jumping. Manya, I love you. I'm flying through space as I wait for an answer. One, two, three, four— (OLGA PAVLOVNA *and her husband hurry out of the house and go to* SENYA.) I love you. Five. Six. Seven.

OLGA PAVLOVNA. What are you up to? Compromising our daughter, with your eyes closed?

SENYA (*opens his eyes*). I've crashed!

OLGA PAVLOVNA. Get this fellow away, Sergey, get him away.

KARAULOV (*takes* SENYA *by the arm and leads him away*). Go for a walk, young man. It's very nice in the woods.

SENYA. Why don't you get to know me, first? Perhaps I am all right.

MANYA. Come to see me, Senya, I like you very much.

SENYA. You do? Me? (*Kisses* KARAULOV.) Oh, Papa! (*Goes out reeling with happiness.*)

MANYA. Why did you drive him away?

OLGA PAVLOVNA. Because you go in for quantity. There are more of them than I can bear. You hold on to Mr. Pribylev, Manya. You don't come across such men twice in your life.

MANYA. What are you talking about?

OLGA PAVLOVNA. We saw how ardently he spoke to you.

KARAULOV. What did he say?

MANYA. A lot of vulgar nonsense.

KARAULOV. What vulgar nonsense?

MANYA. The usual sort.

OLGA PAVLOVNA. Did he show his feelings?

MANYA. You old people are so sexy. "What did he say? How did he say it?" It's positively indecent. I'd like to teach you a lesson, once and for all. Don't look so stunned. Sit down. (KARAULOV *and his wife sit down together on a bench and look at* MANYA *as she walks back and forth*.) I simply can't make out how *I* came to be born of such a family! I forgive Mother—she is a housewife exploited by her husband. But you, Father—you are an artist. Where is your sensitivity? Answer me. And what is it you want, anyway?

OLGA PAVLOVNA. We want your happiness.

MANYA. Oh, fine experts you are, instructors in happiness. Just what is your idea of where I'm to find it?

OLGA PAVLOVNA. In—Fyodor Fyodorovich Pribylev.

MANYA. Pribylev—Pribylev. If I wanted to, I could have a dozen Pribylevs.

KARAULOV. That's just what we're afraid of.

OLGA PAVLOVNA. We want you to settle down, darling, so that we may die in peace.

MANYA. I don't want you to die in peace. Remember, once and for all—I'm going to meet anybody I please—

OLGA PAVLOVNA. Oh!

MANYA. Anywhere I please—

OLGA PAVLOVNA. Oh!

MANYA. And in any way I please.

KARAULOV. All-embracing, indeed.

MANYA. It is. And I will ask you not to interfere in my personal life. It's tactless of you. Try to mend your ways and don't bother me with such trifles as marriage. My mind is occupied with more important matters. I am living a drama. (*Slaps the play script*.) A tragedy. (*Exit*.)

KARAULOV. Why don't you confide in us? You only run to the woods. Is that where you're living your drama?

OLGA PAVLOVNA. A drama. A tragedy. What has befallen us now? (*Enter* ZINA.) Zina, Zina dear. You must help us.

KARAULOV. Yes, Zina, we ask you as an old friend of Manya's.

ZINA. What is it? What has happened?

KARAULOV. Has Manya told you about any tragedy?

ZINA. Why? What has happened?

OLGA PAVLOVNA. We don't know ourselves. But something has happened to her, or is happening right now. Just look at her—

KARAULOV. See how she walks. The poor girl. (*To his wife*.) Let's go into the house or she'll give it to us again. (*They go off. Enter* MANYA. ZINA *quietly steals up behind her*.)

MANYA (*rehearsing*). "What shall I do?" No, that's not the way. "What shall I do? Tell Mother? It will kill her. Go away? But where? And what will happen to my baby, my poor little baby? What kind of life can it have? No, it is better to die."

ZINA. No, no, Manya darling. You mustn't despair. I overheard everything. Surely one does not die because of a thing like that. (*For a moment* MANYA *is at a loss to understand, then she bursts into laughter.*) Of course, you can make your laugh sound natural, you're an actress. But I understand everything.

MANYA. I was just studying my part, learning my lines.

ZINA. That's a lie, Manya. There were tears in your eyes. Of course, one has to tell lies to parents, but to a friend? —I think you're awfully mean. I don't deserve such treatment.

MANYA (*makes a decision*). Very well, then. I do need your help. What shall I do? Tell me. What shall I do?

ZINA. First of all, you mustn't lose courage. Then you must give me your word of honor that you won't try to die, no matter what happens. I won't ask any questions. Tell me just one thing—was it Kostya?

MANYA. I'll tell you later, later.

ZINA. All right. I'll take you to a hospital. No. They might find out who you are. Listen, I know a certain woman, Agrippina Semyonovna. She'll advise you. They all go to her without hesitation.

MANYA. And how do they leave her?

ZINA. With even less hesitation.

MANYA. Let me think. If we go to her, we'll meet those other girls there, those women, won't we?

ZINA. But they don't know you.

MANYA. I'm not afraid of that. I even—but never mind. All right. I'll go.

ZINA. Well, then, we'll take the first train to Moscow, tomorrow morning. I won't ask you any questions, Manya. But was it—Kostya?

MANYA. You'll find out later. But remember, Zina. Not a word to anybody.

ZINA. Manya! (*Points to her own bosom.*) Silent as the grave! (KOSTYA *appears on the balcony.*) Is he the one? He is? I'll leave you alone together. (*Exit.*)

MANYA. I certainly have enough material for my diary today. (KOSTYA, *on the balcony, holds out his hand to* MANYA.)

KOSTYA. I have an awful lot to tell you, Manya.

MANYA. So have I.

KOSTYA. Let's hear.

MANYA. No, you tell me first. (*Pause.*)

KOSTYA. How are you?

MANYA. Fine. (*Pause.*) And you?

KOSTYA. I'm fine. (YAKOV *appears at the door, seizes hold of* KOSTYA *and pulls him inside.*) Blue-nosed governess!

CURTAIN

ACT I

SCENE 2

A room in AGRIPPINA SEMYONOVNA's *apartment. Two doors. A screen.*

AGRIPPINA SEMYONOVNA (*alone, sings*).
> Last night in dreams I saw you
> And drank my fill of joy.
> Ah, could I but thus keep you,
> Nor dawn the bliss destroy.

(*There is a knock at the door.*) Who is it? (*Opens the door. Enter* SENYA.) Oh, it's you! Where have you been? I haven't laid eyes on you for eight long days. Now you turn up during my visiting hours, just when I'm expecting a patient. Do you think I don't see through you? You've chosen to come now so you won't have to stay. And it is for this man that I became a widow.

SENYA. What do you mean? You were made a widow by accident.

AGRIPPINA SEMYONOVNA. No, I became a widow deliberately.

SENYA. Oh, Agrippina Semyonovna!

AGRIPPINA SEMYONOVNA. Agrippina Semyonovna has been my name for thirty years.

SENYA. And what was it the ten years before that?

AGRIPPINA SEMYONOVNA. Are you insinuating that I'm old?

SENYA. Not old, merely not well preserved.

AGRIPPINA SEMYONOVNA. Oh? Then why have you been coming here?

SENYA. On business. You have been getting me gold for dental crowns. But there has been nothing between us.

AGRIPPINA SEMYONOVNA (*weeps*). What is it you feel for me, then?

SENYA. At the moment, only pity.

AGRIPPINA SEMYONOVNA. Then it was out of pity that you hugged me on the couch? For pity that you stayed here for tea? Don't you think you should love me after that rather than pity me?

SENYA. Logically, yes, of course. But physically I can't. You see, Agrippina Semyonovna, in such surroundings as these I am likely to sink to the depths. In the office recently they asked us to write what they called a biography of ourselves. I sat down. There was paper. There was a pen. But no biography. For two whole hours I sat there —and still no biography. Then I began to rake up my past. My whole life lay open in front of me. It was as gray as a mouse. I peeked at what the others were writing. They all had something. One of them had eight dependents. Another one had two convictions. Only I had nothing, as if life had passed me by. I want personal happiness, I tell you. I refuse to live without any biography. Well, I began it yesterday. Prepare yourself. Our relations have exhausted themselves.

AGRIPPINA SEMYONOVNA. Your feelings for me have cooled?

SENYA. Yes, they have. Something lyrical has happened to me. You'd better not ask me what. You won't like it.

AGRIPPINA SEMYONOVNA. Something lyrical, in your spare time? Oh, I must know. Who was it? And where? When?

SENYA. I've met a modern girl. Don't make a pornographic face. There is nothing concrete between us—only abstract strolls in the woods.

AGRIPPINA SEMYONOVNA. In the woods? My God! Who is she?

SENYA (*proudly*). An actress.

AGRIPPINA SEMYONOVNA. An actress? In a theater? Oh, well, if she's an actress, go ahead and ruin yourself. An actress? You're welcome to her. I'm horrified but not jealous.

SENYA. And why not, please?

AGRIPPINA SEMYONOVNA. If I saw a shark swallow you, would I be jealous of the shark? Perhaps you may yet think better of your madness. (*Puts her arms about him.*) Look around—there are plenty of nice women. Look around.

SENYA (*frees himself*). Don't arouse my baser instincts. I have outgrown your apartment. Give me air! Let the fresh breezes of modernity play upon the folds of my topcoat.

AGRIPPINA SEMYONOVNA. But you'll catch a terrible cold. Don't you feel anything for me, Senya?

SENYA. To me you have become a mere experience. Now that I have passed through you, I bid you a farewell. Good afternoon.

AGRIPPINA SEMYONOVNA. Senya dear. (*There is a knock at the door.*) That's a patient. You'll frighten her. Wait here behind the screen— I haven't told you everything yet.

SENYA. No, I'd better go.

AGRIPPINA SEMYONOVNA (*shouts*). We must take leave of each other properly, mustn't we? (SENYA *slips behind the screen. There is another knock at the door.*) Who is it? (*Opens the door. Enter* RAYA.)

RAYA. I telephoned to you. I've come for a consultation.

AGRIPPINA SEMYONOVNA. Step this way. (RAYA *walks into the adjoining room, followed by* AGRIPPINA SEMYONOVNA. *There is a knock at the door.*) Just a moment. Who is it? (*Opens the door. Enter* ZINA.)

ZINA. How do you do? Come in, Manya. Come in. (*She pulls* MANYA *in by the hand. The screen shakes.*)

AGRIPPINA SEMYONOVNA. It's too late for you to be shy, my dear. You should have been shy before. Do both of you want to see me?

ZINA. Oh, no, not I. I'm just her friend.

AGRIPPINA SEMYONOVNA. Wait here, will you? I'll see you in a few minutes. (*Goes into the adjoining room.*)

MANYA (*looks about*). We are the only ones here. I don't think I shall see anybody.

ZINA. Of course not. You mustn't worry about that.

MANYA. You can't imagine how hard it was for me to walk in here. The walls here seem to be ten feet thick and the streets and people a hundred miles away. One feels so alone here, so confined. She must have waited in a room just like this—

ZINA. Who are you talking about?

MANYA. A friend of mine. (*Sits down.*) She sat like this—or like this —probably walked back and forth. (*Paces up and down.*)

ZINA. Manya. Calm yourself. You'll make me cry.

MANYA. I hate the place—I'm going, Zina.

ZINA. Where are you going? Why?

MANYA. Anywhere—but I won't stay here. (*Enter* RAYA, *looking depressed. She sits down and rests her head in her hands. During the following scene* MANYA *frequently turns to look at* RAYA.) I don't understand the women who come here. What drives them to this place? Poverty? Ignorance? Cowardice?

ZINA. You're crazy, Manya. How can you talk of having a child now?

MANYA. When should I have one? When I have a house and furniture and nurses? Is that it? When I'm forty? Then, in addition to the furniture, I shall be permitted to have children as well? How convenient, respectable, and nasty. To be afraid of having a child is to have no faith in the future, no faith in this life of ours— (RAYA *raises her head.*) To destroy what we hold most dear, that gives us more joy than anything. And to remember, perhaps, for the rest of our life this terrible torture chamber. I'm going. (RAYA *springs to her feet and embraces* MANYA.)

RAYA. You're right. Right in every word you say.

ZINA. Now what!

RAYA. I have often thought the same myself. Until the very last moment I couldn't bring myself to do this. And now suddenly you say it so well, in this place, and it is all so true. I'm not coming here again.

MANYA (*rather put out*). Look here. I didn't mean to give anyone advice. I was just speaking for myself. Perhaps our circumstances are different.

RAYA. Are you married?

MANYA. N-no.

RAYA. Neither am I.

MANYA. All the same, my dear, my situation is much better than yours.

RAYA. In what way?

MANYA. It is. Take my word for it. You shouldn't have paid any attention to me.

RAYA. No, no. You spoke wonderfully. I've made up my mind. Let's all go together.

ZINA (*to* MANYA). And your parents? I don't understand you. The thing was discussed thoroughly and you made your decision. Now you change your mind. No, I won't go.

MANYA. Very well. You stay.

ZINA. There's no need of my staying. I think this is indecent of you.

RAYA (*to* MANYA). I would like us to be friends. Shall we?

ZINA. There will be time enough for that. If you've changed your minds you'd better get out of here. (AGRIPPINA SEMYONOVNA *opens the door.*) Oh!

AGRIPPINA SEMYONOVNA. This way, please.

MANYA. I must ask you to excuse me. I've changed my mind.

RAYA. So have I. Pardon me. You mustn't be offended.

ARGIPPINA SEMYONOVNA. Oh, you have both changed your minds? (MANYA *and* RAYA *go out. To* ZINA.) And you?

ZINA. I never had a mind for it at all. I'm only a friend, you know.

AGRIPPINA SEMYONOVNA. But what was the idea?

ZINA. Good-by, Agrippina Semyonovna. Good-by. (*Runs out.*)

AGRIPPINA SEMYONOVNA. Wait a minute. Wait. What's the idea, I wonder. My pocketbook is still here. Perhaps they're from some nosey organization. Perhaps they'll report me. Senya! Come here, Senya. Did you hear them make any threats? Senya! Have you fallen asleep? (SENYA *comes out from behind the screen.*) What's the matter with you? (SENYA *rushes about the room with an expression of utter distress, running into chairs and holding out his hands as if imploring the walls, the door,* AGRIPPINA SEMYONOVNA *to aid him.*) My God! You've gone blind.

SENYA. No, I was blind. Now I've regained my sight. My eyes have been opened. I saw it myself. She was here—in this room—she!

AGRIPPINA SEMYONOVNA. What she? Your actress? My heartiest congratulations. But there were three of them here. Which one was it? Tell me.

SENYA (*sobs*). The one in blue.

AGRIPPINA SEMYONOVNA. Nothing much to look at.

SENYA. Can it have been a hallucination of all five senses? Wake up, Senya. No. She was here. She changed her mind. She went away.

AGRIPPINA SEMYONOVNA. Yes. She went away. Pardon me, but why are you so heartbroken? Is it because she changed her mind that you're worried? Yes, obviously that's it. But—but—wait a minute—why did she choose me, especially? Who told her to come here? And you talk about abstract strolls in the woods? You must have strolled pretty far, indeed. And then after all that you had the nerve to give her my address! My address—to her! Her! My address!

SENYA (*mimics her*). My address! Her! I'm the victim, the sufferer all around. And you—you're just a heartless fool.

AGRIPPINA SEMYONOVNA. Oh? Then everything is all right, thank God.

SENYA. What about my biography?

AGRIPPINA SEMYONOVNA. What about it?

SENYA. It begins with a blot—my usual luck.

CURTAIN

ACT I

SCENE 3

Same as SCENE 1—*in the country.* MANYA *and* KOSTYA *are looking over a plan which is spread out on the table. Gradually their hands and their heads come together.*

KOSTYA. You see this point, Manya? That's where the road will start. From the station, over this way, past your house, like that, then through the woods. Here we'll have a bridge—then follow this line—through the village—and right into the state farm.

MANYA. Pribylev has already shown me all of it.

KOSTYA. Again?

MANYA. What—again?

KOSTYA. No, no. Of course. By all means. We must have absolute freedom, complete faith in one another, and no bourgeois prejudices. We have to outgrow all that. But how can you let him kiss your hand? It's so—

MANYA. So what?

KOSTYA. So unsanitary. As well as vulgar and medieval. Manya, I don't know what we're waiting for. (*Sidles up to* MANYA *and puts his arms about her. Enter* YAKOV.)

YAKOV. May I go through this way?

MANYA. Come here, Yakov.

YAKOV. No. You're hugging each other, what do you want me to do? You only embarrass me, make me feel like the only sober man among a lot of drunks.

MANYA. I need your advice, Yakov. Do you think I should marry him?

YAKOV. Certainly. You would really be doing me a favor. I've had more than enough of him. Do marry him, Manya. You'll make me happy.

KOSTYA (*to* MANYA). I suggest that we tell your family today, and tomorrow we'll go and be registered.

YAKOV. No, that won't do. Better be registered today and tell your parents tomorrow. That's much more certain. As for the wedding celebration, come to the Caucasus with me. It's only two thousand miles away. We'll take an open carriage, stick roses in the horses' manes and tails—curl the bridegroom's hair. It will make you look like a ram—just like a ram. (*To* MANYA.) There won't be any need of curling your hair. We'll fry a mullet. Have you ever tasted mullet? No? Then you've never tasted anything. Also, we'll have a little wine —a bucket of red, another of white. Then we'll give the newlyweds a send-off—at night—with torches—and music—and a big band—a drum, a flute, and a banjo. You'll look about you and there will be the blue sea, the green mountains—but you won't see them, because it will be night—pitch dark. Only the dogs will be barking, and your hearts will melt. Go to the Caucasus. Run and get your tickets.

MANYA. You're a nice man, Yakov.

YAKOV. Of course. A very nice man.

MANYA. Kostya, go get Father. If he starts to scold, pay no attention.

KOSTYA (*walks over to the window. Calls*). Sergey Petrovich— My God, Yakov, I'm too excited to speak.

YAKOV. I can understand your being excited. But why I should be excited beats me. (KARAULOV *comes out of the house.* SENYA *appears from the opposite side. He is extremely agitated and probably not quite sober. In his hand he holds a bottle of wine.*)

KARAULOV. Who called me?

SENYA. I did. (*Puts the bottle on the table with a bang.*) Come on, everybody. Let's make merry at the public memorial services for Senya Perchatkin. He jumped from an airplane—headfirst. But the parachute— (*Points to* MANYA.) though beautiful, was faulty, false, rotten! Yes, rotten! And Senya was smashed to bits. Here before you stands the valiant corpse.

YAKOV. The heat has affected him. Put something on your head, comrade.

SENYA. Shut up, Mohammedan.

KARAULOV. What are you doing here again, may I ask?

SENYA. You're chasing away the wrong man, citizen Karaulov, and anyway it's too late.

MANYA. What's come over you, Senya? Where have you been?

SENYA. Where have you been? Where did you go yesterday afternoon? I loved you decently, in the proper way, and with my own ears I heard you say "I like you, Senya." Why did you say that? Now, goodby. And if the baby you're going to have is a girl, teach her not to tell lies. (*General confusion.* YAKOV *and* KOSTYA *seize* SENYA *by his shoulders.*)

KARAULOV. What baby?

MANYA. It's all nonsense. Don't listen to him. And I didn't go anywhere, either, yesterday. (*Enter* ZINA.)

SENYA. You didn't? (*To* ZINA.) Come here, young lady. Answer as you would on the old-time Judgment Day. Were you at Agrippina Semyonovna's yesterday? I know everything. I can repeat every word that was spoken.

ZINA. Manya dear. I don't understand. I mean I didn't breathe a word to anyone. (KOSTYA *and* YAKOV *release* SENYA.)

SENYA. Is there going to be a little one or not? (ZINA *cries.*) Well? Did I lie? You insulted me, citizen Karaulov, but it turns out that somebody else was the Caruso, not I. (*Exit.*)

ZINA. How did he find out, Manya? I swear it wasn't my fault. Oh,

Manya! (MANYA *pushes her away.* ZINA *runs off.* KARAULOV *stands there stunned.*)

MANYA (*runs up to her father*). It's all a lie, Father. I'll tell you everything. I did go there, it's true, but this is simply ridiculous—

KARAULOV. Ridiculous? You find it ridiculous? Get away from me. Away! (*Staggers into the house.*)

YAKOV. Five minutes ago everything was fine, and suddenly it has all gone wrong, somehow. I'm your friend, Kostya. You understand, don't you? But I wish I understood a little myself. (*Exit.* MANYA *stands leaning against the porch.* KOSTYA *approaches her slowly and looks at her as if unable to recognize her.*)

MANYA. I never thought it would affect Father so.

KOSTYA. Then it is true? No, I don't believe it. I don't believe his foul accusations.

MANYA. Why foul?

KOSTYA. Then it's true?

MANYA. Suppose it is. What difference does it make? We're both new people.

KOSTYA. Both of us? I never did anything rotten. And you—didn't you tell me that you—that I—that for me—oh, it's terrible.

MANYA. I do love you, Kostya.

KOSTYA. But after telling me that— No, not after, before, you allowed some cad, some bandit— Oh—oh—oh!

MANYA. Why a cad?

KOSTYA. Because he's a skunk. Who is it?

MANYA. Do you want to know his social category or his profession?

KOSTYA. I want to murder him.

MANYA. Kostya! Was I wrong about you?

KOSTYA. You?— About me? You have the gall to be wrong about me? That's the limit. (*He rushes off, his hands clasped to his head.* YAKOV *appears at one side, catches him, and leads him away.*)

YAKOV (*as he goes off*). He's a bit excited, isn't he? (*Points at* KOSTYA.) Never mind. He's taken himself in hand already.

MANYA (*calls out*). Kostya, Kostya. (*Stamps her foot.*) So? Very well. (*She cries out after him.*) You call yourself a new man? You're nothing but a hypocrite. (*She runs into the house. Immediately afterward* KARAULOV *comes out, with a towel wrapped around his head. He turns, faces the door, and shouts to* MANYA.)

KARAULOV. Keep out of my sight, wretched girl. It's only by chance that I haven't had a stroke. But your mother will have one. I swear she will. Oh, Lord! How shall I tell her? (*Turns and sees his wife approaching with a bag in her hands.*) Oh!

OLGA PAVLOVNA. What's the towel for? It's not such a hot day.

KARAULOV. It certainly is.

OLGA PAVLOVNA. I haven't noticed it.

KARAULOV. You will. Sit down. (OLGA PAVLOVNA, *still standing,*

takes several small packages from the bag and places them on the table.
KARAULOV, *aside.*) I must begin way back. Olga, there was a country
called Sparta, remember?

OLGA PAVLOVNA. Would you like some buttermilk?

KARAULOV. What I'm telling you is important. There was once a
country called Sparta.

OLGA PAVLOVNA. For all I care.

KARAULOV. Listen to me. It will get more interesting further on.
In that country of Sparta there was a rock from which they hurled
young people.

OLGA PAVLOVNA. They did that to hooligans, I suppose.

KARAULOV. No, no. They did it to all the youngsters.

OLGA PAVLOVNA. My, my. They certainly were strict.

KARAULOV. They did it in order to accustom their youths to every
kind of hardship. A boy would be thrown from the rock two or three
times and then he would come up from under the rock a real man. Do
you understand? They hardened the boys to shocks. When they grew
up the boys could stand anything. If you said to such a Spartan: "Your
daughter, Manya, is going to have—some unpleasantness," he wouldn't
turn a hair. "Let her have as much unpleasantness as she likes," he
would say.

OLGA PAVLOVNA. Really?

KARAULOV. It would be well for you to imitate those Spartans.

OLGA PAVLOVNA. Do you want me to start jumping off rocks? This
weather makes you silly. You'd better come to the point.

KARAULOV. Well, I'm getting—closer to it. Now, take France. A
flourishing country, one might think—Paris, with its Bois de Boulogne
all round it. Yet France is in a fix—there aren't enough children.

OLGA PAVLOVNA. And a good thing, too—there's less mischief done.

KARAULOV. But the nation is dying out— You must think of the
principle of the thing.

OLGA PAVLOVNA. I'm too busy for principles.

KARAULOV. Don't you understand? The poor French women offer up
prayers to this supreme being, as it is now called, to send them children.
And we don't appreciate them.

OLGA PAVLOVNA. Don't appreciate whom?

KARAULOV. Children, I said children. Although I'm not French I
too wish we had a baby.

OLGA PAVLOVNA. We? Your brain's getting soft.

KARAULOV. No, no. I mean if Manya presented us with a grandchild.

OLGA PAVLOVNA. It won't be for a long time yet. First she has to
get married.

KARAULOV. Not so long, any more. Really, not long, I'm telling you.
Sit down.

OLGA PAVLOVNA. Has somebody proposed to her? Who is the man?

KARAULOV. Not proposed, exactly, but something like it. Just sit down. You must prepare yourself for a great—surprise. (*Removes the towel from his head.*) She told me herself. To make it short—Manya's going to have a baby. (OLGA PAVLOVNA *staggers and drops down on a bench.*)

KARAULOV. Didn't I tell you to sit down? (*Puts the towel around her head.*)

OLGA PAVLOVNA. Manya? A baby? What kind of baby?

KARAULOV. Well, just a tiny one.

OLGA PAVLOVNA. Whose baby?

KARAULOV. I can't know all the details, can I? (OLGA PAVLOVNA *hangs her head, as though in a stupor.*) Never mind, never mind. Take a deep breath of air. Remember the Spartans.

OLGA PAVLOVNA. Manya! Where is she? My legs have gone back on me. Manya! (MANYA *comes out of the house. The two women rush into each other's arms.* OLGA PAVLOVNA *cries.*) Manya, my darling.

MANYA. I didn't know you were back, Mother. You've heard? But it's laughable, ridiculous. You mustn't let yourself get worked up like that over such trivial things.

OLGA PAVLOVNA (*pushes her away*). Trivial things? You call that a trivial thing? Your mother has all but had a stroke, and you—you talk and smile as if nothing had happened. A decent girl would cry her eyes out, would jump into the river to drown herself and to spare her parents. Don't you realize? It's a terrible calamity, Manya. A terrible calamity.

MANYA. There hasn't been any terrible calamity and there isn't any now.

OLGA PAVLOVNA. Manya, I won't stand for such cynicism.

MANYA. Very well, then. You won't hear another word out of me. (*Goes toward the house.*)

OLGA PAVLOVNA (*to* KARAULOV). And you allow this?

KARAULOV (*follows* MANYA). Manya. Don't be impertinent.

MANYA (*turns around*). Wha-at?

KARAULOV (*retreats to where his wife is*). I'm afraid of her. (MANYA *exits.* KARAULOV *and his wife sit down together.*)

OLGA PAVLOVNA. What is the world coming to! No God. No shame. Manya's going to have a baby. It's all the doing of the Bolsheviks.

KARAULOV. I don't know. It may be one who isn't a Bolshevik.

OLGA PAVLOVNA. But who is the man, I'd like to know? Who? If the villain is a decent fellow, everything will be all right. If not, it will be terrible. Manya—my daughter Manya. Did she learn such things from us? It's all so sudden, so impossible to understand.

KARAULOV. Science will explain it in time.

OLGA PAVLOVNA. In time. But what shall we do now? (*They both sob. Enter* PRIBYLEV. KARAULOV *and his wife try to appear calm.*)

PRIBYLEV. How do you do, Olga Pavlovna? How do you so, Sergey Petrovich? Are you upset about something?

OLGA PAVLOVNA. No, nothing. On the contrary. (*Dries her tears.*)

KARAULOV. We aren't upset about anything.

PRIBYLEV. That's fine. I may speak to you then?

KARAULOV. Why not?

PRIBYLEV. In these days—parents of grown children—well, I know it is the fashion to ignore them—

KARAULOV. Yes, that does happen in other families.

PRIBYLEV. For myself, I look at the matter in the old-fashioned way, and I have decided to talk to the parents first. I want to speak to you about your daughter. (*The old couple exchange glances.*) I know her. Know her intimately, I might say.

KARAULOV (*with awakening hope*). Oh, yes. Oh, yes.

PRIBYLEV. I love her. But there is something strange in our relations.

KARAULOV. You love her! We're not angry any more.

PRIBYLEV. You have no reason to be angry. I'm ready to marry her tomorrow.

OLGA PAVLOVNA. Then God is still in His Heaven. You're a noble man, Fyodor Fyodorovich. Sergey—

KARAULOV. Olga! (*They fall into each other's arms.*)

OLGA PAVLOVNA. You don't know what a comfort you are, Fyodor Fyodorovich.

KARAULOV. He isn't Fyodor Fyodorovich any more. Fedya! My good boy, Fedya. *(Puts his arms about* PRIBYLEV.)

PRIBYLEV. But your daughter Maria—

KARAULOV. Call her Manya—just Manya.

PRIBYLEV. It seems that Manya has rather whimsical views about marriage. She's full of whims.

OLGA PAVLOVNA. Of course, in her condition, that's to be expected.

PRIBYLEV. Then I can depend upon you to help?

KARAULOV. To help? What a man! He wants us to believe he's shy with women. Oh, Fedya, Fedya! We ought to open a bottle on an occasion like this. Ah! Here's the very thing. (*Fills three glasses from the bottle left by* SENYA.) To Manya, yourself, and—it. (*Drinks.*)

PRIBYLEV. Pardon me, but who is it?

OLGA PAVLOVNA. You're a sly one. But it's too late. We know everything.

KARAULOV. Yes, Fedya. It wasn't nice of you. You might have told us before. Instead, we learned about it only today, and from strangers, too. Like a bombshell it was. Bang! Manya is going to have a baby.

PRIBYLEV. What baby?

KARAULOV. That's just what we asked. My wife nearly lost the use of her legs. (PRIBYLEV *sits down.*) Yes, that's just the way she flopped down. (PRIBYLEV *gets up.* KARAULOV *pours wine into* PRIBYLEV'S *glass.*)

PRIBYLEV. Whose baby?

KARAULOV. Yours, my boy. Yours. (PRIBYLEV *steps away from* KARAULOV. KARAULOV *pours wine on the ground.*)

PRIBYLEV. Are you mad?

KARAULOV. I will be in a minute.

CURTAIN

ACT II

Same as SCENE 1, ACT 1. *Enter* YAKOV. *He makes one or two turns about the open space in front of the house.* KOSTYA *tags after him, holding onto his sleeve.*

KOSTYA. Wait until I've come to the end, Yakov.

YAKOV. I've already heard it twice. You come to the end and then you begin again. You're driving me crazy with your psychology.

KOSTYA. My nerves are all upset, Yakov. I'm almost fit for a lunatic asylum. And I haven't a soul to share my feelings.

YAKOV (*sits down*). All right. Go ahead. I'll take my share.

KOSTYA. Listen. Manya was meeting that fellow before I even knew her. That's so, isn't it? All right.

YAKOV. I don't see how it's all right.

KOSTYA. Wait. You must analyze the thing. Then she fell in love with me. That's a fact. You saw it for yourself. Then, what has changed? Nothing, I say. Absolutely nothing. To be jealous, and especially of the past, is low, it's medieval. You must understand this, Yakov: the love that she felt—no, it wasn't love—merely infatuation—not even that—just momentary forgetfulness—well, that's all over now. It's a thing of the past. Isn't it? You agree with me, don't you?

YAKOV. No, I don't. In the first place, this past you're talking about is pregnant with consequences, so to speak—

KOSTYA. Pregnant, did you say? Oh, yes, pregnant.

YAKOV. In the second place, my opinion of Manya is better than that. She's not the sort of girl to yield to a momentary passion. No, this was a case of genuine feeling. She must have cared for him—

KOSTYA. You think so? But who is he, damn his soul? Well, I'm going to find him. I'll fix him. I'll have my revenge.

YAKOV. You'll have your revenge? Splendid. Tell me how.

KOSTYA. I'd like to knock him down while she's around—I'd like to— Oh, what wouldn't I do to him!

YAKOV. The point is—what *would* you do to him? You don't know. That's not going to get you anywhere. *I'll* tell you what to do. Take this dagger, take it, I tell you. Go to her and make her tell you who the man is. Then find him. Call his name. When he turns around, shoot him six times. Then burn his house. As for her, into the river with a stone around her neck. That's how we do it in the Caucasus.

KOSTYA. You're even worse than I. You're a complete lunatic. Fool! Tie a stone around Manya's neck? Why, I love her, you idiot. *I* was the wrong one, the guilty one. She called me a hypocrite. She was right. I behaved like some little property owner in the Middle Ages. We are men of the new order, Yakov, and look at how I behaved!

YAKOV. We should be of the new order, but the only new thing about you is your cap. Remember, when this—well, let's say he's a boy—when he's born—although he won't be altogether yours, you know—he'll be clever and handsome—not at all like you, of course.

KOSTYA. Yes, another man's child—it's terrible.

YAKOV. Then, just imagine this—you're walking in the street with her and she is greeted by some man. What if he should turn out to be the one! Eh? He, himself!

KOSTYA. I won't allow her to return the greetings of any men. But after all, why not? Let her greet men if she likes.

YAKOV. Here you are sitting on the very same bench where he and Manya probably sat and kissed each other. (KOSTYA *jumps up, picks up a stone and shakes it as if to strike* YAKOV.) The new man of the Stone Age?

KOSTYA. Don't try to frighten me! I'll marry her, no matter what you say, and kill these low feelings in me.

YAKOV. It won't work! Kill the feelings first, then marry afterward. (*Walks toward the house.*)

KOSTYA. Wait. Suppose you fell in love with someone and she left you for another man?

YAKOV. Left me—for another man? Impossible.

KOSTYA. Let's put it this way. Suppose you fell in love and then suddenly you learned she loved someone else. What would you do then?

YAKOV. In that case I would wrap up my love in a clean handkerchief like something precious and I wouldn't show it to anybody.

KOSTYA. Has that ever happened to you?

YAKOV. Never. (*Enter* PRIBYLEV *with a drawing that is rolled up. He stops to observe the students, who do not notice him.*)

PRIBYLEV. Yes, they're both young and they live in the same house with her. But which one is it? I wonder. Let's find out. (*Walks up to them.*) Hello. I want to speak to you. I must submit the plans for the road in five days. But I'm afraid I've made a mistake. (*Unrolls the drawing.*) You know, we have the road crossing the stream twice. Is that necessary?

KOSTYA. Well, the stream bends and forms a loop.

PRIBYLEV. But why do we have to pick just the loop to cross over? Can't we go farther back, say, to this point? Then we'd need no bridges and be much nearer to the station besides. (*Looks at the students intently.*)

YAKOV. Yes, we might do that. You're quite right.

KOSTYA. It would be an improvement.

PRIBYLEV. Then you both agree with me?

YAKOV. Absolutely.

KOSTYA. Entirely.

PRIBYLEV. That's fine. In that case the road will run right through the spot we're standing on now. This house will have to be torn down, of course. (*He looks at* KOSTYA, *then at* YAKOV.)

YAKOV. Couldn't we shift the road to the north a little?

KOSTYA. Or to the south?

PRIBYLEV. To the north we'd run into the ravine and to the south there's the stream.

YAKOV AND KOSTYA (*together*). That's bad.

PRIBYLEV. You both seem to be quite upset about it. Very strange. Of course, I'm sorry too that the Karaulovs' house must come down, but you seem to take it too much to heart. I wonder why. Is it because the party concerned is to be the father-in-law of one of you?

KOSTYA. What father-in-law? We're bachelors.

YAKOV. Wait a minute. I have a better idea.

PRIBYLEV. What's that?

YAKOV. We could start the road the other side of the station. Right there. It would reduce the distance and besides the ground is more level.

PRIBYLEV. Think so? Yes, yes. But then we'd have to— No, no. Your plan won't do.

YAKOV. It will do perfectly. And it will also bring the road so much closer to the station.

PRIBYLEV. No. No. We'll have to find some other solution. Let's go. (*Exit with* YAKOV.)

KOSTYA (*looks at the drawing*). Will it really be necessary to tear down the house? (*Enter* SENYA. *He looks around furtively and notices* KOSTYA. *For a few seconds they stare at each other.*)

SENYA. Hail to the victor—the champion. (*Salutes* KOSTYA *with raised fist and walks past him challengingly.*) Caruso! If it were a real person that had won out over me, I wouldn't mind. But this—! What does Manya see in you? You won't answer? Proud, I suppose, that you're going to be a father. I'm going to make a monkey out of you!

KOSTYA. A father? What are you talking about?

SENYA. Scared, are you? All right. I won't touch you. Just tell me one thing—what did she see in you?

KOSTYA. Oh! So you think I was the one?

SENYA. Weren't you? No? (KOSTYA *shakes his head sadly.*) Do you swear? Oh, hell! And I couldn't sleep all night, thinking it was you. A student, with a lot of cheek, and good looking. So you too were fooled. I'm really glad. (*He shakes hands with* KOSTYA. *Enter* PRIBYLEV. SENYA *nudges* KOSTYA.) I have my suspicions about this fellow, too.

KOSTYA. You're way off! Why, he wants to tear this house down.

SENYA. That's only a blind: he'll tear one down and build another. Diplomacy, I call it.

KOSTYA. Think so? (*The men stroll about, looking at one another suspiciously.* SENYA *passes* KOSTYA *and nods in* PRIBYLEV's *direction.*)

SENYA. A champion if ever there was one. All gloss and polish. A world beater. I swear he's the man. (PRIBYLEV *walks up to* SENYA, *takes hold of his arm, and draws him aside.*)

PRIBYLEV. I believe you met Manya at—that creature's place.

SENYA. Suppose I did.

PRIBYLEV. Tell me. Was there a man with her? (*Nods in* KOSTYA's *direction.*) Was my assistant there?

SENYA (*with evident pleasure*). Your assistant? No. He had nothing to do with it. (*Shouts.*) An error in judgment, Kostya! He too is a victim of misunderstanding. (KOSTYA *walks over and they both shake hands with* PRIBYLEV.) And I thought you were the man. I said to myself, a fellow with a university education is capable of anything. Then it wasn't you? I'm glad to hear it. Sit down, won't you, please? I don't mind having been fooled, as long as it's in such good company. But look here. All the leading men are present and none of them is guilty. Then who is it? The mystery's as thick as ever. Sh-sh—we've overlooked Yakov. Maybe he's the Caruso.

KOSTYA. No, not Yakov. I'm sure of that.

PRIBYLEV. Well, who is it, then? Who is it? (*Enter* YAKOV.)

YAKOV. That's just the place for the road. (*The others walk around* YAKOV *and stare at him.*)

SENYA. He's the only one it could be. I'm positive.

YAKOV. What are you up to? (*The men continue to walk around him.*) Playing some game, are you? I'm going to look the place over from the other side. (*Exit.*)

KOSTYA. No, it's not he, I tell you.

PRIBYLEV (*slaps his forehead*). I have it. She's an actress. We've forgotten about the theater—the actors.

KOSTYA. Actors? Oh, yes. The actors. Yes.

PRIBYLEV. Rehearsals, you know—wings—the stage curtain—it all invites that sort of thing.

KOSTYA (*moans*). Wings—curtains—

SENYA. The prompter's box!

KOSTYA. Might it really have been an actor? Insolent, clean shaven, with padded shoulders? (MANYA *enters and walks toward the house. She stops some distance behind the group.*)

SENYA. I propose that the three of us form a coalition of the Big Four. We'll find him. I'll ransack the—footlights. Comrades, to the theater. (*They all turn around and are overcome at the sight of* MANYA. KOSTYA *takes to his heels.* PRIBYLEV *lifts his hat, bows politely, and walks away.* SENYA *removes his hat and looks about him but has not the courage to leave.*)

MANYA. What are you doing here?

SENYA. I? Well, I was taking a walk—and I lost my way.

MANYA. Yesterday you overheard my secret and betrayed me. Why did you do it, Senya? Have I ever harmed you? Did I ever promise you anything? What did you gain by it? Everybody has deserted me. I'm all alone. Not a soul to speak to. That's what you've done. And you were improving your psychology. You dreamt of horizons. I rather admired you for it. I thought there was something fine, something different, in you. I even thought that you, Senya, that you— (*She leaves him and walks to the house.*)

SENYA. I—I—Manya! (MANYA *enters the house.*) I disgraced her and she—she admired me. (*Sits down on the bench and sings.*)

> A black hat I'll put on
> To the Crimean beaches I'll go,
> For the rest of my life I'll sit upon
> The sands where my tears will flow.

Citizen Semyon Perchatkin is in the dock, standing before the bar of Soviet public opinion. The cross-examination begins.

"Semyon Perchatkin, do you admit you're a skunk?"

"I do."

"Do you admit that you blabbed yesterday like a common fisherman?"

"I do."

"What lies can you invent in defense of your conduct?"

"Citizen Prosecutor, I shall pay for my backsliding. I swear by the holy ikon."

(*Aside.*) The defendant gulps his tears.

"In view of his complete, unreserved confession, the defendant, Semyon Perchatkin, is sentenced to a punch on the jaw." (*He inflicts the punch upon himself.*) "Clear the courtroom."

(*Exit* SENYA. OLGA PAVLOVNA *comes out of the house with* KARAULOV, *who holds a medicine bottle and a wine glass in his hands.*)

KARAULOV. Take the drops, Olga.

OLGA PAVLOVNA. My soul is sick, you can't give drops to it.

KARAULOV. Olga, we must keep calm when we talk to Manya. She's an actress and a very sensitive girl. Yesterday you nearly told her to jump into the river and drown herself.

OLGA PAVLOVNA. "An actress. A successful actress." Lord save us from such success. She got the bouquets, all right. She's famous. She would have done better as a typist without fame.

KARAULOV. But one must help a daughter.

OLGA PAVLOVNA. How?

KARAULOV. Haven't we already decided that?

OLGA PAVLOVNA. We have.

KARAULOV. Then everything is all right. You are a woman of rare beauty—spiritual beauty, Olga. Now I'll call Manya. Don't scold her. Talk to her quietly, with kindness. (*Calls out.*) Manya dear! Manya! (*To* OLGA PAVLOVNA.) Keep cool. God bless you.

OLGA PAVLOVNA. You mustn't get excited either, the Lord help you. (*They make the sign of the cross over each other. Enter* MANYA. KARAULOV *pours the drops into the glass, which he places on the table.*)

KARAULOV. Well, here we are. Manya, for the moment we are not your parents but your friends—yes, friends. We want you to talk to us. You're in trouble. That is, no, perhaps you're happy. Just the same, we want to help you.

MANYA. Thank you very much.

KARAULOV (*to* OLGA PAVLOVNA). You see—everything is all right, we're getting along fine. Manya, we *would* like to know who he is—the guilty one.

MANYA. Nobody. I'm the guilty one.

OLGA PAVLOVNA. You alone? I can't possibly believe that.

KARAULOV. Sh-sh— All the same, Manya, I think you ought to tell us who he is and where he is—I mean your—

MANYA. My lover?

OLGA PAVLOVNA. Oh!

KARAULOV. It's all right. Be brave. (*To* MANYA.) Yes, that's what I mean. Where is he?

MANYA. Gone away.

KARAULOV. Where to?

MANYA. A—construction project.

OLGA PAVLOVNA. Which one? There are so many of them these days.

MANYA. Let's say—Siberia.

KARAULOV. Do you write to him there?

MANYA. No. Since then he's moved to another construction project.

OLGA PAVLOVNA. A fly-by-night!

KARAULOV. Sh—sh— Here, take some drops. (*To* MANYA.) Don't pay any attention to her. She's old, you know. Why, the man was simply transferred, sent to another place, and he went—that's all. And how soon will he be back, Manya?

MANYA. He will never come back.

OLGA PAVLOVNA. Is he dead?

MANYA. No. We just separated.

OLGA PAVLOVNA. Has he deserted you?

MANYA. No, I deserted him.

OLGA PAVLOVNA. You did? Oh, my God! (KARAULOV *quickly reaches for the glass with the medicine.*) These surprises are enough to kill you.

KARAULOV. There's nothing surprising about it. If I were in her place I would not only have deserted him—I would have taken the son-of-a— H'm! (*Drinks the medicine himself.*) Oh, well, now everything has been cleared up, thank God. Everything will be all right,

Manya. Don't be upset. Just go on working, playing. As for the baby, we'll bring it up, we'll nurse it and give it an education. Manya—my silly little girl. (MANYA *impulsively embraces her father, then her mother.*)

MANYA. You're a marvelous old couple. You deserve a medal. You've come through the most difficult test. Soon your trials will be over. Thank you. (*To her father.*) You'll make a fine Young Communist, Father.

KARAULOV. You bet I will.

OLGA PAVLOVNA. Don't corrupt your father, too, Manya. We'll have Mikhailov to act as godfather at the christening.

KARAULOV. He can't. He's a Communist.

OLGA PAVLOVNA. Even a Communist is permitted to do it for friends.

MANYA. But why the christening?

OLGA PAVLOVNA. The child must have a knowledge of God, mustn't it? I wouldn't let it grow up like the Nikolayev children. They weren't even given good Christian names. They called the boy Eros and the girl Erotica. Why, the little pagans don't know God when they see His image. One day they passed a church that had the image of St. Nicholas outside, blessing the passers-by. (*She raises her hand as if making the sign of the cross.*) Eros saw it and asked: "What is the citizen voting for?" St. Nicholas voting! Just imagine! No, you may write to the papers about me but I won't hold an unbaptized child in my arms.

MANYA. And I won't allow the child to be baptized.

KARAULOV. Sh-sh— We'll allow the child to enjoy complete freedom of conscience. When it comes of age it can be baptized any way it likes.

OLGA PAVLOVNA. Summer makes you silly.

MANYA. I don't know what you're arguing about. I'm not going to have the child brought up at home.

OLGA PAVLOVNA. Oh, then you'll let him grow up a guttersnipe?

MANYA. That doesn't follow. There are children's homes and public nurseries.

OLGA PAVLOVNA. Public nurseries are only for public children.

KARAULOV. Hush—or I'll give you the drops. Don't worry, Manya. We'll love it with all our hearts. Of course, if it happens to be a boy, I'll give him a spanking whenever necessary.

MANYA. What, you'll give my son a spanking?

KARAULOV. That is, if he does any mischief.

MANYA. Never. I won't allow my child to be tortured. You'll spank him, will you, the poor little thing? You're a stupid, spiteful old man. I can't entrust his education to you.

KARAULOV. Very well. Good. I won't spank him. Let him grow up to be a ruffian.

OLGA PAVLOVNA. You'll be the first to cry about it.

MANYA. I don't care if I do. I won't let anybody beat him.

KARAULOV. Why beat him? I'll educate him, teach him music. Of course, the cello has gone out of fashion; you prefer a kettle-drum solo. However, I have books that will develop his mind.

MANYA. Some out-dated junk, I suppose.

KARAULOV. Then you don't believe he needs any culture?

MANYA. Bourgeois culture must be taken with reservation. A great deal of the learning that sent you into raptures is now unintelligible and harmful.

KARAULOV. Oh, you find it unintelligible and harmful, do you? You don't trust me? All right. Now I know what to do. (*Runs into the house.*)

OLGA PAVLOVNA. Instead of being grateful to her father, she only tortures him. (KARAULOV *runs out of the house with a pile of books.*)

KARAULOV. I've been saving these "harmful books" as treasures for my grandchildren. Now it seems I've only been wasting my time. They can't understand them. Very well, then. (*Selects a book.*) *A Hero of Our Time.* No, Mr. Lermontov, there are no more heroes and our time is past. You thought your Lieutenant Pechorin was a grand romantic figure. He's nothing of the kind. He's a White Guard officer of the Caucasian front. He is an enemy to be destroyed. (*Throws the book to the ground.*)

OLGA PAVLOVNA (*brings him the medicine glass*). Take this, Sergey.

KARAULOV (*overturns the glass and selects another book*). Un-intelligible. (*Throws it away.* OLGA PAVLOVNA *and* MANYA *run about picking up the books.* KARAULOV *takes another one.*) Turgenev— *Breakfast at the Marshal's.* Is that intelligible? No, what you want is a feed at the Commissar's (*Throws the book after the others.*) The old culture has been sentenced to death. (*Selects another book, brandishes it, then checks himself.*) Pushkin. No, dearest friend, forgive me, I can't throw you away. (*Presses the book to his breast and goes inside the house.*)

MANYA (*follows* KARAULOV *with the books she has picked up from the ground*). You've gone out of your mind, Father. We shall never give these up.

OLGA PAVLOVNA. Hitler. A regular Hitler. He's stripped poor old Turgenev naked. (*Enter* PRIBYLEV. *He makes a bow to* OLGA PAVLOVNA.)

PRIBYLEV. Who's been shouting here? Oh, books on the steps?

OLGA PAVLOVNA (*walks to the house, sobbing a little*). We were just —reading aloud. (*Enters the house.* PRIBYLEV *shrugs his shoulders, pokes around with his cane among the books left on the steps, picks up a notebook, and reads.*)

PRIBYLEV. "The Diary of Manya Karaulova" A diary? (*Opens it, looks about him. Conceals it in the inside pocket of his jacket.*) Interesting. (*Exit* PRIBYLEV. *Enter* RAYA *from the opposite side with* ZINA. RAYA *carries a small traveling bag.*)

ZINA. I recognized you right away at the station. This is the Karaulovs' house. Something terrible has happened here.

RAYA. What is it?

ZINA. They found out everything. That she went to Agrippina Semyonovna and all the rest. Both her parents were stricken. All her admirers have made themselves scarce. And now there's a regular campaign against Manya. (*Calls out.*) Manya! I think it serves her right, though. She was too proud—considering what she did. Of course, I don't wish her anything bad, but let her suffer a little. (*Calls out.*) Manya! There's somebody here to see you. (*Enter* MANYA.)

RAYA. Manya!

MANYA. Raya!

ZINA (*to* MANYA). How thin you've become!

MANYA. Not at all.

ZINA. Of course, one can't bring back the past, but you mustn't lose heart.

MANYA. What makes you speak like that? Nothing has changed for me.

ZINA. I don't know. The boys used to overrun this place. Now they all seem to be on their vacations.

MANYA. That's a lie. They're all here. And if I wish I can be married tomorrow.

ZINA. Is that so? I'd better hurry and prepare a dress for the wedding. (*Exit.*)

RAYA. She's so spiteful.

MANYA. She has always been envious of me. And she's going to envy me still more. Raya, dear. I didn't want to say anything in Zina's presence but it's true that I'm having lots of trouble. It's all harder and more complicated than I thought.

RAYA. Of course it's hard, but what satisfaction one gets in overcoming every obstacle! You know, I've become much calmer again, somehow. And oh—I'll love it so. Will you love yours, Manya?

MANYA. Yes, of course. Raya, there's something I want to ask you: Have you—a—what do they call it—an independent income?

RAYA. No. I'm still at college.

MANYA. Pardon my asking, but is he—going to marry you?

RAYA. No. I haven't seen him for two months. And I don't want to see him ever again.

MANYA. Oh, oh! And your parents?

RAYA. Only my father is living. He's an old man. And the Jews are awfully strict. He doesn't know anything yet but he looks at me strangely.

MANYA. Oh, what have I done! Raya, I feel that I have done something terrible. Why did you believe what I said that time?

RAYA. I still believe it.

MANYA. No, no. I was wrong. There's no earthly reason why a young woman should burden herself with a child. In fact, she mustn't do it. You especially, Raya, in your circumstances. You must forgive me. Please go and see Agrippina Semyonovna again.

RAYA. What's the matter with you, Manya?

MANYA. Nothing's the matter with me. I'm talking about you.

RAYA. It isn't really so bad. This fall I'll have a draftsman's job. I just have to manage somehow for a year. It's Father I'm worried about.

MANYA. I shall never forgive myself. (*Enter* YAKOV.)

RAYA. Yakov? (YAKOV *stops short, disconcerted.*)

MANYA. Do you know him?

RAYA. Of course. We're in the same department. How do you happen to be here, Yakov?

YAKOV. I'm taking a practical course. (OLGA PAVLOVNA'S *head appears in a window.*)

OLGA PAVLOVNA. Manya. Father is tearing up his music! (MANYA *runs to the house.*)

RAYA. Who is her father?

YAKOV. A very fine man.

RAYA. Why haven't you come to see me for six whole months?

YAKOV. I came several times in the beginning but you were out.

RAYA. And then?

YAKOV. Then I was too busy. (*Sheets of music fly out of the window.*) He's suffering from nerves. (*A bound book comes hurtling through the air.*) Let's go somewhere else. We're not safe here.

RAYA (*follows* YAKOV). There have been many changes in my life, Yakov— (*Enter* KOSTYA, *who walks over to them and takes hold of* YAKOV'S *arm.*)

KOSTYA. Raya! How are you? No, I have no time to be surprised. Yakov, I need you—right now—just for a moment— My life depends on it. (*Exit* RAYA.)

YAKOV. If you load a wagon with a fourth of a ton, the ox will drag it. Make it half a ton and the ox will still drag it. But make it a ton and the ox will turn around and kick you to hell. (YAKOV *tries to get away but* KOSTYA *holds him back.*)

KOSTYA. Stop. It's not I who hold you back now. It's an entirely new man, whom you don't know yet. Until now my feelings and my will went their separate ways. Something like Lermontov—

YAKOV. I have no time to talk to Lermontov. Perhaps I'm beginning to get a psychology of my own. (*Tries to break away.*)

KOSTYA (*shouts*). Will you hear me out at least once, you blasted idiot? Yakov, listen! Congratulate me—I'm no longer a Lermontov.

YAKOV. I believe you.

KOSTYA. Listen! Only twenty minutes ago I had fallen so low that I tried with Pribylev and Perchatkin to guess who Manya's friend might be. Now that's all in the distant past. I have definitely rid my-self of the feudal slaveowner, the cheap romanticist, and the Othello in me—

YAKOV. And all in twenty minutes. Good for you!

KOSTYA. Pribylev and Perchatkin are smug Philistines. They both deserted Manya, but I love her as much as ever. I sincerely want to marry her. I have to marry her—I simply must. Yakov, it's absolutely necessary that I should marry her.

YAKOV. Then why try to persuade me?

KOSTYA. It's settled. If she forgives me, come in ten minutes to con-gratulate me.

YAKOV. All right. Only look out, or Leo Tolstoy will come to life in you five minutes before that time. (*Exit in* RAYA's *direction.*)

KOSTYA. I'll knock at the door and say with simple frankness: "Manya, I have erased the past. And now let's go and write our names in the marriage register." (KOSTYA *makes a vigorous gesture and walks toward the house. On the way he crosses* PRIBYLEV's *path.* KOSTYA *stops.* PRIBYLEV *knocks at the door.* MANYA *comes out.* KARAULOV *and his wife look out of the window. During* PRIBYLEV's *speech,* KOSTYA *slowly advances, his face showing increasing amazement.*)

PRIBYLEV. Manya! My love is stronger than anything that has hap-pened in the past. I ask you to be my wife. (KOSTYA *is petrified.*)

OLGA PAVLOVNA. God is still in His Heaven.

MANYA. My good friend, I cannot say that I love you but I cannot help respecting you. (*Looks at* KOSTYA.) While others insult me and run at the sight of me, you act like a real man. My answer is "Yes," and I'll try to love you. (*She holds out her hand to* PRIBYLEV. OLGA PAV-LOVNA *and her husband come out on the porch.*)

OLGA PAVLOVNA. You won't need to try. How can one help loving you, Fyodor Fyodorovich?

KARAULOV. You're a man of shining virtues, Fedya. Don't argue— you are. You—you— (*Collides with* KOSTYA.) Out of my way, young man.

OLGA PAVLOVNA. Come inside and we'll talk things over, Fyodor Fyodorovich. I love to listen to you. You have that wonderful foreign touch. I feel that any moment you'll begin talking German, at least. (*Each taking an arm, the* KARAULOVS *lead* PRIBYLEV *into the house with every mark of admiring attention.* MANYA *throws* KOSTYA *a withering glance over her shoulder. After a pause she turns and follows her parents proudly.*)

KOSTYA. I don't understand—I was going to her—already halfway there— (KOSTYA *steals away. Enter* RAYA *and* YAKOV.)

YAKOV. There *have* been many changes in your life.

RAYA. I saw no point in telling you about them. But you've changed greatly, too. In fact, I don't feel as though you were the friend you used to be.

YAKOV. I'm everybody's friend. A highly qualified specialist in friendship. A walking depository for other people's secrets and experiences. The deposits never stop coming in. Everybody seems to think I'm a bookkeeper of the affairs of the heart. It never occurs to them that I may be a former millionaire myself—that perhaps I invested all my fortune in one splendid enterprise—and lost everything. Now I am only a treasurer—guarding other people's valuables. Come on! I'll take them!

RAYA. What is all this about? I don't understand you.

YAKOV. Forgive me, Raya. I don't understand it myself. However, I'm your friend, your *kardash,* as we say in the Caucasus. And everything is fine. I don't ask you his name. What good would that do? He left you—that means he was bad. And if such a man runs away—good riddance to him. Everything will turn out all right. (*Raising his hand to slap her on the back but checks himself and hardly touches her.*) One must handle you with care, now, like fragile glass. (MANYA *comes out of the house.*) Heavens! Here are some new depositors! The treasurer is going to bolt. (*Exit* YAKOV. MANYA *runs over to* RAYA.)

MANYA. Raya. Forget everything that I said to you today. Don't be afraid of anything. Have your child and go on, bravely. There are new, broad-minded men in the world, and one of them loves me. It's true that I love—no, did love—another. Oh, I'll write forty pages in my diary today, Raya. In the first place, you're going to stay with me. No arguments, please. In the second place, you're getting a job in your department. He's a highway engineer. He'll do anything for me. I won't even have to ask him—he'll do it himself. He's an extraordinarily fine man.

RAYA. Thank you, Manya. It's rather awkward, but unfortunately I do need work.

MANYA (*runs to the house*). I'll send him out. I've already spoken to him. (PRIBYLEV *comes out of the house. Passing* MANYA *on her way into the house, he kisses her hand, nods, and walks toward* RAYA. *As he approaches,* RAYA *gets up.*)

PRIBYLEV. You? (*Looks about him.*) What are you doing here? If you wanted to see me, you could find me in Moscow, or at my summer home, for that matter.

RAYA. I had no intention of looking for you.

PRIBYLEV. What is it you want, then? Money? You refused it once. Perhaps you want to make a scandal because you've heard that I'm going to be married?

RAYA. You're going to marry Manya? So you're the extraordinary man who's so fine? You've certainly managed to fool her. But I know what an expert you can be at that.

PRIBYLEV. I haven't fooled anyone and I'm ready to marry Manya anywhere, even in church.

RAYA. For a month or two? (*Mimics him.*) "Modern marriage does not commit one to any binding obligations." No, you won't do this to her, if I can help it.

PRIBYLEV. Oh, hell! Listen to me, Raya. Don't make a scandal—it's vulgar. Go away, I beg of you. Meet me near my house.

RAYA. Why should I?

PRIBYLEV. Then go home—go wherever you like but don't stand here.

RAYA. The Karaulovs have asked me to stay with them.

PRIBYLEV. Here? Raya! You're a clever girl. You can get even with me later, if you like, but not now. I admit I've been something of a cad, even worse, perhaps, but go. Please go. If you ever loved me, do this for my sake. My God! Don't stand there like the goddess of vengeance! Raya, darling. (*Sees* MANYA *approaching.*) But you won't say anything, at least? Very well, then, I'll see what I can do for you, comrade. We'll go to my house now and I'll give you a note to the chief. Come on, comrade, come along.

RAYA. I'm not your comrade. Stop pretending.

MANYA. What's that?

RAYA. Manya, is this the man you love?— Then I'm sorry for you.

MANYA. What do you mean?

RAYA. I too thought once that he was fine and noble.

MANYA. Oh, then you're the one! You deserted her, in her condition, and then dare to speak to me. You're a scoundrel!

PRIBYLEV. Why a scoundrel? Is my past any worse than yours? I'm taking you, although you're going to have another man's child. (*Pause.*) Or did you think I was a virgin? I didn't make such petty demands of you. I'm not inquiring about your past but if you're interested in mine, all right, I'll keep nothing from you. (MANYA *makes a gesture as if to interrupt him.*) Just a moment. It's true that we were intimate, but that's all over. It was only later that I learned about the child. I sent her money at once and advised her to see a doctor. (MANYA *makes a gesture.*) Wait a minute. Raya agreed with me that she should not have the child and admitted that she no longer loved me. That was two months ago. Is that true?

RAYA. It is.

PRIBYLEV. Then why should you abuse me, Manya?

MANYA. I didn't think—

PRIBYLEV. What about your principles, Manya? What about freedom?

MANYA. Forgive me.

PRIBYLEV. All right. I'm going to reëducate you. As for Raya, she has no claim on me. Here is her letter. (*Fetches the letter from his pocket, at the same time dropping* MANYA's *diary.*)

MANYA. My diary! (*Picks it up.*) My diary in your pocket? You read it? Oh, you contemptible cad! A contemptible cad—that's what you are! (OLGA PAVLOVNA *and* KARAULOV *come out of the house.* YAKOV *descends from the garret.*)

OLGA PAVLOVNA. Come and have some tea, Fyodor Fyodorovich. And there's fresh raspberry jam.

MANYA (*to* PRIBYLEV). If you ever come near our house again I'll drive you away like a dog.

OLGA PAVLOVNA. You'll drive Fyodor Fyodorovich away? Yakov! (*She is about to faint.* YAKOV *supports her.* KARAULOV, *on the other side of* YAKOV, *also reaches out a hand for support.*)

MANYA. You thief! Get out of here!

KARAULOV (*rubs his eyes*). Wake me up, somebody. (PRIBYLEV *on his way out meets* KOSTYA, *who is coming on.*)

KOSTYA. I was hoping I'd see you. I wish—I must admit you're the better man. You love Manya more than any of us and more nobly. Let me shake hands with you.

PRIBYLEV. Get away. (*Exit.*)

MANYA (*runs to* KOSTYA). Don't shake hands with him. Take this. Read it. (*Tosses her diary to* KOSTYA *and runs off.*)

KOSTYA (*goes to* YAKOV). What happened, Yakov? What happened?

YAKOV (*supporting* OLGA PAVLOVNA *with one arm and* KARAULOV *with the other, leads them to the house*). The train is full. No more room. We're off!

CURTAIN

ACT III

Before the curtain rises, voices are heard, raised in argument. The setting is the same as in the preceding scene: before the KARAULOVS' *house. About a table on which a plan is spread out are* KOSTYA, YAKOV, PRIBYLEV, KARAULOV, *and* OLGA PAVLOVNA.

OLGA PAVLOVNA. For thirty-five years we lived under the Czar, for eight months we enjoyed Kerensky's rule, we have been governed by the Bolsheviks for sixteen years (and that's no joke)—but never did we see anything like this.

PRIBYLEV. You're interfering with our work.

KARAULOV (*raises first one hand, then the other*). I would like to say a word. Please let me express my opinion.

YAKOV. You're a man of music, Sergey Petrovich. Won't you please take a pause and hold it for half an hour? (OLGA PAVLOVNA *and her husband draw close together and stand there as if awaiting a verdict.*)

PRIBYLEV. The road will pass this way. I'm sorry to say it, but—the Karaulov house will have to be torn down.

KARAULOV. Fyodor Fyodorovich, according to the first plan, the road went to one side and it stretched away quietly, considerately, without disturbing anyone. But the moment Manya showed you the door, if you will forgive my saying so—the road turned, got crooked at once. Such a spiteful road it became. I shall never believe that it got crooked without prejudice. Decent—roads don't behave like that.

PRIBYLEV. Then according to you I want revenge? Granted. But do you trust my assistants? (*To* KOSTYA *and* YAKOV.) Now, tell us—which is the better plan—the first or the second?

KOSTYA (*sighs*). The second.

YAKOV. The second is better. It's a very good plan.

PRIBYLEV. Do you hear that?

YAKOV. But the third plan is still better. According to that plan, too, comrade Pribylev, only one house will have to be torn down. But it will be your house.

PRIBYLEV. I've been hearing that stupid talk for two days. I'm getting sick of it. Please make the drawing for this project. I'm bringing it up for approval tomorrow.

YAKOV. I'll have it ready. (YAKOV *and* KOSTYA *draw aside.* OLGA PAVLOVNA *and her husband go up to* PRIBYLEV.)

OLGA PAVLOVNA. Fyodor Fyodorovich.

KARAULOV. Fyodor Fyodorovich.

PRIBYLEV. If you think I haven't done the right thing, send in a complaint.

OLGA PAVLOVNA. No, no complaint. We'd rather talk the matter over in the family circle.

PRIBYLEV. In the family circle? Unfortunately, I was not given an opportunity to join your family circle.

KARAULOV. It was the hope of our hearts. Manya hasn't even told us what caused her to change.

PRIBYLEV. Well, appeal to your daughter. I may be willing to tear down my house, yes, my own house, if you can tear down her obstinacy. (*Turns abruptly and goes off.*)

KARAULOV (*raises his eyes to heaven*). Lord! Or Nature! Or whatever there may be! One can't even pray to anybody. Oh, what a life.

OLGA PAVLOVNA. The baby was trouble No. 1, the house is No. 2, and No. 3—we don't know what that will be, but it's sure to come, you may just as well be ready for it, Sergey.

KARAULOV. I'm getting ready for it, all right, Olga, don't worry. (*Goes in.*)

OLGA PAVLOVNA (*sitting down on a bench*). You young men—you're such nice, sympathetic boys—can't you do something to turn this cursed road aside?

YAKOV. All right, we will.

OLGA PAVLOVNA. Will you, really?

YAKOV. I promise you. You may go in and finish a bottle of medicine with your old man. The road will not go through here.

OLGA PAVLOVNA. You're a nice boy, Yakov, even if you aren't an orthodox Christian. (*Enters the house.*)

KOSTYA. Why do you give her false hopes? Why?

YAKOV. I told her the truth.

KOSTYA. Liar. How can you change the location of the road?

YAKOV. I've done it already.

KOSTYA. Another lie. How could you do that?

YAKOV. It's my secret. (*Throws down a sheet of paper on the table.*) Here you are. Now draw up the third project. (KOSTYA *stares at him.*)

KOSTYA. Have you gone mad? You want to map the road right through Pribylev's house?

YAKOV. Those are his orders.

KOSTYA. What orders? When did he give them?

YAKOV. He will, tonight.

KOSTYA. Can you talk sense or not?

YAKOV. Why talk when I have it all written down?

KOSTYA. What a man! What have you written down? When did you do it? Where?

YAKOV. What have I written? An article. When did I write it? Yesterday. Where did I write it? In *The Red Highway Gazette*.

KOSTYA. But Pribylev's project is a damn good one. He's an honest engineer with a great deal of experience, and you, fool that you are, think you can hound him in the papers. You'll be kicked so far down the ladder for this that you'll never be able to climb back.

YAKOV. I, kicked down the ladder? Ha! At home I used to hang over precipices. I climbed Mount Kazbek. I was right up among the eagles. And you try to frighten me with talk about being kicked down the ladder.

KOSTYA. What did you write?

YAKOV. That's my secret. Do the drawing, I tell you.

KOSTYA. I won't. I'll take no part in such idiocy. (RAYA *enters and walks toward the house.*)

YAKOV. Raya, come and help us, please. The plan has to be altered. (*Points.*) Right here. Just the first two kilometers from the station. The rest remains as it is.

RAYA. All right, I'll do it. (RAYA *takes the drawing and walks to the house. At the door she turns around and looks at* YAKOV. *Their eyes meet.* RAYA *turns away quickly and goes inside.*)

YAKOV (*laughs*). A smart girl, Manya. She played the part beautifully, like a first-class actress. "I'm going to have a baby." And everybody believed it. Even I. "Whose baby is it?" First this one is suspected, then another. It's a good thing we didn't get a police dog—it would have gone around in circles. Then the diary—wonderful. And the old folks, Raya, Senya—they don't know the truth even now. A real tragicomedy. When's the wedding coming off, Kostya?

KOSTYA. There isn't going to be any.

YAKOV. No? Who has come to life in you now?

KOSTYA. I love Manya. But marry her— (*Shouts.*) I'm not a cad. When I thought she was in that condition I insulted her. I ran away, acted like a skunk. Now—now anybody would marry her. I'd much rather she had the wretched brat. No, I can't marry her now.

YAKOV. I was mistaken in you, Kostya. You're not Lermontov or Tolstoy. You're Dostoyevsky. Sit down and write *The Idiot.* You could do it well. But didn't you actually start out to propose to her?

KOSTYA. Yes—but I never finished. (*Shouts.*) She doesn't know I started to and I can't prove it to her.

YAKOV. I'm a witness.

KOSTYA. I don't use witnesses to propose.

YAKOV. Will you go to Manya?

KOSTYA. No.

YAKOV. No? Turn around.

KOSTYA. What's the idea? (*Turns around.*)

YAKOV. I just wanted to see something. Stubborn brutes like you can be moved by having their tails twisted. No, I guess you haven't any. You're a disgrace even to your fellow-mules, Kostya. Never mind, old man. You're all right. (*Straightens* KOSTYA's *cap and blouse.*) Douglas Fairbanks has nothing on you. Now, go.

KOSTYA. Right now? Say, you are a fool. You want me to go right away? But you'll have to tell her it's the second time I'm doing it. (*Shouts.*) And don't be hanging around here, will you please. This is intimate.

YAKOV. Anything to please you. (*Exits.*)

KOSTYA. Pribylev won't stop me this time. If she could only forgive. (KOSTYA *takes a few steps toward the house. His path crosses* SENYA's, *who is held back by* AGRIPPINA SEMYONOVNA, RYVKIND, *and a* YOUNG MAN. KOSTYA *stops.*)

AGRIPPINA SEMYONOVNA. Hold him! Hold him! He'll do something abominable!

YOUNG MAN. Stop it, Senya.

SENYA (*runs up the porch steps*). If you don't leave me alone, I'll show you.

AGRIPPINA SEMYONOVNA. He wants to marry an actress with a child on the side. (KOSTYA *makes for* SENYA *but he is stopped by* RYVKIND *and the* YOUNG MAN.)

AGRIPPINA SEMYONOVNA. Let him hear the arguments.

RYVKIND. Comrade Perchatkin. Just look at my familiar face. Don't you recognize me? I'm the dentist, Ryvkind, and you are working for me. (*Walks up to* SENYA.)

SENYA. That's right. I make teeth for you. But now I'll unmake them for you. (*Shows his fist.*)

RYVKIND. I don't enter into your extravagant behavior. Only bring back the teeth—my patients are waiting. (SENYA *turns and knocks at the door.*)

YOUNG MAN. Don't do it, Senya.

KOSTYA. I can't let you. I was here first. Now it's my turn.

SENYA (*over his shoulder*). Just let anybody else try to butt in! (MANYA *comes out of the house.* SENYA, *on the middle step, goes down on one knee. He holds out one hand to* MANYA *and the other to his friends.*)

SENYA. This is Heaven, and this, to be nice about it, is the earth. Comrade Manya, last week you were a young woman like other young women, and I spoke to you of love. Those were not words that left my mouth. Just Indian nuts. (*Spits, as if he were eating Indian nuts.*) Everything I said to you then was a lie. But now that you have been discovered with a mysterious child and you are proudly lit up like a lighthouse with a lamp inside, I have been able to make out their dirty physiognomies in the illumination that you give out. (*To his friends.*) You don't mind that. (*To* MANYA.) Now I understand what love is. You have made a new citizen of me. I invite you to become my strictly legal wife. And if anybody at all, even your own mother, should ever smile at you, I'll wipe them out. There. (OLGA PAVLOVNA *and her husband come out of the house.*)

MANYA. Senya, you're a dear. I'm really touched. In three days you've grown up. Thank you. Only why must you get married? It's not the thing for you.

SENYA. It is. I swear it is.

MANYA. Anyway, you're my best friend. Come in. I want to show you something. (MANYA *goes inside.* SENYA *starts after her but stops.*)

SENYA (*to* MANYA's *parents*). Well, Papa and Mama, it was a hard job to get you. But don't worry: I'll take care of you from now on. (*Gives his friends a look of triumph and walks inside.*)

AGRIPPINA SEMYONOVNA. You didn't stop him. And you call yourselves men!

YOUNG MAN. Wild horses couldn't have held him back.

RYVKIND. Let's go and hold a conference in the bushes. (SENYA's *friends leave.* KOSTYA *throws himself down on a bench in despair.*)

OLGA PAVLOVNA. One yesterday and another one today. It's enough to make you dizzy. Well, I suppose it can't be helped. Let's go. We'll have to get everything ready—bread and salt and the ikon. We must give them our blessing.

KARAULOV (*sighs*). Yes, I suppose so. (*They go inside. Enter* YAKOV —*he walks around to* KOSTYA.)

YAKOV. Well? Didn't you go to her?

KOSTYA (*cries*). I went, all right. But I didn't make it. Foiled again—

this time by Perchatkin. They are all new men. I'm the only medieval relic. (*Exits abruptly.*) I'm through. This is the end of everything.

YAKOV (*shouts after* KOSTYA). I'll be your agent. And listen, buy me
a copy of *The Red Highway Gazette*. (RAYA *comes out of the house
with a drawing in her hand.*)

RAYA. I can't make this out, Yakov. Is this a stream? (*Sits down at
the table.*)

YAKOV. Certainly it is. Oh, what streams we have in the Caucasus,
Raya. You look at some river and all of a sudden it vanishes—goes
underground. Then it comes out again—and falls, hangs from a rock
like a silver ribbon. And all about you are lizards lying on the stones
—hundreds of them—sunning themselves. We have white rivers, blue
rivers, yellow rivers. And the roads! They wind in and out among the
chasms, and overhead the mountains rise straight up to heaven.

RAYA. I have never been in the Caucasus.

YAKOV. You're lucky, then.

RAYA. How is that?

YAKOV. Well, *you're going* to the Caucasus—for the first time. It's
the most beautiful country on the globe. Ah! Adjaristan—Batumi—
(*Carried away, he hums a few bars of an Adjar song.*) When you stand
high above the valleys and see the river highways flow on beneath you
—and the air is filled with an immensity of mist, gilded by the sun and
stretching to the end of the world—your eyes grow large with wonder
—and your soul, that was like this (*indicates the size with his hands*)
swells until it is as large as this (*Again.*) Please be my wife, Raya.

RAYA (*rises*). What?

YAKOV. Marry me. We'll go to the Caucasus. (RAYA *holds out her
hand to* YAKOV, *draws it back instantly, and runs inside the house.*)
She's running to buy the railroad tickets. (YAKOV *walks off in the opposite direction. Enter* AGRIPPINA SEMYONOVNA, RYVKIND, *and the*
YOUNG MAN. MANYA *walks backward out of the house. She is followed
by* SENYA, *a bewildered smile on his face and* MANYA's *diary in his
hand.*)

SENYA. I don't understand. Then there really is no child? You were
simply pretending, as one does in the theater? And you're no heroine
but just an ordinary young lady—like all the rest? And instead of a
hero it seems I am only a fool? Why, my eyes were filled with tears of
admiration when I looked in the mirror at night. I began to respect
myself. And now, suddenly—it's all over. The child is no more. My
heroism is no more. I have been deceived, dishonored. Give me back
my child—my child by another man. (*Enter* ZINA. KARAULOV *and his
wife come solemnly out of the house, walking side by side. He is carrying an ikon. She holds a plate with half of a French loaf and a salt-
cellar.*)

KARAULOV (*solemnly*). Come, children.

SENYA. Put away your ikon. Remove the feed. I have changed my mind. (KARAULOV *and* OLGA PAVLOVNA *sink down on the porch steps.*) I have been deceived in a cultured house!

ZINA (*to* SENYA's *friends*). Why? What's happened? Is he deserting her, too? (*Enter* YAKOV. *He sees the old couple.*)

YAKOV. The ambulance is here. (YAKOV *helps* OLGA PAVLOVNA *and* KARAULOV *to stand.*)

KARAULOV (*breaks away from* YAKOV *and turns to* SENYA). Ruffian! I challenge you to a duel.

YAKOV. You can demand satisfaction only through your second. (*Leads away the* KARAULOVS.)

AGRIPPINA SEMYONOVNA. Come, Senya dear. I'll give you satisfaction.

YOUNG MAN. Come on, Senya.

SENYA (*points to* MANYA, *then at his friends*). Heaven is compromised and the earth makes me sick. I dangle between them like —like a flower on top of a mountain. (*To his friends.*) Don't wait— the worm is coming back to you. (*Exit* SENYA. *His friends run after him.*)

ZINA (*to* MANYA). How do you explain it, Manya? You're pretty and an actress. And yet you're so unfortunate.

MANYA (*advances upon* ZINA *and forces her off the stage*). It's not true. I am very fortunate, more than you will ever be. (*Alone now.*) My fortune will come to me in the theater. I know what life is, now. My Kostya, the one man I love, has left me. My girl friends rejoice at my troubles. Even my father seems to be willing to sell me so that he can keep his wretched house. But I have gained an understanding of my part. "What awaits my child? Almost before he has learned to speak, he will have to beg in the streets, a tiny tot. I can see him holding out his thin dirty little hand. I see the people in their heavy furs brush him by, indifferently. I see his starved, bony frame through his torn shirt. No. No. Anything but that." (*Throws herself down on a bench. Cries. Gets up again.*) Now I shall know how to play it. Here is my baby. So warm and tiny and alive. Here he is, in my arms. I am alone on the stage. The audience is silent. Nobody will dare to cough now. (YAKOV *comes out of the house. He wrings out a towel and places a medicine bottle on the table.*)

YAKOV. The old people have gone completely cuckoo. You must tell them the truth. They've had enough of this tragicomedy.

MANYA. Yes, you're right. The place for acting is on the stage. I'll tell them everything. But how can I explain to Raya? I wouldn't be able to open my mouth. Yakov, darling. You talk to her. Make her understand that she'll be ruined if she has a child. She's penniless. And her father is a fanatic—he'll kill her.

YAKOV. All right. I'll talk to her. Produce the woman. (MANYA *runs out.* YAKOV *sings. Enter* RAYA.)

RAYA. Manya wants me to have a talk with you.

YAKOV. Oh, no. It's I who want it. Will you please manage to have your boy, father unknown, resemble me?

RAYA. Why a boy?

YAKOV. When I say a boy it's a boy. I promise that for me he'll be no different from my own. And there will be quite a lot of them. I shall need at least three sons, besides as many girls. One is already with us, God be praised. He will be an engineer. Another will be an aviator. And the third a writer.

RAYA. Why a writer?

YAKOV. Every family must have its freak.

RAYA. Why didn't I see you before, as you are, and understand you? I am so happy now. For the first time in six months I feel like singing.

YAKOV. Sing, then, by all means.

RAYA. All my life I'll be thankful to you.

YAKOV. Don't mention it. We'll balance our accounts some day. (RAYA *embraces and kisses* YAKOV, *after which they both walk off in different directions.* YAKOV *stops around the corner of the house and feels his cheek carefully, as if to make certain that the kiss was really placed there.* RAYA *runs into* PRIBYLEV *as he enters.*)

PRIBYLEV. How gay and beautiful you are today. Happy too?

RAYA. Yes. (YAKOV *listens.*)

PRIBYLEV. I look at you and I can't understand how I could ever have left you. Raya, little Raya, I'm a cad.

RAYA. It's possible I agree with you.

PRIBYLEV. Come back to me. I used to kiss those lips—remember? Weren't they once mine?

RAYA. Let me pass.

PRIBYLEV (*takes hold of her arm*). We are bound to each other by the child. (YAKOV *is all attention.*) I'll marry you. No, don't misunderstand me. I'll marry you really, for good. I'm getting old, Raya. I'll never be unfaithful to you again. Do you remember—

RAYA. Let go of my arm. I shall always think of you as a bad dream. I'm in love with a wonderful man. He's brave, handsome, strong— Go away. Don't spoil my happiness.

PRIBYLEV (*takes hold of her arm once more*). I won't let you go. (YAKOV *comes out with a resolute air.*)

YAKOV. If I met a man like you on a mountain path not wide enough for two, this is what I would do— (*Steps back and sweeps his arm to one side.*) On your way, please. (PRIBYLEV *raises his elbow for a moment as if to protect himself, then slinks away.*) Happy journey! (*Pause.*) I heard everything. So Pribylev is the man? It's his child?

RAYA (*apologetically*). I was blind then— (YAKOV *laughs, as he squats and slaps his knees.*)

YAKOV. Pribylev! Oh, that's fine! Thank you, darling! I was afraid your first man was young and handsome—and that you would remember him. Now I'm not afraid. Pribylev! Why, I'm a better man than he! (*Dances.* RAYA *runs inside.* ALEXANDER MIRONOVICH *enters from the side facing the house. He wears an old suit, very neat. He takes off his cap and wipes his head with a handkerchief.*)

ALEXANDER MIRONOVICH. Will you tell me, please, if a beautiful young girl by the name of Raya lives in this house? Please note that I have already asked the same question twenty-six times.

YAKOV. A substantial depositor. (*To* ALEXANDER MIRONOVICH.) Won't you have a seat? A beautiful young girl, you say? Raya? Oh, yes, she's staying here. She's out walking just now. (*They size each other up.*)

ALEXANDER MIRONOVICH. Do you know Raya well?

YAKOV. Why, we're fellow-students at the institute.

ALEXANDER MIRONOVICH. I see—you're a comrade of hers, a colleague. Well, I'll tell you who I am. I'm Raya's uncle. On her mother's side.

YAKOV (*sighs with relief*). And I thought you were her father.

ALEXANDER MIRONOVICH. Her father? Why on earth would her father be dragging himself all this way in the sweltering heat? He's in Moscow now, sitting at the window, with a frown on his face, and repairing watches. I'm Raya's uncle. So you're her friend?

YAKOV. That's right—a friend, a kardash.

ALEXANDER MIRONOVICH. A kardash? Does that mean a good friend?

YAKOV. The very best kind of friend.

ALEXANDER MIRONOVICH. Then let me tell you a secret. Raya's father is greatly worried about her. He's gotten wind of something. I, her uncle—I know everything—the whole affair. But her father is beginning to guess it, too.

YAKOV. That's too bad. They say her father is an old brute?

ALEXANDER MIRONOVICH. A brute? Raya's father a brute? I would like to see the scoundrel who said that.

YAKOV. Well, not altogether a brute, just partly.

ALEXANDER MIRONOVICH. Many thanks for the "partly."

YAKOV. There is nothing for her papa to worry about. You must explain to him that Raya's child will be well cared for.

ALEXANDER MIRONOVICH. Raya's child! Oh, my God! (*Places his hand to his heart.*)

YAKOV. What's the matter?

ALEXANDER MIRONOVICH. Nothing's the matter with me. But wait till her father hears about it. It'll be much worse. I know him. A child! How did she get it? It's probably a joke, but you almost killed me. I mean, her father—he may die of such humor. If you don't mind, I must get used to it a little.

YAKOV. By all means. Have you heard that Raya is going to be married?

ALEXANDER MIRONOVICH. A fine business! What a country this is!

You'd think they had turned enough things upside down. Now, tell me, is it really so hard to get married first and have the rest of it afterward?

YAKOV. That's the bridegroom's fault— He was—sent away on business.

ALEXANDER MIRONOVICH. But is it compulsory to do this before going away on a business trip? And where is the bridegroom now? Where is the good-for-nothing? Come on, finish me off, I'm dying of curiosity anyway.

YAKOV. He's not so bad.

ALEXANDER MIRONOVICH. He has some occupation, I suppose. Or is he simply a movie extra with nothing but a long beard?

YAKOV. Please don't insult him. He does some important work—on the roads, you know.

ALEXANDER MIRONOVICH. Oh! A bridegroom who does road work. Could I have a look at him? Just at his profile, at least?

YAKOV. You go for a walk, Uncle, and I'll call him. (YAKOV *walks toward the house and* ALEXANDER MIRONOVICH *in the opposite direction.*)

ALEXANDER MIRONOVICH. All of a sudden a child and a bridegroom —to hell with parliamentary procedure! (*Disappears among the bushes.*)

YAKOV. Raya! Raya! (RAYA *comes out on the porch.*) Raya, darling, your uncle is here.

RAYA. What uncle? I have no uncle.

YAKOV. No? Try and remember—perhaps you'll recollect.

RAYA. Don't be funny. What uncle? What does he want?

YAKOV. It's your old uncle, on your mother's side, he says. There he is, you can see him walking in the bushes.

RAYA. That's my father. (YAKOV *clasps his hands to his head.* RAYA *runs after* ALEXANDER MIRONOVICH. *Enter* KOSTYA.)

KOSTYA. When are they going to register?

YAKOV. Who?

KOSTYA. Manya and Senya Perchatkin.

YAKOV. So far only Perchatkin has signed—a confession of his stupidity—then he went away.

KOSTYA. What? Went away? Where to?

YAKOV. I'll tell you later. Now I want you to take off your pants. Take them off, please.

KOSTYA. What do you mean?

YAKOV. Just take them off. I want to borrow your white pants. I'm going to introduce myself to my father-in-law.

KOSTYA. Father-in-law?

YAKOV. Can't you take off your pants without all this psychology? (YAKOV *leads* KOSTYA *out.* ALEXANDER MIRONOVICH *enters from the other side, followed by* RAYA.)

ALEXANDER MIRONOVICH. I'm not your father. Your father's in the zoo, sitting in a cage. A beast. Or better still, your father's in the museum, hanging in a gilt frame. He's Ivan the Terrible killing his— daughter. The artist made her a son because he didn't know you.

RAYA. Please don't get excited.

ALEXANDER MIRONOVICH. Am I excited? I'm raging. I'm a savage beast. I ought to be locked up. I have been tried by so many things in life, I can be tried on a criminal charge as well.

RAYA. Papa, darling.

ALEXANDER MIRONOVICH. Raya, my little baby. I used to make your bed and comb your hair. You had such honest eyes. Now I don't recognize my little girl. The first man I meet here—a kardash, on this bench, presents me with a grandchild. What is the world coming to! And still we go on living. (*Enter* YAKOV, *wearing white trousers and a tie. He goes up to* RAYA *and her father.*) Ah, here you are, comrade. You promised to bring me the bridegroom.

YAKOV. There's no need of bringing him. He'll come himself. (*Walks around a bush.*) It's as easy as that. Here he is. (*Pause.*) Is he very bad?

ALEXANDER MIRONOVICH. Why, you were only a kardash.

YAKOV. And you were only an uncle. I'm not angry with you, am I?

ALEXANDER MIRONOVICH. The young people are so sly nowadays.

YAKOV. And you tried to be an old fox yourself, if I may say so. (ALEXANDER MIRONOVICH *walks all around* YAKOV, *studying him from every side.* RAYA *gazes now at one, now at the other.*)

ALEXANDER MIRONOVICH. May I ask you a question? What is your religion?

YAKOV. I'm an atheist.

ALEXANDER MIRONOVICH. Of course, naturally. We are all atheists when we fill out the questionnaires. But for yourself?

YAKOV. Also an atheist.

ALEXANDER MIRONOVICH. You can't fool him. Well, what was your father's religion?

YAKOV. He was a Mohammedan.

ALEXANDER MIRONOVICH. It would be something like that. A Mohammedan. But Raya, their law permits him to have forty wives.

YAKOV. Quite right. Only Mohammed commanded that each wife should have a separate room.

ALEXANDER MIRONOVICH. Well, then there's nothing to worry about. As for the Soviet regime, what have you to say?

YAKOV. Everything. I say: everything *for* the Soviet regime!

ALEXANDER MIRONOVICH. No, I can't catch him. I really should curse these Bolsheviks, yet, somehow, I can't get mad at him. What am I to do now? (*Sighs and holds out his hand to* YAKOV.) I'm very glad.

YAKOV. Good. (RAYA *throws her arms around her father.*)

ALEXANDER MIRONOVICH. No, don't. Your father is a brute! He may bite you. (*All three walk away, changing their positions twice. In the end* RAYA *is between the two men.* ALEXANDER MIRONOVICH *and* YAKOV *try to put their arms around her but only succeed in placing them on each other's shoulders.* ALEXANDER MIRONOVICH *continues, on their way out.*) Still, why couldn't it have been after the business trip? (KARAULOV *and* OLGA PAVLOVNA *enter from the house. She is knitting a baby's cap.*)

OLGA PAVLOVNA. Tearing down the house and breaking up our lives. Now we'll have no place to die.

KARAULOV. They have to give us another house. Out there they're building new bungalows. That's where you're going to—live.

OLGA PAVLOVNA. I live in a bungalow? Summer makes you silly. What have I done that they should put me in a bungalow? Every piece of wood in the old house is like an old friend. I know every board by its creak. Sergey, try and persuade Manya to marry Pribylev. We'll go down on our knees before her. We have only a little time left to live. We must save the house. My chickens are here. They would die in a bungalow.

KARAULOV. We'll get others.

OLGA PAVLOVNA. Do you expect me to get used to strange chickens? (*Enter* MANYA.) Plead with her.

MANYA. Mama, Papa. I've come to open your eyes at last.

OLGA PAVLOVNA. You'd better come and close our eyes. Give us a chance to die with a roof over our heads.

MANYA. Nobody's dying yet. What are you making there?

OLGA PAVLOVNA. I'm knitting a baby's cap. I wonder if it's the right size. I have no idea what newborn babies are like nowadays.

MANYA. Then this is for—my baby? (*Embraces her mother and goes to her father.*) Forgive me. I didn't know you. Only now have I realized what I did. Well, I'd better tell you—it's possible that I may not have any child, after all.

KARAULOV. What's that? You won't have a child? Why not? Do you mean you want to— Don't dare to do such a thing. I beg of you, I command you—there must be a child. The theater is the most important thing, of course, but you won't be tied down. We'll take care of the little one. So remember—don't dare. (*Draws* MANYA *aside.*) I've become attached to it. (OLGA PAVLOVNA *walks over to them.*)

OLGA PAVLOVNA. Manya, darling. Have pity on us. Marry Pribylev—

KARAULOV. I'm talking now. Yes, Manya. We see things in the right perspective. Between the two of us we have lived a hundred and ten years. It is late—we are in the evening of our lives. Your path lies in the morning. Go your own way. Don't look back at us. Go. Have no fear. (*Gently he pushes* MANYA *toward the porch. She goes in.* KARAULOV *takes a cello from the porch and returns to his wife.*)

OLGA PAVLOVNA. What did you say to her? (KARAULOV *bows over*

the cello without replying and begins to play a sad old tune. His re-
marks while playing are spoken in a simple, natural tone. Sometimes
the words are interpersed with long, arbitrary pauses.)

KARAULOV. We mustn't stand in her way. (*Plays.*) Think of when
you were twenty. (OLGA PAVLOVNA *quietly walks over to her husband.*)
You were so lovely. (*He is carried away by the music. Then he stops
playing. Rises.*) Let's not hinder her, Olga. If we have to give up the
house and leave this place, won't we be going together? Won't you be
with me? (OLGA PAVLOVNA *weeps.*) There, there, old girl, there's nothing to cry about. House, garden, and lawn. I don't need the wretched
house. I can call on my old friend Tchaikovsky. I can visit Mozart. And
even Beethoven himself in his palace. Garden and lawn. How much
land do I need? Only a single point—where I can rest my cello. Art
has no need of a house. The hand, the body, the musician himself,
are only an extension of the bow. Let Pribylev do as he likes. He shall
never have our Manya. Wants to tear down our house, does he? Why,
I'll raze it to the ground myself. (*Pulls an old window shutter from its
hinges and throws it on the ground.*) Enough. The devil with it. We're
going to Moscow. Tie up your bundle, Mother. (*Runs into the house.*
OLGA PAVLOVNA *walks after him.*)

OLGA PAVLOVNA. Trouble No. 3 has come at last. (MANYA *appears
on the porch.*)

KARAULOV (*off stage*). Manya. Get ready. We're leaving for Moscow.

MANYA. Just a minute. I'm in such a muddle. What should I do
now? (*Enter* RAYA. MANYA *runs over to her.*) Raya. Forgive me. Has
Yakov told you?

RAYA. Yes. I'm so happy.

MANYA. Happy? What did he tell you?

RAYA. That he'll stay with me forever. That he'll love my child. I
want your child and mine to be like brothers. Manya, you have done
so much for me. I'll tell my son all about you. He will sit on my lap,
listening and staring with his big black eyes—like Yakov's—yes, like
Yakov's. What would you like yours to be? A boy or a girl? (ALEX-
ANDER MIRONOVICH *appears for a moment behind the bushes.*)

ALEXANDER MIRONOVICH. Raya. This Yakov of yours is a storyteller.
Who ever heard of building railways in the air? They make up such
stories only in Odessa. (RAYA *runs to her father.*)

MANYA. Is it possible that I envy her? Yes, I do. She's going to have
a son—a real one. And I'll have only a lifeless doll that the assistant
director will shove into my hands just before I come out on the stage.
A property child! I want a real one. I want to see it breathe—and fall
asleep, a trusting little creature—my very own. Today I saw its cap—
(MANYA *cries. Enter* YAKOV.)

YAKOV. Make your deposit, comrade. The bank is closing up.

MANYA. What is Kostya doing?

YAKOV. Just what you're doing—only he's in the bushes. I swear by everything that Kostya was the first who tried to propose to you. Marry him. Please do.

MANYA. Will he have me?

YAKOV. He'll jump at the chance. I'll give him a convenient push.

MANYA (*entering the house*). Do. (*Enter* PRIBYLEV *and* KOSTYA, *the latter carrying some small stakes.*)

PRIBYLEV (*at the porch*). Sergey Petrovich! Olga Pavlovna! (KOSTYA *and* YAKOV *stand a little distance away. Enter* KARAULOV.) What has your daughter decided?

KARAULOV (*with the same formality*). After considering the matter carefully with our daughter, we have decided not to marry you.

PRIBYLEV. Thank you.

KARAULOV. You're welcome. (*Goes to the porch.*)

PRIBYLEV (*to* KOSTYA). The road will go through here. Plant the stakes. (KOSTYA *sighs and hammers in the stakes.*)

KARAULOV (*from the porch*). You think you've buried me and you're driving a stake into my heart? Well, sir, you're mistaken, and I shall play at your funeral yet. (*Enters the house.*)

PRIBYLEV (*to* YAKOV). Is my drawing ready?

YAKOV. Here it is. (*Puts a drawing on the table.*) You can sign it now. (PRIBYLEV *takes out his fountain pen.* KARAULOV *and his wife, dressed for the train, come out of the house.* KARAULOV *is carrying a cello wrapped up in a cloth cover. His wife carries a hamper.* MANYA *follows them out of the house and locks the door.* OLGA PAVLOVNA *closes the shutters.*)

YAKOV. Off to the Caucasus?

OLGA PAVLOVNA. You shouldn't laugh at the misfortunes of others. Even with a dark complexion you can't escape the wrath of God. (*Bows to the house.*) Sergey. Manya. Let's sit down—for the last time. (*The old couple sit down on the porch steps.*)

PRIBYLEV. This is certainly not very pleasant. Say! What's this?

YAKOV. The drawing. The plan for the road project.

PRIBYLEV. But according to this it's my house that has to come down.

YAKOV. Absolutely true.

PRIBYLEV. I don't permit any joking in such a serious matter.

YAKOV. Neither do I.

PRIBYLEV. You're dismissed from the job.

YAKOV. I don't think so.

PRIBYLEV. This is fraud. You tried to slip this drawing in, hoping I would sign it without first looking at it.

YAKOV. On the contrary. You'll sign it only after you look at—this. (*Hands* PRIBYLEV *a newspaper.*)

PRIBYLEV. What's this? A newspaper?

YAKOV. At the bottom of page three. Here: Engineer F. F. Pribylev.

(KARAULOV, OLGA PAVLOVNA, MANYA, *and* KOSTYA *come closer. Later* RAYA *appears and stands at* YAKOV'S *side.*)

PRIBYLEV (*reads*). "Although he has come from the ranks of the prerevolutionary engineers, F. F. Pribylev has recently given convincing proof that he is a true citizen of our era. While drawing up the plans for a highway project, engineer Pribylev became convinced that the most satisfactory route was one which required that his house be torn down. Without a moment's hesitation, Pribylev decided to sacrifice his own interests and issued orders for the demolition of his home. By this action, engineer Pribylev has given further indication of the growth of socialist consciousness in our ranks. The Pribylevs are the pride of our profession." Who wrote this vile thing?

YAKOV. I did.

PRIBYLEV. You'll be prosecuted for this, and I shall write to the paper today, denying the report.

YAKOV. Yes, write to them. Tell them that you, eningeer Pribylev, are not a citizen of our era—that your consciousness has not grown, and that you are not the pride of our profession. Go ahead, write your denial. (*Pause.*)

PRIBYLEV. I feel like an idiot and I can't do anything about it.

YAKOV. You're right for once.

PRIBYLEV. But, damn it, why are you so terribly anxious to save the house for the Karaulovs?

YAKOV. Because they're old and not very rich. It will be better for them as well as for the road that they should keep the house.

PRIBYLEV. I'm not going to present this plan for approval—damn it! I don't want to laugh at myself all the way to the office.

YAKOV. Just you sign it and I'll do both the other things—take it down to the office and laugh at you.

PRIBYLEV (*hesitates, studying the drawing*). Hell! What an idiotic situation. It's awful! Should I save my house or my reputation?

YAKOV. Your reputation, if you please.

PRIBYLEV (*signs the plan*). You've played a dirty trick. But you do have brains, damn you. (*Walks away quickly.*)

OLGA PAVLOVNA (*embraces* YAKOV). I can't believe that a boy like you could be born in the God-forsaken Caucasus.

KARAULOV. We're grateful, of course. But for us artists property is a mere trifle. (*With a show of indifference he opens the shutters, unlocks the door, and enters the house.*)

OLGA PAVLOVNA (*Goes behind the house*). Here, chickie, chickie, chickie. We're going to stay, chickies. (KOSTYA *pulls out the stakes. He and* MANYA *look at each other, then turn away. She enters the house, he goes to the woods.*)

RAYA. Manya! (*Runs after her.*)

YAKOV. Kostya! (*Catches him at the edge of the woods.*) Go to Manya.

She's proposing to you. She has promised to marry you right away. Hurry, before somebody else gets ahead of you again.

KOSTYA. There's nobody left to do that now. (*Takes a step toward the house.* ALEXANDER MIRONOVICH *crosses* KOSTYA's *path.* KOSTYA *pounces on him from behind.*) No, you don't. I'll break your legs first.

ALEXANDER MIRONOVICH. Help! Murder! (YAKOV *comes running from the woods,* MANYA *from the house.* KOSTYA *lifts* MANYA *up in his arms.*)

KOSTYA. Get out of my way, everybody! Or I'll do something you'll never forget!

ALEXANDER MIRONOVICH (*as* YAKOV *picks him up*). Is he a bandit or a lunatic?

YAKOV (*leads him away*). Just a crank who shows signs of becoming a bandit.

KOSTYA. Manya, I'm going to carry you to the registry office.

MANYA. All right. Only we'll have to tell my parents first. (KOSTYA *puts her down, looks about, and grabs her hand.*) Papa. Mama. (KARAULOV *and his wife come out on the porch.*) We have loved each other for a long time.

KARAULOV (*indifferently*). That's fine.

OLGA PAVLOVNA (*indifferently*). The bridegrooms are growing inferior in quality. Well, never mind. I'll give you my blessing. (*Goes into the house.*)

KOSTYA. We would like to register.

KARAULOV. Is that so? You want to go and register your love—that beautiful, sweet emotion? Why do you stand there as if paralyzed? Sit down. (KOSTYA *and* MANYA *sit down together and with their eyes timidly follow* KARAULOV, *who walks up and down in front of them.*) I know very little about you, young man. But you—you are an actress. Where is your sensitivity? Register! What kind of ideas will you give to my grandchild? Can't one love without records and official red-tape? (*From the porch, as he goes into the house.*) Love must be free.

KOSTYA. We'll have to register on the quiet.

MANYA. And another thing. Can we have a child—in a hurry?

KOSTYA (*thoughtfully*). I'll do what I can. (OLGA PAVLOVNA *comes out of the house, carrying an ikon.*)

OLGA PAVLOVNA (*as if speaking about something very trivial*). Come and be blessed.

KOSTYA. Excuse me—it will have to be either I or St. Nicholas.

OLGA PAVLOVNA. You're ignorant, even if you are a student. St. Nicholas! What have you been studying, if you don't know the difference between St. George and St. Nicholas?

KOSTYA. It's all the same—you'll have to choose between us.

OLGA PAVLOVNA. I certainly won't exchange a saint for a student.

(She goes inside with the ikon. YAKOV *and* ALEXANDER MIRONOVICH *enter from the woods.* KARAULOV, RAYA, *and* OLGA PAVLOVNA *enter from the house.)*

MANYA. Get acquainted, comrades (ALEXANDER MIRONOVICH *shakes hands with* OLGA PAVLOVNA *and her husband—he nods to* KOSTYA *from a distance. Enter* ZINA.)

ZINA (*to* MANYA). May I congratulate you at last?

MANYA. You may. I'm getting quite used to it.

ALEXANDER MIRONOVICH (*walking arm in arm with* KARAULOV). I'm a watchmaker. I know all there is to know about time. But they treat time as if it were their servant. They give it orders. Stop! Go faster! Five years they make into four years and even three. And the marvelous thing is that the mechanism stands up to it. (*They walk off to one side.*)

YAKOV. I'll have a wedding in the Caucasus. We have everything there—a Roman bridge going back to the fourth century and right alongside it a power station built in the fourth year of the Five-Year Plan.

RAYA. That's what we have to learn—to build as strongly as the Romans and as swiftly as the Bolsheviks.

ALEXANDER MIRONOVICH. Hear that? This girl wants to build a bridge. Everything is possible today. Well, I'll make sure that I'm not the first one to cross that bridge. (PRIBYLEV *is seen passing in the distance.*)

YAKOV. I don't like that—a man walking in the woods all alone, like a bear. Comrade Pribylev! Come have a glass of wine with me! (PRIBYLEV *approaches diffidently. Makes a bow all around.*)

PRIBYLEV. I'm afraid I'll spoil your festivities with my presence. (*He looks about and notices* ZINA *standing alone. He goes over to her. The rest are busy opening bottles and setting the table. To* ZINA.) What's your name?

ZINA. Zina.

PRIBYLEV. Zina, little Zina—have you ever been in love?

ZINA. Oh, what are you saying! (*He takes hold of her arm and they stroll about. Enter* POSTMAN.)

POSTMAN. A telegram for Pribylev. (*Hands him the telegram and goes out.*)

OLGA PAVLOVNA (*to* PRIBYLEV, *after he has read the telegram and stands there scratching his head and smiling*). Some bad news?

PRIBYLEV. No, not at all. (*Reads.*) "After reading *The Red Highway Gazette,* a group of fellow-workers send you thanks and their warmest regards."

YAKOV. I've made his career.

PRIBYLEV (*draws* ZINA *aside*). Zina, little Zina.

MANYA (*holds up a glass of wine*). My dears. I've caused you a great deal of unpleasantness, but I'll make up for everything. I promise you

I'll play my part brilliantly—and not on the stage alone. What little I still have to learn about babies—

KOSTYA. Oh, I'll attend to that.

KARAULOV. And I still think bad little boys should be spanked.

OLGA PAVLOVNA. Or thrown down from the Spartan rock? Oh, summer always makes you silly.

CURTAIN

FAR TAIGA

BY ALEXANDER AFINOGENOV

THE virgin Siberian forests, called the "taiga" by the Russians, stretch across nearly the entire length of Siberia in its southern, more temperate region. The Trans-Siberian Railway cuts through the taiga as it wends its way along the Siberian border from west to east, skirting the great Lake Baikal, following the Amur River for some distance, and terminating at Vladivostok, on the Pacific shore. Until recently this railway was single-tracked, so that numerous sidings were necessary to permit passage of trains in opposite directions. One of these sidings, somewhere near Lake Baikal, provides the setting for Alexander Afinogenov's play.

Russian colonization of Siberia, which began in the sixteenth century, was the work of fugitive serfs and Cossacks who were later joined by common criminals and political exiles. It produced a sturdy pioneer stock with some admixture of native blood (some Siberian tribes are distant relatives of American Indians) whose members played an active part in the civil war and in the liberation of eastern Siberia from the Japanese and the Japanese-supported Whites. Under the Soviets the Special Far-Eastern Army took over the task of protecting the region. Exceptional care was lavished on this army by the Government, and all Russians, especially in Siberia, came to regard it with pride and affection.

Alexander Nikolayevich Afinogenov (born in 1904, killed in an air raid on Moscow in 1941) began his career as a dramatist with a play, "Robert Timm" (1924), which dealt with the labor movement in England. His other plays were: "The Other Side of the Slit," "Turning Point," "Look Out," "The Wolf's Trail," "Raspberry Jam," "The Odd Fellow," "Fear," "The Portrait," "Far Taiga" (1935), "Hail, Spain," "Second Track," "Mother of Her Children," "Mashenka," and "On the Eve."

A. B.

FAR TAIGA

CHARACTERS

ALEXEY YEFIMOVICH KORYUSHKO (ALYOSHA), agent of siding "Far Taiga" in Siberia, age 52

GENNADY MIRONOVICH TOMILIN, telegrapher, age 33

ZHENYA, KORYUSHKO's daughter, age 15

IVAN MAKAROVICH MAKAROV, head switchman, age 56

VLASS FILIPPOVICH TONKIKH, second switchman, age 48

SULIN, Adjutant to Corps Commander MALKO, in charge of the saloon car, age 30

LAVRENTY PETROVICH BOLSHEV, track walker, age 26

MATVEY ILYICH MALKO, Corps Commander of the Far-Eastern Soviet Army, age 48

VERA NIKOLAYEVNA, his wife, age 43

GLAFIRA IVANOVNA BOLSHEVA (GLASHA), LAVRENTY's wife, age 22

LYUBOV SEMYONOVNA (LYUBA), KORYUSHKO's wife, age 46

TIME: The middle 30's. The action spans twenty-four hours, from one August morning till the next

ACT I

Railway tracks. A platform. A small, neat building with a signboard: "FAR TAIGA. Moscow—6782 kilometers. Vladivostok—2250 kilometers." Seen through an open window, a telegraph office. Beyond the house the taiga, the virgin Siberian forest stretching the length of the continent. A single saloon car, blinds drawn, is standing alongside the platform.
Everything is quiet except for the voice of KORYUSHKO, the siding agent, who is in the office dictating telegrams to GENNADY TOMILIN.

KORYUSHKO. "Far Taiga to Transbaikal. Saloon car number nine-four-three uncoupled Moscow express account broken tires period. Send reserve locomotive comma tires comma workers immediately as per order head office." Go to bed, Gennady Mironovich, it's time for me to take over now.

GENNADY. You come on at seven, and it's only six-thirty. Besides, I'm not going to bed just when something's happening.

KORYUSHKO. Yes, we've never had anything like this before. I'm dictating, Gennady Mironovich. "Far Taiga to head office. Confirming receipt head office order, *re* immediate dispatch reserve locomotive." That fellow's no ordinary conductor, no, sir! Sent one telegram after another and here's the result—an order.

GENNADY. I'm all jumpy. Can't imagine why. (*In another window the curtain is pulled aside and ZHENYA, not entirely awake yet, sticks her head out.*)

ZHENYA (*sees the railway car, rubs her eyes, and stares at it again, at the same time shouting*). Daddy! Daddy! Where are you?

KORYUSHKO. Is that you, Zhenya dear? (*Lays telegram down before GENNADY and steps out of the office.*) You should be sleeping.

ZHENYA. Where's Mother?

KORYUSHKO. Hunting in the taiga. Went out last night.

ZHENYA. And what's that?

KORYUSHKO. A car, Zhenya, a saloon car. It's been uncoupled. The tires snapped. Go back to bed.

ZHENYA. Who's traveling in it?

KORYUSHKO. Some military man. From Khabarovsk to Moscow. We'll know all about it pretty soon, now. Go to sleep, dear, build up your strength. You've grown thin in the city. That's what being a student does to you.

ZHENYA. A military man! From Khabarovsk! That means one of the higher-ups!

KORYUSHKO. Sh-sh, Zhenya.

ZHENYA. Now I'll see a real live leader in the flesh. I'm going to get busy right away and organize a reception.

KORYUSHKO. Zhenya! (*But* ZHENYA *has already disappeared behind the drawn curtain.*)

GENNADY. Alexey Yefimovich! I'm going to shave and put on my uniform.

KORYUSHKO. Yes, go ahead. Then I'll do the same thing—I've let my bristle get too long. (GENNADY *goes off.* KORYUSHKO *walks up and down the platform. The telegraph instrument is heard clicking.* KO-RYUSHKO *rushes in to take the message.* MAKAROV *slowly comes onto the platform from the left. Rolling a cigarette, he walks silently past the saloon car and stops at the office window.*) Big doings, Ivan Makar-ovich, eh? No passenger train ever stops here, and then, all of a sud-den, a saloon car.

MAKAROV. Are they asleep?

KORYUSHKO. The only one I've seen is the adjutant. A smart fellow, I must say. A regular hurricane. (ZHENYA *rushes on.*)

ZHENYA. I've got it all figured out. This is the plan. The siding will report to the army on its accomplishments. We'll all line up as though it were a military review and wait till he comes out. Then you step forward—like this—one, two—one, two—and make the report.

KORYUSHKO. No, no! I'm no good at that. Let the young people talk. Let Gennady Mironovich do it, or say Ivan Makarovich here—he's your front-line element, a candidate for party membership.

ZHENYA. Makarov hardly speaks seven words a day. Just rehearse the thing and you'll get it. Suppose I'm the leader. I come out of the car— (*Gets onto the steps of the car.*) and you come up—don't be afraid—don't hunch over.

KORYUSHKO (*raising his hand as in salute*). Dear comrade, I greet you with all my heart— No, I can't do it—I just can't. You'd better do it yourself—after all, you've been studying railway engineering.

ZHENYA. You're a funny one, Daddy. I'll come up after your report and ask him to give us a statement on the Red Army and our immedi-ate tasks.

KORYUSHKO. Do you think all that's really necessary? And what if he doesn't come out?

ZHENYA. He's sure to come out. Then we'll give him a guard of honor—though I'm afraid maybe that's just for funerals—and Ma-karov will call a meeting and invite our distinguished visitor. Of course, it can't be a party meeting, since he's the only full-fledged party member here. That'll be a first-rate program. And to top it all off, Glasha can treat him to dinner.

MAKAROV. Glasha has other things to think of.

ZHENYA. Why, what's happened?

MAKAROV. Lavrenty is definitely leaving.

KORYUSHKO. Leaving? My goodness! He wants to be a hero, of

course, and what chance is there for heroic deeds in the taiga? Our life here is a narrow one.

ZHENYA. He's dying to get to Moscow—wants to see his picture in the papers. Life on a siding is much too dull for him. What kind of heroism is that, to run away from your wife and child? I hate him.

MAKAROV. His wife is my daughter. His son is my grandson. Let him go. (*Enter* GENNADY, *clean shaven and in uniform.*)

GENNADY. Now you can go, Alexey Yefimovich.

ZHENYA. That's right. And put on your shantung jacket. Hurry up or it'll be a disgrace—the masses are ready but not the leading citizen. Run along. (KORYUSHKO *goes off.*) I wish he'd come out quick! (*Tries to peek into the window.*) No, you can't see a thing. Do you suppose he's young, Gennady?

GENNADY. I'm so jumpy. I feel terribly nervous, Zhenya. (*The instrument is heard clicking.* GENNADY *rushes into the office.*)

ZHENYA. Now, what shall we give him for a gift? Oh, we can let him have one of Mother's bearskins. She did the bear in with her own hands—that makes it worth more as a present. (VLASS, *a heavy, disheveled-looking man, appears on the platform, right.*)

VLASS. Burning up with impatience? Waiting for the superior authority? When thou sittest down to partake of food with thy master, let not thyself be tempted by his flavorsome viands—it is a deceiving food.

ZHENYA. The priestly prattle has started.

VLASS. I've never been a priest. I was a sectarian, a Molokan. Today I'm a switchman. Thus speaketh the wisdom of Jesus, the son of Sirach.

ZHENYA. Keep quiet, you old church windbag! Why are you here, anyway?

VLASS. To expose.

GENNADY. It would be a good thing if you washed your face, Vlass Filippovich.

VLASS. Vanity. My boots are worn through and my clothes are shabby, but those who expose wickedness will be loved. Give me a cigarette, Gennady.

GENNADY. I don't smoke.

VLASS. That's a matter of common knowledge.

ZHENYA. Go away. We have a definite program and you're in our way. Tell him to go, Ivan Makarovich.

MAKAROV. Let him be.

VLASS. Verily I say unto him: Let him be! I've been waiting for this moment for four years. The powers that be have arrived in a saloon car and I'm going to talk to them.

GENNADY. Vlass Filippovich—

VLASS. Keep still, you two-legged guitar!

GENNADY. My guitar has nothing to do with this.

VLASS (*singing in a falsetto voice*).
> Once there was a fruiterer,
> Who tootled on a fluterer.
> His wife gave him a booterer,
> The fruiterer kaputered her.

ZHENYA. Oh, stop clowning, Vlass Filippovich! An old man like you—I should think you'd know better.

VLASS. It's the weariness of the spirit, virgin.

ZHENYA. Don't call me by that stupid word, please.

VLASS. Do you mean you're already a wanton?

ZHENYA. I'm a Young Communist, and please—

VLASS. Can't Young Communists be virgins?

ZHENYA. Don't bother me with your mystic nonsense.

VLASS. You ought to enlighten me. We live in the taiga, there's nobody to teach one. That's why Lavrenty's going away. (*To* MAKAROV.) Your son-in-law is going, Ivan, eh? Leaving his wife to the mercy of her passions, eh? Don't worry. She'll be picked up. Gennady will play something moving on the guitar for her.

GENNADY. I'll ask the scandalmongers to hold their tongues. It's none of their business. (*Slams down the office window.*)

MAKAROV. People will blab.

VLASS. Yes, won't they? (*Enter* KORYUSHKO, *freshly shaved, in a white shantung jacket.*)

KORYUSHKO. Good morning, Vlass Filippovich. Fine day, isn't it?

ZHENYA. Daddy, tell him he can't do that. He wants to push ahead of everybody.

KORYUSHKO. He's joking, Zhenya. Look, my friend, seeing this is a special day, you ought to clean yourself up a little.

VLASS. I have no uniform, no shantung jacket.

KORYUSHKO. This is just an old one; I've had it eighteen years. Real Chinese material—gets softer every year.

ZHENYA. Turn around. Now again. Looks all right. Let's have a salute. Oh, it's split under the arm.

KORYUSHKO (*lifting his arm and peering under*). So it is—along the seam. I'll have it sewed up in no time.

VLASS. Sewing is the duty of the mistress of the house.

KORYUSHKO. My Lyuba has no time for that. She's a brave woman, busy hunting in the taiga—has no time for us. She's a splendid girl! I darn socks too, I don't mind telling you, and do it damn well. (*The door of the saloon car opens. Taken by surprise, everybody steps back.* SULIN *emerges.*)

SULIN (*holding a bucket*). Good morning, comrades.

KORYUSHKO (*stepping in front of the others*). I'm very happy to see you. We've already met, so to speak. (*Stretches out his hand but, recalling the split under his arm, hastily withdraws his hand again, keeping his arm bent at the elbow.*) Excuse me, some little disorganization. Did you sleep well?

SULIN. Very. I wonder if I could get some water, comrade Koryushko. It's time for the samovar.

KORYUSHKO. Water? We'll fix that right away. Take the bucket, Vlass Filippovich.

VLASS (*to* SULIN). Don't give yourself airs and don't set yourself up in the place of the mighty.

ZHENYA (*under her breath*). Oh, the nerve of him!

VLASS. Because it's better to be told "Come up here" than to be abased before a high personage. (*Goes off, rattling the bucket.*)

KORYUSHKO (*to* SULIN). He has odd ways, you know.

ZHENYA. One of the priests that's escaped the ax. What's your name?

SULIN. Sulin. And yours?

ZHENYA. My name is Zhenya. I'm a student at the technical institute in Sretensk. Member of the Communist Youth League—membership card No. 00523.

SULIN. Tell me, can we get some food here?

ZHENYA. We have bear-meat sausage. Would you like that?

SULIN. How about some milk and vegetables?

KORYUSHKO. Makarov has a cow and a truck garden. He'll supply you.

SULIN. Will you sell us some milk, comrade Makarov?

MAKAROV. I can give it to you but I'm not in the selling business. (*Goes off.*)

KORYUSHKO. He'll bring it. He'll bring everything, don't worry. It's a fine day, I must say. Of course, this is the taiga, a wilderness—it's like living on an island. You won't find much excitement here. But an order for an engine has already been issued and by lunch time, I hope, we'll be able to send you off.

ZHENYA. Who's traveling in your car? Don't nudge me, Father. An army leader?

SULIN. A corps commander of the Special Far-Eastern Army, comrade Malko by name—Matvey Ilyich. (*Enter* GENNADY.)

GENNADY. Comrade adjutant, telegrams for you—I mean your chief —three of them. Please sign this receipt.

ZHENYA. Three telegrams? Wow! Who else is with him?

SULIN. His wife, Vera Nikolayevna.

ZHENYA (*excitedly, to herself*). She'll give us a talk on women's work. (*To* SULIN.) Is this his own car?

SULIN. You do want to know a lot. The car belongs to the Commander of the Far-Eastern Army.

ZHENYA (*impressed*). Oh! How soon will comrade Malko be up?

SULIN. He's getting up now.

KORYUSHKO. Ah! You play the host here a while, Gennady Mironovich. (*Pointing to his sleeve.*) I have a little repair job. (*Hurries off into the building as* VLASS *comes on.*)

VLASS. Running? You're all in a hurry to live, but all for nothing.

KORYUSHKO (*to* VLASS, *in a low voice*). Vlass Filippovich, please re-

frain from preaching today. I beg of you. You'll only do yourself harm.
(*Goes off.*)

VLASS. I've had enough harm done to me to last till I rot. Receive
the water and drink it for your solace. (*Enter* LAVRENTY. ZHENYA *draws
him aside for a quick résumé of what has been happening.*)

SULIN. Thank you, citizen.

VLASS. Tell your chief that Vlass Tonkikh, a former member of the
Molokan sect, is living at the siding and that said Vlass proposes to
ask a few questions about the meaning of life and the universe, re-
questing that he be granted this opportunity.

SULIN. Your request will be transmitted to him.

LAVRENTY (*approaching*). Comrade Sulin? My name is Lavrenty
Bolshev, a track walker here and a former soldier of the Special Far-
Eastern Army. Of course, comrade Malko won't remember my face
but I remember him very well—especially in the last maneuvers where
our regiment distinguished itself in crossing the Bureya. I would like
to have a talk with the comrade commander.

SULIN (*shaking* LAVRENTY's *hand*). I'll report this without fail, although he's forbidden to tire himself—so the conversation mustn't
be too long.

ZHENYA. How about the lecture?

SULIN. What lecture?

ZHENYA. We've been planning one—about the Red Army.

SULIN. Don't even mention it to him, I beg of you. He's not well
and he's very tired. (*Goes into the car.*)

ZHENYA. I see. Well, all right, we'll drop the lecture. But we'll make
our report. (*At the station window.*) Are you ready, Daddy?

KORYUSHKO (*popping his head out*). Can't find a needle.

ZHENYA. I'm asking about the report.

KORYUSHKO. In a minute, Zhenya dear, in a minute. Right away.

ZHENYA (*to* LAVRENTY). What's he like? Young—stern—tall—fair?

LAVRENTY. Rather gray. But broad shoulders! A strong fellow. Jolly
too. Many's the time I used to see him. He's one of the common
people—used to be a mechanic in the Tula armament works. A
hero!

ZHENYA. How many decorations?

LAVRENTY. Two. Won them in the civil war. Oh, that was a time!
What names! Budyonny, Kotovsky, Klementy—

GENNADY. Which Klementy?

LAVRENTY. There's only one Klementy—Voroshilov. Great men!

GENNADY. Siemens was a great man too. So were Hughes, and
Baudot, and Morse.

LAVRENTY. Were they Bolsheviks?

GENNADY. No, inventors. They invented telegraph apparatus.

LAVRENTY. And who invented the guitar?

GENNADY. The Moors.

LAVRENTY. Well, let the Moors have your telegraphers. Imagine comparing Morse with Budyonny!

GENNADY. I certainly will compare him.

LAVRENTY. Go play your guitar to Budyonny.

GENNADY. I certainly will play it to him.

LAVRENTY. A bourgeois instrument. A tear-jerker. It's fit to lure other men's wives, not the leaders of the people.

GENNADY. I won't bother to reply to such rudeness.

VLASS. No, no. You mustn't keep quiet. You must argue against him, prove your case, defend yourself. Tell him you love Glasha immeasurably and call on him to compete with you.

GENNADY. Comrade Tonkikh! I'll have to request you—I've no desire— And if others— (*Goes off quickly.*)

VLASS. Heh! Heh! I love it when people get cross. And I love to make them that way. For an open denunciation is better than a secret love.

ZHENYA. Lord, but you make me sick! Get out of here—at once! (*She advances on him.* VLASS *falls back a step toward the car.*) You hear me? (*Retreating farther,* VLASS *reaches out and grabs the handrails of the car.* ZHENYA *tries to pull him away. The door opens and* MATVEY MALKO *appears. He is of medium height, stocky, with a big, deeply grayed head, set on broad shoulders.* ZHENYA, *frightened, dashes away from* VLASS *toward the house and climbs in the window.*)

VLASS (*stepping back from the car*). H'm! H'm! (LAVRENTY *comes forward, draws himself up before* MATVEY, *and salutes him.*)

MATVEY. Good morning, comrade Bolshev. What's going on here? Setting-up exercises?

LAVRENTY. Just a slight argument with a bit of physical persuasion, comrade Commander.

MATVEY. Any injuries?

VLASS. Injuries and suffering elevate man.

MATVEY. You're the Molokan, I take it?

VLASS. I renounced God six years ago.

MATVEY. Do you always dwell on the past?

VLASS. I have no memory of the past nor shall I have any of what's to come.

MATVEY. My, my. You come from the Volga, from Yaroslavl, don't you?

VLASS. Verily. You have guessed it.

MATVEY. Well, what is it you want to ask me?

VLASS. Why does man fear death?

MATVEY. H'm.

LAVRENTY. Comrade Commander, pay no attention to his prattle. (*Enter* KORYUSHKO, *followed by* ZHENYA.)

KORYUSHKO (*giving a military salute, with his elbow pressed to his side*). Comrade Commander, I beg to be permitted to make a report on the condition and work of the siding Far Taiga.

MATVEY (*shaking hands with him*). Who am I to be receiving a report?

KORYUSHKO. You're our dear guest, so to speak. Of course, this is the taiga, a wilderness—our work is unimportant—perhaps I shouldn't bother you?

ZHENYA. No, no. What if it is unimportant?

MATVEY. You're right, Zhenya.

ZHENYA. How do you know I'm Zhenya?

MATVEY. I can tell by your eyes.

ZHENYA. We want to welcome you—and in your person the Red Army. Please don't say "no." We're so glad your car broke down— No, of course we're not glad—but we regard ourselves as part of the Far-Eastern Army.

MATVEY. I understand. (*Draws himself up and speaks in a sterner voice.*) Present your report, comrade agent.

KORYUSHKO (*agitated*). During the six months just past, the siding Far Taiga has carried out its entire work program according to plan. There have been no delays of freight trains. No cases of absence from work. Disciplinary fines—one. (MATVEY *turns his head toward* VLASS.) That's right. But he's done better since. There've been no accidents. I should like to request that the state of the siding and signaling equipment be inspected in person. Also, we're in a state of readiness for defense.

LAVRENTY. All along my section of the line, too, comrade Commander.

KORYUSHKO. The siding is competing for the yearly banner of the Trans-Baikal Railroad.

MATVEY. Any hopes?

KORYUSHKO. Ours is an inconspicuous siding, so there isn't much hope. Nevertheless—

MATVEY. I accept your report with pleasure. However, I note an underestimation of the siding and of your own work. We have no inconspicuous sidings.

ZHENYA. What did I tell you? Lavrenty!

MATVEY (*turning to* LAVRENTY). Are you going to make a report too?

LAVRENTY. No. Mine is a personal matter. Please inspect the office and the line, comrade Commander. (VERA *appears at the door of the car—a simple dress, almost completely gray hair, and a very young face. Behind her is* SULIN.)

VERA. It's time for breakfast, Matvey.

MATVEY. I'll be back shortly. Look, while we're looking things over, you organize an alfresco breakfast for all of us. You have no objections, comrade agent?

KORYUSHKO. The next train is at 11:28. We have plenty of time. Zhenya dear, lend a hand; get the cups, the chairs—the tablecloth is in the left-hand bottom drawer—get the jam—

MATVEY. Oh, no. Permit me to be the host.

KORYUSHKO. No, no, no. I'm glad of the opportunity. You're our honored guest. I can't agree to any other arrangement. Zhenya dear, you know what to do, don't you?

ZHENYA. I should say so. (MATVEY, KORYUSHKO, *and* LAVRENTY, *followed at some distance by* VLASS, *go off, left.*) Let's get acquainted. (*Shakes* VERA's *hand.*) You'll give us a lecture on women's work. A very serious question here. Lavrenty—you saw him—with curly hair—he's leaving his wife. And she has a baby. What's to be done?

VERA. Has he stopped loving her?

ZHENYA. He says the family strangles his development.

SULIN. Have you a small table, comrade Zhenya?

ZHENYA. We have everything—tables, chairs, and cups. I'll hand them to you and you'll carry them—and Vera Nikolayevna will set them out. A conveyer-belt system. (*Goes into the house and hands out furniture, china, and table linen through the window,* SULIN *passing them on to* VERA.)

VERA. How old are you, Zhenya?

ZHENYA. Just fifteen. I'm a member of the Communist Youth League. All the others here are nonparty, except Makarov.

VERA. And Lavrenty?

ZHENYA. He's been back from the army eighteen months and he's still a nonparty man. Funny, isn't it? If you ask me, he's an anarchist, has to have his own sweet way all the time—the fool! "I'm bored here in the taiga where nobody knows me," he says, "I want to go to Moscow." What I say is people should leave Moscow and come to us, to the Far East.

VERA. We'll have to talk this over. Yes.

ZHENYA. And why are you going to Moscow?

VERA. We've been called by the People's Commissar.

ZHENYA. To receive a new decoration?

VERA. No, not a decoration.

ZHENYA. I get it. It's a secret. What's your own occupation? A housewife?

VERA. No, I teach school.

ZHENYA. Then you're on leave. What is he ill with?

VERA. Just overwork.

ZHENYA. Ask the Makarovs to give you some roots. Glasha dries all different kinds of herbs and uses them as a cure. (*Enter* GLASHA *carrying a basket. Behind her is her father,* MAKAROV, *with a bottle of milk.* ZHENYA *scrambles out the window.*) Glasha, give them some of your herbs. This is Glasha, the one—you know.

VERA. Good morning, Glasha. Where's your baby?

GLASHA. He's asleep. This is for you. (*Sets the basket down near* VERA. MAKAROV *places the milk bottle on the table.*)

ZHENYA. We'll all have breakfast together. (*Takes the food out of the basket.*) Dumplings, beets— (*To* VERA.) Glasha has her own way of cooking. She puts in herbs and lots of other things—but it comes out simply delicious!

VERA. Have you a girl, Glasha?

GLASHA. No, mine's a little Petka.

VERA. Do let me play with him. I love babies.

GLASHA. You haven't one of your own then?

VERA. No— Somehow we never—

GLASHA. There's worry in your face—a kind of waiting for something.

VERA. No—I just—didn't get enough sleep. Have you finished laying the table, Zhenya? (SULIN *brings on a samovar.*) A lovely breakfast. (*To* MAKAROV.) Does your daughter tell fortunes?

MAKAROV. She has a special eye for people. (*Enter* GENNADY.)

GENNADY. Telegrams—two of them. Please sign. Permit me to introduce myself. (*Mumbles his name.*)

VERA. Sorry, I didn't quite catch it. (GENNADY *mumbles again.*) What?

GENNADY. I'm jumpy.

ZHENYA. He plays the guitar—and sings.

GENNADY. No, the guitar has nothing to do with it. I'm sorry. (*Makes a movement to leave. Enter* MATVEY, KORYUSHKO, LAVRENTY, *and* VLASS.)

KORYUSHKO (*introducing* GENNADY). Our radio fan. Graduated as a radio operator by correspondence. Dreams of receiving signals from Mars. Picks up Japanese stations. Studies Japanese grammar. What's a locomotive in Japanese, Gennady Mironovich?

GENNADY. *Kisya.*

MATVEY (*shaking hands with him*). The Japanese are a gentle people. With them a locomotive is a kisya, and they tried to smother us with kisses in Manchuria, didn't they?

KORYUSHKO. Matvey Ilyich—allow me to introduce—Ivan Makarovich—Glasha.

MATVEY (*looking at* GLASHA). Ah, what eyes. (*To* MAKAROV.) Her mother was a Yakut, wasn't she?

MAKAROV. She was. She died three years ago.

MATVEY. You have a beautiful wife, Lavrenty. (*To* GLASHA.) Have you ever been to Khabarovsk?

GLASHA. I was at Nerchinsk once.

MATVEY. A familiar face. Do you recall it, Vera?

VERA. No, Matvey.

MATVEY. Ah, I've got it. Have you any brothers?

GLASHA. Two. Both in the army.

MATVEY. Bring the newspapers, Sulin. (SULIN *goes off*.) Of course, the Makarov brothers. (*To* MAKAROV.) Your sons took first prize in the rifle shoot—a watch for each of them. And they both have slanting eyes, just like Glasha's. Beautiful boys. Did you get the latest army paper?

MAKAROV. Not yet.

MATVEY. I'll be damned! I've beat the mail. (SULIN *hands him the paper*.) Then you haven't seen this?

MAKAROV. No.

MATVEY. There it is—their pictures too. (*Everybody crowds around him, looking at the paper*.) You do have fine sons, Ivan Makarovich. Real Far-Eastern soldiers.

MAKAROV. That's them, all right. The spit and image of them. (*Suddenly laughs*.)

ZHENYA. Ha-ha-ha! Makarov's laughing! Makarov's laughing! (*Everybody laughs*.)

MATVEY. We'll drink a toast. Sulin, drag out the bottle, we'll drink a toast.

KORYUSHKO. Pardon me, Matvey Ilyich. Of course, I understand—a happy occasion, and all that. But permit me to ask you—put it off till evening because—well, there's a notice up on the board—drinking during the performance of duty— We had to impose a disciplinary punishment on Vlass Filippovich for the very same thing—

MATVEY. Sulin, it's off till evening.

VERA. We'll drink Makarov's health in tea.

ZHENYA. Take your seats, comrades. Let's do things on an organized basis. (*All take their places*.) Glasha, you sit next to comrade Malko and see that he gets enough to eat. Lavrenty, you sit with Vera Nikolayevna. (*Whispers to* VERA.) That's the fellow. Oh, Father doesn't have a seat!

KORYUSHKO. I'll stand. I don't mind. You go ahead and eat. I don't like sitting.

MATVEY. Move up, Glasha. Sit down, Alexey Yefimovich, there's a seat for you, sit down. (KORYUSHKO *sits down*.) Now we can begin.

ZHENYA (*rising*). Dear comrades—

KORYUSHKO. Bravo, daughter.

ZHENYA. Here at Far Taiga we have among us a leader of the Red Army, and we must—

MATVEY. The subject is dismissed. Now look, comrades. An accident is a particular case of necessity, as they say in clever books. We've got stuck here by accident, but personally I'm very glad it happened.

VERA. And so am I.

ZHENYA. We, too.

MATVEY. No denying it—you do live in a far-off place. But it's no accident that I've met Makarov here. Nor is your good work here an accident, because you're bound up tightly with the entire country and share its interests in your own life. And so with all of us who love our jobs, who realize our part in the great community of effort; mere distance is nothing to be afraid of, no matter how vast.

VLASS. People loved their work in the old days too.

ZHENYA (*under her breath*). Devil, devil, devil!

MAKAROV (*raises his hand, then rises*). The old days—huh! The old days! In the old days I was a common switchman.

VLASS. And now?

MAKAROV. Now I've got full responsibility for all the switches on the siding. There's a difference. (*Sits down.*)

ZHENYA. That's true.

VERA. Let comrade Lavrenty give us his view.

LAVRENTY. Why choose me?

ZHENYA. Yes, you, you.

VERA. Do you agree with Matvey Ilyich? (LAVRENTY *makes no answer.*) There you are.

ZHENYA. No, he doesn't agree with him! No, he doesn't!

LAVRENTY. There's some truth in what comrade Malko said, looked at in a certain way. But it's not altogether true.

VLASS. Verily.

LAVRENTY. Keep quiet, you sectarian deacon. I've never had a united front with you. Comrade Commander, they've been hounding the life out of me here. They keep calling me a deserter and all sorts of things. You say one can't be afraid of living far away. One can be afraid, comrade Commander. In the old days it probably didn't make any difference where folks like me kicked the bucket. But today all that's been changed. A person can't spend his life in the taiga—like a nameless pine tree, when all around him there's heroism. We've rescued the Cheluskin party in the Arctic, we're flying into the stratosphere, we knock down all sorts of records like ninepins—with our canals, Dnieprostroys, Ural Machine Plants— Everybody wants to be a hero, but I have to rot—because there's nobody here even to write about us. Nobody can see us—that's the trouble. Don't interrupt me, Zhenka. If one could only prevent a train accident or pull the siding out of some kind of jam. But not a chance. Everybody's right on the job. And I can't live like this—when I was in the army I was always in the thick of things.

MATVEY. How would you like to live?

LAVRENTY. I want everything around me boiling over—I want to work where other people can see me, and show them the kind of stuff I'm made of.

ZHENYA. He wants a medal.

LAVRENTY. Yes, I do. Our Commander here has medals. He's been decorated a hero and stands out for everyone to see. I want to stand out too, so the working class can be proud of me—and the newspapers write me up.

ZHENYA. Tell him where to head in, Glasha. "The newspapers!"

GLASHA. No, Lavrenty must go. He must. I make it too cramped for him here. I spoil his life. I realize it. Don't hold Lavrenty back, let him go. He has to become a hero. I beg of you, do let him go. (*Everybody is silent.*)

KORYUSHKO. Yes—that's how things are with us out here. (*Enter* KORYUSHKO'S *wife,* LYUBOV SEMYONOVNA [LYUBA], *a tall, strong shaggy-looking woman, carrying a rifle and with a bag over her shoulders.*) Ah, Lyubov Semyonovna! And we're having breakfast without you. Allow me to introduce to you, ladies and gentlemen, my wife, if I may.

LYUBA. Quite a crowd! Good morning. I'm tired. Help me off with my bag. (KORYUSHKO *takes it off.*) Whom has God sent us?

ZHENYA. God hasn't. These are guests.

LYUBA. Guests are always welcome. You're a military man? Tell me what you think of this rifle? I've been hunting with it for seven years.

MATVEY (*takes the rifle*). H'm! Sulin, go get my popguns. (SULIN *goes off.*) I'd say this one was so-so.

LYUBA. I killed a bear with it—how's that? Is this your wife? Good morning. Pour me a little of that hot tea, will you? So you don't approve of my rifle?

MATVEY. In this business we're comrades. I've been hoping to meet a real hunter for a long time. What do you shoot?

LYUBA. Black grouse, wood grouse. We set traps for sables and in the winter we go after squirrels. (*To* KORYUSHKO.) Have you showed off my sables? Haven't got around to them yet? Slow poke!

MATVEY. How about going today? Making a day of it till sunset? Or are you tired?

LYUBA. Don't make me laugh. We can leave in an hour. I'll show you our taiga marshes. Do you have high boots?

MATVEY. I'll find a pair. By Jove, I'm lucky! (SULIN *brings a rifle.*) Now it's your turn to appraise.

LYUBA (*takes it and looks it over*). Ah—this is all right—good workmanship. (*Takes aim.*)

ZHENYA. Mother!

KORYUSHKO. Lyubov Semyonovna, you know—you should be careful—

LYUBA (*fires and looks up*). Eh! (*Goes off.*)

VLASS (*also looking up*).

> A baby bird dives headlong down
> From high up in the tree,
> And naturally it cracks its crown.
> So will your ending be.

MATVEY. Impromptu poetry?

VLASS. No, I read this one in a book thrown off an express train. (LYUBA *returns with a bird in her hands.*)

LYUBA. It picks off a swift on the wing. Lord Jehovah, what a gun! (*Examines the rifle.*)

MATVEY. What did you fill your bag with today? (*Tries to open the bag.*)

LYUBA. Don't touch that bag. It's not yours. Ah, what a gun!

VLASS (*picking up the bird*). Dead. It was flying and psst! Nobody knows the hour of his death. That's why they fly and fuss around and look for better places to live in. Had they known—who and at what siding would be dropped into a grave—

MATVEY. What then?

VLASS. Then they wouldn't be so anxious to get decorations, wouldn't worry about wisdom and heroism.

MATVEY. They'd rather get drunk?

VLASS. Heh—heh! Yes, they'd go on one final rip-roaring binge! Oh, yes!

VERA (*to* GENNADY). I believe you play the guitar?

GENNADY. No, no! I only do it for myself.

VERA. Do play us something.

ZHENYA. Do as you're told.

GENNADY. No, I can't. No, really.

GLASHA. Play something, Gennady Mironovich—just for the guests.

GENNADY. I'm no good at it. (*But* ZHENYA *is already dragging him off to fetch his guitar.*)

LYUBA. A wonderful rifle. (*Hands it back to* MATVEY.) A rifle like this is worth more than an eye. Take care of it. (*Rising, to* KORYUSHKO.) Come along. I have something to tell you. Bring the bag. (*To* MATVEY.) We'll set out in an hour. (*Goes off with* KORYUSHKO.)

VERA. Matvey.

MATVEY (*as if waking up*). What?

VERA. Here are some telegrams for you.

MATVEY. Telegrams? Oh, yes, and I haven't even answered the ones that came earlier. (*Reads and writes his answers.*) Just left them unanswered—forgot about them. (*To* LAVRENTY.) Planning to go away? I see. Afraid of dying in obscurity? I see.

VLASS. And it's all wrong. One's better off eating a handful of flour in peace than a whole loaf in weariness and toil. For, though people die in the taiga, they won't save you from death in Moscow either. No, they won't.

VERA. What's happened to the guitar player?

MAKAROV (*who has been reading the army papers all this time, erupts into laughter again*). They're my sons all right, Glasha. (*Rises and bows to* MATVEY.) You've made fine men of my sons, Matvey Ilyich. I'll thank you for them to the end of my days.

MATVEY (*shaking his hand*). To the end, Ivan Makarovich. To the last long end, good brother. (*Enter* ZHENYA, *followed by* GENNADY, *carrying his guitar.*)

VERA. Hurry up, comrade.

GENNADY. I'm jumpy. (*Strums his guitar.*) I don't know how to begin. All the songs seem to have flown right out of my head. I'm jumpy.

VERA. Sing something jolly.

GENNADY. All right. Here's something jolly. (*Closes his eyes, strikes a chord, and sings. But he does not really sing—only speaks the words quickly and expressively, sometimes intoning the ends of the lines. An uneven, rather hoarse voice; words now shouted, now whispered, occasionally a pause, while he continues to twang the strings. But everybody listens with rapt attention, even* LAVRENTY, *who has been looking askance at him the whole time.*)

> With every step our land grows great,
> And step by step our years increase.
> Each Five-Year Plan, each project marks
> > A date to reckon by.
>
> But comrades, see how blissful youth
> Goes down those selfsame steps of time.
> While as a souvenir it leaves
> > Gray hair and duller eye.
>
> For some it still trips joyfully,
> Yet, for myself, I cannot grasp
> That youth, unlike the gentle dove,
> > Lies warm in no man's hand.
>
> Hard is it, too, to see the days
> Frittered away, marked by no thought,
> And realize, friends, that each day means
> > Another graying strand.
>
> Farewell, good comrade Youth, farewell.
> We've reached the crossroads; let us part
> With one last smile, one last embrace
> > To speed us on our way.
>
> Take heart, good friends, dear comrades all:
> We've scarcely yet begun to live—
> Our years will still be happy ones,
> > Even with hair turned gray.

MATVEY (*after a pause*). There, now! That's wonderful! Ah, Gennady! Thank you, thank you heartily.

GENNADY. Really? You think it's not so bad?

MATVEY. It's magnificent, Gennady—simply wonderful. Give us

another one. Something a little more touching—to wring our hearts. Come on.

GENNADY (*closes his eyes, pauses absorbed in thought, plays the introductory bars, and begins to sing*).

> There's no one to understand me,
> And no one my sorrow to share.
> My secret is silent inside me,
> And I've almost learned not to care.
>
> Oh, Sasha, dear Sasha, my darling,
> How long must I love you in vain?
> I know I shall never forget you
> Till death sets me free from my pain.
>
> Then gently to rest let them lay me,
> Let them bury me deep in the ground
> Where no longing can trouble my slumber,
> Far from thy sight and thy sound.

(VERA *has been listening with a tense and nervous air.* GENNADY *has been carried away himself but, as he reaches his last lines,* VERA *springs to her feet and hurries into the car. Everybody turns to look at her.* GENNADY *opens his eyes, looks after her, and breaks off his song.*)

MATVEY. Ah? Go on, Gennady, go on.

CURTAIN

ACT II

A railway track in the taiga with a semaphore indicating that the siding is not far away. A clearing. Twilight. A song is heard from the direction of the siding. It is being sung by VERA, GLASHA, *and* ZHENYA *who enter on the last verse. They come on the march, carrying hampers with food and dishes.*

> (SONG)
> Then always we shall cherish,
> To be our guiding lights,
> Grim days of Volochayevsk
> And Spassk's embattled nights.

GLASHA. Here! (*Stops.*) This is where they went off into the taiga and this is where they'll come back.

VERA (*looking around*). Is there a trail? I don't see one.

GLASHA (*pointing out the evidence*). The tall young man broke off a twig that was in his way. Then he lit his pipe just as he was about to start his long walk. (*Picks up a match.*) And Lyuba, right behind him, stamped out the match. This is a dry summer, anything will set off a fire. Last year the taiga was burning far away but we could smell the smoke.

ZHENYA. Our Glasha is like a witch. She can read everything in the taiga.

VERA. Who taught you that?

GLASHA. My eyes. I have Yakut eyes. Let's make a campfire—to drive away the midges. We'll cook a salamata stew.

VERA. A campfire! Yes, we must have one. Come on, girls, let's collect firewood! One, two, three! (*They scatter in different directions, though keeping within sight of one another, and finally, arms full, they gather at the spot they started from.*) We'll wait right here for them.

ZHENYA (*unpacking the food and dishes*). This is so much fun, I can hardly believe it!

VERA. Come and stay with us for a few weeks in Moscow— I'll give you our address.

ZHENYA. Oh, I will! The only thing I really need is a place to sleep. In the daytime I'll be out in the streets sight-seeing. I'll see everything down to the last paving stone. And the first thing I'll do will be to go to Lenin's Tomb in Red Square and stand in line. I'll stand in line seven times in a row. That's my dream—seven times in a row.

GLASHA. My place in Moscow will be taken by Lavrenty.

ZHENYA. I hate your Lavrenty.

GLASHA. Don't run him down. Please don't. What sort of life does he have with me? There's not even anything to talk about but the taiga and our Petka. But in Moscow he'll be a hero.

VERA. You'll find it hard to be alone, without a husband.

GLASHA (*lighting the fire and hanging up a kettle*). I'll have my little son with me.

VERA. You do have a wonderful little son.

GLASHA. The best ever. When he grows up he'll fly through the sky —higher than anybody; and he'll read books—the cleverest boy of all.

VERA. Do you like books?

GLASHA. I read one once about Chapayev. That was exciting! But the ending was wrong. He's a hero and then suddenly he drowns! Why should a hero drown?

VERA. That's how it happened in real life.

GLASHA. No, that's wrong. As I see it, he only pretended to drown. He went down to the bottom, then crawled quick over the bed, and got out on the other side of the river. Then the Reds met him, gave him a horse, and he jumps on and back he goes! The Whites saw a dead man galloping, swinging his sword, and they went down plop on their knees, thinking it was Judgment Day. That way, of course, it gives us a complete victory. That's the ending I've thought up.

VERA. No, Glasha dear, one has to die for victory too.

GLASHA. Let the Whites die. Our Red commanders must live on.

VERA. I wish it were so. What other books have you read?

GLASHA. Arithmetic. Gennady is teaching me.

ZHENYA. What does twenty-eight times thirty-two make?

GLASHA (*moving her lips and counting on her fingers*). Eight hundred and ninety-six. What I'd like to get is a book about the way trees live, and animals. And another one that explains why the stars in the sky are getting fewer and fewer.

VERA. Who told you they're getting fewer?

GLASHA. Why, they keep falling—so there are fewer left.

VERA. Yes, you must do some studying. I'll send you books and exercise books and everything. But it'll be difficult for you all alone.

GLASHA. Never mind. Just send me the books. I have a Yakut rug, made of pelts. I'll give it to you—you can sell it in Moscow and send me books.

ZHENYA. We'll read together. And when I leave for Sretensk, I'll raise the question of organized help for you. We'll have a brigade, with me as chairman. We'll take you in tow, and to hell with Lavrenty after that!

GLASHA. Oh, no! Lavrenty is Petka's father. When Petka grows up, he'll send me to hell too.

ZHENYA. Nonsense! Superstition!

GLASHA (*stirring the kettle*). For real superstition take my mother and father's wedding. At the wedding feast my grandfather, a Yakut man, ate a whole side of beef and a trough of fat—topped everybody —so that my mother would have plenty of food in her married life— that was superstition. But to respect one's parents—that's not superstition. I love children. And I respect my father—he was a partisan at the time of Admiral Kolchak.

VERA. You know, girls, I feel so at home with you!

ZHENYA. It's simply wonderful! As if we've known one another a hundred years. Stay here a week, Vera Nikolayevna, won't you?

VERA. Can't be done, Zhenya.

ZHENYA. Promise that you'll come next year, then. Otherwise I won't let you go.

VERA. All right, next year.

ZHENYA. Next summer. We'll tidy up the station, whitewash it, hang slogans on the walls.

GLASHA. Petka will be walking by then.

ZHENYA. We'll build an enormous campfire.

GLASHA. What's the matter, Vera Nikolayevna? Don't turn your head away—tell us.

ZHENYA. Vera darling, what is it?

VERA. Oh, just—I don't know.

GLASHA. Won't you come next year?

VERA. No.

ZHENYA. Why not?

VERA. Because Matvey Ilyich— You see, he doesn't know. He thinks
—it's just overwork. The Commander of our army gave him his saloon
car and a special assignment, and the War Commissar sent for him in
Moscow. The Commander and the Commissar know everything.
Matvey has a serious illness, girls, an incurable disease—a sarcoma of
the lungs. He doesn't know. In three months—

GLASHA. He'll be dead? (VERA *nods.* ZHENYA *draws in her breath
sharply. It is still. Only the tops of the pine trees sigh in the wind.*)
Only you mustn't— Please, don't— Let me stroke your hair—like this.
(*She sings in a low, drawling voice.*)

> A hawk is flying over the steppe.
> In the Baikal lake an omul is swimming.
> But I am held prisoner by the taiga pines.
> Come across the steppe to the taiga,
> Walk through the taiga to the station.
> There I await you, pale sorrow of my life.

When my mother was dying, I didn't cry—I walked in the taiga for
two days singing sad songs to get rid of my terrible heavy feeling
through the throat. When you're left alone, come back here. I'll be
alone too—I'll wait for you. Your hair has turned gray with your
heaviness—ah!

ZHENYA (*springing suddenly to her feet.*) Matvey Ilyich! Matvey
Ilyich! (*Runs off into the darkness.*)

VERA. Zhenya! Zhenya! You mustn't take it like that! Wait, dear!
(*Runs after* ZHENYA.)

GLASHA (*following the two women with her eyes*). Here he comes
and my heart doesn't beat any faster. (*Enter* GENNADY.)

GENNADY (*in a low voice*). Glasha. (GLASHA *turns her head toward
him.*) Glasha. (*Sets down the box he has been carrying and walks up
to the campfire.*) Good morning, Glafira Ivanovna.

GLASHA (*looking up at him uncomprehendingly*). Are you here
too?

GENNADY. I've brought it here. Tonight or never. Because tomorrow
Matvey Ilyich will be gone. Let him say his weighty word. I'm terribly
—jumpy. (*Opens the box, putters around, mumbles something to himself.*) Of course it's not perfect yet. Nevertheless—it's a new development of the old crystal set. Five years of work have gone into it. Now
it may prove useful, I hope, at tractor stations, collective farms—also
for the Red Army.

RADIO (*faint voices and crackling audible in the stillness of the
taiga*). Chita— Chita—comrades, young electors— Irkutsk— In its
size the future Angora power plant— Novosibirsk— Sverdlovsk—
Moscow— Moscow—

GENNADY. There! Do you hear, Glasha?

RADIO. The new model light automobile— Die kommunistische
Revolution und proletarische Diktatur— (*Distant music.*)

GENNADY. Do you hear? Do you hear, Glasha? Six thousand eight hundred kilometers! Don't feel sad, Glasha. If Lavrenty leaves, we'll listen to the radio together here. We can pick up fifteen countries from this siding. We'll read books together, too. No, don't speak. Sit quietly and listen. Because I know you'll never love me. Only don't say "no," and I'll be happy. You are like the joy of getting some far-away place on the radio—my farthest removed happiness. Farther than Moscow. Farther than Mars. I don't know what I want to tell you. I'm in a hurry. I have to talk to you and hold your hand in mine. Only, don't say "no." You're my happiness, my sorrow!

GLASHA. You mustn't, Gennady Mironovich.

GENNADY. I mustn't? So I mustn't. I know myself I mustn't. Now I'll shut up again—for a long time. (*Turns the dial sharply.*)

RADIO. Khabarovsk—Khabarovsk. A concert by the artists of the Moscow Grand Opera Theater is being broadcast from the Red Army House.

GENNADY. I wonder what I could do to soothe your feelings, to calm you. Shall I get the guitar?

GLASHA. Why must people die? In Khabarovsk, and everywhere—

GENNADY. Why do you ask? Anybody in your family?

GLASHA. Not only in my family. (*Enter* LAVRENTY.)

GENNADY. Lavrenty Petrovich.

LAVRENTY. That's me. (*Pointing at the radio.*) Working?

GENNADY. Yes, we've picked up Moscow, Khabarovsk— (*Turns it off.*)

LAVRENTY. Quite a distance. You deserve a prize.

GENNADY. How's the car?

LAVRENTY. They're finishing it. Who's the campfire for?

GENNADY. We're waiting for Matvey Ilyich to come back from the hunt.

LAVRENTY. What a man! He's worn me to a frazzle. What trails are there in the taiga? Where does the Shilka flow into the Arguin and the Arguin into the Amur? And where do they have their sources? Can one walk through the taiga to reach the frontier? Are there badgers here and how do you catch them? I got wet through with perspiration, I tell you. "You don't know your own region, you live as if you were blind," says he. He showed me the map. Our siding is on it, and all around are different signs, each with a meaning of its own. The first thing a soldier must do, says he, is to fit himself to the terrain.

GENNADY. That's geography—science.

LAVRENTY. Why don't you say something, Glasha? Perhaps I'm in your way?

GENNADY. No, no. Quite the contrary. (*There is a pause.*)

GLASHA. What else did he talk about?

LAVRENTY. Asked me what books I'd read. About heroes, about the class war, I answer. I've read, I say, even about Cicero, but as soon as I read a book I forget it. So he began to bawl me out again.

GENNADY. Yes, he's a hero. (*Rises.*) Incidentally, if you translate the name Cicero it means Mr. Beans.

GLASHA. Who was Cicero?

GENNADY. A Roman. (*Goes off.*)

LAVRENTY. Glasha, I want to tell you something—

GLASHA. Say it, Lavrusha.

LAVRENTY. Glasha darling. Of course I act on the spur of the moment, get worked up over everything. But I see no other course but to go away from here. It's easy for him to bawl me out—all he has to do is put his wife in a saloon car and today he's in Chita, tomorrow in Khabarovsk. But I have to carry my wife and Petka on my back. The family weighs me down, Glasha, yes, the family. It's like a hump to me now. I didn't realize it but I got myself a son much too early. I thought that would tame me, make me calmer. Only it hasn't. I'm still on fire and I'm off to Moscow. But I'm off alone—I must go alone, Glasha dear.

GLASHA. Go your way, Lavrusha. We've already settled that, haven't we?

LAVRENTY. I'm going tomorrow.

GLASHA. Tomorrow?

LAVRENTY. I'll leave with Matvey Ilyich. We had a talk and I begged him to take me with him to Moscow—particularly as it's my time for a leave. He finally agreed.

GLASHA. Tomorrow.

LAVRENTY. You don't want me to?

GLASHA. No, you go.

LAVRENTY. Glasha, my darling! I love you just as much as ever. Even more. But a man must walk the earth freely, without a load. Otherwise life isn't worth a damn.

GLASHA. You don't value life very highly.

LAVRENTY. What good is it when you're tied down, chained? You couldn't make me a present of life on those terms.

GLASHA. Give it to Matvey Ilyich then. He needs it more than you do.

LAVRENTY. His own will last him long enough.

GLASHA. In three months Matvey Ilyich will be—dead.

LAVRENTY. Don't joke, Glasha!

GLASHA. He doesn't know about it—and he mustn't know.

LAVRENTY. That's a dirty lie, Glasha.

GLASHA. Vera Nikolayevna said so herself—he's going to die.

LAVRENTY. Gla— Matvey Ilyich? Comrade Malko? (*Enter* VERA *leading the silent* ZHENYA.)

VERA. They're not back yet? Let's call them—all of us together. (*Shouts.*) Mat-vey! They don't answer. Mat-vey! (*A pause.*)

GLASHA. They're coming. I hear things crackling.

VERA. What a wife you have, Lavrenty! She sees everything, hears everything. Do you help her with her education?

LAVRENTY. What? Education? Why education? Matvey Ilyich! Ah, damn it. Oh, yes. Do I help her? I need help myself.

VERA. You worry too much about yourself. It's always me, and I, and myself. Zhenya, more combustibles. (*She and* ZHENYA *gather brushwood and throw it into the fire.*) Is the salamata ready?

GLASHA. I'm stewing it.

VERA. I can't quite make out what it smells like.

GLASHA. There's mare's milk in it, flour, fir-tree bark, dried fish, and berries, all mixed together.

VERA. Have you tried it, Zhenya? Is it good?

ZHENYA. I want to go home.

VERA. What do you plan to do in Moscow, Lavrenty?

LAVRENTY. I don't know. (*Enter* MATVEY, GENNADY, LYUBA, *and* SULIN.)

MATVEY. Moonlight! A campfire! Comrades, what a life! Go get your guitar, Gennady. I haven't the words to express it! How did your song go? (*Sings in a low voice.*)

> There are no words to tell by name
> The power that sets men's hearts aflame.

GENNADY.

> My father gave me good advice,
> "Beware black brows that arch blue eyes."

I'll fetch it, Matvey Ilyich. And we'll sing all through the night! There's only one thing—(*Looks at the radio set.*) All right. We can see to that later. No hurry. (*Goes off.*)

MATVEY. Hey, women at the campfire! Greet the hunters! Glasha, let's have some of your salamata.

GLASHA. The salamata is ready. Please be seated. (*Pours the salamata into cups.*)

MATVEY. What a day we've had, Vera dear! Lyubov Semyonovna, what's your tally?

LYUBA (*counting in her bag*). Wood grouse—four, ducks—three.

MATVEY. And what do we have, Sulin?

SULIN. Six ducks and another six wood grouse.

MATVEY. Ah! What a land, Vera! Lyubov Semyonovna! Sulin! Come on! (*Pours some vodka into cups, offers one to* LYUBA.) I ought to stay on with you for good and go out hunting every day.

LYUBA. I wish you would. I'd round up a bear for you, a deer, a boar.

MATVEY. Let's drink to our friendship, Lyubov Semyonovna.

LYUBA. Well, just a drop! (*They drink.*)

MATVEY. Hope you don't object, Vera. (*Kisses* LYUBA.) Now, then, let's do it up right. Take this Winchester, Lyubov Semyonovna. Take it; I say. Take it.

LYUBA. O-o-oh! Your rifle? O-o-h! That's too much! (*Clasps the rifle.*) Won't they take it away from me? You'll go, and they'll take it away.

MATVEY. If I give it to you, it's yours. Read the inscription: "To comrade Matvey, a fellow-hunter." You need it more here. There are no bears in Moscow. And in exchange you'll give me your old one—

LYUBA. And how will I go after fowl without a fowling piece?

MATVEY. You say you need the fowling piece? All right, then, keep that too.

LYUBA. Oh, my stars! Let me bow low to you, Matvey!

MATVEY. As in the days of Ivan the Terrible.

LYUBA (*moves closer to the fire and begins to clean the rifle*). Zhenya, you be the hostess, feed the guests, see they're taken care of—your mother's busy!

VERA. Come on, hunters, you can begin.

MATVEY. A blessed land!

LYUBA. The best piece of land on the face of the earth! When God finished creating the world, he brushed all the remaining seeds into his hand and threw them down. That handful fell across the Baikal. That's why animals and plants from all over the world are gathered here. Yes, sir!

ZHENYA. God again. Such a primitive outlook—it's simply amazing!

LYUBA. This is a legend, Zhenya darling, a legend!

MATVEY. Wonderful salamata, Glasha.

GLASHA. Gennady Mironovich has invented a radio. Would you take it to Moscow and see that it gets to the right party, so that collective farmers and the Red Army can have the use of it?

MATVEY. Where is the radio? Is this it? Sulin! (SULIN *flicks on the switch and turns a dial. A throaty voice and distant noise are heard.*) Where's that from?

SULIN. Japan. Matvey Ilyich—Yokohama, as nearly as I can make out. (*They all listen silently to a Japanese military march.*)

MATVEY. Oh, Yokohama! Well, we're not going to give this land to anybody. We'll live here, hunt here ourselves. Won't we, Zhenya?

ZHENYA (*springing to her feet*). I'll—I'll be right back—I'm going home— (*Runs off.*)

VERA. Zhenya darling—

LYUBA. She'll be back. It's Elijah's Day today, Elijah the Thunderer's.

MATVEY. Peter-Paul an hour stole, Elijah's Day steals two away.

LYUBA. The swifts were flying. There was thunder and lightning. The wood devil needed a coat in a hurry. He sat under a pine tree and began sewing one, while Elijah thundered. Every time the lightning flashed, the devil pushed the needle through the cloth, muttering "Why don't you flash more often, lightning?" Elijah got angry and, bang, let a thunderbolt fly at the devil—it smashed the tree to smithereens but the devil dodged it. Yes, these are the things that used to happen here—and now we pick up Yokohama on the radio.

VERA. I'm going in, Matvey, and lie down. Don't stay up too late.

MATVEY. It's all this fresh air. Puts you to sleep, drugs you with pine, if you're not used to it. You go ahead—we won't be long. (VERA *goes off*.) So, Lyubov Semyonovna, it's settled, you'll have a breeding farm. We've decided, Glasha, to breed sables in Far Taiga. We'll set off some territory for a preserve, fence it in, keep it in a natural state, and we'll put it all under Lyuba's management. Of course, it would hardly become the War Department to concern itself with sables. But being a member of the regional government, I can act.

GLASHA. I wrote to a newspaper once and asked why use traps for catching sables? Let them live and breed their kind.

LAVRENTY. You wrote? To a newspaper? When was that?

GLASHA. When you were in the army. They didn't answer.

MATVEY. Sulin!

SULIN. I've already made a note.

MATVEY. Another thing: I had quite an argument with Lyubov Semyonovna as we were walking home—

LYUBA. No, there isn't. I've waded through all the streams—not a trace of it.

MATVEY. You didn't wade very well. What do you say, Glasha? Is there or is there not gold in this district?

LYUBA. There isn't.

MATVEY. There is.

LYUBA. Glasha wouldn't know.

GLASHA. There must be gold here.

MATVEY. Jot this down, Sulin. Glasha—I mean Glafira Ivanovna Bolsheva—is to be put in charge of prospecting for gold. Have we got some canvas boots? Give her yours, Sulin. Leave an order at the nearest depot to send her digging tools. Regular contact to be maintained with her by telegraph.

SULIN. As you say.

MATVEY. You ought to have Lavrenty for an assistant, but that one will be on his way tomorrow. Have you heard about it, Glasha?

GLASHA. I'll get along without Lavrenty.

LYUBA. How do you like that? Tomorrow. The fellow *is* quick on the take-off. And his wife is supposed to bill and coo all by herself? Feeling sorry to be left without a husband, Glasha?

GLASHA. We'll find gold.

LYUBA. Stupid! (*Enter* KORYUSHKO, *followed at some distance by* VLASS.)

KORYUSHKO. I wish to report, Matvey Ilyich—repair of your car has been completed. It can be picked up by the morning express, if we get orders to that effect from the head office. I'd like to ask comrade Sulin to come with me to the office.

MATVEY. Sulin will see to everything. Sit down, mine host.

KORYUSHKO. Thank you. I'd be delighted but we're clearing the Vladivostok express, and that's what's holding Gennady Mironovich up. Pardon me, Lyubov Semyonovna, a word with you on household matters. (*Takes her aside.*) Have you figured out something?

LYUBA. Now, you keep out of it, Alyosha.

KORYUSHKO. I can't. I can't, Lyubov Semyonovna, because—

LYUBA. We'll talk about it at home. Because nothing!

KORYUSHKO. I can't. We must tell everything.

LYUBA. Home with you! Get! (*In a louder voice.*) Thanks for the treat. I'm off. Carry the game, Alyosha.

KORYUSHKO (*with a sigh*). Good appetite—and rest. Delighted. (KORYUSHKO, LYUBA, *and* SULIN, *the latter carrying the radio set, go off.*)

VLASS (*coming forward*). Killed birds, burning wood—everything dies and turns to dust.

LAVRENTY. Leave off, deacon.

VLASS. I'm no deacon. I'm a Molokan. And I've come to settle an argument—let the superior authority judge between us.

LAVRENTY. I won't blather with you.

VLASS. You always fall back on that—for want of arguments, because you don't know how to answer me.

MATVEY. A former Red Army man doesn't know how to answer a deacon? I don't believe it. Well, proceed, Vlass Filippovich.

VLASS. Hearken to the voice of the wise man, Lavrenty. And answer me, why be wise? I had been in the deacon line for fifteen years. I'd read the Gospels—great wisdom that! Then I lapsed into heresy, joined the sectarians, suffered persecution by the old regime for eight years, roamed the country from one end to the other, was exiled to Siberia. And then, when the godless ones seized power, and God bore with it, I spat in his beard and renounced him. Renounced everything. To hell with it! I might just as well be a switchman and tread the path of a fool! I don't believe in anything. For a wise man and a fool will both die. What good is book learning then? What good are worldly concerns?

LAVRENTY. It's better to live the life of a man for one year than ten years as a pig. We have to improve the lot of the working people.

VLASS. In time to come both the fight and the wisdom will be forgotten.

LAVRENTY. Lenin won't be forgotten.

VLASS. The author of Ecclesiastes has been forgotten. They'll forget Lenin too.

LAVRENTY. Fool!

VLASS. Always the same tune! Nevertheless, you have to disprove my unbelief, as formerly you used to disprove God.

LAVRENTY. If a man doesn't believe in our cause, he's a class enemy, and an argument with an enemy is a brief one.

VLASS. Through the rifle barrel? Threatening me with death? But isn't death a transformation of matter from one guise into another, as the materialists teach? I used to be a deacon. Now I'll become a mushroom.

LAVRENTY. A toadstool.

VLASS. Even a toadstool. But why frighten people with death? It's because you don't feel like mere matter yourselves and are afraid of death.

LAVRENTY. We're not afraid of death. But we don't want to die.

VLASS. The early Christians did want to die. Went out with joyous hearts to face the lions. Because they believed in the life in heaven, in another life.

MATVEY. That's because they had no real life on earth and so deceived themselves.

VLASS. That's what I say. They deceived themselves. But they believed. I too deceived myself for many years—and lived in peace. But when I realized that my heaven was empty and a fraud, I began to worry—I became afraid of death, of turning into a mushroom, a worm.

MATVEY. A grave situation—a worm can be easily trampled underfoot.

VLASS. You'll be trampled underfoot too.

MATVEY. No, I'll live on even after death. Not up there, beyond the stars, but here upon the earth, in the memory of men, in my deeds.

VLASS. We know your deeds. Sending munitions trains past the siding—to make war on Japan.

MATVEY. Japan will make war on us—that is, the Japanese imperialists.

VLASS. And you?

MATVEY. What about us? We're the Special Far-Eastern Army.

VLASS. You'll have to die, no matter what. And where there is war, there is death.

MATVEY. If necessary, we'll go through death too.

VLASS. Why is it necessary?

MATVEY. How else? We're building our happiness on this earth, aren't we?—and so we have to defend our happiness.

VLASS. And if they kill you?

MATVEY. Lavrenty will be left, Glasha, Petka—

VLASS. What do you care? You won't be here.

MATVEY. What of it? Tomorrow I won't be at this siding either. But the sable farm soon will be. And gold will be found by Glasha. The more I manage to do on this earth for the happiness of those near and dear to me, the longer I shall live.

VLASS. How many are there near and dear to you?

MATVEY. Plenty. All the workers the world over. My country. My party. Our children. Their life, Molokan, is my life. It is myself living in their persons. Not in three persons but in millions of persons. Your God is no match for me there.

VLASS. I have no people close to me, nor children, nor anybody. Nor do I want anybody, except myself. I want to live to pleasure my own eyes. The rest can be wiped off the face of the earth—I won't stir a muscle.

MATVEY. That's why you're afraid of death, deacon. You live alone like a mushroom, and like a mushroom you'll turn into dust, into nothingness.

VLASS. You're just as afraid. Yes, you are. You can make these beautiful speeches just so long—till you find you're facing death yourself.

LAVRENTY (*leaping to his feet*). I'll paste you one, you sniveling sectarian!

VLASS. Words! You're all brave with words. But let the old man with a scythe rise up before you and your beard will tremble and your hair stand on end. It would be interesting to have a look at you then.

MATVEY. Well, look at me, deacon. Look well. Do you see?

VLASS. Now, here—do I see what?

MATVEY. In another three months I'll be dead! (*A noise increasing to a roar drowns the cry that has been torn from* GLASHA *and* LAVRENTY. *Like a shadow the Vladivostok express shoots by. It is gone and all is still again. Only the rhythmic clicking of the wheels on the rails is heard. Everybody is silent. Rising,* MATVEY *speaks.*) Let's go!

CURTAIN

ACT III

Inside the saloon car. Windows look out on the platform. A corridor and doors lead to the bedroom and to the exit. It is early morning. MATVEY *is seated in front of a mirror, shaving.* KORYUSHKO *stands before him.*

MATVEY. Sit down, please. Sit down.

KORYUSHKO. It's all right. Don't upset yourself. I'm more comfortable standing. You wanted to see me, Matvey Ilyich?

MATVEY. That's right, Alexey Yefimovich. Sit down, I tell you. (*Looks for and finds a paper on his desk.*) This is a brief statement about your work and the condition of your siding. I may as well tell you right away—it's a very favorable statement. (*Hands over the paper.*)

KORYUSHKO (*having just sat down, gets up again*). I'm happy to hear it. In the name of the working masses at the siding—we—

MATVEY. How soon are we going to be coupled to the train?

KORYUSHKO. In half an hour, Matvey Ilyich. You've made me so happy—so happy. I was worried, thinking I was going to be fired—or something like that. And suddenly, a testimonial. Of course, we live in the taiga and are humble, uninteresting people—

MATVEY (*sternly*). Comrade siding agent, I'll take my testimonial back.

KORYUSHKO. I apologize. I'm heartily moved by your attention and friendliness. And, Matvey Ilyich, if you can remember this, please tell them in Moscow, tell your colleagues, that you passed through Far Taiga and you found everything there as one would expect of Soviet railway men. Don't try to remember our names, it's not necessary. But just tell them simply: the siding Far Taiga is bound up with the entire country.

MATVEY (*rising, and shaking* KORYUSHKO's *hand*). I will, Alexey Yefimovich, rest assured.

KORYUSHKO. Thank you. Please forgive my interrupting you while you're busy shaving. Good morning. (*Starts toward the door.*)

MATVEY. Anything else on your mind?

KORYUSHKO. Anything else? What do you mean?

MATVEY. Just asking. Maybe there's something you'd like to talk about?

KORYUSHKO. No. No, there isn't. What makes you think there is?

MATVEY. I can tell by your walk. Well, out with it—I'll be glad to help you if I can.

KORYUSHKO. You will?

MATVEY. I will indeed.

KORYUSHKO. Seeing as you've shown so much sympathy— (*Whispers.*) Please bring your influence to bear on Lyubov Semyonovna. But she mustn't know that it comes from me—understand? We're having an argument.

MATVEY. Go on.

KORYUSHKO. This spring Lyuba found some gold dust—but she's keeping it a secret. Pretends to be going out hunting—but actually on the quiet she's panning for gold. I've been telling her we must send in a report, notify the government. But she won't let me. She just pans and puts it by—pans and saves. Now, what's the sense of that? You can make her do the right thing, Matvey Ilyich, particularly as she respects you very, very much. (*Enter* LYUBA.) Ah, here's Lyubov Semyonovna to pay you a call. Excellent; I'll go. Forty-one will soon be asking for clearance. (*Goes off.*)

LYUBA. Take this. (*Presents* MATVEY *with some game.*) I shot it at dawn with the rifle you gave me. There's enough to last you beyond Moscow. Lord, how it shoots! It takes your breath away.

MATVEY. How about the sable farm? Have you drafted a report?

LYUBA. I sat up all night over it. My hunters' hand isn't used to writing. Will you be able to make it out?

MATVEY. I'll manage somehow. Sit down, Lyubov Semyonovna. (*Finishes shaving.*)

LYUBA. Just a minute. (*Yanks out some sable pelts.*) Give these to Vera Nikolayevna—from Lyuba. And something in return for your rifle too—sables for a collar.

MATVEY. But the pelts are for Vera.

LYUBA. So they are. And for you— (*Looks about and closes the door to the exit.*) Ah, my good man, Matvey Ilyich. As we tramped through the taiga together, I realized you're a good man, a fine man. I've heard from Zhenya—you're ill.

MATVEY. From Zhenya?

LYUBA. She told me in secret. But the Moscow doctor won't cure you. Go to the warm countries—they'll cure you there. And to pay for the journey—take this. (*Places a small bag on the desk.*) Sell the bag and go.

MATVEY (*weighing the bag in his hand*). It's heavy—

LYUBA. There's dust in it. Gold dust. I know a stream—I go there quietly and pan. Take it.

MATVEY. Well, what do you know! (*Hands the bag back.*) If there is such a need, they'll send me to a warm climate. And money will be found too. Our country is not so poor. All the same, I thank you for your kindness. Our toast to friendship isn't just empty words, it seems. Keep the bag but help Glasha look for placers.

LYUBA. Help Glasha? My, you are sly!

MATVEY. You have to be sly.

LYUBA. Why should we go prospecting? You won't get the gold, will you?

MATVEY. Will you get the sables from the sable farm?

LYUBA. That's different. I'm fond of animals. But if we discover gold, people will come here with machines, there'll be noise and pother, and it'll be good-by to our peaceful taiga.

MATVEY. Good-by to the isolation and backwardness. It's about time, too, Lyubov Semyonovna.

LYUBA. Alexey keeps me awake nights pestering me: "Make it public for the common good." I like that, "for the common good"! (*Enter* VLASS.)

VLASS. Teach how to live.

LYUBA. Have you been drinking?

VLASS. I've been drinking despondency, not vodka.

MATVEY. Just have a seat for a minute. (*To* LYUBA.) So we understand what's what, don't we?

LYUBA. So we do. Take this, eh?

MATVEY. What am I to do with it? I don't need it. Oh, hold on there —I almost forgot. (*Gets a box out of a drawer and hands it to her.*) Cartridges for the Winchester. Sulin will see that you're kept supplied.

LYUBA. You're a brick! Will you be out to say good-by?

MATVEY. Certainly. (LYUBA *goes off.* MATVEY *looks out the window.*) Where does she come from? The Amur?

VLASS. That's right. A fisherman's daughter.

MATVEY. The whole taiga is stirring. It's sure to rain. Even the pines smell. It's a fine Indian summer.

VLASS. I've come to clear myself before you, to repent in the fullness of my heart.

MATVEY. "The heart is deceitful above all things, and it is exceedingly corrupt, who can know it?"

VLASS. What's that from? Jeremiah?

MATVEY. Right the first time.

VLASS. Well, I didn't know but that you might be angry with me about yesterday—my verbal license—what I said about Japan. I wasn't quite myself then, having taken one too many for courage.

MATVEY. "Woe unto them that tarry late into the night till wine inflames them," warned Isaiah.

VLASS. Heh-heh! Truly spoken. You understand, my words can be misinterpreted. You'll go but I'll stay on, and others here, particularly Makarov—you can figure it out yourself. Makarov has been waiting for an opportunity for a long time. As for my words, they were idly spoken, forget them.

MATVEY. "Every idle word that men shall speak—they shall give account thereof in the day of judgment."

VLASS. Am I to take this as coming from Matthew or from you?

MATVEY. Well, I am Matthew, you know.

VLASS. Where did you come by all this?

MATVEY. I've had it a long time. I worked on the antireligion front. Used to quote the Bible.

VLASS. Everything concerns you.

MATVEY. We can't do without the Bible.

VLASS. I once had a case. I was reciting Psalms from memory at some merchant's funeral, when I saw a fly crawling slowly down the dead man's nose. I began to feel as if I were being tickled, and it got so I started shaking with violent laughter and couldn't stop. Well, I made my voice sound like sobbing—and, believe it or not, nobody noticed the difference, some people even complimented me on showing so much feeling. And I could have been an opera singer and earned fame and honors. How can an unbeliever go on living under such conditions? Tell me.

MATVEY. My advice to you is go home and shave. Buy yourself a razor and shave. That's the way you'll save yourself.

VLASS. I feel humiliated and crushed.

MATVEY. "Blessed are the meek."

VLASS. Well, how about yesterday's incident, Matvey Ilyich? All I ask is that you trust me to switch points. I want nothing more. (*Enter* MAKAROV, GLASHA, *and* LAVRENTY, *the last carrying a traveling case.*)

MATVEY (*shaking hands with the new visitors*). What do you say, Ivan Makarovich, should we trust him to switch points?

MAKAROV. That we can't.

VLASS. "Vengeance is mine, and recompense." You have no call to vent your spite on me.

MAKAROV. You haven't seen me vent any spite yet. (*To* MATVEY.) He has renounced God but doesn't believe in you either. That means he's an empty man. And you can pack an empty man with anything you like. Maybe gunpowder, maybe poison. You can't trust an empty man.

VLASS. But what if I feel the ache of my own emptiness? What if I'm looking for a new faith—perhaps have already found one? What if I prostrate myself before the one who's strong and place my spirit in his hands? Maybe he's the prophet for me? Maybe, like Christ, he's trampling down Death by death, and I'm saving myself through him!

MATVEY. Sit down, my dear guests. My wife has a headache but she'll be up soon. Make yourself at home, Lavrenty. Well, Vlass Filippovich, you've said all you had to say and you've had your answer.

VLASS. My eyes perceive the shadow of your greatness! (*He rises, bows low, and goes out.*)

MAKAROV. The shadow, that's just the point. The other day a strange old man was passing by. Vlass asked him into the booth and they had a good long talk. The old man wanted to know how you get to the Arguin River through the taiga. And, I suppose, how you get from the Arguin to the Amur by boat, eh? And across the Amur is a foreign country, eh? They call themselves sectarians!

GLASHA. Last night, Matvey Ilyich, we had a special meeting—on account of—

MAKAROV. On account of your departure.

GLASHA. We went on record with our decisions. Not all of us will have a chance to fight the Japs bayonet to bayonet. But we have to take on certain obligations. We have to prepare ourselves as guides in the taiga. We have to watch all strangers that may be passing through. (*Reads.*) "Resolved: Comrade Makarov shall give an account of his experiences in guerrilla warfare in enemy territory. Also a group shall be organized for the study of conversational Japanese—"

MAKAROV. With Gennady as the teacher.

GLASHA. We ask you to accept this statement and to check on it some time in the future. So that every fighter who has been lost may be replaced by—

MATVEY (*rising and drawing himself up to full height*). I thank you for your trust in me, comrades and friends. Not all of us will still be alive when these events take place. But those to whom this honor will be granted—

GLASHA. We'll be alive then, all of us, no question about it. My dad here was condemned to death for guerrilla fighting by Admiral Kolchak himself. He was caught with six other comrades, and the Whites led them off, tortured them—twisting their arms—and shot them down! He lay in the snow wounded and freezing the whole day. Mother found him—warmed him, and there he is, still alive. The bullet is in him to this very day. Feel it!

MAKAROV. I'll load my rifle with this bullet and I'll plant it right in the forehead of a White general—no less. So I have to live on at least until I am a hundred.

MATVEY. You're of the guerrilla, the taiga breed—as strong as an oak. Let 'em have one for us, too, Ivan Makarovich. I'll keep in touch with you, comrades. (*Accepts the paper from* GLASHA.) And who's to take Lavrenty's place on the track here?

GLASHA. Well, I'm staying on, Matvey Ilyich. I've been put on the job starting today.

MATVEY. So you've arranged it between you?

LAVRENTY. We went for a walk together last night.

MATVEY. Bequeathing your beat to her?

LAVRENTY. No, we just strolled in silence.

MATVEY. Saying good-by?

LAVRENTY. Thinking.

MATVEY. Well, it's never too late to think. Lyubov Semyonovna will help you, Glasha. She's found a stream with some placer deposits—gold.

LAVRENTY. Found a stream? But she insisted—

MATVEY. She was joking.

GLASHA. I knew it—by her boots. They have river clay on them.

MATVEY (*producing a camera and equipment—to* GLASHA). Can you take pictures?

GLASHA. Gennady knows how.

MATVEY. Let him teach you. Take this. Learn to use it. Make some shots of Far Taiga, of Petka, paste them in an album, and send them to me. And I'll show them to him. (*Pointing at* LAVRENTY.)

GLASHA. I'll send them. And you must give me a picture of yourself —autographed.

MATVEY. Agreed. (*Looks for a photograph, finds one, and inscribes it.*) We've spent only one day together but we've become lifelong friends. Because we have the same goals and share the same interests. That's what makes us strong, friends, what makes us invincible. During my absence I leave comrade Makarov as my representative to check up daily and to educate you nonparty people in the party spirit.

MAKAROV. I'll strive to the utmost to be worthy of my candidate's rank. Of course, I'm the only party man here, so no party meetings are held. Nevertheless, we read the papers aloud. Maybe you have some interesting books?

MATVEY. We certainly have. (*Takes all the books from the shelf, stacks them up, and hands them to* MAKAROV.) Read them and remember a friend.

GLASHA. I've brought you an infusion of Chinese root. Take it a drop a day, Matvey Ilyich. The Chinese crawl across the border on their bellies to get it. Please take it.

MATVEY. Thank you, Glasha dear. (*Reads his inscription on the photograph.*) "Your taiga is far, but we all have a far goal—Communism. This is what we think of, this is what we live for—to the last second of the last hour." And if we die, we'll die fighting. Right? (GLASHA *steps forward, gazes into* MATVEY's *eyes, kisses him, and goes out.*) H'm, h'm! Well, you'd better go, friends. I'll come out to the platform presently. (MAKAROV *and* LAVRENTY *leave in silence.*) H'm, h'm! (*Paces the car with long strides.*) H'm! "Across the steppe the Cossacks are riding, the Red Army heroes are riding along—" There you have it, comrade Malko. (*Enter* ZHENYA.)

ZHENYA. Good morning, Matvey Ilyich. Vera Nikolayevna's not in? (*Turns to go.*)

MATVEY. Just a minute. What is it? Secret business?

ZHENYA. No, no. I just wanted to say good-by to her.

MATVEY. Only to her?

ZHENYA. No, to you too, of course.

MATVEY. Sit down, then. (ZHENYA *sits down obediently.*) And what are the secrets that you have with Vera?

ZHENYA. Why, none. What gave you that idea?

MATVEY. I know.

ZHENYA. What do you know?

MATVEY. Everything.

ZHENYA. You know, Matvey Ilyich? As a member of the Lenin Young Communist League— I mean, Matvey Ilyich, I give a solemn Young Communist oath that I shall stay at my post and continue to serve our aims. We'll not waver, Matvey Ilyich, when the enemy crosses our border. Good Matvey Ilyich, take my blood for a transfusion. Take it, I beg you. Take me to Moscow, Matvey Ilyich, let them transfuse my blood to you, Matvey Ilyich.

MATVEY. So that's it! Who gave you the idea? Who told you, Zhenya? You have truthful eyes. Who told you, daughter?

ZHENYA. Matvey Ilyich. we Young Communists—

MATVEY. Glasha? (ZHENYA *shakes her head.*) Lavrenty? (ZHENYA *shakes it again.*) Vlass? (*And again.*)

ZHENYA. Don't ask me! Don't ask me, Matvey Ilyich.

MATVEY (*walks over to her, draws her to his breast, and caresses her*). Don't squander your young blood, daughter. You'll need it one day. (*Enter* VERA. *Seeing her,* ZHENYA *breaks away, seems about to say something, then—afraid that she may cry—rushes out.* MATVEY *and* VERA *exchange glances. There is a pause.*)

VERA. That one—what's the matter with her?

MATVEY (*sternly*). Who gave you the right to deceive me?

VERA. Matvey!

MATVEY. Who gave you the right not to trust me? Am I no longer a commander of the Red Army? Am I to be disregarded as though I were already a squeezed lemon?

VERA. What's come over you, Matvey? What are you saying?

MATVEY. Why wasn't I told the truth?

VERA. Zhenya—

MATVEY. You, Sulin, the chief, and this car—what am I to say about you all? You've bundled me off quietly to Moscow on a made-up special mission—afraid I might feel depressed, succumb to pessimism if I found out the truth. You doubted my ability to face the facts. Comrades turned conspirators!

VERA. We didn't mean it that way, dear. That wasn't in our minds at all.

MATVEY. What was in your minds? The fear that I might be seized with despair? But I'm not only a sick man, I'm also a Bolshevik. And I don't recognize anything as being hopeless. There is no such thing!

VERA. Of course, Matvey, of course!

MATVEY. Who told you I'd lost hope? The doctor? But is it impossible for him to have been mistaken in his diagnosis? If he couldn't have been mistaken, there's no point in dragging me to Moscow, and yet that's what you're doing. So you have hope yourselves. So you think, who knows, he may get over it. And if there's an iota of hope, how can one give up the fight? Is this what we teach the soldiers in the Red Army? We have to fight for the hope, damn it! Fight, and not bow our heads with humility saying, just as Vlass does, we'll die anyway. You've placed me on the same level with Vlass! (*Enter* SULIN.) I'm busy! (SULIN *withdraws instantly.*)

VERA. Matvey! All we wanted was to see you in harness as a commander of the Red Army until your last day.

MATVEY. I'm going to put up a struggle for my life, fight for it! In Moscow I'll stir up all the institutes, all the doctors—I'll try every experiment. I'd rather die under a surgeon's knife, in a glorious attempt to conquer death, than fold my arms in meek resignation. Do I make myself clear?

VERA. Yes, Matvey, you do. That's why we're going to Moscow. We still have time and there's still hope.

MATVEY. That's more like it! Come here. Look at me. Well, I've put the fear of God into you, haven't I?

VERA. Matvey! Oh, Matvey! (*Clings to him.*)

MATVEY. It'll be better now, believe me. All the more, since I've known everything anyway.

VERA. You've known? Since when?

MATVEY. We were still in Vladivostok. I forced the doctor to tell me the truth.

VERA. And never a word to me!

MATVEY. I didn't think you could stand up under it. Forgive me.

VERA. My dear! It's the first time I've ever seen you like this. Well, we're at one again. There's no more need to dissimulate. Nor to hide my tears. And there won't *be* any more tears either. My dear!

MATVEY (*holding her in a firm embrace*). Siding Far Taiga. Far. We could have gone right by. But what seemed far turns out to be close. And the people here too are like our closest friends. Here the taiga hums. Here the devil sews himself a coat. Then, bang, Elijah hurls a thunderbolt—and the old devil runs away—coat and all. Vera dear! (*Enter* SULIN *carrying a box. After him come* GENNADY, *with a guitar, and* LAVRENTY.)

SULIN. Everything's in order and will be delivered safely. I expect comrade Tomilin will have to come down to Moscow later to give detailed information. (*Sets the radio on the desk and turns it on.*)

MATVEY. You think so? Better start training your substitute, Gennady.

GENNADY. Zhenya is willing, if the occasion arises. She can already take messages by ear, without looking at the tape, and does it very well. Comrade Sulin has been very complimentary about my work on the radio.

MATVEY. So he has. Is the guitar going to Moscow too?

GENNADY. I want to sing you a good-by song, Matvey Ilyich—with your permission.

MATVEY. Of course—I insist. How about the train, Sulin?

SULIN. Due in about five minutes.

MATVEY. Sing us something gay, my friend, something cheerful—full of the zest of living.

GENNADY. Sure thing. (*Quickly picks a tune, cocks his head, and sings, as usual, half-whispering his words, but very expressively and strikingly.*)

> Ah, hear the troika sleigh bells ring,
> And hear the merry song they sing.
> Our steeds, as through the snow they race,
> Spray silver powder in our face.
>> No star shines in the wintry sky,
>> But lights of earth go flitting by.
>> The cheerful tinkling in my ears
>> Banishes all black cares and fears.
> Fly off, my soul, brave dreams to find—
> Faint hearts and faces left behind,
> While close beside me in the dark
> Two dear eyes glow with tender spark.
>> O chattering sleigh bells, simple friends,
>> Accomplices to love's sweet ends,
>> Speak not my private thoughts, nor bare
>> My ardent secrets to the air.
> Fall back, all you who bar the way!
> I thirst for life—no hand can stay

My headlong passage through the night.
For love and hate I've boundless might!

MATVEY. That hits the spot! (GENNADY *leans back. A brief pause. Then, suddenly, the roar of a passing train. The engine hoots. The brakes screech. The train stops.*)

GENNADY. Forty-one. They'll couple the car on now.

MATVEY. Let's step out to the platform. They've asked us. Come on, Vera dear. (MATVEY, VERA, *and* SULIN *go off.*)

GENNADY (*to* LAVRENTY). Lavrenty Petrovich! I'd like—I wish you the best of luck, Lavrenty Petrovich. (*They shake hands.*) May I say frankly—I don't envy you. I'm sorry for you, Lavrenty Petrovich. (*Goes off. Voices—words of farewell are heard through the windows.* LYUBA *enters hurriedly.*)

LYUBA (*holding a big bunch of autumn foliage, looks around, places the leaves on the desk, then notices* LAVRENTY). Sitting here? You *are* a cut-off thumb! You might at least kiss Petka good-by. (*Goes off. Enter* GLASHA.)

GLASHA. You here? I thought you'd come out. Good-by, Lavrusha. Write to me when you feel like it. And don't worry about me—I've found my job.

LAVRENTY. What if I—come back? Will you take me in?

GLASHA. A father is always welcome.

LAVRENTY. And a husband?

GLASHA. I don't know. You had your chance. And you won't be too heartbroken. (*The car jerks as it is being coupled to the train.* GLASHA *puts her arms around* LAVRENTY *but rushes out as* MATVEY *and* VERA *enter.*)

LAVRENTY (*dashes to the window, then darts nervously about the car*). Comrade Commander—are we leaving?

MATVEY. We are, comrade Bolshev.

LAVRENTY. I've been a track walker, comrade Commander. Millions of rubles of the people's money have been entrusted to my care. I've had to guard every spike so all the trains would pass safely. And another thing. The border is a long way from here, of course, but even here strange old men snoop around.

MATVEY. Glasha has sharp eyes.

LAVRENTY. She's been assigned to gold prospecting, Matvey Ilyich. And so it turns out I'm only sick with my own discontent, as Vlass is, and have earned no respect for myself. Take even Lyuba Koryushko —you think more of her than of me, and she even shoots better than I do. Of course, one should move ahead and rise, but not like that— gain fame and that sort of thing, and give up one's job, one's work—

MATVEY. What are you driving at? I don't follow you.

LAVRENTY. I only understood it myself last night. But I was ashamed to turn back. Now I want to be like you, to live like you, comrade Commander. (*The car begins to move.*) Like you, comrade Malko—

here at my old siding! (*Throws his traveling case out the window and dashes off into the exit corridor. Those standing on the platform are seen slipping slowly past the windows, waving their hands and caps.*)

KORYUSHKO (*running along the platform*). Matvey Ilyich! Many thanks! Heartily delighted! (*His voice dies away. The train gains speed.*)

MATVEY (*sees the bunch of leaves and picks it up*). Lavrenty has stayed behind, Vera dear. Ah, what wonderful people are coming up. And we too will go on living. Yes, we will—we will!

CURTAIN

THE SQUARE OF FLOWERS

BY VASSILY ILYENKOV

THE name of this play, a translation of *Campo dei Fiori*, a square in Rome in which Giordano Bruno was burned at the stake at the hands of the Inquisition, suggests a parallel between the fate of the great Italian philosopher and poet and the martyrdom of countless Russians who in the territory occupied by the Germans refused to renounce their faith and conscience and accept the overlordship of the brutal invader. Seventy million Russians were reduced to the condition of slavery at the height of the German invasion. Millions of them were driven off to Germany. Great numbers were held in concentration camps. Some of the bolder spirits rebelled and formed partisan bands. But the majority suffered their fate in silence hoping for liberation by the Red Army, frequently only to be cheated of delivery by the intensified terror of the retreating Germans. There was also a small though not negligible minority who for personal gain or under pressure accepted service under the Germans, filling the numerous ranks of local officials, policemen, spies, and even hangmen. "The Square of Flowers" pictures representative types of both groups, the suffering majority and the subservient minority, whose conflict of moral values forms the subject of the play.

The author of the play, Vassily Pavlovich Ilyenkov, was born in 1897. After some years as the head of the Board of Public Education in two provincial cities that later were devastated by the Germans, he began writing short stories. A collection of these was published in 1931, and was followed in 1933 by a novel, "Driving Axle," an English translation of which was published in this country the same year. He afterward wrote another novel, "Sunny City," and brought out three volumes of short stories comprising some of the work he had contributed to the *Red Star* as a frontline war correspondent. "The Square of Flowers," the only play he has written, was published in 1944.

A. B.

THE SQUARE OF FLOWERS

CHARACTERS

Anna Sergeyevna, age 52
Tatyana Sergeyevna, age 55
Nadezhda Sergeyevna, age 50
Sergey Petrovich Kashirin, age 75, their father
Katya (Katerina Petrovna), age 20, daughter of Anna Sergeyevna
Ivan Ivanovich Mushkin, age 30
Anatoly Berkutov, a flier, aged 30
Lieutenant Gütner, a German officer
German Soldiers
A Messenger, an old man
An Interpreter, a German

The action takes place in a small town a thousand kilometers from Moscow.
Time: Autumn, 1941, to spring, 1942.

ACT I

A bright, cheerful room. Left, two windows and a glass door giving onto a veranda which overlooks a garden. Right, a curved staircase leading to a room on the second floor. Beyond it, upstage, a door to the kitchen and a Russian tile stove. Under the staircase, an arch, covered with a curtain, leading to another room.

In the center, a table with a lamp and a samovar. Left, beneath one of the windows, a sofa. A profusion of flowers in vases. A clarinet case and a clock with a huge pendulum hang on the wall. A big mirror in the right corner. A sideboard, with a brass mortar on it, in the left corner. It is late at night. A kerosene lamp glows under its white shade. The windows and the glass door are covered over with blankets. ANNA SERGEYEVNA *is drying dishes and glancing anxiously every now and then at the clock.* TATYANA SERGEYEVNA *is knitting.* NADEZHDA *is seated on the sofa smoking. The sound of gunfire drifts in from the distance.*

ANNA. It's late, and Katya's still out.

TATYANA. No cause to worry, Anyuta. Ivan Ivanovich will see her home.

NADEZHDA. Fine lot of protection he is! Miserable insect!

ANNA. You mustn't speak like that, Nadya. Ivan Ivanovich is a very pleasant and decent man.

TATYANA. Nadezhda hates him.

NADEZHDA. You've guessed it, Tanya. I can't understand how Anyuta can still have any respect for that—that nobody.

ANNA. Ivan Ivanovich is the only man left we can turn to for advice. We are defenseless women, and how much do we understand of what's going on? Everybody's run away, including our Communist leaders—just as panicky as all the rest. Only Ivan Ivanovich has shown any self-control.

NADEZHDA. Why should he run away? It makes no difference to an insect which flower it lights on.

ANNA. How can you talk like that, Nadya? Ivan Ivanovich is the secretary of the town soviet; he's a responsible official.

NADEZHDA. The responsible ones have left to fight the Germans. The insects have stayed on.

TATYANA. We've stayed on.

NADEZHDA. Because we're insects.

ANNA. But, Nadya, think, where would we go? Four women and an old man. It would be certain death.

NADEZHDA. Yes, you're right, Anyuta. A snail can move anywhere it wants—it carries its own house on its back. But how can we carry ours?

ANNA. That's just it. What are we without this house? Our whole life's wrapped up in it.

NADEZHDA (*ironically*). Life?

ANNA. It's easy enough for you, Nadya, to solve such problems. You've never let everyday cares and worries affect you. But I've put everything I've had—all my strength—into these walls. Father struggled a lifetime to build the house, to make sure we had a roof over our heads. Tanya poured all her money into it—her entire salary for dozens of years of teaching. Now all of a sudden to leave everything to the mercy of fate and flee to some place in Siberia, become charity cases in some strange family, be given a corner to sleep in, and humble ourselves for every potato, when we have everything—potatoes, pickled cucumbers and apples here in the cellar—why, it would be madness, Nadya, and I for one am happy that Ivan Ivanovich has opened my eyes.

NADEZHDA. Just see that he doesn't help shut them, Anyuta.

ANNA. Take this brass mortar. It's over a hundred years old. Our great grandmother pounded rusks in it. It's something sacred to me. How can I leave it behind? I'm a plain, down-to-earth sort of person—for me everything here, every rag and scrap has meaning. And you—you're just the same as when you were young. You live in a world of fancy, in the clouds, you despise ordinary life.

TATYANA. There you go fighting again. All your lives. You've never understood each other.

NADEZHDA. And never will. Life's passed us by—big, shining, beautiful life. Others it caught up in its swirl, carried them off somewhere, like a river in spring. But we, the Kashirins, we've been left behind our high fence to die surrounded by the things we love—brass mortars, flowers, chickens.

ANNA. Well, has it been such a bad life? We haven't had riches but we've always had enough for our needs, eaten our own bread, got everything by our own efforts. We've lived quietly, harmed nobody, never set the world on fire, just led a modest life, like everybody else.

NADEZHDA. Like everybody else—like all the gray little people. All right, then, so we've lived our time, we can't go back. But why do you force the same fate on Katya? Why have you got her tied to your fence? You refused to let her go to Moscow and study acting. You're killing an actress in her. You're rushing her into a marriage with that contemptible Mushkin. You stopped her from being evacuated with the Kramskies. Out there, in Siberia, she would have been out of all danger. What's going to happen to her now? Have you thought about that?

ANNA. You know, the Germans may not be quite as bad as these writers make them out. They're just hard on the people who resist them. And we'll live quietly, inconspicuously. Katya will always be at home, with us— (*Dull rumblings of gunfire are heard. The window-panes rattle.*)

TATYANA. Why, for heaven's sake, did Katya have to go out at a time like this?

NADEZHDA. I asked her to get me a book from the library. I have to finish a translation from the English.

ANNA (*irritably*). Dear God! Who's going to read your translations now? Your foreign languages! (SERGEY PETROVICH *pushes aside the curtain and enters.*)

TATYANA. Papa, more firing again, do you hear it?

SERGEY PETROVICH. There's always plenty of firing in a war. Even killing. You're a school teacher and ought to know these elementary things.

NADEZHDA. The Kashirins know life only from books, and in books war is pictured as an interesting event.

ANNA. Please, Nadya, please, stop your sarcasm. You can see I'm trembling all over. Oh, God! Where's Katya? (*She begins to move nervously and distractedly about the room, bumping into the furniture. Some fragile object falls off a table and breaks.*)

SERGEY PETROVICH (*putting on a light winter coat*). Goodness, we've gone and left those gladiolas out in the garden—the ones we dug up.

ANNA (*in despair*). Papa, this is no time to think about gladiolas. You're not going anywhere!

NADEZHDA. I'll go get them. (*Opens the door to the veranda.*) Turn down the lamp, Papa. Oh, it's pitch black! And something's burning— way off over there. (*They all hurry to the door.*)

TATYANA. It seems to be in the center of town.

ANNA. No, it's the railway station. (*A loud explosion is heard.*)

NADEZHDA. That's our fliers bombing the town. We're being bombed by our own men.

TATYANA. How do you mean, our own? Why should they be bombing our town?

NADEZHDA. Our town is German now. We too are German, and we must be bombed, and will be.

ANNA. It gives you an eerie feeling. Our house is on the outskirts, almost in the fields. It would be more cheerful if we were closer to other people.

SERGEY PETROVICH. Oh, no, Anna Sergeyevna, I deliberately chose this place because it wasn't near other people. There's a fire over there —all right, let it burn. But it's quieter here. You didn't forget, did you, to pick the Antonovka apples? They're supposed to be left on the tree until just before the frost.

ANNA. Papa, you're like a child—Antonovka apples, gladiolas. Look at the horrors out there. And Katya's not back yet. I'm sure I'll go mad.

SERGEY PETROVICH. It's too early to go mad. The war is only beginning, my dear Anna Sergeyevna. We'll have need of our intelligence.

Granddaughter will come but the Antonovkas will get frostbitten, and they're our bread. You can trade Antonovkas for a lot of flour. Have you dumped all the potatoes down in the cellar? (*Nobody answers him. There is another loud explosion—and a pause.*)

NADEZHDA. They're bombing the railway station. It was such a beautiful building. And it gave you such a pleasant feeling to meet the trains and think of all the people going to distant parts, to Moscow. Now we'll never see Moscow. We're German. What a horrible—shameful thing! (*She covers her face with her hands and stands motionless.*)

TATYANA. I don't understand why our men had to retreat. I don't understand a thing.

SERGEY PETROVICH. Nothing could be clearer. We're Russians, a peaceful and hard-working people. We've been spending our time building, planting gardens—

NADEZHDA. While the school teacher Tatyana Kashirina was taking her pupils out into the fields and telling them about the flowers. Now you see the blossoms. Fine blossoms—like Mushkin!

TATYANA. Man needs flowers too—for his soul, his heart. Who knows, maybe my pupils are now fighting Germans all the more bravely because I taught them to love flowers, fields, their native land.

SERGEY PETROVICH (*cheerfully*). That's the truth, Tatyana Sergeyevna! Flowers. "By this sign ye shall conquer!"

NADEZHDA (*ironically*). Flowers against tanks!

TATYANA. Yes. Tanks are powerless against men who love the flowers of their land.

SERGEY PETROVICH. That's right, Tatyana Sergeyevna, flowers. "By this sign ye shall conquer!" Therefore, we'd better bring in the gladiolas after all. (*Goes off to the veranda.*)

ANNA. I'll die if Katya doesn't come at once.

TATYANA. Don't get all worked up, Anyuta. It's bad for you. Calm down, dear. I'll put on my coat and go meet her. (*Begins to put on her coat and hat.*)

ANNA (*to* NADEZHDA.) If anything happens to Katya you'll be to blame. And generally speaking, you have a bad influence on her.

NADEZHDA. I love Katya no less than you do—or Tatyana. But you're ruining her life with your kind of love.

ANNA. You've never been a mother, and can't understand.

NADEZHDA. Yes, I've been deprived of that happiness—the greatest happiness a woman can have.

ANNA. But Colonel Berkutov was married.

NADEZHDA. And the Kashirins are convinced that loving a married man is a great sin.

ANNA. The same old reproaches again. One would think you were still a girl of twenty.

NADEZHDA. It's harder to bear at fifty, knowing you can never repair what was smashed in your youth. You killed the mother in me. Now you're killing Katya. (SERGEY PETROVICH *returns from the garden, carrying a box of flower bulbs.* TATYANA *takes it from him.*)

SERGEY PETROVICH. They'll have to be put in the cellar, Tanya. It's too warm up here.

TATYANA. Right away, Papa. (*She moves the sofa and pulls up the rug which covers the trap door to the cellar.*) Give me a light, Papa.

SERGEY PETROVICH (*taking the lamp*). By the way, how are the bees doing down there? Maybe some water's got in?

TATYANA. How could it? It's a wonderful cellar, dug right out of the sand. Only you, Papa, could have chosen such a fine place for the house. (*Enter* KATYA, *pale and frightened. She is followed by* MUSHKIN, *wearing a hat and neatly pressed coat, and carrying a cane.* ANNA *rushes up to* KATYA.)

ANNA. At last—Katya darling. I've been worried to death.

MUSHKIN. Good evening, Anna Sergeyevna. My compliments, Sergey Petrovich. How do you do, Nadezhda Sergeyevna? (*Shakes hands all around.*) Well, I've brought your Katerina Petrovna, safe and sound. Please sign a receipt.

KATYA. Am I a package?

MUSHKIN. A figure of speech, as it were.

NADEZHDA. A witty remark by a man of education. Did you bring me the book, Katya dear?

KATYA. The books are burning. Everything's burning. Everything.

MUSHKIN (*moving about the room*). Everywhere bombs are bursting, there's shooting, and fires have broken out. I must confess that even though I'm a man it gives me quite a creepy feeling. War is a terrible sight. Our Serdechensk has never seen anything like it since the day it was founded. It's a nightmare.

SERGEY PETROVICH. Serdechensk saw Tartars once and Polovetsians beneath its walls.

MUSHKIN. What sort of war was that, Sergey Petrovich? Arrows, spears, boiling pitch. You should see German tanks, sir. Tigers! Lions! Elephants of iron and steel! They bellow, roar, thunder. It's terrible, simply terrible!

NADEZHDA. If it's so terrifying, why do you stay on?

MUSHKIN (*surprised*). Why? Do you still fail to see the reason? (*Emphasizing every word.*) I've stayed on because you, the Kashirins, are staying. How could I possibly desert you in such a terrible hour? Desert you, defenseless women and an elderly man? It would have been despicable. You are my friends. You have warmed my solitary life with your kindness and love. If I'm to lose my life, let it be only with you.

ANNA. I've always regarded you as our friend, Ivan Ivanovich. Thank you, thank you.

MUSHKIN. Believe me, Anna Sergeyevna, my life is your life. I've lived through so much since that day.

ANNA. Yes, of course. You're in great danger, Ivan Ivanovich. You hold a responsible post, and the Germans pounce first of all on just such Communists as you.

MUSHKIN. I'm not a party man, Anna Sergeyevna. I was going to apply for membership but kept putting it off. I had some sort of premonition, as if somebody was whispering in my ear, "Hold on!"

NADEZHDA. But you served the Soviets?

MUSHKIN. I did, in a manner of speaking. But look at this clock. It was made by Paul Bourré! A fine clock, but it doesn't go by itself. Somebody has to wind it. And in that way it's been going for half a century. It ticks. Once it ticked in the office of some bourgeois director, then the director vanished, but the clock went on ticking. Later it was sold, and you bought it. It ticked just as well under the Soviets, it's served you, and so we say this is a fine clock! You and I—all of us, there are millions of us—we're a kind of clock too. Somebody pulls up the weight each morning; the weight, following the Newtonian law, pulls down the tiny wheel of our fate, and we act, not of our own free will, so to speak, but mechanically. We tick. Now the weight of our life will be pulled by other hands and we'll tick again, because clocks are still needed.

ANNA. You do explain everything with such marvelous simplicity, Ivan Ivanovich. Right away I feel ever so much calmer. And really, if you stop to think of it, there's probably nothing to fear. We're plain, ordinary humans and we're not answerable for the way things were before.

NADEZHDA. A clock can't be accused of treason. Hurray!

MUSHKIN. Well, I leave you to judge. Let's take your family, for instance. You've lived like thousands of others. You puttered about in your garden, grew vegetables, and provided for yourselves, so to speak. Anna Sergeyevna managed the house. Tatyana Sergeyevna taught children to solve little problems, to write. Nadezhda Sergeyevna made translations from foreign languages. Sergey Petrovich grew gladiolas and apples. As for Katerina Petrovna, she's of course completely guiltless of anything. Now, have you done anything that could be charged against you? You never mixed up in politics, made no speeches at meetings, didn't push yourselves—you merely lived quietly, peacefully, like harmless insects, so to speak. You lived in your quiet little house, behind a high fence, and you were not in the least concerned about the preaching and building of socialism or the people who were doing it. You lived in your little state, so to speak, following your own quiet laws, and you're not responsible for anything. (*The* KASHIRINS *gaze at* MUSHKIN *with awe, as if he were pronouncing a death sentence on them. Only* NADEZHDA's *face breathes contempt and hatred.*)

TATYANA. But I taught children in a Soviet school, Ivan Ivanovich.

I taught them to hate slavery, coercion, fascism. I tried to develop in them the feeling of love for all mankind.

MUSHKIN. Yes, Tatyana Sergeyevna, I well remember your words, "Children, all human beings are brothers." That's a romantic hallucination, Tatyana Sergeyevna. As the poet says, "Dearer than a host of lowly truths we hold deceit that lifts aloft our souls." You spun a cloud of golden dreams over us, Tatyana Sergeyevna. Well, you were mistaken. And a mistake, as the saying goes, is not counted as deceit. Particularly since you didn't speak your own words, but mechanically, so to speak, repeated what others were saying. The teacher resembles a phonograph, which plays any old song.

SERGEY PETROVICH. But I've received the gratitude of the Soviet authorities, Ivan Ivanovich. I was awarded a medal for my flowers when I showed them at the National Agricultural Exposition. I've served my people with all my heart. I'm not a phonograph or a clock. My gladiolas have brought beauty into people's lives.

MUSHKIN. But your gladiolas have no relation to politics, have they, Sergey Petrovich? They are nonparty creatures, like me, like all of you. Flowers adorn the luxurious palace of a rich man as dispassionately as they do the humble cabin of a woodsman. Now, I feel your high fence itself is the symbol of your aloofness from politics. Like quiet Switzerland you preserve neutrality in every war. Incidentally, Moscow has been taken by the Germans.

NADEZHDA. That cannot be.

MUSHKIN. It's true, Nadezhda Sergeyevna. The Red Army is withdrawing behind the Urals. The ship that was taking you to the land of socialism has run upon the rocks, so to speak. What of it, though? You have your Solitude Island and your faithful servant Friday. Let the ocean rage around you— Anna Sergeyevna can go on raising chickens and pickling cucumbers.

ANNA. Ivan Ivanovich, we've lived our time, but Katya—I'm afraid for her. A young and pretty girl—and the Germans. You say yourself they're lions.

MUSHKIN. Anna Sergeyevna, let any lion try and touch her with his paw. I'll be the first to jump into his cage and wrest Katerina Petrovna from his fangs. And it's an open question who has more courage, the one who jumps into a lion's cage without any weapons, in order that he may save the victim, or those who run home for a gun.

NADEZHDA. Oh, yes, you'll go into the cage, Mushkin—I have no doubts about that—and you'll remain alive, as did that little dog that went to live in a lion's cage. Remember? The lion got so attached to the little dog that he was upset when it died. But it died all the same, the poor little dog.

MUSHKIN. This touching story you've recalled is very much to the point. It's very instructive. It shows that a lion too has a heart.

SERGEY PETROVICH. When he's in a cage. But right now he's at large, isn't he?

MUSHKIN. Who knows what he's like when he's at large? Who has observed his conduct in that state?

SERGEY PETROVICH. We've heard a thing or two about it.

MUSHKIN. Those are the tales of timid people, Sergey Petrovich. But what are the facts? Take my case. I too was a little apprehensive. Then they came. At the time I was making an inventory of our fire-fighting equipment. Lieutenant Gütner entered the office. He introduced himself politely, praised me for continuing with my work, and offered me the post of secretary of the town administration. Salary, four hundred rubles; bread ration, two hundred grams—

ANNA. There you are. That's splendid.

KATYA. And you—agreed?

MUSHKIN. I could, of course, assume the pose of an insulted patriot and refuse. That would have been a beautiful gesture, but stupid. Yes, I agreed, because I thought of you, Katerina Petrovna, of your future, of your aunts, your mother, your aged grandfather.

ANNA. My God, the trouble we've caused you. I'll never forget it.

NADEZHDA. It's certainly unforgettable.

MUSHKIN. Now, what is required of you? Only that you live as before, quietly, peacefully, maintaining neutrality, so to speak, keeping your door shut to others. Well, it's time for me to leave. Oh, I nearly forgot. Nadezhda Sergeyevna, Lieutenant Gütner offers you a job as his interpreter. Two hundred grams of bread.

ANNA. Isn't that fine, Nadya? You see, your foreign languages have come in handy.

NADEZHDA. You can tell your Gütner that Nadezhda Kashirina is a human being, not a dog that can be beckoned with a piece of bread.

MUSHKIN. You're wrong to refuse it. Two hundred grams and a job! That shows they trust you. Think it over, Nadezhda Sergeyevna. Good-by. I'll stop in tomorrow morning. By the way, Sergey Petrovich, tomorrow you may expect a man from the town hall who will call for flowers to be placed on the graves of the fallen German soldiers.

SERGEY PETROVICH. Flowers in autumn? They're all dead. (*Pointing at the flowers in the vases.*) That's all that's left.

MUSHKIN. They'll do. They'll testify to your nonpartisan sentiments, so to speak. Good-by. I'll call tomorrow. (*Bows, kisses* KATYA'S *hand, and goes off. There is a general silence for a few seconds.*)

KATYA. How shameful—and awful!

TATYANA. A phonograph—I'm a phonograph.

NADEZHDA. At last he's gone, unspeakable man!

ANNA. Nadya, this is impossible. I demand you respect my friends. I do so as the mistress of this house, as your elder.

NADEZHDA. You're no longer the mistress, Anyuta. Now it's the lion who is the master, and you're only a little dog, a wretched, miserable little dog.

ANNA. You're getting absolutely unbearable. You tear at everybody's nerves. And it's hard enough as it is.

SERGEY PETROVICH. Yes, the clock is going. (*Approaches the clock.*) But *my* clock I'll wind myself, with my own hands.

KATYA (*putting her arms around him*). Darling Grandpa! (*There is a knock on the door. Everybody is petrified. The knock is repeated.*)

SERGEY PETROVICH. It's the wind. The apple tree is rattling its branches. Good Lord, we've forgotten all about picking those apples. (*Another knock.* KATYA *walks bravely to the door.*)

ANNA. Katya, don't, for heaven's sake. You'd better go to your room. (*Pulls her away from the door and up the staircase.*)

TATYANA. Who's that? (*A faint, indistinct voice is heard.*)

NADEZHDA. Open the door and ask. What are you afraid of? (*Walks to the door and opens it. A man in a flier's suit crawls in.*) Who are you? What's wrong with you?

FLIER. I'm a friend. My plane crashed. Please help. (KATYA *runs down the stairs.*)

KATYA. Were you shot down?

FLIER. Yes. I'd already dropped my load on the railway station.

NADEZHDA. So it was you who bombed our station?

FLIER. Yes, I did that. And right on the bull's-eye—the main building. But a shell knocked out my engine. A fire started. Then I bailed out—and I must have sprained my ankle. I saw your house—

KATYA. Aunt Nadya! Aunt Tanya! Why don't we do something? Mama!

ANNA. I don't know your name, comrade, but—

FLIER. Anatoly Berkutov.

NADEZHDA. Berkutov?

ANNA. You see, comrade Berkutov, we understand—you're in a terrible situation. You must be suffering severe pain too. But we're defenseless women, everything frightens us—

KATYA. Mama!

NADEZHDA. Tanya, bring some bandages—quick. Katya, there's iodine in my room, on the little table— (KATYA *runs upstairs.*)

ANNA. We can't help you. They must be looking for you, they may even be on your track already. My God, shut the door, Tanya! What are we going to do? They'll be coming here.

BERKUTOV. If you're afraid—I'll go. I'll drag myself somewhere else.

NADEZHDA. You ought to be ashamed, Anna. Tanya, help me lift the comrade. (*They try to lift the wounded man, helped by* SERGEY PETROVICH. KATYA *comes down with iodine and gauze.*)

BERKUTOV. Help me out of my flying suit, quick, will you, and give me some civilian clothes.

NADEZHDA. Are you from Moscow?

BERKUTOV. Yes, that's right.

KATYA. Then Moscow is still ours.

BERKUTOV. I took off from Moscow at eight o'clock tonight.

NADEZHDA. Thank you for the good news.

BERKUTOV. Thank you for your good heart. My leg does hurt very badly. I must have broken it.

ANNA. You see, you need a doctor. And what can we do? Yes, we'd better take you to the doctor—he doesn't live very far from here—Dr. Skvortsov, Nikolay Pavlovich, is his name.

KATYA. Mama!

BERKUTOV. I'll get to the doctor's later. Right now I've got to make a quick change. Hide my outfit—throw it away—

SERGEY PETROVICH. Throw it down in the cellar, Tanya. I'll get you a coat and pants. (*Goes off through the curtained arch.*)

BERKUTOV. If the Germans come here, tell them I'm a relative of yours—wounded during the bombing of the city. And don't call me Anatoly—use some other name. I think I lost my papers. They may find them.

NADEZHDA. We'll call you— (*she is agitated*) Victor.

BERKUTOV. That was my father's name.

NADEZHDA (*startled*). It was? Victor Berkutov—

TATYANA. Nadya, you'd better help me take off his boots.

KATYA. Does it hurt very much?

BERKUTOV. Please hide me somewhere. And forgive me for causing so much trouble. As soon as I get better I'll go.

ANNA. Ivan Ivanovich will think up something. He'll hide you some place. Our house is so small.

KATYA. Mama! (SERGEY PETROVICH *brings a coat and pants.*)

BERKUTOV. I'll go. You don't have to worry. I understand.

SERGEY PETROVICH. Here are the pants. Only they'll be too short for you.

KATYA. We'll hide you in the wardrobe. It's in my room—a huge one.

BERKUTOV. In a wardrobe—anywhere. But do it quick.

SERGEY PETROVICH. Katya dear, you can't coop a man up in a wardrobe. We'll have to take him down into the cellar.

KATYA, NADEZHDA, AND TATYANA (*happily*). The cellar. Into the cellar!

ANNA. But it's crowded with boxes, sacks, barrels of pickles. No, no —anywhere but the cellar.

KATYA. I'll make a bed there right away. I'll bring down my own mattress. (*Runs upstairs.*)

BERKUTOV. I don't need a mattress. A couple of boards will do. Well, now I do look like an ordinary resident of Serdechensk. Thank you, where is the cellar?

SERGEY PETROVICH. Open the trap, Tanya. Somebody has to stand downstairs and give a hand. But we're all so old and feeble, devil take it. (KATYA *brings down a mattress, a sheet, and pillow, disappearing with them into the cellar.*)

ANNA. Now, why a down pillow? That blanket too—I'll go get another one. (*Goes off behind the curtain.*)

SERGEY PETROVICH. Take care you don't disturb the beehives. (TATYANA *and* NADEZHDA *pull* BERKUTOV *to the trap door.*)

KATYA (*popping her head out of the cellar*). Everything's ready.

TATYANA. Hold his feet, Katya dear. Here we go.

BERKUTOV. There's a gun in my suit, give it to me.

SERGEY PETROVICH (*cautiously pulling a pistol out of the suit*). It won't go off, will it? I'm awfully scared of these things. (*There is a loud knock on the door.*)

NADEZHDA. Close the trap, Tanya, quick.

TATYANA. But Katya's down there.

NADEZHDA. Quick. (*Slams the trap door.*) Push the sofa back where it was. (ANNA *enters with an old torn blanket and gazes alarmedly at the door. The knocking is repeated more strongly. Loud voices are heard.*)

SERGEY PETROVICH. I think it's the lions roaring.

ANNA. My God, we're lost. I told you. (TATYANA *turns the carpet back over the trap door and pushes the sofa into place.*)

NADEZHDA. Papa! Lie on the sofa quick—you're dying.

SERGEY PETROVICH (*lying down on his back*). What do you mean, I'm dying? I don't want to die, even if I know how. (TATYANA *opens the door. Several* GERMAN SOLDIERS *and* LIEUTENANT GÜTNER *burst in.*)

GÜTNER. Stehen Sie ruhig!

NADEZHDA. He orders us to stay quiet. Stehen Sie ruhig!

GÜTNER (*looking her over with an expression of surprise*). Sprechen Sie Deutsch? Wo ist Ihre Waffe?

NADEZHDA (*smiling*). We're women. Unsere Waffen sind Tränen.

TATYANA. Our old father is dying.

NADEZHDA. Ja. Wir weinen am Sterbebett unsers Vaters.

GÜTNER. Wo haben Sie den russischen Soldaten verborgen?

NADEZHDA (*pointing at her father*). Da is unser alter russiche Soldat. Er hat bei Port-Artur gekämpft.

GÜTNER (*turning a flashlight on the old man*). Oh, he's a new dead. Soon you have to dig a grave. (*To the* SOLDIERS.) Durchsuchen!

NADEZHDA. Well, you can search the house. (*The* SOLDIERS *inspect the room. Some go up the staircase.* GÜTNER *takes the case with the clarinet off the wall.*)

GÜTNER. Oh, mein Liebling! (*Puts the clarinet to his lips and plays a children's tune.*) I respect very much old men. I also have old Grossvater—Grosmutter. (*Lays the clarinet on the table. A* SOLDIER *grabs it and shoves it into his bag.*) Lassen, Fritz! (*The* SOLDIER *pulls the clarinet out of the bag and lays it on the table.*) Auf wiedersehen. (*The Germans go off. The three sisters stand petrified.*)

SERGEY PETROVICH (*still lying on the sofa*). It almost feels as if I really were dead. How do you like that? There was once a man named Sergey Petrovich Kashirin, a resident of the town of Serdechensk. He lived for seventy-five years—three quarters of a century. Quite a time, the devil take it. And now he's dead. He's lying on a sofa in his own house, and his daughters are weeping over him. His neighbors will come to the wake—they love reminiscing about a man when he dies. In a year or two they'll forget him, and Sergey Kashirin will die for the second time, lost even to memory. Strictly speaking, why should he be remembered? What did he do in his long life? Let's draw up a balance sheet. He built a house, planted and cultivated a garden. He brought up three daughters—one to pickle cucumbers, breed chickens, and cook a dinner. The second he taught to help the first. The third—learned five languages so she'd have more ways of not understanding anybody. It was a bad life the old man lived, a very bad one. (*Gets up, walks to the sideboard, takes a decanter of raspberry brandy, and pours himself a glass.*) Daughters! Sergey Petrovich Kashirin is dead. Weep for him—because he lived three quarters of a century to no good purpose, in slothful futility. To Sergey, newly deceased servant of the Lord. (*Drinks.*) Yes, to a servant—a slave— (*Pours more and drinks.*) To the new dead! (*Snatches the flowers from their vases, throws them to the floor, and tramples on them.*)

TATYANA. Papa, what are you doing?

CURTAIN

ACT II

The following morning. The same room. The blankets have been taken down from the windows. Through the glass doors can be seen trees with golden autumn leaves. The faces of the KASHIRIN *family show the signs of a sleepless night.*
ANNA *speaks in a dead-tired voice, holding a hand to her head and wincing with pain.*

ANNA. No, I can't stand this torture. My head's splitting.
TATYANA. And this is only the first day. What will it be like later on?
ANNA. We're all worn out, afraid to turn around, and expecting something dreadful to happen.
SERGEY PETROVICH. The wise men of the past used to say: "The beginning of wisdom is fear." Pour me some tea, Tanya. Make it strong.
ANNA. I wish Ivan Ivanovich would hurry up and come. He'd advise us what to do.

NADEZHDA. Do you seriously mean to tell him what's been happening here?

ANNA. Who else can advise us? You? I can't go on living like this. I can't.

NADEZHDA. But if you must—if we all have to?

ANNA. But why should we, of all the families here, be the ones to go through this torture? If this Berkutov—if he were a relative of ours, even a distant one—well, I'd understand. But as it is, he's an utter stranger.

NADEZHDA. Anybody who doesn't happen to be named Kashirin is a stranger to you. To me he's as close as if he were one of us.

TATYANA. Nadya is awfully fond of imagining things. Yesterday she even got the idea that this Berkutov is somehow related to Colonel Victor Berkutov. But that would be too much. Such coincidences only happen in stories, Nadya.

SERGEY PETROVICH. We ought to give him some tea—find out how he's getting along down there. Then the next thing is to think up something in the way of medical treatment.

TATYANA. He has a broken leg. He needs a surgeon. We can't do anything for him, Papa.

ANNA. Of course, he should be taken to a doctor—put in a hospital —given proper treatment.

NADEZHDA. Are we to go to the Germans—tell them we have a wounded Soviet flier in our house who needs hospitalization? Is that it?

ANNA. But why not, Nadya? You saw yourself last night—they're not brutes. They didn't take Papa's clarinet—they were polite.

NADEZHDA. Oh, they're very polite. They will politely hang the wounded man on our own apple tree, right there by the window, so we can enjoy a free show.

SERGEY PETROVICH. But why is it really necessary to have a doctor, a surgeon? What's a broken bone? What's so terrible about it? In my garden such accidents happen every year. (KATYA *comes down the staircase. She tiptoes over to the others and speaks in a whispe*r.)

KATYA. Well, how are things down there? (*Points to the floor.*)

TATYANA. Oh, Katya, I was so frightened last night when the Germans began knocking on the door and you were still in the cellar. I don't remember how the trap door got shut. Were you scared?

KATYA. Not a bit, Aunt Tanya. But all of you up here—you must have been.

ANNA. But they could have opened the trap, and what would have happened to you? I nearly died of fright.

KATYA. Why, Anatoly had a gun. He said they wouldn't get him alive—not in a million years! It gave me a creepy feeling being there. But it was interesting. Complete darkness and quiet—and you could hear everything—the scuffing of their feet, their voices. We held our breath. I felt a bit scared. Then I thought—I'm in good health, after all, but he has a broken leg and wants to groan, but mustn't. Then all my fright suddenly disappeared. Anatoly kept reassuring me and begged to be forgiven for causing us so much trouble.

NADEZHDA. He probably comes of a refined family.

KATYA. Yes, he's wonderful. It's hard enough not to moan when you have a toothache, and he had a broken bone.

TATYANA. It's terrible. I remember once when I hit my finger with a hammer, it made me—

ANNA. It made you run to the doctor, where you got a cold compress and then a hot one. And you want a man with a broken leg to do without a doctor. Tanya, go call Dr. Skvortzov right away.

KATYA. Anatoly asked us not to tell anybody he's here.

SERGEY PETROVICH. If that's the case, it's up to us to supply medical aid ourselves.

ANNA. You're so naïve, Papa. Think of it, a fracture of the leg.

SERGEY PETROVICH. That's nothing. Remember that time a storm snapped your favorite apple tree, the brown Antonovka, right in two? There was just a thin skin holding the parts together. I made splints out of wood, bandaged it all up tight, spread window putty around the wound, and the tree came to life again.

TATYANA. That was a tree, and this is a live human body.

SERGEY PETROVICH. Man is more tenacious than a tree. And so we begin the operation. Katya dear, bring me my box of garden tools. (KATYA goes off.)

ANNA. You've gone mad, Papa!

SERGEY PETROVICH. I'll certainly go mad if you keep telling me that. I have enough intelligence to last out my lifetime. And Sergey Kashirin has no intention of trying to borrow other people's. Nor will you, if you take my advice, Anna Sergeyevna.

TATYANA. Katya certainly looks like a new girl—there's more life in her, her eyes are burning—and she's prettier than ever.

NADEZHDA. People are always more beautiful when their souls are caught up in something big. (KATYA brings the box of garden tools. SERGEY PETROVICH rummages through it, making a clatter.)

SERGEY PETROVICH. If a surgeon is needed, I'll be a surgeon.

ANNA. But it's impossible.

SERGEY PETROVICH. If it's necessary, a man must perform everything, even the impossible. Katya darling, get me the sticks I hid in the attic—the walnut ones. They're in the corner near the stove flue. (KATYA rushes up the stairs. An old man, a MESSENGER, enters.)

MESSENGER. I've been sent here from the town hall—I'm supposed to get flowers—for a wreath for the dead Germans.

SERGEY PETROVICH. The flowers have been killed by the frost. You understand? The frost.

MESSENGER. I understand, Sergey Petrovich. Flowers are like human beings—they too love the sun. And it's bitter cold out. It chills you through.

SERGEY PETROVICH. That it does. (*Sings.*)

> Chrysanthemums have long since died in the garden,
> But my love still lives in my aching heart—

Colonel Berkutov used to sing that awfully well. Oh, those were the days!

MESSENGER. But you're still the same, Sergey Petrovich. As long as I've known you, you never seem to grow any older. So you want me to tell them—the flowers are dead?

SERGEY PETROVICH. That's right. Tell them the only thing left alive in the garden is nettles. If they want nettles, they're welcome to them.

MESSENGER (*laughing understandingly*). Nettles? Heh-heh-heh! That's just their style. (*Goes off through the door to the veranda.*)

SERGEY PETROVICH (*singing*).

> But my love still lives in my aching heart.

ANNA (*tearfully*). We'll all be lost. My God, what have we done to deserve such suffering? (KATYA *brings down the sticks.*)

NADEZHDA. That Mushkin—he used to be a pupil of yours, didn't he?

TATYANA. Yes, I'm sorry to say, Mushkin was my pupil. And I must admit he was a fine boy at school. Ah, those children! I remember once I gave them dictation: "Why is it harmful to drink too much tea or coffee? Because they are the two caffein drinks." Mushkin wrote: "Because they are the two coffin drinks." I asked him "Why did you write coffin, Vanya?" He answered, "That's what you said, isn't it? People who drink too much tea or coffee end up in a coffin." I never could convince him that caffein and coffin weren't the same thing. He was a stubborn one.

SERGEY PETROVICH. You wasted your breath. He's twice as poisonous as caffein himself.

KATYA. Up there in the attic you can see the smoke rising from the buildings. And it's such a gorgeous morning, the gardens are all crimson. It made me want to cry. I felt so sorry for our poor little town. The houses looked so small and pitiful and drab!

NADEZHDA. Is the railway station still burning?

KATYA. Yes, it is, Aunt Nadya. Now I won't see Moscow for a long time.

NADEZHDA. Did you ask him, Katya, what street he lived on?

TATYANA. Colonel Berkutov lived on Bozhedomka Street, didn't he?

SERGEY PETROVICH. Now, let's go. Tanya, open the trap.

KATYA. He must be hungry. Have we anything left from supper, Mama?

ANNA. I don't know. I don't know anything. Do as you please.

TATYANA. There's a cabbage pie on the sideboard—some eggs too.

SERGEY PETROVICH. And while you're at it, bring the raspberry brandy and a glass. Better make it two glasses, Katya dear.

ANNA. Are you taking some putty?

SERGEY PETROVICH. What putty?

ANNA. The kind you use for sealing up windows in winter.

SERGEY PETROVICH. Oh, no, Anna Sergeyevna, you won't catch me on that. I haven't gone that crazy. (*Goes down into the cellar, followed by* KATYA.)

NADEZHDA. You stand at the window, Tanya—make sure that nobody sees anything. I'll watch the door. And you, Anyuta, you go into the kitchen and see if the door there is locked.

ANNA. No, I won't be able to stand this torture much longer. (*Goes off.*)

NADEZHDA. Tanya, I don't like Anyuta's attitude. She can ruin everything. I can't handle her—you do it much better. I ask you, Tanya dear, keep your eyes on Anyuta. The war has come to our house. We'll have to go through a terrible battle to save this man. And another thing I ask you—don't remind me of Berkutov. Don't touch the wound. It hasn't healed and never will as long as I live. This Berkutov is such a striking likeness of him. Perhaps he's Victor's son.

TATYANA (*embracing her*). Forgive me, Nadya.

NADEZHDA (*looking through the glass door*). Mushkin's coming! Close the trap, Tanya, quick!

TATYANA (*shouting down into the cellar*). Papa! Katya! Mushkin's coming! Get up here, quick!

SERGEY PETROVICH. Are you crazy? I'm operating. (TATYANA *slams the trap door and pushes the sofa back into place.* MUSHKIN *knocks on the door.* NADEZHDA *pauses.*)

NADEZHDA. Just a minute, Ivan Ivanovich. The key's stuck. (*Opens the door.*)

MUSHKIN. Well, how did you make out last night? I worried about you. To make it still worse, the whole town was in a state of turmoil. A few planes were shot down and the Germans were looking for fliers all night. I had to help. All the fliers got killed when they crashed, except one or two who made off.

TATYANA. They came here—during the night.

MUSHKIN. Who—the fliers?

NADEZHDA. No, the Germans, your masters.

MUSHKIN. God! Why do they bother you? I told them there were only old women in the Kashirin house. I spoke to Lieutenant Gütner and he promised not to disturb you. How did they behave? (*Enter* ANNA.)

ANNA (*happy to see* MUSHKIN). Oh, Ivan Ivanovich! You've come at last. We've gone through such torture. (*Cries.*)

NADEZHDA. Haven't we? Armed men broke into our house, searched it for some Russian soldiers. And they did that in the Kashirin house, of all places.

ANNA (*crying*). It was such an awful, such a horrible experience!

MUSHKIN. Yes, I can imagine how upset you were. And Katya, where's she?

NADEZHDA. She's somewhere around.

TATYANA. Tell us what's happening in town. Out here we know nothing.

MUSHKIN. It's quiet there now. The streets are being patrolled. But I have a pass, of course. Listing of the population is being rushed through. I have to help. They're introducing numbers for each inhabitant.

ANNA. I don't understand, Ivan Ivanovich. What are the numbers for?

MUSHKIN. They're instead of a passport. You'll have your number, Anna Sergeyevna, say six hundred and sixty-six. And you'll wear it on your chest. That's all. Nothing terrible.

NADEZHDA. How do you mean, nothing terrible? There used to be a human being called Anna Sergeyevna Kashirina. Suddenly there is no human being; there's only number six hundred and sixty-six.

TATYANA. Will I have a number too?

MUSHKIN. Certainly.

TATYANA. You mean—like ordinary objects, like books in a library? Like a number in a stock inventory?

MUSHKIN. We are a stock.

NADEZHDA. But this is an offense to a human being. It's like a brand on an animal.

MUSHKIN. I see nothing offensive in that. It's a way of keeping order. But where's Katerina Petrovna?

TATYANA. Probably up in her room. Katya! Ka-tya! (*A suppressed cry comes from below.* TATYANA *shifts the table, jarring plates and glasses on it.*)

NADEZHDA. She's taking a bath.

TATYANA. Or perhaps she's in the attic—hanging up rowan berries to dry.

MUSHKIN. I know the attic is her favorite spot. I'll get her down. (*Goes up the staircase.* TATYANA *quickly pushes aside the sofa and opens the trap.*)

TATYANA. Katya, quick! (KATYA *climbs up.*)

NADEZHDA. Anyuta, let us do the talking and acting. You keep silent. Or we'll be lost.

KATYA (*in a low voice*). Oh, how he frightened me! Where is he?

TATYANA. Gone upstairs to look for you. Tell him you've been taking a bath. How is it down there?

KATYA. Grandpa began with the raspberry brandy, of course. To steady his hands, he said. Anatoly had some too. He needed it—it may lessen the pain. (MUSHKIN *is heard shouting,* "Katerina Petrovna! Katya!" *His voice draws nearer.*)

TATYANA. Anyuta darling, not a word!

ANNA. Oh, do as you please. Only leave me alone. (MUSHKIN *comes down the stairs and smiles as he sees* KATYA.)

KATYA. I was in the bathroom. Had a lovely bath.

MUSHKIN. But your hair is dry.

KATYA. I only wash it in rain water. The soap is so bad.

MUSHKIN. I've brought you a cake. It's beautifully scented. (*Pulls a cake of soap out of his pocket and smells it.*) German.

NADEZHDA. It smells awful. Like corpses. (*From below comes the voice of* SERGEY PETROVICH: "Open it.")

KATYA. Heavens! I've locked Grandpa in! Poor Grandpa! (*Moves the sofa and tries to lift the trap.*)

MUSHKIN. Allow me, Katerina Petrovna. I'll help you. (*Starts toward her.*)

KATYA (*in a frightened tone*). No, no! I'll do it myself. Stay where you are, please. I'm not such a helpless female as all that. Sit down. (*She opens the trap.* SERGEY PETROVICH *climbs out.*)

KATYA. Grandpa darling! Forgive me for shutting the trap door on you.

SERGEY PETROVICH. Everything's all right. I put bandages on. (KATYA, *embracing and kissing him, whispers something into his ear.*)

MUSHKIN. Who were you treating, Sergey Petrovich?

SERGEY PETROVICH. Treating? Yes, I was.

MUSHKIN. You look just like a surgeon—your sleeves rolled up.

SERGEY PETROVICH. I treated a barrel, Ivan Ivanovich. A barrel of pickled cucumbers went dry in the staves. So I treated it. Tightened the hoops. Why, I can do everything, Ivan Ivanovich. I'm a gardener, a beekeeper, a horticulturist, a cooper, a cabinetmaker, and a surgeon for all maimed—objects in the household.

TATYANA. Ivan Ivanovich says the Germans are going to hang some numbers on us.

KATYA. What do you mean?

MUSHKIN. Just ordinary numbers, so to speak—tallies with figures on them.

KATYA. I like that! Will I have to walk around with a tally?

MUSHKIN. You, too, Katerina Petrovna.

KATYA. Rats!

ANNA SERGEYEVNA. Where do you get such expressions, Katya?

SERGEY PETROVICH. So it's tallies? Such as I tie to my apple trees? Little pieces of wood with a number and a name?

MUSHKIN. No, only a number, no name.

SERGEY PETROVICH. But look, Ivan Ivanovich, there are different kinds of apple trees—Brown Bark, Antonovka, the Anise kind, the Warped kind— You see, even the trees have names. Aren't we as good as they are?

MUSHKIN. Well, you have an apple tree you've called the Sweet Kashirin. But if you'll forgive me, the apple is really awfully sour. In the same way a man's name doesn't express anything. It's just an empty sound, so to speak. But a number is something precise and indisputable. My number, for instance, I already know—it's ten.

NADEZHDA. One stands for Lieutenant Gütner and the zero alongside is Mushkin. Yes, it's very accurate.

KATYA. "Mushkin the Tenth"—sounds like a royal title.

MUSHKIN. It does have an imposing sound. You'll be hearing it in due time, Katerina Petrovna. You're all so gay, but if you only knew how my heart sank when I stepped on your porch. I saw blood on your steps. And I thought— (*Everybody stands frozen.*)

KATYA. What did you think, Ivan Ivanovich?

MUSHKIN. I thought that something terrible had happened to you. And I also said to myself, "I hope to God that flier that the Germans are after hasn't crawled onto this porch."

SERGEY PETROVICH. Why, that was the hen I killed this morning. Remember the speckled hen we had?

KATYA. Yes, it had speckles all over it.

TATYANA. Why, of course, that was the hen. It was spotty and lame.

SERGEY PETROVICH. Oh, what an idea! Ha! Ha! Ha! (*All laugh, including* MUSHKIN.)

MUSHKIN. The speckled hen, you say? (*Laughs, holding his sides.*)

ANNA (*sobbing*). Oh, my God, my God! I can't stand this nightmare.

KATYA. Mama darling, do calm yourself.

SERGEY PETROVICH. And don't forget, Anna Sergeyevna, that you're the hostess and have to treat your guest to dinner.

MUSHKIN. Well, Anna Sergeyevna, I must confess I'm hungry. As you know, I love chicken with noodles—and so now we'll go to work on the speckled one. (*He laughs. The others are silent.* MUSHKIN *regards everybody with suspicion.*)

ANNA. I'll go get dinner ready. (*Goes off.*)

MUSHKIN. She's terribly shaken up about something. Tell me, has anything very unpleasant happened here. Are you in any danger?

TATYANA. No, no, Ivan Ivanovich. It's just nerves.

MUSHKIN. I have a heavy feeling today. And there's something strange about all of you. It feels close in here— You have blood on your hands, Sergey Petrovich.

SERGEY PETROVICH. Oh, this—this is from the speckled hen. I forgot to wash it off. (*Goes off.*)

MUSHKIN. Just now, coming to your house, I found a pocketbook in your garden. (*Pulls a leather case from his pocket and opens it.*) An identification certificate in the name of Anatoly Berkutov—a photo-graph—

KATYA. May I look at it?

MUSHKIN. Certainly, Katerina Petrovna. See you don't fall in love—he's young and handsome.

TATYANA. You shouldn't make such cheap jokes, Ivan Ivanovich. You know yourself who holds first place in Katya's heart.

KATYA. It's an interesting face. He must be very brave.

MUSHKIN. Well, I don't know. It doesn't take much courage to drop a bomb and fly away. It's really easy.

KATYA (with feeling). You think it's easy to fly a thousand versts—from as far as Moscow?

MUSHKIN. How do you know he's from Moscow? (KATYA is at a loss what to say. There are a few moments of silence broken by the desperate death cry of a hen.)

NADEZHDA. Naturally, it would be Moscow. Only Moscow can send planes so far away.

MUSHKIN. But Moscow is in German hands.

KATYA (having regained self-control). How could it be easy, Ivan Ivanovich? There's his certificate in your hands. He was knocked down, wounded; suffered terribly. Had to throw away everything. Look, even his medal is in the pocketbook. The Order of the Red Banner. I've never seen it so close. How beautiful. It's given only to heroes.

NADEZHDA. What are you going to do with these things now?

MUSHKIN. The things themselves, without their owner, don't inter-est me. But Katerina Petrovna, I see, is quite taken with this toy. Even her eyes sparkle. I can make you a present of it, Katerina Petrovna.

KATYA (putting the order to her chest musingly). No, I could never wear such a high award.

MUSHKIN. Well, take a good look at it and throw it away out of sight. Who knows, the Germans might notice it, and you realize what that would mean—

KATYA. All right, I'll just look at it. I won't keep it.

TATYANA. She's still such a child, Ivan Ivanovich, isn't she? (SERGEY PETROVICH comes in, wiping his hands on a towel.)

MUSHKIN. You are awfully angry with the hens today, aren't you, Sergey Petrovich? Killed another speckled one?

SERGEY PETROVICH. The Germans will gobble them up if we don't.

TATYANA. I couldn't kill even a hen. How can anybody do it—to a human being?

MUSHKIN. I feel awfully depressed today. Katerina Petrovna, sing my favorite song from "The Queen of Spades": "Oh, I'm so wearied, so worn out."

KATYA. No, I can't, Ivan Ivanovich. I'm not in the mood today. It's true of me, too: "I'm so wearied, so worn out."

TATYANA (*dutifully*). Yes, "the cloud came and brought a storm—gone were the happiness, the hopes." I still remember the time I saw "The Queen of Spades."

MUSHKIN. Queen of Spades stands for secret ill will.

TATYANA. I got so terribly frightened when Herman walked up to the old countess with a pistol in his hand—and she died of terror. I felt so sorry—

MUSHKIN. For the countess?

TATYANA. No, for Herman. He killed out of love for Liza. Life has such strange patterns—to kill for the sake of love.

NADEZHDA. Love knows no obstacles.

MUSHKIN. For the first time, I think, I have to agree with you, Nadezhda Sergeyevna. You're right, love knows no obstacles. People in town are already calling me a traitor. Let them. I'm prepared to do anything for the sake of my feeling—my love.

NADEZHDA. I'm not speaking of your love. Herman's crime, like yours, remains a crime and nothing can excuse it. But there's a higher love, and in its path the sin of killing becomes a heroic deed.

KATYA. There they go. I hate listening to talk about death. Ivan Ivanovich, here's a riddle for you. I think it's very funny.

MUSHKIN. I like a good riddle.

KATYA. Well, guess this one: What's the difference between caffein and coffin? And how are they alike?

MUSHKIN. I see we're starting in on death again.

ANNA. Katya!

MUSHKIN. In what way are caffein and coffin alike? Well, it must be —you can't squeeze a lemon with either of them.

KATYA. No, you haven't guessed it. And what's the difference?

ANNA. Katya!

MUSHKIN. The difference is that one gets into you, and you get into the other.

KATYA. You still didn't guess it! You didn't guess it. The resemblance is that both are caffein. And the difference is that caffein, spelled "caffein," is something you drink, and caffein, spelled "coffin," is the same thing when the schoolboy Mushkin spells it out.

MUSHKIN. "Caffein—coffin." Oh, yes, I remember! Oh, yes! (*Laughs.*) You will have your little joke, Katerina Petrovna. Now I really do feel light and easy, I swear. In fact, I suddenly have a craving for pickled apples. It's all your fault, Katerina Petrovna. I'm afraid I'll have to go down into the cellar to get some.

SERGEY PETROVICH. Those—pickled ones—are not too good yet, Ivan Ivanovich. In two or three months—they'll be really delicious.

ANNA. Just in time for the wedding, Ivan Ivanovich.

MUSHKIN. No, that's too long to wait. Gütner said to me: "Hurry up with your wedding while I'm still the master of the town, Mr. Mushkin. I'll make it a feast for the whole town." I beg of you not to put it off, Anna Sergeyevna. Two weeks are quite sufficient for all preparations.

KATYA. Oh! (*Faints.*)

ANNA. What's the matter, dear? Ivan Ivanovich, she's fainted. Help her, quick! (MUSHKIN *rushes to* KATYA. *General confusion.*)

CURTAIN

ACT III

*A month later. The cellar. A clutter of barrels, boxes, sacks, beehives. *BERKUTOV* is lying on a bed made out of boxes, with a small kerosene lamp lit beside him. *SERGEY PETROVICH* is feeling *BERKUTOV'S* leg.*

SERGEY PETROVICH. Does it hurt here?

BERKUTOV. No, it doesn't hurt there either.

SERGEY PETROVICH. Liar. It must hurt. You can't fool me, my friend. You can play hide-and-seek with Katya but to me you've got to tell the truth. I'll now press one of the condyles. It says in the anatomy book: "The lower extremity of the thighbone presents two rounded protuberances or condyles which form articulations with the shinbone and the kneecap." Does this hurt?

BERKUTOV. No. Not at all.

SERGEY PETROVICH (*sits down and pulls a wine bottle out of his pocket*). I can't figure out what kind of a man you are. (*Pours some wine into a glass.*) Let's have a drink. It'll do you good, and me too—I have a kind of circumduction in my head.

BERKUTOV. What's that—a disease?

SERGEY PETROVICH. That's the scientific name—in anatomy. It means circular movement, in plain words, giddiness. (*Drinks.*) I can tell by your eyes it hurts a lot. Come on, out with it.

BERKUTOV. It does hurt.

SERGEY PETROVICH. Why don't you groan, then?

BERKUTOV. Will power. It's stronger than pain.

SERGEY PETROVICH. I see. So you're a man of iron? That's just what Katya says about you.

BERKUTOV. No, I'm an ordinary man. Like everybody else.

SERGEY PETROVICH. And Nadezhda says you're extraordinary. Did you volunteer?

BERKUTOV. No, I was drafted. I used to be a construction engineer. I'm really a peace-loving fellow. I built railway stations, sanitariums, houses. I love building. It's a good feeling when something beautiful takes shape under your hands. It makes life on this earth a little more cheerful.

SERGEY PETROVICH. I see. Then you weren't very anxious to go to war?

BERKUTOV. Hardly. I'd never intended to do any fighting. But when the time came and it had to be done, there wasn't much choice.

SERGEY PETROVICH. I see. Did you have a little house of your own, a family, young ones?

BERKUTOV. No—no house. I'm single.

SERGEY PETROVICH. Then what are you fighting for?

BERKUTOV. So that after the war I *can* have a house of my own, a family—kids. I want to build houses again. One for myself, too. A pretty house, with shrubs and flowers all around.

SERGEY PETROVICH. I see. This is the kind of strategy I like. But if you listen to my women-folk—"He's a hero," they say. "An extraordinary man. He's like Giordano Bruno," they say. That's Katya. "Bruno defended his faith—an idea. And for that he was burned at the stake. In Rome. In the Square of Flowers—the Campo dei Fiori, the Italians call it—burned alive! And he's remembered for the very reason that he lost his life not for any personal interest but for the sake of all mankind." Now that I've talked to you, I feel a little easier in my mind. It turns out you're no different from us. You dream of building yourself a little house and want to have some kids. And Katya and Nadezhda have made you out to be a saint. I don't like saints. It makes me nervous to be around them. They don't feel pain. I do. I don't understand them and they don't understand me. So I was afraid you might be a saint. But I see you feel pain. That makes you near and dear to me. Let's have a drink. (*He drinks.*) I've come to you with my own pain. You see, I haven't a soul to talk to. I used to have a friend, Dr. Skvortsov, but he's taken to skulking in corners like all the rest; he's afraid to go out in the street. Nowadays everybody in town avoids everybody else—they all keep looking around to see who's following. Each one's worrying about himself. No one wants to visit his friends. You have to wear a tally, and it makes you ashamed to appear in public: you feel like a horse or a sheep. Let me explain things to you in proper order. All my life I've been building this house, putting every hard-won kopeck into it. The house itself is insured for fifty thousand and the contents are worth another twenty. Now it turns out that all my work has been for nothing. It'll all go down the drain, straight to hell. Nadezhda, she says, "Serves us all right for being so smug." So it means I'm a dirty skunk because it gives me the shakes to think about losing my house. They've got it all figured out I'm supposed to act differently—as Katya says: "Burn the blasted house so the Germans won't get it." And maybe they expect me to be like Bruno and burn up in the fire myself, eh? Then mankind would remember that once there lived a certain Sergey Petrovich Kashirin, who put on quite a show. But I'm weak in spirit. I can't act like Bruno. I'd be sorry to lose this house. Now, you understand me. You sympathize with me. It's frightening to be alive today, my friend, isn't it?

BERKUTOV. It is. In addition to my plane two others were shot down. And there were thirty men in their crews. They were all burned to death.

SERGEY PETROVICH. Thirty? A-ah! Thirty men.

BERKUTOV. I feel sorry for my comrades. But it can't be helped. We had to save you, Sergey Petrovich. So for your sake thirty men lost their lives.

SERGEY PETROVICH. I see. Burned to death? In a fire, eh? For me? For my house?

BERKUTOV. Yes, for the sake of your happiness. The road to happiness has always been through fire.

SERGEY PETROVICH. So that's where you've led me? I see. I came to you with my pain. And you cheered me up with your little house, your children. Now you've brought me right up to the fire. "Jump, Sergey Petrovich," you say, don't you? Like Bruno? "People burn for you, and now you must burn." Is that it? For the flowers? For the little house?

BERKUTOV. Our whole country was covered with flowers. Flowers were everywhere, even in the factory yards and around the smelting plants. Yes, we lived in the Square of Flowers. Then the enemy set the torch to that square—started a huge conflagration. They're burning us now for our faith in man, in his happiness upon this earth, in his triumph over the primordial evil of the world. We're burning. But like Giordano, we'll never renounce our faith in human reason so long as there's breath in our bodies. (NADEZHDA *comes down the cellar stairs.*)

SERGEY PETROVICH. You're right, Nadezhda. He's a saint. He scares me.

NADEZHDA. Tell me, Victor, where's your gun?

BERKUTOV. Right here. What's happened? (*He searches under the pillow.*) That's funny. This morning it was under the pillow.

SERGEY PETROVICH. Where could it have disappeared to? Nobody's been here today.

BERKUTOV. Katya was down this morning. She brought me my tea.

NADEZHDA. That explains everything. (*Sits down wearily.*) That girl's going to make trouble.

BERKUTOV. What's happened?

NADEZHDA. What should have been expected—what I've been afraid of. Mushkin suspects that we're hiding you. He's just like a bloodhound on your trail, straining at the leash to get down here. It takes every ounce of our strength to hold him back. Now he's changed his tactics. He knows that Anna's the weakest member of our garrison and he's terrorizing her. Anna's afraid of everything. So he demands that he and Katya get married at once. And Anna's agreed.

SERGEY PETROVICH. She's trading Katya for the house—says if Mushkin joins the family, the Germans won't touch it.

BERKUTOV. And Katya?

NADEZHDA. She says death is preferable to such dishonor. We'll have to think up something, or there's going to be a catastrophe.

SERGEY PETROVICH. Yes, Katya's capable of doing anything. She takes after me. Hot blooded, impetuous.

NADEZHDA. Mushkin's coming soon for his final answer. (*A pause.*)

SERGEY PETROVICH. You're a military man. Give the command. Our fortress is besieged. Like Port Arthur. At Port Arthur I served as cook to General Stoessel. We'd never have surrendered if that general hadn't turned traitor. Now I'm back at Port Arthur again—and there's no one to take command over us but you.

NADEZHDA. We've got to make Katya give up that gun. You've got to, Victor. She'll listen to you. You're the only person who has any influence.

SERGEY PETROVICH. I'll go tell Katya to come down. (*Points to* NADEZHDA.) She used to be like that too, when she was young—unmanageable. (*Goes up the stairs.*)

BERKUTOV. Do you have any relatives or friends here? I could move to their place and make it easier for you.

NADEZHDA. It wouldn't be possible, Victor. People are afraid. In any case, we'd never agree to such a thing—to shift our burden onto somebody else. No, we have to go through the ordeal to the bitter end. Fate itself has sent you here. To us you're Moscow. We've dreamed of it all our lives and never seen it. Now Moscow has come to us. You're our dear guest.

BERKUTOV. I've brought trouble to your house.

NADEZHDA. Tell me, is your father an officer?

BERKUTOV. No, he's a private. (KATYA *rushes down the stairs.*)

KATYA. Did you want me?

NADEZHDA. A private—

BERKUTOV. Please give back my gun, Katya.

KATYA. I need it.

BERKUTOV. It's a dangerous article, Katya. You've got to know how to handle it.

KATYA. I do know. They taught us at school how to take it apart, load it, take aim.

BERKUTOV. What do you need a gun for?

KATYA. Somebody has to guard the house. Anything could happen. And you're helpless. You can't even defend yourself, can you? What if the Germans break in?

BERKUTOV. Then the gun will give me a final way out.

KATYA. No. No. You must live. You will live. I—all of us—want you to live.

BERKUTOV. And I want you to live. Give me the pistol, Katya.

KATYA. We can't have it both ways. If you're to live, someone has to die.

NADEZHDA. Katya, what's in your mind?

BERKUTOV. It's not as easy as you think to kill a man. I certainly cannot permit you to do anything of the sort—for my sake. Give me back the gun.

KATYA. Oh, how I hate him! (BERKUTOV *tries to rise.*)

NADEZHDA. Why are you getting up, Victor?

BERKUTOV. I don't want to be the cause of your destruction. I'll go. (*Struggles to his feet but loses his balance.*)

KATYA (*supporting him*). You'll do no such thing.

NADEZHDA. Victor dear—you're going out of your way to get killed.

BERKUTOV. I'm a soldier. It makes no difference to me.

KATYA (*holding him back*). You can't even stand up. You must be insane!

BERKUTOV. I'll crawl.

KATYA. I won't let you go. Pull down the trap door, Aunt Nadya.

NADEZHDA. You're hurting our feelings, Victor. You're like one of the family. Saving you isn't a duty; it's something we want to do because we love you. (*Starts toward the door.*)

KATYA. If you go, that'll only leave one way out for me. (BERKUTOV *slowly lowers himself onto the bed.* NADEZHDA *retraces her steps.*)

NADEZHDA. There's another way out, Katya. Only listen to me calmly. Tanya and I have been thinking it over and this is what she suggests. We have to gain time until Victor gets better. Perhaps two or three months. We have to trick Mushkin. We'll take him prisoner, disarm him, and at the same time allay Anyuta's fears. She understands everything that's going on, you know, and whenever you're down here and don't come right up again, she gets terribly upset.

KATYA. That's why she's in such a hurry to marry me off. But it's not going to be that way.

NADEZHDA. Katya, listen calmly, my dear. You must consent to your mother's wishes. For a time—

KATYA. No, never! I won't listen to any more. Don't dare to talk to me about it.

NADEZHDA. I'm sorry but I have to. You'll tell Mushkin you agree to be his wife but you won't actually go through with it. Make believe you're on the stage. After all, you want to be an actress. And some day, when you're in a play, you may have to kiss an actor you can't bear. Here you have to play the part of a bride-to-be. It's a good chance for you to practice. You'll test your talent.

KATYA. God, what a horrible, detestable part!

BERKUTOV. It's certainly not an easy one. Deception is the most unpleasant kind of weapon. But it's war now, and to deceive an enemy by any means so as to defeat him—that's as honorable as to fight with a gun in your hand.

NADEZHDA. In two or three months Victor will be well again and we'll take him to the partisans, to White Moss—I've heard that's where they are— From there he'll be able to go to Moscow.

KATYA. Yes—to Moscow—to Moscow.

NADEZHDA (*embracing* KATYA). Katya, darling, it's up to you to save him. (*Goes off.*)

BERKUTOV. Give back my pistol, Katya. Your weapon now is cunning.

KATYA. What a shameful part!

BERKUTOV. It's hard on you, Katya, I know—very. But has it been easy for me? Before the war I built railway stations. But the enemy has forced me into the hard rôle of a destroyer and now I drop bombs on my own railway stations. When I press the button to release the bombs I feel like crying out with pain. Afterward I do cry, but nobody has ever seen my tears—or ever will.

KATYA. It's horrible. Life is so cruel.

BERKUTOV. We'll go to Moscow together, Katya.

KATYA. Together? But that wouldn't be possible, would it?

BERKUTOV. Can I leave you here for certain doom? No, I don't want to—I can't—buy my life at the price of yours.

KATYA (*returning the pistol*). Now you've disarmed me. (ANNA *comes down the steps with a plate of steaming meat dumplings.*)

ANNA. Here's some hot dumplings for you. (SERGEY PETROVICH *and* TATYANA *follow her.*)

SERGEY PETROVICH. Hold on, there! Dumplings without raspberry brandy—that's no treat.

BERKUTOV. Thank you, Anna Sergeyevna. I don't know when or how I'll ever be able to repay you for all this pampering.

TATYANA. We've been saving up this pampering for half a century. We didn't know what to do with it. Good appetite.

KATYA. Mama, I've made up my mind. I'm willing.

ANNA. Katya dear, that's fine. I'm so glad. (*Embraces her.*) Anatoly Victorovich, Katya is going to marry Ivan Ivanovich.

SERGEY PETROVICH. What? Are you crazy, Katya?

KATYA. Grandpa darling, it has to be.

SERGEY PETROVICH. I don't want it. I won't permit it.

TATYANA. Papa, a storm is brewing over our house, and we need a lightning rod.

SERGEY PETROVICH. No lightning rods for me! Let everything burn, and the devil with it. I don't want it. I say I don't want it—that's all. I'll set fire to the house. I don't give a damn about anything!

ANNA. Anatoly Victorovich, maybe you can calm the old man. He's lost his head completely.

SERGEY PETROVICH. No, I've found my head, Anna Sergeyevna. And to sell Katya for the house—that's something I won't permit. I'm not that low. Thirty men have given their lives for me—for all of us. Am I going to begrudge my house then? I'll set fire to it!

ANNA. Won't you understand, Papa, that that would mean the end of us? I can't stand this torture any longer, I can't. (*Goes off.*)

TATYANA. There's nobody on guard upstairs. We're so careless! (*Hurries up the steps.*)

SERGEY PETROVICH. Just like General Stoessel—all of you. But I don't intend to surrender my Port Arthur! I don't intend to retreat!

BERKUTOV. Sometimes, to achieve victory, you have to retreat, execute a maneuver, outflank and surround your enemy. Do you have faith in me, Sergey Petrovich?

SERGEY PETROVICH. In you? Yes.

BERKUTOV. In that case carry out my orders. Submit to discipline. You're a private of our besieged garrison. Hide me behind these boxes, leave the trap open. Let Mushkin come down. Katya will stay here. He'll declare his love, and a little while later you'll join them and make the thing official according to the custom of your Orthodox ancestors. Is that clear? (NADEZHDA, KATYA, *and* SERGEY PETROVICH *hide* BERKUTOV *behind the boxes. Just as they are finishing, a knock is heard upstairs.*)

NADEZHDA. Listen! Tanya's giving a signal.

KATYA. He's here! Get out quick! (NADEZHDA *and* SERGEY PETROVICH *run up the steps.* MUSHKIN'S *happy voice can be heard, saying,* "At long last!") Life is cruel!

MUSHKIN (*coming down the stairs*). At long last, Katerina Petrovna!

KATYA. Oh, Ivan Ivanovich! Don't come down here, please! I'm all mussed up. The pickled apples were getting mouldy and I'm sorting them out.

MUSHKIN. I'm so glad we're alone—here, in the cellar. (*Looks around suspiciously.*) Anna Sergeyevna has told me—

KATYA. Yes, I agree, Ivan Ivanovich.

MUSHKIN. You make me very happy, so to speak. (*Kisses her hand.*) I can hardly believe my ears, Katya. I'm so happy!

KATYA. And I'm so happy, too. I'm even ashamed—of my happiness.

MUSHKIN. You have no reason to be ashamed of your happiness, Katya. I've paid a high price for it. I've gone through much torment, much suffering. All the time I had the feeling you were playing with me like a cat with a mouse, so to speak—that you didn't love me—

KATYA. Whatever put such a monstrous idea into your head?

MUSHKIN. Forgive me, Katya. It's true. I've grown suspicious. I can't get rid of the idea that I'm constantly being deceived, that people are lying in wait for me around corners, ready to hit me from behind. When I walk down the streets in town, I see how they look at me. They hate me. And I don't trust anybody. (*Glances about.*) Who's been eating dumplings down here?

KATYA. Oh, that was—Grandpa. He was so happy to hear that we were to get married soon, he had a few drinks and came down here, with a plate in his hand, to congratulate me.

MUSHKIN. No, I can't believe my fortune. (*Kisses her hands.*) Now I can be frank with you, Katya. I had the impression that you were hiding something from me. I guess without my realizing it my suspiciousness must have been getting to be a mania. I even imagined that here, in this cellar, you were hiding—that flier.

KATYA. Oh, yes, you're sick, Ivan Ivanovich. Just think what you've said! Ask my forgiveness at once! Down on your knees!

MUSHKIN (*kneeling*). Forgive me, Katya. I'm so ashamed of myself. (ANNA, TATYANA, *and* SERGEY PETROVICH *come down*, ANNA *carrying an icon.*)

TATYANA. Oh, this is where they are, the two doves—billing and cooing—

ANNA. My children. Let me give you my blessing. I wish you happiness.

MUSHKIN. Believe me, my life is your life, Mother. (*Kisses her hand.*)

SERGEY PETROVICH. Now let's see you love birds seal it with a kiss! (MUSHKIN *kisses* KATYA.)

ANNA. Well, what are we standing here for? Let's go upstairs.

MUSHKIN. I suppose the pickled apples are ready now, Mother.

TATYANA. Yes, now they're ready, Ivan Ivanovich. (*Everybody goes up, except* SERGEY PETROVICH, *who stands, decanter in hand, filling his glass and drinking.*)

SERGEY PETROVICH. Listen, commander. It's all going according to plan, but I wonder if we won't be sorry. The maneuver is a very risky and objectionable one. It's given me such a circumduction in my pate. (*Drinks.*) Yes—in the Square of Flowers. Burned alive! That was a man!

CURTAIN

ACT IV

Scene 1

The end of April. There is a bustle of activity at the KASHIRINS'. *Storm windows are being taken down by* TATYANA *and* NADEZHDA. SERGEY PETROVICH *and* KATYA *are bringing up beehives from the cellar and carrying them out to the garden.* ANNA *is pounding something in the brass mortar.*

Through the open veranda door can be seen the greenish haze of apple trees with tender new leaves.

TATYANA. How lovely! Spring again—and sunshine. It makes me feel so carefree, just as if there hadn't been any terrible winter.

NADEZHDA. Let's get these storm windows up to the attic as fast as we can, Tanya, so Victor can enjoy a real breath of fresh air before he goes.

SERGEY PETROVICH. Careful there, Granddaughter. The other way—hold it on this end. Bees don't like to be rushed. You have to handle them calmly.

KATYA. We have to hurry, Grandpa dear. Time's getting so short. Mama darling, hurry with the coffee. (*She carries the beehive out through the glass door.* ANNA *goes off to the kitchen.*)

TATYANA. I don't know why, but I always feel a little sad in spring, and I keep wishing something would happen—something unusual. I get restless—I want to say tender, gentle things to people.

NADEZHDA. People need tender, gentle deeds, Tanya. (TATYANA *and* NADEZHDA *pick up a window frame and carry it upstairs. For a moment the room is empty. Then* MUSHKIN *comes in through the glass door and, glancing cautiously about, hides behind the curtain.* ANNA *enters and sinks wearily into a chair.*)

ANNA. I'm like a prisoner in my own house. They don't trust me, they watch my every step, my every word. Even Katya's been avoiding me. She's hiding something. I might just as well be a stranger. But he'll go today, and tonight for the first time I'll be able to sleep in peace. (TATYANA *and* NADEZHDA *return.*)

NADEZHDA. Anyuta, make the coffee right away. I'll shut the windows. I think the room's been aired enough. Let's set the table just so—make everything as beautiful as we can. This is the first chance he's had to sit down with us like a normal human being. (ANNA *goes off.*)

TATYANA. He'll go, and we'll be all alone again.

NADEZHDA. Today is our feast day. Let everything be beautiful so we'll remember it as long as we live.

TATYANA. I do hope that terrible Mushkin won't spoil the feast. I think he knows everything. Lately he's seemed so ill at ease and bitter. Could it possibly be that Anna— (SERGEY PETROVICH *and* KATYA *come in.*)

SERGEY PETROVICH. Well, we've let the bees out. Now let's bring our prisoner up into the air and let him dry. He's had such a time waiting. Katya, shut the door. In a minute you'll see that my surgery has triumphed after all. (*He lifts the trap door.* TATYANA *spreads a clean tablecloth.* NADEZHDA *sets flowers on the table.* ANNA *comes in and takes up the mortar.*)

NADEZHDA. Coffee ready yet, Anyuta?

ANNA. I'm going to pound the beans now. (*Pounds with the pestle.*)

SERGEY PETROVICH (*solemnly*). Lazarus, take thee from off thy couch—and come and have coffee! (BERKUTOV *climbs out of the cellar. He*

*smiles, squinting in the unaccustomed daylight. He walks leaning on
a cane but with a firm and assured step. His eyes rove excitedly over
the members of the family.*)

BERKUTOV. Everything looks so strange after the darkness. The light
hurts my eyes. Hello! Hello, dear friends. (*His excitement checks his
speech. The* KASHIRINS *gaze at him with happy smiles, with tenderness
and wonderment.*)

TATYANA (*wiping her eyes*). You look so pale.

BERKUTOV. In the daylight you all seem like different people—fes-
tive, radiant.

NADEZHDA (*impulsively embracing and kissing him*). My dear one—
I don't deserve such happiness!

SERGEY PETROVICH. Don't hold us up, Nadezhda—or he'll be hugging and kissing all day, and we haven't much time to spare. (*Goes to
the sideboard and the decanter of raspberry brandy.*)

ANNA. Please forgive me for having been so unkind that first
night.

BERKUTOV. I'm the one, Anna Sergeyevna, who ought to ask forgiveness for all the anxiety and suffering I've caused you.

SERGEY PETROVICH. That's all over and done with! Now, then, take
a few steps. Let's see how you walk. I did bandage your leg tight, didn't
I? Come on! Stamp your foot! Step lively there! (BERKUTOV *moves
across the room toward the curtain.*) That's the spirit!

BERKUTOV. I must embrace you, my marvelous surgeon! (*He and*
SERGEY PETROVICH *embrace.*) Thank you. Thanks to all of you, my
good, dear friends.

SERGEY PETROVICH. Let's go! (*Fills the glasses.*) To our guest!

NADEZHDA. To our son!

BERKUTOV. To this little house, to you the Kashirins! You're brave
people, all of you.

TATYANA. No, no, Anatoly! We're just ordinary, little people—like
millions of others. Oh, goodness—we're forgetting to keep an eye out.
I'll watch the window, you watch the door, Nadya. The kitchen door's
locked, isn't it?

NADEZHDA. What a lucky man you are, Victor. You'll soon be in
Moscow. Moscow! Is it really beautiful?

BERKUTOV. It is. I live not far from the Kremlin—about two hundred yards—near the Okhotny Arcades.

NADEZHDA. Not on Bozhedomka?

BERKUTOV. No, in Geörgievsky Alley. Properly speaking, it's got
lost now. They've built a huge house and made the exit from our
alley through an archway in that house—so it's quite a job to find it
these days. Well, the Kremlin is just a stone's throw. At night I always
hear two things: the clock on the Spassky Tower striking and a rooster
crowing.

ANNA. A rooster? I didn't know they kept chickens in Moscow.

BERKUTOV. My father is a passionate poultry farmer and he has a vociferous cock which crows every night.

KATYA. The cock will remind us of this house, won't it, Tolya?

ANNA (*staggered*). Katya, I don't understand—what are you talking about?

KATYA. Oh, yes. We—I forgot to tell you, Mama, that—

SERGEY PETROVICH. Everything's clear, Katya. Everything. Let's drink to your happy life, to our future great-grandsons and great-granddaughters.

ANNA. I'm under the impression I'm your mother, Katya. Yet I don't seem to know or understand a thing.

SERGEY PETROVICH. There's nothing to understand. They love each other. They're going to get married and live in Moscow. The only thing I feel sorry about is I'll never have a chance to visit Geörgievsky Alley.

ANNA. What is all this? What does it mean? I don't understand. Haven't I already given you and Ivan Ivanovich my blessing?

SERGEY PETROVICH. To hell with this Ivan Ivanovich! The retreat is over.

BERKUTOV. Anna Sergeyevna, I love Katya—I've loved her for a long time. Now we've decided to live as husband and wife.

ANNA. But you're going away, aren't you?

BERKUTOV. I am, and Katya's going with me.

ANNA. It's impossible. How can you? You're taking away everything I live and breathe by. We've saved you from death—nursed you—suffered for you. And now you're robbing us—me. You're—

KATYA (*rushing to her mother*). Mama! Darling! Don't take it so hard!

ANNA. I don't want to hear another word. You organize plots against me, conspire—it's driving me mad! You're not going anywhere, Katya. I won't let you go to certain death. You're the only one I have.

KATYA. Mama darling, don't you understand?

ANNA. I don't want to understand anything. I'll go to Ivan Ivanovich. I'll—

TATYANA (*putting her arms around* ANNA). Anyuta dear. Katya loves Anatoly. You mustn't stand in the way of her happiness.

ANNA. I've been robbed, cheated. (*Sobs.*) I'm to be left all alone—an old woman— No, I'd rather die.

TATYANA. Anyuta, you want Katya to live, don't you? Then she must leave with Anatoly. That's the only way. They'll go to the woods, to the partisans, and from there they'll get to Moscow.

ANNA. To the woods? Partisans? Certain death? No, that will never be. Never! Never!

SERGEY PETROVICH. Anna, you have to take a sensible view of things and not go raving mad before your time. We're old people. We've lived out our days. But Katya's just beginning her life. I'm all for it.

ANNA. Very well. They love each other. All right. Let them wait until the war's over—then they can live together. We'll all live together. But why now?

TATYANA. You don't seem to realize, Anna—if Katya doesn't leave immediately, that'll be the end of her—Mushkin will see to that. Make your choice.

ANNA. No, I don't believe it! Ivan Ivanovich is not that kind of man. He won't do that. He loves Katya.

TATYANA. That's exactly why he will do it. He's a rapacious little beast. He'll destroy her out of hatred for us. He certainly must have guessed what's going on. We've been putting off the wedding from day to day. He's gotten irritable and suspicious. I'm sure he knows everything and is just waiting for the right time to destroy all of us.

NADEZHDA. Katya won't be separated from us very long. Later the war will end, and we'll all go to Moscow to Geörgievsky Alley.

SERGEY PETROVICH. All of us? And who'll stay at home? Just like a woman! Never thinks! Here I've got a garden, bees, flowers—for that matter, a house! How can I leave all that and go away?

KATYA. I must go. I have to take Anatoly into the woods to the partisans. I know the way. We used to drive there to pick mushrooms. It's at the White Moss survey mark. I can come back home, if you insist. I'll wait with you for the end of war. Just decide.

TATYANA. No, of course you mustn't return—not until the war's all over. You'll have to reconcile yourself to that, Anyuta.

ANNA. No, Ivan Ivanovich won't hurt Katya. I'll explain everything to him as a mother—and he'll understand. You can't make yourself loved by force.

TATYANA. Even if he takes it all right, there'll still be the Germans. Do you imagine for one minute they'll consider your feelings, Anyuta? You know as well as I do that they send all the pretty girls to those terrible houses for soldiers. Think what a horrible fate's waiting for Katya.

KATYA. I'd kill myself first.

BERKUTOV. Whatever you decide, I will not leave Katya here. She's my wife, and I have the right to act as I consider necessary. I cannot condemn Katya to certain death.

SERGEY PETROVICH. Now, that's something I can understand—a husband talking. I've been waiting and waiting to hear the men speak up. How can you argue with them? So, it's settled. Let's have one last drink.

ANNA. What about me? How shall I live?

TATYANA. To our future, Anyuta.

ANNA. But what are we going to say to Ivan Ivanovich? How can we explain Katya's disappearance to him?

SERGEY PETROVICH. We'll say she's gone to her grandmother's.

ANNA. He knows there is no such person.

SERGEY PETROVICH. There wasn't before but she's suddenly appeared. Anything can happen in wartime.

TATYANA. That's really a serious question. Mushkin isn't such a fool that he'll believe anything.

BERKUTOV. Tell him some German soldiers broke into the house at night and carried Katya away.

ANNA. Oh, my God! More lies, more pretending. More endless torment. We'll be all alone—old, weak, and helpless.

SERGEY PETROVICH. Don't worry, Anyuta. We'll put up a fight yet. We've already won the main battle. The rest doesn't matter so much.

KATYA. Darling Grandpa! (*Embraces him.*)

SERGEY PETROVICH. Now, look here, Katya. See that my great-grandchildren take after him. (*Pointing to* BERKUTOV.) To the devil with the meek ones. Look, even gladiolas have leaves like swords. Gladiolus means a sword in Latin. By this sign ye shall conquer!

BERKUTOV. Well, Katya, it's time we were getting ready to leave. I'll go down and take a last look at my prison. Oh, how I dislike saying good-by to this lovely spring day! (*Goes down into the cellar.*)

NADEZHDA. Moscow—Moscow— You're so fortunate, Katya. (MUSH-KIN *glides out quickly from behind the curtain, slams the trap door shut and locks it with a big padlock he has whipped out of his pocket. While this is going on, the whole* KASHIRIN *family stand motionless, watching with mute horror.*)

MUSHKIN. You didn't foresee, of course, how your conspiracy would end? Don't speak. It's my turn to talk. There's a lot I want to talk about. (*Tries to speak calmly but cannot keep his voice steady.*) You have nothing to say. You've said everything, and I've heard it all. Now I, Ivan Ivanovich Mushkin, will speak. I was a friend of your family. I was attached to you. I loved you, Katerina Petrovna, loved you as only a lonely heart can love. I gave you everything—my love, my devotion, my friendship. I realized that staying on with the Germans I made myself a traitor, so to speak. But I became one out of love for you. I know what's in store for me if the Soviets return. I disregarded all that for your sake. What have you done with me? How have you paid back all I've done for you? You've been hiding black betrayal in your heart. That morning I saw blood on the steps, I already guessed you were concealing the flier in your house. I saw it in your faces. No, I didn't believe in your speckled hen, Sergey Petrovich. Mushkin is not as naïve as you think. You, Katerina Petrovna, played your little comedy of fainting to distract my attention from the cellar. You didn't do it very well, Katerina Petrovna. You'll never make an actress. Still, all I had to go on were suspicions, conjectures of a wounded heart. I said to myself, no, it's only my own mistrustfulness, the Kashirins wouldn't be capable of such meanness. I was in an agony of doubt for a long time—until Anna Sergeyevna disclosed the whole secret to me. (*The* KASHIRINS *look at* ANNA *with horror.*)

TATYANA. Anyuta. Oh, God! Is it possible?

ANNA (*gasping with excitement*). I—I didn't—I never said a word. Why do you say such things?

MUSHKIN (*with malicious, gloating joy*). Of course, it's hard for you to admit it, Anna Sergeyevna, since it makes you a traitor too.

ANNA. Don't believe him. I never—said anything.

MUSHKIN. Then how did I get here behind the curtain and hear everything, if you didn't help me?

SERGEY PETROVICH. So there's been a Stoessel in our family?

TATYANA. You've betrayed us, Anyuta? I curse you! (ANNA *sobs.*)

NADEZHDA. Stop it, Tanya. Don't you see he wants us to kill Anna with our own hands? He's afraid to do it himself—he's a coward. He wants us to be his executioners.

ANNA. I thought you were an honest man. You lie—you lie! (*Weeps.*)

MUSHKIN. Katerina Petrovna, why don't you comfort your poor mother?

KATYA. Mama—what have you done, Mama? (*Cries.*)

MUSHKIN. Cry, Katerina Petrovna. I cried, too, at your despicable betrayal. You made fun of me, of my deepest feelings. You put on an act of loving me. You deceived me, lied to my face, brazenly. You turned me into a clown. You could have told me honestly that you had ceased to love me.

KATYA. I never loved you.

MUSHKIN. You lie. You gave me your kisses up there in the attic, near the stove flue. Have you forgotten?

KATYA. Yes, I did kiss you. But only to convince myself how repulsive you were. I had to do it to hate you more.

MUSHKIN. You went even further, Katerina Petrovna, showed more daring, so to speak, real impatience—

KATYA. Shut up, you filthy—

MUSHKIN. No, I won't. Let him hear it! (*Stamps on the trap door with his foot.*) Hey, you! Miserable lover! Do you hear? Before you put your arms around her, she was mine. You were deceiving Berkutov, and Berkutov was deceiving you, Katerina Petrovna. He never told you, did he, that he's been married for a long time?

KATYA. It's not true. You're making it up!

MUSHKIN. Here's a letter from his wife, Verochka. It was in his pocketbook with the other things, but I didn't show it to you. (*Tosses her the letter.*) A pleasant discovery, isn't it?

KATYA (*picks up the letter, reads it, turns pale, and with clenched fists rushes to* MUSHKIN). You're wicked—bad!

TATYANA (*holding her back*). You mustn't, Katya darling. Nobody believes him. You're pure—you're a saint. (*Shouting.*) You're a monster! Anyuta dear, forgive me—I wronged you. Now I see that—

MUSHKIN. Keep quiet, you old procuress! Didn't you keep telling me that the heart of this treacherous snake belonged to me? Have you forgotten?

SERGEY PETROVICH. You're crazy, Ivan Ivanovich. Completely crazy. (*Looks around for the decanter and fills his glass.*)

MUSHKIN. Shut up, you old clown. This time you won't take me in with your speckled hen. I know whose blood was on your hands, you quack surgeon.

SERGEY PETROVICH. Why quack? I did heal a man's leg. (*He is still holding the decanter and looking at the brandy against the light.*) I performed my job honestly. I've always lived honestly.

MUSHKIN. Why don't you say something, Nadezhda Sergeyevna? You're the only one who's been honest toward me. You've openly hated me.

NADEZHDA. I have. And I've taught everybody else to hate you.

MUSHKIN. That for you! (*Spits on the floor.*)

SERGEY PETROVICH. I won't allow you to spit in my house, Ivan Ivanovich. Go out into the street and spit there as much as you like, but not in my house.

MUSHKIN. This house is no longer yours. Today the Germans are taking it over. The master of the house is Lieutenant Gütner. He'll be here in a few minutes.

KATYA. Well. He can go whistle!

SERGEY PETROVICH. Yes, let him whistle one of his German tunes. I'm not afraid!

MUSHKIN. He will—and you'll damn well dance to his tune. And you, Katerina Petrovna, will change your tune too. It won't be from "The Queen of Spades." You'll sing what Lieutenant Gütner tells you and you'll dance for him.

KATYA. No power in the world can force me to do that. I'll go where I please.

MUSHKIN. To the woods? The partisans? Moscow? No, Katerina Petrovna, no. You won't go anywhere. And he, your lover— (*Stamps on the trapdoor.*) he won't go anywhere either! Do you hear? Nowhere! He belongs to Lieutenant Gütner. You, too, Katerina Petrovna, belong to Lieutenant Gütner. You're German property, so to speak. You'll have a tally hung on your neck, and you'll get sent to a house where you'll have lots of fun! You'll have all the lovers you want there. (*Pressing the pestle to her breast,* ANNA *lunges at* MUSHKIN.)

ANNA. That will never be! It won't, it won't!

NADEZHDA (*catching* ANNA *by the arm*). Tanya! Katya! Help me— help me hold up Anna. She's terribly weak. (TATYANA *and* KATYA *hurry to* ANNA'S *side and support her. Slowly, without taking her eyes off* MUSHKIN, ANNA *moves toward him, as do the other women around her.* SERGEY PETROVICH *stands holding his empty decanter by the neck like a hand grenade.*)

MUSHKIN (*shouting triumphantly*). They will take her! To a brothel! Do you hear? To a brothel! I'll visit her there! Ha! Ha! Ha! (ANNA *advances, holding the pestle on high. As if at a signal, all the* KASHIRINS *pounce on* MUSHKIN.)

CURTAIN

ACT IV

Scene 2

The same room half an hour later. It gives evidence of a struggle—overturned chairs, flowerpots scattered on the floor. TATYANA, NADEZHDA, ANNA, *and* KATYA *are disposed about the room in attitudes suggesting utter exhaustion.* SERGEY PETROVICH *is standing over the open trap door.*

SERGEY PETROVICH. Bury him as deep as you can. In the left corner—it's sand there—easier to dig. Devil take it! I built the cellar to keep the bees through the winter and for pickled apples and potatoes and my gladiola bulbs. Now I have to hide carrion there. (*Walks over to the table, looking for the decanter, and sees broken glass on the floor.*) The decanter's smashed. I hit him on the head with it. I don't remember a thing. I killed him.

ANNA. I did it.

KATYA. No, Mama dear. It wasn't you.

NADEZHDA. We—all the Kashirins——killed him.

TATYANA. We couldn't kill a hen without crying. Now we've killed a man.

NADEZHDA. Not a man—a louse.

SERGEY PETROVICH. A louse? No, a spider. Forty sins are forgiven him who kills a spider. He was a spider. (BERKUTOV *climbs up out of the cellar. He has managed to change into* MUSHKIN'S *clothes and now tends to resemble him. The* KASHIRINS *stare at him with frightened expressions, as if he were a ghost.*)

TATYANA. Oh, you frightened me! I thought it was—Mushkin.

BERKUTOV. He'll never be back in this life. But his clothes have come in very handy, particularly the certificate made out to the secretary of the Serdechensk city administration, with the genuine German seal. With documents like these we don't have to be afraid to set out even in broad daylight. Are you ready, Katya?

ANNA. She's not going with you. You've deceived us.

BERKUTOV. I don't understand. What's happened?

ANNA. You deceived Katya. It's enough to drive a person mad!

BERKUTOV. Katya, please explain it to me. I don't understand a thing.

KATYA (*handing him the letter*). This is a letter from your wife.

BERKUTOV (*taking it*). Yes, it's from Verochka. (*Kisses the letter.*) From my sister. Her last letter. She was killed in an air raid. On the third day of the war. She looked quite a lot like you, Katya. However, it's time to go, dear. Good-by!

TATYANA. Good-by!

NADEZHDA. Good-by, Victor—my son! It doesn't matter that he's a private. We're all privates. Good-by.

SERGEY PETROVICH. Not good-by, but au revoir. Oh, you women! (*Goes off, wiping his eyes.*)

KATYA. Mama darling—please forgive my being so cruel. It pains—it shames me to desert you when you're defenseless. Forgive me. (BERKUTOV *and* KATYA *leave. There is a pause. The women look out the windows, following them with their eyes.*)

TATYANA. We ought to clear up the room—and close the trap. I'm scared, Nadya.

NADEZHDA. I'll close it, Tanya dear. (*Does so.*)

TATYANA. But how are we going to live after this? It's like a cemetery here. It frightens you.

NADEZHDA. We'll just live, that's all.

TATYANA. I ought to wash my hands. I did it with my bare hands. (*Shuddering.*) God, what our enemies have done to us!

NADEZHDA. Pick up the pestle and wash it. We'll have to look everything over carefully, so as not to leave any traces.

TATYANA. But how are we going to live, Nadya? How? If anybody told me that I, Tatyana Kishirina, with my own hands—these hands which corrected my pupils' notebooks, checked their problems—that I would—kill my own pupil—

NADEZHDA. Tanya, that's something out of Dostoyevsky. Better help me put things back in place. (*Returns the flowers to the table.*) Everything must be in order. Let the Germans see that the people living here are quiet and peaceful.

ANNA. It's dark and empty in my soul—I'm frightened.

NADEZHDA. It would be more frightening still, if in the hour of common misfortune we stood aside from other people. Now we too are fighting. The time will come when people will remember us, the Kashirins, and thank us. Isn't that what makes happiness? (*The voices of the approaching Germans are heard.*)

TATYANA. Here they come.

ANNA. Katya—Katya—

NADEZHDA. Call papa, Tatyana. (TATYANA *goes off. The* GERMANS *burst in. They include* GÜTNER, *a fidgety young German* INTERPRETER, *and several* SOLDIERS.)

INTERPRETER. Is this the residence of the Kashirin family?

NADEZHDA. What is it you want?

GÜTNER. I remember you. Sprechen Sie Deutsch?

NADEZHDA. Today I'll speak only Russian, my own language. (SERGEY PETROVICH *and* TATYANA *come in.*)

INTERPRETER. In the name of Lieutenant Gütner I notify you that you must leave this house at once.

NADEZHDA. What have we done that you deprive us of our own home?

INTERPRETER. You've been hiding a Russian flier here.

NADEZHDA. There's no Russian flier in our house.

INTERPRETER. We'll take steps to prove it to you. (*To the* SOLDIERS.) Search the cellar. (*The* SOLDIERS *go down into the cellar.*) We have precise information that you're hiding a Russian flier.

NADEZHDA. Did Mushkin tell you that?

INTERPRETER. Yes. He's a close friend of yours, isn't he?

NADEZHDA. He told you a lie.

INTERPRETER. He'll be here in a minute to confirm it.

NADEZHDA. He's not coming.

INTERPRETER. We know better than you.

NADEZHDA. No, I know better than you. He won't come. He was here and told us that he'd had enough of being a traitor—that his conscience had awakened in him—that he wanted to recover his honor. He won't serve you any more. He's gone away, far away to atone for his guilt. (*The* INTERPRETER *translates this to* GÜTNER.)

GÜTNER. Sie lügen!

NADEZHDA. No, I'm not lying. I'm speaking the truth. (*The* SOLDIERS *come up from the cellar eating pickled apples.*)

A SOLDIER. Oh, der Keller ist sehr gut! Goot cellar. Much—much to eat.

INTERPRETER. Didn't you find anybody? (*Repeats the question in German.*)

A SOLDIER. Dort ist niemand!

GÜTNER. Durchsuchen! (*The* SOLDIERS *search the rest of the house.*)

INTERPRETER. Leave the house. You could have been punished more severely. But you've been spared on account of your age.

TATYANA. But we have to collect our things.

INTERPRETER. All your things are to remain here. They are now the property of the German Army. (*To the* SOLDIERS.) Bring everything you find in the cellar and carry out the more valuable objects. What have you down there?

SERGEY PETROVICH. Different kinds of food—cabbage, potatoes, pickled cucumbers and apples, and even coffee beans chock full of caffein.

GÜTNER. Oh, I like very much gut caffein.

SERGEY PETROVICH. I've been saving it especially for you. Drink it with my best wishes. It's very good to settle the stomach if you're bothered with circumduction.

GÜTNER. Cir-cum-duction? I do not understand.

SERGEY PETROVICH. You know, a circular rotation in the belly. (*The* INTERPRETER *translates to* GÜTNER. *The latter smiles delightedly and slaps* SERGEY PETROVICH *on the back.*)

GÜTNER. The old man is very gay. Cir-cum-duction! (*The* SOLDIERS *bring up sacks, barrels, boxes, beehives from the cellar. They carry out the furniture from the living quarters.*)

SERGEY PETROVICH (*taking the clarinet off the wall*). Well, you don't need this, and it'll be useful to me.

GÜTNER (*snatching the clarinet*). Russische musik is sad. Deutsche musik is jolly. (*Plays a crude tune.*)

SERGEY PETROVICH. Well, it doesn't matter now, let him play—we've got to get out of here. Let's go!

INTERPRETER. First put on the tallies with your numbers. (*Looks in his notebook.*) Your numbers are from 601 to 605 inclusive. Where are your tallies?

TATYANA. We never left the house, so we didn't need them.

INTERPRETER. Now you're leaving and must wear them. (TATYANA *takes the tallies from the sideboard, puts on her own, marked "602," and hands the others to* ANNA *and* SERGEY PETROVICH *who put theirs on too.*)

TATYANA. Take it, Nadya, yours is 604.

NADEZHDA. I won't wear it. I'm not an animal. I'm a human being.

INTERPRETER (*looking in his notebook*). Six hundred and four. Katerina Petrovna Kosheleva, age twenty. Where's she?

TATYANA. She—she's gone to visit friends in town.

INTERPRETER. Without her tally?

TATYANA. Yes, without her tally.

INTERPRETER (*to* NADEZHDA). Why don't you put yours on? It's number six hundred and five.

NADEZHDA. I told you, I'm not an animal, I'm a human being.

GÜTNER. Sofort! (NADEZHDA *throws the tally on the floor.*)

INTERPRETER. You'll get into trouble for this.

GÜTNER (*shouting*). Sofort! Ohne Widerrede! (NADEZHDA *stands motionless.* GÜTNER *pulls a revolver out of his holster.*)

ANNA. For God's sake, Nadya, put it on.

NADEZHDA. No, Anna. I want to die a human being, not a groveling insect.

SERGEY PETROVICH. That's right, Nadezhda, that's right—a human being.

GÜTNER. Sofort! (*Advances toward* NADEZHDA *with a raised revolver.*) Unverzüglich! (NADEZHDA *spits in his face. There is a shot.* NADEZHDA *drops to the floor.*)

SERGEY PETROVICH. That's right, Nadezhda, that's right—a human being.

GÜTNER. Fort! Hinaus! (*Indicates with a gesture that the* KASHIRINS *must leave the house. They start for the veranda. From the cellar a* SOLDIER *brings up* BERKUTOV's *flier's suit.* GÜTNER *regards it narrowly and, barring their way to the veranda, shouts in a fierce voice.*) Sie lügen! Zurück! Zurück!

SERGEY PETROVICH (*pointing to* NADEZHDA's *dead body*). But we can take this with us, can't we? You don't need it. (*The* INTERPRETER *translates to* GÜTNER.)

GÜTNER. Oh, nein! For an old man it is difficult to dig a grave. We cannot make an old man do difficult work. We'll make a crematorium —and we will play a jolly German march. (*He goes off through the veranda, playing a march tune on the clarinet. The* SOLDIERS *and the* INTERPRETER *follow him in military step. The* KASHIRINS *stand motionless near* NADEZHDA. *A* SOLDIER *slams the doors from outside. Smoke appears beyond the windows, then the crackle of fire is heard.*)

ANNA. They've set our house on fire! Let's get out quick! (*Rushes to the door but finds it locked.*)

TATYANA. Oh, my God! They've locked us in!

ANNA. Quick! Through the windows! (*Rushes to a window and opens it. A shot is heard.* ANNA *falls dead.*)

TATYANA. They want to burn us! Monsters!

SERGEY PETROVICH. Yes, this is our bonfire, our Square of Flowers. Our little house will burn down. But some day Berkutov will build beautiful big houses here. And there will be a Square of Flowers in the great new city—and flowers everywhere. The red petals of the gladiolas will absorb our blood and the color of these flames—in memory of us. Tanya dear, pin my medal to my chest. (*He takes off the tally, flings it on the floor, and pulls a medal out of his pocket.* TANYA *pins it to the lapel of his coat.* SERGEY PETROVICH *puts his arm around her. Flames break into the room. As the curtain slowly comes down, there are heard the crackle of fire, the wild march played by* GÜTNER *on the clarinet— the symphony of war, destruction, death. In the burning room stand two immortal Russians, and the brass pendulum of the wall clock, blazing like the sun, swings in broad sweeping movements.*)

TWELVE MONTHS

BY SAMUEL MARSHAK

IN A note to the Russian edition of this play the author states that he has based his play on the motifs of Slovak and Czech folk tales about the Month Brothers. It is worth noting that he has added a great deal to the story that is not to be found in his folk-tale source. The latter relates the adventure of a young Girl whom her Stepmother has sent to the woods on a cold winter night to gather snowdrops for her Stepsister. In the woods the Girl meets the Twelve Month Brothers who are moved by her story and instantly change the seasons to enable her to pick her snowdrops. On her return home her Stepsister learns how she got the flowers and decides to go to the woods and make the Month Brothers give her several other things she wants. She too meets the Month Brothers, but she is so rude and brash in her demands that instead of presenting her with gifts the Month Brothers let loose a snowstorm which completely buries her. The same fate befalls the Stepmother who goes to the woods to look for her daughter. It will be recognized by the reader that Samuel Marshak's "Twelve Months" tells a substantially different story, besides enriching the original folk tale with poems and newly imagined characters.

Born in 1887, Samuel Yakovlevich Marshak entered literature as a translator of Blake, Wordsworth, and English folk ballads. Sixteen years later, in 1923, he produced his first book of children's verse, "Children in a Cage," which was followed by a long succession of similar books. "Twelve Months" was written on the eve of the war and has been accepted for production by the Moscow Art Theater. During the war Marshak published a great deal of satirical verse, and since the war has been busy translating poems of Shakespeare, Keats, Burns, and other English poets.

A. B.

TWELVE MONTHS

CHARACTERS

Wolf
Raven
First Squirrel
Hare
Second Squirrel
Stepdaughter
Soldier
Two of the Twelve Months (December and January)
Fox
Queen
Professor of Arithmetic and Calligraphy
Chancellor
Old Woman
Daughter of the Old Woman
The Other Months
Ambassador of the Western Kingdom
Ambassador of the Eastern Kingdom
Lady in Waiting
Commander of the Royal Bodyguard
Royal Prosecutor
Head Gardener
Officer of the Royal Bodyguard
Young Soldier
Guests, Musicians, Courtiers, Pages, Gardeners, Servants, Ladies of the Court, Coachman, Guards

ACT I

Scene 1

A snug-looking clearing in a wintry forest. Clean snow lies in wavy drifts and covers the trees with downy caps. It is still. For a few moments the scene appears empty, almost dead. Then a ray of light runs over the snow and illumines, in turn, the whitish-gray head of a WOLF *peeping out among the trees, a* RAVEN *perched on a pine tree, and a* SQUIRREL *nestling between the forking branches over a hollow in a trunk. There are sounds of rustling, of flapping wings, of crunching dry twigs. The forest is coming to life.*

WOLF. Ow-oo-oo! To look around you'd think there was nobody in the forest, that the place was empty, deserted. But you can't fool me. I know the Hare is somewhere about, the Squirrel's in the hollow, the Raven's up on a twig, the Partridges are under the snowdrifts. Ow-oo-oo! How I'd love to eat them all up!

RAVEN (*rolling his "r's"*). Cr-roak! Cr-roak! Liar-r! You can't eat up ever-rybody.

WOLF. Shut up. I'm so hungry my belly is twisted with pain and my teeth are chattering.

RAVEN. Cr-roak! Cr-roak! Go your-r way, str-ranger! That'll keep you fr-rom danger. I'm a sharp-eyed r-raven and from this tree I can see all of thirty miles away.

WOLF. Well, what do you see?

RAVEN. Croak! Croak! A soldier is coming up the road. He's carrying the wolf's death across his back, and at his side the wolf's peril is swinging. Croak! Croak! Where are you off to, Wolf?

WOLF. You bore me with your talk, old fellow. I'm going to look for a quieter place. (*Runs off.*)

RAVEN. Croak! Croak! So that scared you, gray pelt, made you take to your heels? Yes, the deeper into the forest you go, the safer you'll be. Well, I fooled you this time. The soldier is not coming after you at all. He's coming to get a fir tree and is pulling a sled behind him. Brrr! It's cold. It's New Year's Eve tonight, and we're having a regular New Year's frost—you can hear it crackle. It would be a good thing to spread out my wings, do a little flying, and warm myself. But I've grown too old—too old. Croak! Croak! (*He hides himself among the branches. A* HARE *leaps out into the clearing. Up on the tree, near the hollow, another* SQUIRREL *appears beside the one already there.*)

HARE (*clapping his paws*). My stars, it's cold—so cold it takes your breath away, and your feet freeze to the snow as you run. Come on, you Squirrels, let's play burn.

FIRST SQUIRREL. All right, Hare. Who's going to be it?

HARE. We'll count out.

FIRST SQUIRREL. As you please.

> Squint-eye, squint-eye, have a care—
> Leave no tracks for wolf or bear.
> If your overshoes you wear,
> Your bandy legs will get you there.
> O-U-T spells out—you burn.

HARE (*stepping forward as the two* SQUIRRELS *stand behind him*).

> Fire, burn high—
> Flame, never die!
> Birds are singing,
> Bells are ringing.

FIRST SQUIRREL. Catch me, Hare!

SECOND SQUIRREL. You'll never get me. (*The two* SQUIRRELS, *passing the* HARE *on either side, race away over the snow; the* HARE *runs after them. During this race a young girl, the* STEPDAUGHTER, *enters the clearing, pulling a sled. She wears a tattered kerchief, an old jacket, shabby boots, and coarse mittens, and carries a small hatchet stuck in her belt. Stopping between two trees, she watches the* HARE *and the* SQUIRRELS, *who are so preoccupied with their game that they do not see her. The* SQUIRRELS, *outdistancing the* HARE, *run full tilt up a tree.*)

HARE. Where are you going? You can't do that—it's not fair. I won't play with you.

FIRST SQUIRREL. Come on, Hare, jump!

SECOND SQUIRREL. That's it, jump!

FIRST SQUIRREL. Swing your tail and up you go.

HARE (*after a few attempts to jump, pitifully*). My tail is too short! (*The* SQUIRRELS *laugh. So does the* STEPDAUGHTER. *Noticing her, the* SQUIRRELS *and the* HARE *vanish instantly.*)

STEPDAUGHTER (*drying her eyes with a mitten*). Oh, dear Heaven! I never heard anything so funny! It's made me hot in spite of the frost. "My tail's too short," he says. His very words! I wouldn't believe it if I hadn't heard it with my own ears. (*A* SOLDIER *comes into the clearing. He has a hatchet tied to his belt and is drawing a sled. He is not too young, has a big mustache, and altogether looks like one who has seen life.*)

SOLDIER. Hello, my pretty one! What's making you so happy? Have you found a treasure trove or heard some good news? (*The* STEP-DAUGHTER, *shaking with laughter, waves her hand at him helplessly.*) Come on, tell us what's so funny! Maybe I can have a laugh with you too.

STEPDAUGHTER. You won't believe me.

SOLDIER. I don't know about that. We soldiers have heard and seen

lots of things in our lives. We believe all right but we don't let anybody fool us.

STEPDAUGHTER. Here, on this very spot, a hare and two squirrels
were playing burn a minute ago.

SOLDIER. Is that so?

STEPDAUGHTER. Cross my heart! Just like our kids playing in the
streets. "Fire, burn high— Flame, never die!" The hare was tearing
after the squirrels, when oops!—up a tree they went—and not only
that—they kept teasing him from the tree: "Come on, jump up here."

SOLDIER. And they spoke like that in our own language?

STEPDAUGHTER. They did.

SOLDIER. What do you know!

STEPDAUGHTER. You see, you don't believe me.

SOLDIER. Not believe you on a day like today? Oh, no. Today, you
know yourself, is the end of the old year and the beginning of the new.
And I heard my grandfather say that his grandfather used to tell
him that on a day like today anything can happen in the world—all
you have to do is to look sharp not to miss it. That's no great wonder,
to see squirrels and hares play burn. Even more marvelous things
happen on New Year's Eve.

STEPDAUGHTER. What things?

SOLDIER. Well, my grandfather told me that once on New Year's Eve
his grandfather met all the twelve months together.

STEPDAUGHTER. Did he really?

SOLDIER. Cross my heart! The old man saw the whole year, winter
and summer, spring and fall, all at the same time. It was such a sight
he could never forget it. He told his son about it and ordered him to
tell the grandchildren. That's how I come to know the story.

STEPDAUGHTER. But I don't see how winter, summer, spring, and
fall can all come together. That's impossible.

SOLDIER. Well, I only say what I know. But what has brought you
here on such a cold day? I take orders from my superiors—and I've
been sent here. Who sent you?

STEPDAUGHTER. I haven't come here of my own free will either.

SOLDIER. Are you in service?

STEPDAUGHTER. No, I live at home.

SOLDIER. Then how did your mother happen to let you out?

STEPDAUGHTER. My mother wouldn't have let me out but my stepmother did—she told me to get some brushwood.

SOLDIER. I see. So you are an orphan? That's why you have such
hand-me-down gear. I'm sure the wind blows right through you. Well,
I'll give you a hand and afterward I'll see to my own business. (*The*
STEPDAUGHTER *and the* SOLDIER *gather brushwood and pile it on the
girl's sled.*)

STEPDAUGHTER. And what's your business?

SOLDIER. I have to cut a fir tree for a grand party—the best fir tree in the forest—so tall, so straight, and so green that there's none like it.

STEPDAUGHTER. Who will you be cutting it for?

SOLDIER. Who? The Queen, of course. Tomorrow the palace will be full of guests—so we must have a holiday surprise for them.

STEPDAUGHTER. What are you going to hang on your tree?

SOLDIER. The same as everybody. All sorts of toys, and knicknacks, and trinkets. Only, other people make them out of gilt paper and colored glass, and we have them all of pure gold and diamonds. Other people have dolls and rabbits made of plain cloth, ours are made of satin.

STEPDAUGHTER. Do you mean to say the Queen still plays with dolls?

SOLDIER. Why shouldn't she? She may be a queen but she's no older than you are.

STEPDAUGHTER. I gave up dolls years ago.

SOLDIER. Well, you must be too busy for that, and she has lots of time. Nor has she anybody to give orders to her. Since the old king and queen died, she's been giving orders to everybody.

STEPDAUGHTER. Then the Queen too is an orphan?

SOLDIER. It looks that way.

STEPDAUGHTER. I'm sorry for her.

SOLDIER. Who wouldn't be? There's nobody around to put good sense into her head. Well, your job is done. You have enough brushwood to last you a week. And it's time I turned to my own job—started looking for a tree—or I'll get it in the neck from my little orphan—she stands for no nonsense.

STEPDAUGHTER. Just like my stepmother, and my stepsister, too. You can never please them, no matter what you do. Whichever way you turn, it's always the wrong way with them.

SOLDIER. Don't worry, you won't have to put up with it forever. You're still young and you'll see better days. Take our army service. It's long enough, isn't it? Yet it too comes to an end.

STEPDAUGHTER. Thank you for your kind words—and for the brushwood. I've finished my chores early today. Now let me show you a fir tree I know here—it may be just what you want. It's a beautiful tree; every twig on it matches every other twig.

SOLDIER. I'll be glad to have you show me. You seem to be at home in the forest. No wonder squirrels and hares play burn as you look on. (*Leaving their sleds, the* STEPDAUGHTER *and the* SOLDIER *disappear among the trees. For a moment the stage is empty. Then the branches of the two old snow-covered fir trees move apart, admitting two tall old men, the months* DECEMBER *and* JANUARY. JANUARY *wears a white fur coat and cap.* DECEMBER *wears a striped black and white fur coat and a white cap trimmed with black.*)

DECEMBER. There you are, brother, take over the management. I think everything is in order. There's enough snow—the birches have it up to their waists, the pine trees up to their knees. Now it'll do no harm if the frost lets itself go. We've lived behind the clouds most of our time but you can have the sun to play with during your turn.

JANUARY. Thank you, brother. I can see you've done a good job. And how is your ice on the streams and lakes—is it strong?

DECEMBER. It holds up all right. But it wouldn't be a bad idea to freeze it a little more.

JANUARY. I'll freeze it. You can depend on me. Well, and how are the forest people?

DECEMBER. As they're supposed to be. Those who have to sleep, sleep, and those who don't have to—they either skip about or wander. I'd better call them so you can look them over. (*Claps his mittened hands. A* WOLF *and a* FOX *peek out among the trees.* SQUIRRELS *appear on the branches. A* HARE *leaps into the center of the clearing. Ears of other* HARES *can be seen stirring behind snowdrifts. The* WOLF *and the* FOX *eye the little animals, ready to jump on them, but* JANUARY *shakes an admonishing finger.*)

JANUARY. What are you up to, Red? And you, Gray? Do you think we've called the hares for your special benefit? Oh, no. You'll have to get your provender without our help. What we want is to count all you forest people, the hares, and the squirrels, and you too, the fellows with sharp teeth. (*The* WOLF *and the* FOX *subside. The two old men unhurriedly count the animals.*) All right. You're all counted. You can go to your homes and your jobs now. (*The animals disappear.*) And now, brother, it's time we made ready for the holiday—freshened up the snow in the forest, silvered up the trees. Wave your sleeve, will you? You're still the master here.

DECEMBER. Isn't it too early yet? Nightfall is quite a while off and I see somebody's sled there. That means there are people wandering about the forest. If I dump more snow on the trails, they won't find their way out.

JANUARY. You don't have to give it all you've got right away. Blow a light wind first, then add some whirling snow, and the visitors will guess it's time to go home. If you don't hurry them up, they'll stay till midnight gathering fir cones and twigs. They always want something—these human beings.

DECEMBER. All right, we'll start lightly.

> Hear ye, snowstorms,
> Blow and fall,
> Cover trails
> And pathways all.
>> Let none intrude
>> By foot or sleigh,

Nor man nor devil
Find his way
Into the woods this year's last day.

(*Behind the curtain of snow the two old men in white fur coats and caps can scarcely be distinguished from the trees. The* STEPDAUGHTER *and the* SOLDIER *return to the clearing, treading heavily through the snowdrifts and covering their faces against the snow as they pull along a big tree.*)

SOLDIER. Good lord, what a snowstorm, a regular New Year's blizzard. I can't see a thing. Those sleds we left here, where can they be?

STEPDAUGHTER. Look, here they are—these two snowdrifts. The lower and longer one is yours; the other one, shorter and higher, is mine. (*Brushes the snow off the sleds with a branch.*)

SOLDIER. Now I'll tie the tree to the sled and we'll get going. Though why should you wait for me? In your clothes you'll be frozen stiff in no time. My, my, how it blows!

STEPDAUGHTER. I'll be all right. I'm used to this. (*She helps the* SOLDIER *tie the tree.*)

SOLDIER. Well, that's that. Now, I'll walk in front and you follow my trail—it'll be easier for you that way. Let's go.

STEPDAUGHTER. Let's go! (*Starts.*) Oh!

SOLDIER. What's the matter?

STEPDAUGHTER. Look. Two old men in white fur coats are standing there, behind those pine trees.

SOLDIER. What old men? Where? (*Takes a step forward. The trees draw together and screen the old men.*) There's nobody there. You're seeing things. Those are just fir trees.

STEPDAUGHTER. I swear I saw them—two old men in fur coats and caps.

SOLDIER. Today even trees wear coats and caps. Let's get going. And just keep looking straight ahead. In a New Year's storm, deep in a forest, worse things may leap before your eyes. (*The* STEPDAUGHTER *and the* SOLDIER *go off.* DECEMBER *and* JANUARY *reappear from behind the trees.*)

JANUARY. Are they gone?

DECEMBER. They are. (*Peers after them, shading his eyes with his hand.*) They're quite a distance away, too. I can just see them going down the hill.

JANUARY. Well, your last visitors, it seems. There'll be no more human beings in the forest this year. Let's call our brothers and start a campfire. We'll boil gum for glue, set honey to brew.

DECEMBER. And who's to find wood for the fire?

JANUARY. We the winter months.

DECEMBER. Then who'll get the fire?

VOICES FROM THE FOREST (*chiming in*). The spring months.

DECEMBER. Who's to fan the fire?

VOICES. The summer months.

DECEMBER. Who's to damp the fire?

VOICES. The fall months. (*Shapes of forest folk flit among the trees in the distance. Lights flicker through the branches.*)

JANUARY. Well, brother, it looks as if everybody's here who should be. Lock the forest for the night. No more going in or out.

DECEMBER. All right. I will.

> Winter storm, grim and white
> Whip the snow into flight.
> Make it curl,
> Make it whirl,
> In a dance of fury swirl.
> Spread your cloak upon the ground,
> Wall the woods with snow around.
> Turn the key
> In the lock,
> Every path and passage block.

(*A curtain of falling snow hides the forest.*)

CURTAIN

ACT I

Scene 2

The QUEEN's *classroom in the royal palace. The blackboard has an elaborate gold frame. At the desk, which is made of rosewood, the fourteen-year-old* QUEEN *is sitting on a velvet cushion writing with a long gold quill. Standing before her is the* PROFESSOR OF ARITHMETIC AND CALLIGRAPHY. *He has a gray beard and in his mantle and odd doctor's cap with a tassel resembles an old-time astrologer.*

QUEEN. I detest writing. It stains all your fingers with ink.

PROFESSOR. You are perfectly right, Your Majesty. It's a highly unpleasant occupation. The ancient poets knew what they were doing when they dispensed with all writing implements. That's why science classes their work as oral literature. However, I make bold to request Your Majesty to inscribe four more lines with your royal hand.

QUEEN. All right. Dictate them.

PROFESSOR.

> Soft and green is the grass,
> The sun is in the sky;
> The swallow at our door
> Announces spring is nigh.

QUEEN. I'll write only "Soft and green is the grass." (*Writes.*) Soft and green is— (*Enter the* CHANCELLOR.)

CHANCELLOR. Good morning, Your Majesty. May I kindly request you to attach your signature to one proclamation and three decrees?

QUEEN. More writing? Oh, well. But in that case I won't write "the grass." Give me your papers. (*Signs the papers.*)

CHANCELLOR. Thank you, Your Majesty. Now I beg leave to ask Your Majesty to inscribe—

QUEEN. Inscribe again?

CHANCELLOR. Only signify your royal will on this petition.

QUEEN (*impatiently*). What is it I have to write?

CHANCELLOR. One of two things, Your Majesty—either "hang" or "pardoned."

QUEEN (*to herself*). Par-doned. Hang. I'll write "hang." It's shorter. (*The* CHANCELLOR *takes the papers, makes a bow, and goes off.*)

PROFESSOR. Permit me to ask Your Majesty what seven times eight makes.

QUEEN. I cannot recall. It never interested me very much. Did it interest you?

PROFESSOR. Of course it did, Your Majesty.

QUEEN. How extraordinary! Well, good-by. Our lesson is finished. Tonight being New Year's Eve, I have an awful lot to see to.

PROFESSOR. As it may please Your Majesty. (*Obediently, with a sad air, picks up the books.*)

QUEEN (*leaning on the desk with her elbows and watching the* PROFESSOR *vacantly*). Really, it's much better to be a queen than an ordinary schoolgirl. Everybody obeys me, even my teacher. Now tell me, Professor, what would you have done with another pupil if she had refused to answer you what seven times eight makes?

PROFESSOR. I dare not say, Your Majesty.

QUEEN. It's all right, I permit you.

PROFESSOR (*timidly*). I'd have put her in the corner.

QUEEN. Ha! Ha! Ha! (*Pointing at the corners.*) Which corner? This or that?

PROFESSOR. It doesn't make much difference, Your Majesty.

QUEEN. I would have preferred this one—it looks cosier. (*Walks into the corner.*) And what if she had persisted in refusing to tell you what seven times eight makes?

PROFESSOR. I would have—I beg your forgiveness, Your Majesty—I would have made her go without dinner.

QUEEN. Without dinner? But she may be expecting guests—say, ambassadors of some foreign power or some foreign prince.

PROFESSOR. I'm not talking about a queen, Your Majesty, but an ordinary schoolgirl.

QUEEN (*drawing an armchair into the corner and sitting down*). Poor ordinary schoolgirl! I expect you're a very cruel man. Do you know I can have you executed? This very day, if I want to?

PROFESSOR (*shaking*). Your Majesty!

QUEEN. Yes, I can, I can. And I see no reason why I shouldn't.

PROFESSOR. But what have I done to displease Your Majesty?

QUEEN. Well, I don't know. You are a very willful person. When I write something, you say it's incorrect. When I give you an answer, you say it's wrong. I like people to agree with me.

PROFESSOR. I swear by my life, Your Majesty, I'll never disagree with you against your wishes.

QUEEN. You swear by your life? Splendid. In that case we may continue with our lesson. Ask me some question. (*She goes back to her desk and sits down.*)

PROFESSOR. What does six times six make, Your Majesty?

QUEEN (*looking at him with her head drooping to one side*). Eleven.

PROFESSOR (*with a melancholy air*). That's perfectly correct, Your Majesty. And how much is seven times eight?

QUEEN. Three.

PROFESSOR. Correct, Your Majesty. And how much is—

QUEEN. Always how much. You're such an inquisitive man—keep asking questions. Why don't you tell me something interesting yourself?

PROFESSOR. You want me to tell you something interesting, Your Majesty? What sort of thing?

QUEEN. I don't know. Something about the New Year, perhaps. Today is New Year's Eve, isn't it?

PROFESSOR. Yes, Your Majesty. A new year will begin tomorrow. A year consists of twelve months, Your Majesty.

QUEEN. Does it really?

PROFESSOR. Exactly twelve months, Your Majesty. The months are —January, February, March, April, May, June, July—

QUEEN. What a number of them! And you know each one by its name? You do have a wonderful memory.

PROFESSOR. Thank you, Your Majesty. August, September, October, November, and December.

QUEEN. Imagine that!

PROFESSOR. The months follow one another. Immediately one month ends, the other begins. There was never known a case when April came before March, or September before August.

QUEEN. And what if I should want April to come immediately?

PROFESSOR. That couldn't be done, Your Majesty.

QUEEN. Arguing again?

PROFESSOR (*in an imploring tone*). It's not I who argue with Your Majesty. It is science and nature.

QUEEN. My goodness! But suppose I pass such a law and stamp it with the Great Seal?

PROFESSOR (*spreading out his arms helplessly*). I'm afraid that won't help either. But your Majesty will hardly need such a change in the calendar. After all, each month brings us its gifts and pastimes. Decem-

ber, January, and February give us ice skating, the holiday tree, car-
nival week. In March a thaw sets in, and in April the first snowdrops
peep out from under the melting snow—

QUEEN. I want it to be April now. I love snowdrops. I've never
seen them.

PROFESSOR. April is only a short time off, Your Majesty, just three
months or ninety days.

QUEEN. Ninety? I can't wait for three days. I'm having the New
Year's reception tomorrow, and I want those—what do you call them?
—snowdrops to decorate my table.

PROFESSOR. But the laws of nature, Your Majesty—

QUEEN (*cutting him short*). I'm going to pass a new law of nature.
(*Claps her hands.*) Hey, there! Send me the Chancellor. (*To the* PRO-
FESSOR.) Now you sit at my desk and write. It's my turn to dictate.
(*Pauses.*) Well, soft and green is the grass, the sun is in the sky. Yes,
write as I say. Soft and green is the grass, the sun is in the sky! And
spring flowers are blossoming in our royal forests. Wherefore we gra-
ciously command that a basketful of snowdrops be delivered at our
palace for New Year's Day. The person carrying out our sovereign
wish will be rewarded by us right royally. What could I promise them?
Wait, don't write that down. Oh, I know. Now write. We will give
that person as much gold as will fill his basket, present him with a
velvet coat lined with silver foxes, and will permit him to take part in
our royal New Year's drive through the city. Have you written that?
You are so slow!

PROFESSOR. Lined with silver foxes. It's a long time, Your Majesty,
since I've taken dictation.

QUEEN. Never mind. Now hand me the quill and I'll inscribe my
royal name. (*Scribbles her name quickly and waves the sheet to make
the ink dry. As she is doing this the* CHANCELLOR *enters.*) Put the seal
here and here. And take measures that everybody in the city may know
my decree.

CHANCELLOR (*runs his eyes over the paper*). Put the seal on this? As
Your Majesty commands.

QUEEN. Yes, it is my command and you must carry it out.

CURTAIN

ACT II

Scene 1

*A small house on the outskirts of the city. Inside, a hot stove warms
the room. Outside, glimpsed through the windows, a snowstorm is
raging. The day is drawing to a close. The* OLD WOMAN *is rolling*

dough. Her DAUGHTER *is sitting before the fire. Near the girl, on the floor, lie a few baskets. The* DAUGHTER *compares them with one another, first picking up the smallest, then the one next in size, then the biggest.*

DAUGHTER (*holding the smallest basket*). Do you think, Mother, this basket will hold a lot of gold?

OLD WOMAN. Quite a bit.

DAUGHTER. Enough to buy a fur coat?

OLD WOMAN. Not only a fur coat, my dear—there will be enough for a whole trousseau—for coats and capes, for skirts and scarves.

DAUGHTER. And how much will this one hold?

OLD WOMAN. That one will hold a lot more. There'll be enough there to buy a fine brick house, a horse and a harness, a ram and a lamb.

DAUGHTER. And this one?

OLD WOMAN. With that one—why!—you'll have a house in the country, a house in the city, and a handsome husband to treat you pretty.

DAUGHTER (*with a sigh*). The trouble is you can't get any snowdrops. The Queen must have issued that proclamation only to make fun of us.

OLD WOMAN. She is young and full of whims.

DAUGHTER. And what if somebody does go to the forest and finds snowdrops there? He'll get a big basketful of gold.

OLD WOMAN. Not a chance! No snowdrops will be seen until spring comes. And look at those snowdrifts—they're almost up to the roof.

DAUGHTER. Yes, but they may be growing quietly under the snowdrifts. I'm going out to look for them.

OLD WOMAN. No, no, dear. I won't let you step out of the house. Look out the window—see what a snowstorm is blowing? It'll be a million times worse as night falls.

DAUGHTER (*grasping the biggest basket*). I said I'm going and I will. To get into the royal palace, attend the Queen's party, and win a whole basketful of gold—it's a chance that comes once in a lifetime!

OLD WOMAN. You'll freeze to death in the forest.

DAUGHTER. Then go to the forest and pick the snowdrops yourself and I'll take them to the palace.

OLD WOMAN. Don't you care at all for your mother?

DAUGHTER. Of course I care for you. But I care for gold too, and most of all I care for myself. Why don't you go? You've been out in a snowstorm before. Wrap yourself up good and warm, and go.

OLD WOMAN. A fine daughter I have, I must say. On a day like this one wouldn't drive a dog out into the street, to say nothing of one's mother.

DAUGHTER. Drive you out? Not you. You won't put yourself to that much trouble for your daughter. I can see how I'm going to spend the holiday, thanks to you—sitting by the stove in the kitchen, while others will be riding with the Queen in a silver sleigh and shoveling gold with a spade. (*She cries.*)

OLD WOMAN. Now, now, dear, don't cry. Here, have a piece of pie. (*She takes a pie pan out of the oven.*) Fresh from the oven, piping hot. Just taste it—it'll hit the spot.

DAUGHTER (*through her tears*). I don't want any pie. I want snowdrops. If you refuse to go out yourself and won't let me go, then make Sister do it. She'll be back from the forest pretty soon. Send her out again to get snowdrops.

OLD WOMAN. That's an idea. I don't see why I shouldn't send her. The forest is near, it won't take her long to pick 'em. If she brings the flowers, you and I will take them to the palace. And if she gets frozen—well, such is her fate. Nobody will shed any tears over her.

DAUGHTER. Certainly not I. I'm sick and tired of her. I can't go outside the gate without hearing our neighbors talking about her: "Oh, the poor orphan!" "Oh, what a worker she is—she has golden hands!" "Oh, how beautiful she is—you can't take your eyes off her." Is she any better than I am?

OLD WOMAN. Why, darling, you're the one who's better, as far as I'm concerned. But not everybody sees that. She's so sly, you know, lays it on so thick, bowing to this one, smiling at that one. That's why everybody feels sorry for her. "The poor orphan!" they say. And what is it that the poor orphan lacks? I gave her my own kerchief—it was quite a good kerchief. I'd worn it less than two years and had only used it afterward to cover the kneading-trough. I also gave her your last year's shoes—let her wear them, I'm not mean. And the amount of bread I give her—a crust in the morning, a hunk for dinner, a chunk for supper. At the end of a year it all adds up. Another girl wouldn't know how to thank you enough, but you never hear a word of thanks from that one.

DAUGHTER. That's right. So let her go to the forest. She can take the biggest basket—the one I've picked out.

OLD WOMAN. No, no, dear. That's a new basket. I only bought it the other day. We'll give her that one—if it's lost we won't miss it.

DAUGHTER. Pity it's so small. (*Enter the* STEPDAUGHTER. *She removes her kerchief and shakes off the snow, then walks up to the stove and warms her hands.*)

OLD WOMAN. Is it snowing hard outside?

STEPDAUGHTER. So hard you can't tell the ground from the sky—as if you were walking on clouds. I don't know how I managed to get home.

OLD WOMAN. Snowstorms are what you expect in winter.

STEPDAUGHTER. There hasn't been anything like it this year and there won't be again.

DAUGHTER. How do you know there won't?

STEPDAUGHTER. That's simple. This is the last day of the year.

DAUGHTER. Oh, I see! You haven't been so badly frozen, it seems, that you can't talk in riddles. Have you warmed yourself enough? You have to go somewhere else now.

STEPDAUGHTER. Where to? Is it far?

OLD WOMAN. Not so near, but not too far either.

DAUGHTER. You have to go to the forest.

STEPDAUGHTER. The forest? What for? I've brought enough brush-wood to last a week.

DAUGHTER. Who wants more brushwood? You're to get snowdrops.

STEPDAUGHTER (*laughing*). Oh, snowdrops, at this time of the year! Of course! I didn't realize you were joking at first—for a minute I was scared. There's nothing easier than losing your life today—it just whirls you around and blows you over.

DAUGHTER. I'm not joking. Haven't you heard about the royal proc-lamation?

STEPDAUGHTER. No.

DAUGHTER. You don't seem to know anything. Everybody's talking about it in town. Why, the Queen has promised a basketful of gold, a fur-lined coat, and a ride through the city in her sleigh to anybody who brings her fresh snowdrops tomorrow.

STEPDAUGHTER. This is no season for snowdrops—this is winter.

OLD WOMAN. If it were spring you wouldn't be offered gold for them, but coppers.

DAUGHTER. Well, no more arguing. Here's your basket.

STEPDAUGHTER (*looking out the window*). It's getting dark.

OLD WOMAN. You shouldn't have stayed so late getting brushwood.

STEPDAUGHTER. Maybe I'd better go tomorrow morning. I'll get up early, at daybreak.

DAUGHTER. Tomorrow morning? I should say not! What if you don't find the flowers till evening? They won't sit waiting for us at the palace—they need the flowers for the New Year's party.

STEPDAUGHTER. I never heard of flowers growing in the forest in winter time. And how can I see anything in the dark?

DAUGHTER (*munching her pie*). All you have to do is to bend lower and look sharper.

STEPDAUGHTER. I'm not going.

DAUGHTER. What do you mean?

STEPDAUGHTER. Don't you have any pity for me at all? I'll never get back from the forest.

DAUGHTER. Then am I to go there instead of you?

STEPDAUGHTER (*lowering her eyes*). I don't need any gold.

OLD WOMAN. You don't need anything, of course. You have every-thing you need, and what you haven't got you know you can get from your stepmother or stepsister.

DAUGHTER. She's the rich one in our family. She can turn up her nose at a whole basketful of gold. Well, are you going or not? Yes or no? No? Where's my coat? (*Choking back her tears.*) Let her warm herself at the stove here and fill herself with pies, while I wander in the forest till midnight, wading through snowdrifts— (*Snatches her coat from a peg and rushes to the door.*)

OLD WOMAN (*catching her by the skirt*). Where are you going? Who gave you permission? Sit down, you fool. (*To the* STEPDAUGHTER.) Now, you there, quick! Put a kerchief over your head, take a basket, and get! And mind you, if I learn you've been sitting it out at some neighbor's, I won't let you back into the house—you can freeze outdoors.

DAUGHTER. Run along and see you don't return without snowdrops. (*The* STEPDAUGHTER *covers herself with the kerchief, picks up a basket, and goes. There is a pause.*)

OLD WOMAN. (*glancing at the door*). She wouldn't even shut the door properly. Such a draft! Shut it tight, dear. And lay the table. It's time for supper.

CURTAIN

ACT II

Scene 2

The forest. A heavy snow is falling. It is twilight. The STEPDAUGHTER *is plodding through the deep drifts. She draws her tattered kerchief tighter and blows on frozen hands. It is getting darker. A cushion of snow falls noisily from the top of a tree.*

STEPDAUGHTER (*starting*). Who's there? (*Glances around.*) A snow cap falls, and I imagine somebody's jumping out at me from behind the tree. And who could it be at a time like this? Even the animals are all hiding in their holes. I'm the only one out. (*She moves on, stumbles, gets caught in some fallen twigs, and halts.*) I'm not going any farther. I'll stay here. It makes no difference where I freeze to death. (*Sits down on a fallen tree.*) Heavens, it's dark. I can't even see my hands. Where am I? I don't know. It's easy enough to get lost here in daytime, and now it's the dead of night. I couldn't possibly find my way around the forest or turn back now. So it's death. Life hasn't been very good to me, but even so I'm afraid to die. Maybe I ought to cry out, call for help. Somebody may hear me—some huntsman or some woodsman going home late. Yoo-hoo! Yoo-hoo! Help! (*Pause.*) No answer. What am I to do now? Just sit here and wait for the end? And what if wolves come? They can smell a human being a long way off. Oh, I hear a crackling sound, like something creeping up. Oh,

I'm scared! (*Walks up to a tree and regards its thick, knotty, snow-covered branches.*) Shall I climb up? They won't reach me there. (*Draws herself up on one of the branches and, seating herself in a fork, dozes off. For a while all is still in the forest. Then the WOLF peeps out from behind a snowdrift. Glancing cautiously about, he comes forward and, raising his head, begins his lonesome wolf song.*)

WOLF.

> Oh, this frost—
> It's fierce!
> How this frost
> Does pierce!
> It could nail
> Your tail
> To the ice-hard trail.
> In the cold the sheep
> A sheepskin has.
> In the cold the fox
> A fox coat wears.
> The shaggy old bear
> Has foot-long hair,
> And the sables pad
> In sable clad.
> Oh, it's just my luck
> To be good and stuck
> With an old wolf-skin
> All ragged and thin.
> What a life I've got—
> What a cursed lot!

(*Pauses and pricks up his ears, then resumes his song.*)

> Now in den and nest
> All have gone to rest,
> All the hares asleep,
> All the bears asleep.
> In their holes they sleep,
> Or in thickets deep.
> Husha, hushaby,
> Pretty little hares!
> Husha, hushaby,
> Lazy, grouchy bears.
> But no rest for me,
> Only misery—
> Only misery,
> All there is for me.
> Weary wolf am I—
> Sleep has passed me by.

Be it night or day,
Hunger dogs my way.
Where to look for food
In this frozen wood?
Hunger, frost, and snow—
This is all I know.

(*He prowls around until, sniffing the air, he stops before the* STEP-
DAUGHTER'S *tree.*) Ow-oo-oo! I smell human flesh. Now I'll have a fine
supper for New Year's Eve. (*The* RAVEN *appears on a treetop.*)

RAVEN. Croak! Croak! Watch out, gray one! The prey is not for
you. Croak! Croak! Croak!

WOLF. Oh, it's you again, old wizard? You fooled me this evening
but you won't do it this time. I sense a prey. I do.

RAVEN. Well, if you sense it, perhaps you'll tell me what's on your
right, what's on your left, and what's right ahead of you.

WOLF. You think I don't know? A bush on my right, a bush on my
left, and a dainty morsel right ahead.

RAVEN. You lie, my friend. You have a snare on your right, poison
on your left, and a pitfall right ahead. The only road left for you is
the one going back. Where are you off to, gray one?

WOLF. I run where I please. Mind your own business. (*Disappears
behind a drift.*)

RAVEN. Croak! Croak! The gray one has run away. The wolf is old
but I'm older. He's cunning but I'm more so. I'll trick him many a
time yet. And you, pretty one, wake up. You mustn't doze in a frost—
or you'll freeze to death. (*A* SQUIRREL *appears high in the tree and
drops a cone on the* STEPDAUGHTER.)

SQUIRREL. Don't sleep—or you'll freeze to death.

STEPDAUGHTER. What? Who spoke to me? Who's there? No, I must
have imagined it. It was just a cone that fell on me and woke me up.
And I was having such a nice dream—it even made me feel warm.
Now, what did I dream of? Oh, dear, I can't remember. Oh, yes. I have
it. I saw my own mother walking about the house carrying a lamp,
and the light hit me right in the eyes. (*Raises her head and with her
hand brushes the snow off her eyelids.*) Why, I think I see light—
down there, in the distance. But what if that's a wolf's eyes? No, the
wolf has green eyes and this is a golden light—it trembles and twinkles
like a star caught in the branches of a tree. I'll run to it. (*Jumps off the
branch.*) It's still glowing. Maybe some forester has a cabin near
here, or woodsmen have lit a campfire. I must get there, I must. Oh,
my legs—they're frozen stiff and I can hardly move. (*She stumbles on
through snowdrifts and over fallen trees.*) If only the light doesn't go
out! And it isn't going out! It burns brighter and brighter. I seem to
smell warm smoke. Can it be a campfire? I'm sure it is. Maybe I'm
just imagining but I seem to hear the brushwood crackling in the fire.
(*She walks on, pushing her way through the branches of the thick,*

high fir trees. It grows constantly lighter. Reddish spots of light keep flitting over the snow and the trees. Suddenly the girl finds herself at the edge of a small round clearing in the center of which a big camp-fire is blazing. Around the fire are seated Twelve Men: *three are old men, three middle-aged, three young, and three mere striplings. The young people sit close by the fire, the old ones farther away. Two of the old men wear long white fur coats and shaggy white fur caps; the third one a white coat with black stripes and a white cap trimmed with a black fur border. The three middle-aged men are dressed in clothes of different colors—one in golden red, another in rusty brown, and the third in buff. The remaining six wear embroidered caftan coats of various shades of green. One of the young men has a fur coat slung over his shoulders, atop his green coat, another has a fur coat hanging from one shoulder. The* Stepdaughter *stops between two fir trees and, hesitant to advance any further, listens to what the twelve brothers are saying.)*

January (*throwing an armful of brushwood into the fire*).

> Burn, burn brighter—
> Warm the winter air,
> Bring a hotter summer,
> And a spring more fair.

All.
> Fire, burn high—
> Flame, never die!

June.
> Burn with a crackle—
> That berries soon may grow
> In the woods and copses
> Covered now by snow.

May.
> Let the bees make honey
> For the world to eat.

July.
> Let the fields turn golden
> With waving stalks of wheat.

All.
> Fire, burn high—
> Flame, never die!

(*Having mustered up courage, the* Stepdaughter *slowly moves forward into the clearing. The twelve brothers stop singing and turn toward her.*)

Stepdaughter (*bowing to everybody*). Good evening.

January. And a good evening to you.

Stepdaughter. I hope I'm not intruding. If not, may I warm myself by your fire?

January. What do you say, brothers? Shall we permit her?

February (*shaking his head*). There's never been a case before of a stranger sharing this fire with us.

May. True enough. But if somebody has seen our light, let him warm himself.

April. Let her warm herself. It won't make our fire any colder.

JANUARY. Well, come up, my beauty, come up. But mind you don't burn yourself. You see what a fire we have—it fairly blazes.

STEPDAUGHTER. Thank you, Grandpa. I won't come too close. I'll stand aside. (*She approaches the fire, carefully avoiding touching anybody, and warms her hands.*) It's wonderful here! Your fire is so light and hot—it's gone right to my heart. I'm warm now. Thank you. (*There is a brief pause. Only the crackling of the fire can be heard.*)

JANUARY. That's a basket you're carrying, isn't it, my girl? Have you come to gather cones on New Year's Eve, and in such a snowstorm?

FEBRUARY. The forest needs rest too—you can't go on stripping it of everything.

STEPDAUGHTER. I haven't come here of my own free will, nor to pick cones.

AUGUST (*smiling*). Mushrooms then?

STEPDAUGHTER. Flowers, not mushrooms. My stepmother has sent me here to gather snowdrops.

MARCH (*laughing and nudging* APRIL). You hear, brother? She's come for snowdrops. Receive your guest then. (*They all laugh.*)

STEPDAUGHTER. I'd laugh with you, too, but I'm past laughter. My stepmother has told me not to come back without snowdrops.

FEBRUARY. What does she want snowdrops for in midwinter?

STEPDAUGHTER. She doesn't want flowers. She wants gold. Our queen has promised a basketful of gold to anyone who brings her a basketful of snowdrops. That's why she's sent me to the forest.

JANUARY. You're in a bad way, my dear. This is no time for flowers. You'll have to wait for the month of April.

STEPDAUGHTER. I know that, Grandpa. But I had nowhere else to go. Well, thank you for letting me warm myself and for your kindness. Forgive me if I have intruded on you. (*Takes her basket and slowly walks toward the trees.*)

APRIL. Wait, don't go yet, girl. (*The* STEPDAUGHTER *halts.* APRIL *walks up to* JANUARY *and bows to him.*) Brother January, give me your place for an hour.

JANUARY. I don't mind, but April can't come before March.

MARCH. Don't worry about me. What do you say brother February?

FEBRUARY. All right, brother March, I won't argue. I'll withdraw for an hour too.

JANUARY. That being so, I bow to your wish. (*Strikes the ground with his ice-covered staff.*)

> You winter frosts
> That crackle and shine,
> Stop gnawing the bark
> Of birch and pine.
> Stop chilling the blood
> Of crow and hare,
> Stop freezing the peasant
> And his mare.

(*The forest grows still. The storm subsides. Stars cover the sky.*) Now it's your turn, brother February. (*Hands his staff to the lame and shaggy February.*)

FEBRUARY.   Winds, storms and hurricanes—
    Blow now with all your might!
    Whirlwinds, gales and squalls—
    Go sweeping through the night!
    Roar, you in the clouds,
    Shaking the world below!
    Twist down over the fields—
    A white snake in the snow.

(*The wind howls in the branches of the trees. Snow flurries whirl across the clearing.*) It's your turn next, brother March! (MARCH *takes the staff, which instantly turns into a long budding twig. As he speaks, the tinkling of bells can be heard like water dripping in a spring thaw.*)

MARCH.   Now the snow is darker,
    Melting on the ground.
    The ice is breaking on the lake,
    Crackling all around.
    The sky looks higher, bluer,
    And clouds race faster now;
    The sparrow chirps and twitters,
    Perched up on the bough.
    Trails and paths grow muddy,
    Each day brings brighter dawn,
    And all the pussy willows
    Put silver earrings on.

(*The snow has turned darker on the ground and ceased falling; the thaw has set in. The trees, like the staff, begin to bud.*) Now you take the staff, brother April. (APRIL *takes the staff, which is instantly covered with green young leaves. He puts a shepherd's pipe to his lips and plays a short, rousing song, then speaks in a voice ringing with youthful vigor.*)

APRIL.   Flow, streams, to every side—
    Puddles, spread out wide.
    Ants come into the sun—
    A warmer time's begun.
    The bear trudges along,
    The lark sings his song;
    And here before the showers,
    The early snowdrop flowers.

(*Everything in the forest and clearing undergoes a transformation. The last snow melts away. Blue and white flowers appear on the hillocks under the trees. All around there is dripping, flowing, and gurgling. The* STEPDAUGHTER *stands spellbound in wonder.*) Why do you stand still? Make haste. My brothers have given you and me only one hour.

STEPDAUGHTER. But I don't understand what's happened. Can it be true that just for my sake spring has come in the middle of winter? I can't believe my eyes.

APRIL. You can believe it or not, as you please, but hurry up and pick your snowdrops. Or winter will be back before you've filled your basket.

STEPDAUGHTER. Right away! Here I go! (*She disappears among the trees.*)

JANUARY (*in a low voice*). I recognized her the moment I saw her. She has the same torn kerchief and worn-out boots she had this afternoon. We winter months know her very well. One day she's at the ice hole with buckets, another day in the forest with a sledful of brushwood. And she is always so cheerful and pleasant and always singing. But today she's sad.

JUNE. We summer months know her just as well.

JULY. We certainly do. Before the sun is up she's down on her knees in the back garden pulling out weeds, tying up stems and picking off caterpillars. Or we see her in the forest taking care not to break a twig needlessly, or picking a ripe berry but leaving a green one on the bush to grow and ripen freely.

NOVEMBER. Many's the time I've drenched her with rain. I'm sorry for that but it can't be helped—that's what a fall month is for.

FEBRUARY. She's seen very little kindness from me either. I've made her shiver in the wind, freeze in the cold. Yes, she does know February, and February knows her too. One doesn't mind making up a gift of an hour of spring to such as her.

APRIL. Why only an hour? I'd be satisfied to spend my whole life with her.

SEPTEMBER. She's certainly a fine girl. No better housewife is to be found anywhere.

APRIL. Well, if she's agreeable to all of you, I'll give her an engagement ring.

JANUARY. Go ahead. You're young and it's natural for you to feel the way you do. (*The* STEPDAUGHTER *returns, carrying a basketful of snowdrops.*) A whole basketful? You do have quick hands.

STEPDAUGHTER. There are untold numbers of them down there. They are everywhere—on the hillocks and under the hillocks, in clearings and in thickets, under the trees and under the stones. I never saw so many snowdrops in my life. And they're all so big, with such downy, velvety stems, and petals clear as crystal. Thank you, Brother Months, for your kindness. If it weren't for you, I'd have never seen the sun and the spring snowdrops again. As long as there's breath in my body, I'll thank you for every flower I pick, every day I live. (*Bows to* JANUARY.)

JANUARY. Don't thank me. Thank my young brother April. He pleaded for you and he brought the snowdrops out from under the snow so that you might pick them.

STEPDAUGHTER (*turning to* APRIL). Thank you, Month of April, I've always welcomed you, and now that I've seen you face to face, I'll never forget you.

APRIL. And to make sure that you don't forget me, here's a ring for you. Look at it from time to time and think of me. And if you ever find yourself in trouble, throw it on the ground, or into water, or into a snowdrift and say:

> "Roll on, my little ring,
> Onto the porch of spring,
> Into the summer hall,
> Through the house of fall,
> Over winter's carpet white
> To the brothers' campfire bright!"

And we'll all come to your help—all twelve of us, one after another. Have you remembered what to say?

STEPDAUGHTER. I have. (*Repeats.*)

> Over winter's carpet white
> To the brothers' campfire bright!

APRIL. Well, good-by, and take good care of the little ring. If you lose it, you'll lose me.

STEPDAUGHTER. I won't lose it nor shall I ever part with it. To me it will always be the dearest thing I have in the world.

JANUARY. Now I must tell you something. It has come to you, this last night of the old year and this first night of the new, to meet all the twelve months at once. August is not due for a long time yet but here he is standing before you. The April snowdrops won't blossom till several moons from now but you already have a basketful of them. You've come to us by the shortest road, the others tread the long road —day after day, hour after hour, minute after minute. That's how it should be. So don't disclose or show this short road to anybody. This is a forbidden road.

STEPDAUGHTER. I'd rather die than tell anybody.

JANUARY. That's better. Remember what I've told you and what you've replied. Now run along home before I let loose a snowstorm.

STEPDAUGHTER. Good-by, Brother Months.

TWELVE MONTHS. Good-by, little sister. (*The* STEPDAUGHTER *runs off.*)

APRIL. Brother January, she'll find the road back too dark. Ask the moon to light the way for her.

JANUARY. That I will. But where has it gone to? Ho there, Moon, will you please come out from behind that cloud? (*The moon sails out and pauses over the clearing.*) Do me a favor, Moon—show our little guest the way out of the forest so she may get home quickly. (*The moon moves across the sky in the direction the* STEPDAUGHTER *has gone. There is a brief silence.*)

DECEMBER. Well, brother January, our wintry springtime is coming to an end. Take the staff back.

JANUARY. Wait a while. It isn't time yet. (*The clearing lights up again. The moon returns from behind the trees and halts overhead.*) You've seen her home then? Well, thank you, Moon. And now let me have the staff, brother April. My turn has come.

> Hark ye, sisters of the north,
> Through your silver doors come forth!
> Blizzard, hurricane, and gale,
> Fill the earth with moan and wail!
> Let your stormy dance begin,
> Set your carousel a-spin!
> Through the woods and fields
> blow free,
> Sound your New Year's revelry!

(*He strikes the ground with the staff. A snowstorm begins howling. Clouds race across the sky. Heavy snowflakes fill the stage.*)

CURTAIN

ACT III

Scene 1

The OLD WOMAN's *cottage. The* OLD WOMAN *and her* DAUGHTER *are dolling themselves up. A basket filled with snowdrops stands on a bench.*

DAUGHTER. I told you to give her the big new basket and you begrudged it. Now blame yourself. How much gold will this one hold? A handful or two, that's all.

OLD WOMAN. Who would ever have thought she'd get back alive, to say nothing of bringing snowdrops? It's unheard of. I just can't figure out where she found them.

DAUGHTER. Haven't you asked her?

OLD WOMAN. I didn't have time. She came home all excited and happy, her eyes shining, her cheeks flushed. You'd think she'd been to a fair, instead of a forest. And no sooner did she put the basket on the table than she slipped behind her curtain. By the time I took a look at what was in the basket she was already asleep—and so soundly you couldn't wake her. The sun was up and she was still asleep. I had to make the fire and sweep the floor myself.

DAUGHTER. I'll go wake her up. In the meantime you can take the big new basket and put the snowdrops in it.

OLD WOMAN. Won't the basket look rather empty?

DAUGHTER. Not if you spread the flowers out. (*Throws the big basket to her.*)

OLD WOMAN. You are a clever girl. (*The* DAUGHTER *goes off behind the curtain. The* OLD WOMAN *transfers the snowdrops.*) And how am I to place them to make the basket look full? Maybe I ought to add some dirt. (*Takes some flowerpots from the window ledge, empties the earth in them into the basket, places the snowdrops in it, and arranges the green leaves from the pots around the basket's border.*) Good. Flowers like earth. And where there are flowers, there are leaves too. My darling daughter seems to take after me. And between the two of us we have no shortage of brains. (*The* DAUGHTER *tiptoes out from behind the curtain.*) Look how I've arranged the snowdrops. Isn't it wonderful?

DAUGHTER (*in a low voice*). You look at this. Isn't this wonderful?

OLD WOMAN. A ring! And such a marvelous one. Where did you get it?

DAUGHTER. Where! I walked in there and began to wake her. She was dead to the world. I grabbed her hand and there was this ring shining on her finger. I pulled the ring off quietly but didn't try to wake her—let her sleep.

OLD WOMAN. Ah, so! Just as I thought.

DAUGHTER. What did you think?

OLD WOMAN. It's clear she didn't pick the snowdrops all by herself. Somebody was helping her. There's an orphan for you! Show me the ring, dear. My goodness, how it sparkles! I've never seen one like it in all my life. Put it on your finger, dear.

DAUGHTER (*trying to put it on*). It won't go. (*The* STEPDAUGHTER *appears from behind the curtain.*)

OLD WOMAN (*whispers*). Hide it. Put it in your pocket. (*The* DAUGHTER *hides the ring in her pocket. The* STEPDAUGHTER, *looking at the flowers, slowly walks to the bench, then to the door, and out into the hall.*) She's noticed it's missing. (*The* STEPDAUGHTER *returns, walks up to the basket with the snowdrops, and searches among the flowers.*) What's the idea of mussing up the flowers?

STEPDAUGHTER. Where's the basket I brought the snowdrops in?

OLD WOMAN. What do you want it for? There it is. (*The* STEPDAUGHTER *looks into the basket.*)

DAUGHTER. What is it you're looking for?

OLD WOMAN. She's a great one for looking for things. Who ever heard of anybody finding such a heap of snowdrops in midwinter? Yet she found them.

DAUGHTER. And she argued there were no snowdrops in winter. Where did you get them?

STEPDAUGHTER. In the forest. (*Bends and peers under the bench.*)

OLD WOMAN. For God's sake, what are you looking for?

STEPDAUGHTER. Have you found anything around here?

OLD WOMAN. What could we find here? We haven't lost anything.

DAUGHTER. Apparently you've lost something yourself but are afraid to say what it is.

STEPDAUGHTER. Do you know what it is? Have you seen it?

DAUGHTER. How can I know? You never told me or showed me anything.

OLD WOMAN. If you tell us what you've lost we may be able to help you find it.

STEPDAUGHTER (*forcing herself to speak*). I've lost a ring.

OLD WOMAN. A ring? But you never had one.

STEPDAUGHTER. I found it in the forest last night.

OLD WOMAN. Aren't you the lucky girl? You find snowdrops—then you find a ring. Quite the little finder, I'd say. So if you look for what you've lost, you're sure to find it. As for my daughter and me, it's time for us to go to the palace. Wrap yourself up well, daughter. It's very cold. (*They dress and preen themselves.*)

STEPDAUGHTER. What do you need my ring for? Give it back to me.

OLD WOMAN. What's that? You're crazy. How can we have it?

DAUGHTER. We've never even caught a glimpse of it.

STEPDAUGHTER. Sister dear, darling, you have my ring. I know. Don't make fun of me. Give it back. You're going to the palace. They'll give you a whole basketful of gold there and you'll be able to buy yourself anything you want. And all I had was this little ring.

OLD WOMAN. Leave her alone, will you? It looks to me as if you didn't find the ring at all but it was given to you and it's dear to you as a remembrance.

DAUGHTER. Tell me, who gave it to you?

STEPDAUGHTER. Nobody. I found it.

OLD WOMAN. Oh, well, it's no pain to lose what's been easily found. It's not like something you've earned. Come along, dear. Take the basket. They must be waiting for us at the palace. (*The* OLD WOMAN *and the* DAUGHTER *go off.*)

STEPDAUGHTER. Mother! Sister! Please wait! They don't even want to listen to me. What am I to do now? Who can I go to? The brother months are far away. I can't find them without the ring. And who else will help me? Maybe the Queen, if I go to her palace and tell her what's happened. After all, I picked the snowdrops for her. The soldier said she was an orphan. Maybe an orphan will take pity on another orphan. No, they'll never allow me to see her if I come with empty hands, without my snowdrops. (*Sits down in front of the stove and gazes into the fire.*) Now it feels as if nothing had ever happened, as if it was all a dream. The snowdrops are gone, the ring is gone. Only the brushwood remains out of all I've brought from the forest. (*Throws an armful of brushwood into the fire.*)

Fire, burn high—
Flame, never die!

(*The fire in the stove flares up and crackles.*) It does burn brightly—

merrily. As if I were by the campfire in the forest, among the brother months. Good-by, my New Year's fortune. Good-by, Brother Months. Good-by, April.

CURTAIN

ACT III

Scene 2

The throne room in the royal palace. In the center of the room stands a tall, lavishly decorated tree. Before the door to the interior apartments a crowd of elegantly attired GUESTS *waits for the* QUEEN *to make her appearance. Among the* GUESTS *are the* AMBASSADORS *of the* EASTERN *and* WESTERN KINGDOMS. *The* MUSICIANS *play a fanfare. The door opens and in come the* COURTIERS *headed by the* COMMANDER OF THE ROYAL BODYGUARD, *with the* ROYAL PROSECUTOR *behind him; after them the* QUEEN *accompanied by the* CHANCELLOR *and a tall, bony* LADY IN WAITING. PAGES *carry the* QUEEN's *long train. The* PROFESSOR, *toddling along modestly, brings up the rear of the procession.*

EVERYBODY. A happy New Year, Your Majesty! A happy New Year!

QUEEN. Thank you. But the New Year hasn't arrived yet. (*General surprise.*)

CHANCELLOR. However, Your Majesty, today is the first of January.

QUEEN. You're mistaken. (*To the* PROFESSOR.) How many days has December?

PROFESSOR. Exactly thirty-one, Your Majesty.

QUEEN. Then today is the thirty-second of December.

LADY IN WAITING (*to the* AMBASSADORS). This is a delightful New Year's joke by her Majesty. (*Everybody laughs.*)

COMMANDER OF THE ROYAL BODYGUARD. A very witty remark, more pointed than my sword, isn't it so, Mr. Royal Prosecutor?

ROYAL PROSECUTOR. The acme of wit.

QUEEN. I'm not joking. (*All stop laughing.*) Tomorrow will be the thirty-third of December, the day after tomorrow the thirty-fourth of December. How does it go? (*To the* PROFESSOR.) You continue.

PROFESSOR (*taken aback*). The thirty-fifth of December. The thirty-sixth of December. The thirty-seventh of December. But it's impossible, Your Majesty.

QUEEN. You're at it again.

PROFESSOR. Yes, Your Majesty, again and again. You can cut off my head, you can throw me in jail, but there's no such thing as the thirty-seventh of December. December has thirty-one days. Exactly thirty-one. It has been proved by science. And seven times eight, Your Majesty, is fifty-six, and eight times eight, Your Majesty, is sixty-four. This, too, has been proved by science. And I value science more than my own head.

QUEEN. Well, well, dear Professor, calm yourself. I forgive you this time. I've heard somewhere that monarchs like to be told the truth. All the same, December won't end until a basketful of snowdrops is brought in here.

PROFESSOR. As you wish, Your Majesty. But snowdrops will not be brought here.

QUEEN. We'll see. (*General confusion.*)

CHANCELLOR. I beg leave to present to Your Majesty the Ambassadors Extraordinary of two friendly nations, who have just arrived— the Ambassador of the Western Kingdom and the Ambassador of the Eastern Kingdom. (*The two* AMBASSADORS *step forward and bow to the* QUEEN.)

WESTERN AMBASSADOR (*he is tall, close shaven, and bald headed*). His Majesty, the King of my country, has instructed me to convey to Your Majesty his best wishes for the New Year.

QUEEN. Convey my best wishes to His Majesty too, if the New Year has already arrived in his country. In my country, as you observe, the New Year has been delayed this year. (*The* WESTERN AMBASSADOR *bows gracefully, but somewhat confusedly, and steps back.*)

EASTERN AMBASSADOR (*he is short and stout and has a long black beard. He bows to the* QUEEN). My lord and master has ordered me to convey his greetings to Your Majesty and to offer you his congratulations on—

QUEEN. On what?

EASTERN AMBASSADOR (*after a pause*). On the excellent state of your health and the great wisdom which is so rare at such a tender age.

QUEEN (*to* PROFESSOR). Did you hear? And you're still trying to teach me something.

PROFESSOR. People of wisdom, Your Majesty, learn as long as they live.

QUEEN. They probably have nothing else to do. Kings and queens have too many cares as it is. (*The* PROFESSOR *sighs and bows. The* QUEEN *sits down on the throne and with a movement of her hand summons the* CHANCELLOR *to her side.*) I'm surprised there are still no snowdrops. Does everybody in the city know my decree?

CHANCELLOR. Your Majesty's wish has been fulfilled. Flowers will immediately be cast before your feet. (*He waves a handkerchief. The doors open wide. Enter a procession of* GARDENERS *carrying baskets, vases, and bouquets of flowers in great variety. The* HEAD GARDENER, *an important-looking man with side whiskers, presents the* QUEEN *with a huge basket filled with roses. Other* GARDENERS *place tulips, narcissuses, orchids, hydrangeas, azaleas, and other flowers around the throne.*)

LADY IN WAITING. What gorgeous colors!

WESTERN AMBASSADOR. A real feast of flowers.

EASTERN AMBASSADOR. A rose in the midst of roses!

QUEEN. Are there any snowdrops here?

CHANCELLOR. Very probably.

QUEEN. Please find them for me.

CHANCELLOR (*bends over, puts his spectacles on, and with a suspicious air begins to scrutinize the flowers in the baskets; finally picks a peony and a hydrangea*). I believe one of these flowers is a snowdrop.

QUEEN (*to the* PROFESSOR). What's your opinion?

PROFESSOR. I regret to say I know only the Latin names of plants. As far as I can recall this is a *peonia albiflora* and this is *hydrangea opuloides*. (*The* GARDENERS *shake their heads disapprovingly and resentfully.*)

QUEEN. *Opuloides?* It sounds more like the name of some disease. (*To the* GARDENERS.) You tell me what these flowers are.

GARDENER. This is a hydrangea, Your Majesty, and this is a peony or Mary's root, as the country folk call it, Your Majesty.

QUEEN. I don't want any Mary's roots. I want snowdrops. Are there or are there not some snowdrops here?

GARDENER. Your Majesty—how can snowdrops grow in a royal greenhouse? The snowdrop is a wild flower, you might say, a weed.

QUEEN. Where do they grow then?

GARDENER. In their proper place, Your Majesty. (*Contemptuously.*) Somewhere in a forest, under hummocks.

QUEEN. Then bring them to me from the forest, from under the hummocks.

GARDENER. Yes, Your Majesty. Only there aren't any snowdrops in the forest at this time of the year. They won't appear before April.

QUEEN. What is this? A conspiracy? Everybody keeps saying April —April. I don't want to hear it again. If I end this day without snowdrops, some one of my subjects is going to end it without a head. (*To the* ROYAL PROSECUTOR.) Who do you think is responsible for my not having snowdrops?

ROYAL PROSECUTOR. In my opinion it's the Head Gardener, Your Majesty.

HEAD GARDENER. Your Majesty, I answer with my head only for garden plants. For forest plants the Head Forester is responsible.

QUEEN. Very well. If I don't get snowdrops, I'll order both of you to be hanged. My Lord Chancellor, have the decree prepared.

CHANCELLOR. I have everything ready, your Majesty. All that's left is to put in the name and affix the seal. (*A door opens. Enter an* OFFICER OF THE ROYAL BODYGUARD, *followed by the* OLD WOMAN *and her* DAUGHTER, *the latter carrying a basket covered with a napkin.*)

OFFICER. Your Majesty. In compliance with the royal decree these two women have brought here a whole basketful of— (*Pauses.*) snow-drops.

QUEEN (*rising*). Oh, let me have them! (*Runs to the basket and tears off the napkin.*) So these are snowdrops?

OLD WOMAN. They are, Your Majesty. Fresh forest snowdrops, right from under the snowdrifts, picked with our own hands!

QUEEN (*both hands full of the blossoms*). Now, these are real flow-ers, not like your—what do you call them?—*opuloides* or Mary's roots. (*Pins a bunch to her breast.*) Today let everybody wear snowdrops in their buttonholes or pinned to their dresses. I don't want to see any other flowers. (*To the* GARDENERS.) Out with you!

HEAD GARDENER (*delighted*). Thank you, Your Majesty. (*The* GAR-DENERS *pick up their flowers and go off. The* QUEEN *hands out snow-drops to the* GUESTS.)

LADY IN WAITING (*pinning some to her dress*). These sweet little flowers remind me of the time when I was a tiny thing and used to run about the paths in the park.

QUEEN. You mean to say you were ever a tiny thing and ever ran around through the park? (*Laughs.*) That must have been very funny. How annoying that it was before I was born.

COMMANDER OF THE ROYAL BODYGUARD (*receiving a snowdrop from the* QUEEN). This is my new decoration, Your Majesty. The pity is it will die soon. I prefer decorations which last a long time.

QUEEN. You have a great many of them already. Mind that they too don't die soon. And this is for you, Mr. Royal Prosecutor. Pin it to your black cloak, it will make looking at you a more cheerful experi-ence.

ROYAL PROSECUTOR (*pinning a snowdrop to his cloak*). This is the best New Year's gift I've received, Your Majesty.

QUEEN. I'm very glad. From now on I'll present you with a flower every year. Next year it will be a forget-me-not, then a daisy, then a pansy. Well, have you all got a snowdrop? Everybody? Splendid. That means a new year has started in my kingdom too. December is ended. You may offer your congratulations now.

ALL. A happy New Year, Your Majesty. A happy New Year!

QUEEN. A happy New Year! A happy New Year! Light up the tree. I want to dance. (*The* WESTERN AMBASSADOR *solemnly and respect-fully bows to the* QUEEN. *She gives him her hand. The dancing begins. The* QUEEN *dances with the* WESTERN AMBASSADOR, *the* LADY IN WAIT-ING *with the* COMMANDER OF THE ROYAL BODYGUARD. *Other pairs of dancers follow them.*) My dear Ambassador, I wonder if you would mind tripping up my Lady in Waiting? It would be such a jolly sight to see her stretched out in the center of the hall.

WESTERN AMBASSADOR. I beg to be forgiven, Your Majesty, but I don't think I quite understand you.

QUEEN. Oh, I just asked if you like my palace. You know, it's very ancient. It was built when my Lady in Waiting was just a tiny thing.

WESTERN AMBASSADOR. Was it really? I love antiquities.

QUEEN. I can't say I do very much. I have too many of them—the palace, the various ruins in the park, the statues, the Lady in Waiting, the Chancellor, the Commander of the Royal Bodyguard—

LADY IN WAITING (*dancing*). Have you been talking about me, Your Majesty?

QUEEN. Just as a change from your constant talking about me.

LADY IN WAITING. Who else can we talk about if not Your Majesty? (*To the* COMMANDER OF THE ROYAL BODYGUARD *as they move away from the* QUEEN.) Oh, I'm afraid the Queen may start on some mad prank today. You can expect anything from her. She's such an unmannerly little chit.

COMMANDER OF THE ROYAL BODYGUARD. My dear lady, haven't you been in charge of her upbringing?

LADY IN WAITING. Oh, what could I do with her? She's taken after her father and mother—her mother's caprices and her father's pranks. In winter she wants snowdrops and in summer she'll demand snow.

QUEEN. Well, thank you. I'm bored with dancing. (*Everybody stops instantly. The* QUEEN *proceeds to her throne.*)

OLD WOMAN. Permit us to offer you our New Year's greetings, Your Majesty.

QUEEN. Oh, you're still here?

OLD WOMAN. Yes, ma'am, we're still here, waiting with our basket.

QUEEN. Oh, yes. My Lord Chancellor, order this basket to be filled with gold.

CHANCELLOR. Filled with gold?

OLD WOMAN. As promised, Your Excellency. As much gold as there were flowers.

CHANCELLOR. But their basket contained much more earth than flowers, Your Majesty.

OLD WOMAN. Flowers die without earth, your Excellency.

QUEEN. Is that true?

PROFESSOR. Absolutely, Your Majesty.

QUEEN. Pay them in gold for the snowdrops. As for the soil, in my kingdom it's already my property. Isn't that true, Mr. Royal Prosecutor?

ROYAL PROSECUTOR. Absolutely, Your Majesty. (*The* CHANCELLOR *takes the basket and goes off.*)

QUEEN (*regarding a bunch of snowdrops*). And so, April hasn't come yet, but snowdrops have already blossomed out. What do you say to that now, dear Professor?

PROFESSOR. I still consider it wrong.

QUEEN. Wrong?

PROFESSOR. Yes, Your Majesty. Such things don't happen.

WESTERN AMBASSADOR. This is indeed an extremely rare and remarkable case, Your Majesty. It would be very interesting to hear how these women found such delightful spring flowers at the coldest season of the year.

EASTERN AMBASSADOR. I'm all ears and dying to hear the wonderful story.

QUEEN (*to the* OLD WOMAN *and her* DAUGHTER). Go on, tell us where you found the flowers. (*The* OLD WOMAN *and her* DAUGHTER *remain silent.*) Why don't you speak?

OLD WOMAN (*to her* DAUGHTER). You tell it.

DAUGHTER. Tell it yourself.

OLD WOMAN (*steps forward, bows, and clears her throat*). It's an easy matter to tell the story, Your Majesty. It was a much harder job to find the snowdrops in the forest. As soon as we heard the royal proclamation, we both decided: we may risk our lives, we may get frozen to death, but we'll fulfill Her Majesty's will. We took a broom and a spade each and went into the forest. With the brooms we swept a path before us, with the spades we dug up the snowdrifts. It was dark and cold in the woods. On and on we went but we got only deeper and deeper into the forest. I could see my daughter was frozen stiff—shivering in every bone. Now we're lost, I thought to myself—

QUEEN. Well, what happened after that?

OLD WOMAN. After that it was worse than ever, Your Majesty. The snowdrifts grew higher and higher, the cold more and more bitter, the forest darker and darker. Suddenly we see two trails, but who made them you can't tell—maybe a wolf, maybe a bear, and maybe some unknown beast. Well, I say to my daughter, "What's to be is to be!"

LADY IN WAITING (*throwing up her arms*). My, how frightening!

QUEEN. Don't interrupt, please. Go on with your story.

OLD WOMAN. Yes, Your Majesty. So on we went, I down the left trail, she down the right one, and—lo and behold! we came to the same place. And what a place! So marvelous looking, you can't even describe it. The snowdrifts stood higher than the trees, and right in the middle there was a lake—just like a plate it looked, it was so round. The water in it hadn't frozen, there were ducks swimming on it, and its banks were smothered with flowers—

QUEEN. All snowdrops?

OLD WOMAN. All kinds of flowers, Your Majesty. I'd never seen some of them before. (*The* CHANCELLOR *brings in a basket with gold and sets it down beside the* OLD WOMAN *and her* DAUGHTER. *Casting glances at the gold, the* OLD WOMAN *continues her story.*) The whole land seemed covered with a carpet of flowers.

LADY IN WAITING. That must have been beautiful! Flowers, birds!

QUEEN. What birds? She never mentioned birds.

LADY IN WAITING (*embarrassed*). The little ducklings.

QUEEN (*to the* PROFESSOR). Are ducks birds?

PROFESSOR. Swimming birds, Your Majesty.

COMMANDER OF THE ROYAL BODYGUARD. Do mushrooms grow there too?

DAUGHTER. Mushrooms too.

ROYAL PROSECUTOR. And berries?

DAUGHTER. Strawberries, raspberries, whortleberries, bilberries—

WESTERN AMBASSADOR. Are there any plums there?

EASTERN AMBASSADOR. And nuts?

DAUGHTER. Everything is there.

QUEEN. That's wonderful. Go back to the forest at once and bring me some strawberries, nuts, and plums.

OLD WOMAN. My goodness, Your Majesty.

QUEEN. What's the matter? You don't want to go?

OLD WOMAN (*plaintively*). It's such a long journey there, Your Majesty.

QUEEN. It can't be so very long seeing that I signed my decree yesterday and you brought me the flowers today.

OLD WOMAN. That's true, Your Majesty, but we got so frozen on our trip.

QUEEN. Frozen? That's all right. You'll be given a couple of warm fur coats. (*To the* SERVANTS.) Bring two fur coats, quick.

OLD WOMAN (*to her* DAUGHTER *in a low voice*). What are we to do?

DAUGHTER (*in a low voice*). We'll send her.

OLD WOMAN (*in a low voice*). Will she find what the Queen wants?

DAUGHTER (*in a low voice*). She will.

QUEEN. What are you whispering?

OLD WOMAN. We're putting our heads together to decide which trail to follow—the right or the left one.

QUEEN. But you said both trails meet at the same place.

OLD WOMAN. They do, Your Majesty, they certainly do. So order them to give us each a fur coat and we'll go. (*Picks up the basket with the gold.*)

QUEEN. You'll be given the coats presently. But leave the gold here for the time being. When you return you'll get two baskets at once. (*The* OLD WOMAN *puts the basket down, whereupon the* CHANCELLOR *hastily moves it away. The* OLD WOMAN *and her* DAUGHTER *look displeased.*) And see you get back quickly. We need strawberries, plums, and nuts for our New Year's dinner today. (*SERVANTS hand coats to the* OLD WOMAN *and* HER DAUGHTER, *who put them on and look each other over.*)

OLD WOMAN. Thank you for the coats, Your Majesty. We need have no fear of the cold in them. They may not be lined with silver fox but they're warm. Good-by, Your Majesty. Wait for our return with nuts and berries. (*She and her* DAUGHTER *bow and hurry off to the door.*)

QUEEN. Wait. (*Claps her hands.*) Give me my fur coat too. Give everybody a fur coat. And have the horses harnessed.

CHANCELLOR. Where do you propose to drive, Your Majesty?

QUEEN (*almost bouncing on her throne*). We are driving to the forest, to that round lake, and there, on the snow, we'll gather strawberries. That'll make something like strawberries and ice cream. Let's go! Let's go!

LADY IN WAITING. I knew it. What a delightful idea!

WESTERN AMBASSADOR. One couldn't think of anything better for a New Year's entertainment.

EASTERN AMBASSADOR. The idea is worthy of Haroun-al-Rashid himself.

LADIES OF THE COURT (*wrapping themselves up in fur capes and coats*). This is wonderful! Isn't it fun?

QUEEN. Put these two women in the first sleigh. They'll show us the way. (*The* QUEEN *and her suite continue their preparations.*)

DAUGHTER. Oh!

OLD WOMAN. Your Majesty!

QUEEN. What is it?

OLD WOMAN. Don't be in such a hurry, Your Majesty. Allow me to tell you something.

QUEEN. Go on.

OLD WOMAN. Your Majesty mustn't go to the forest.

QUEEN. What is there to stop me?

OLD WOMAN. There are terrible snowdrifts there—absolutely impassable.

QUEEN. If you could clear a way for yourself with a broom and a spade, there will be no difficulty in clearing a wide road for me. (*To the* COMMANDER OF THE ROYAL BODYGUARD.) Have a regiment of soldiers armed with spades and brooms proceed to the forest at once.

COMMANDER OF THE ROYAL BODYGUARD. Your will be done, Your Majesty.

QUEEN. Well, is everybody ready? Let's go!

OLD WOMAN. Your Majesty!

QUEEN. I don't want to hear another word out of you. You'll keep silent until we reach the lake. You can use your hands to show us the way.

OLD WOMAN. What way? That lake is gone, Your Majesty.

QUEEN. What do you mean?

OLD WOMAN. Just what I said. The lake is gone. It was frozen over before we left it.

DAUGHTER. And buried under mountains of snow.

LADY IN WAITING. What happened to the ducks?

OLD WOMAN. They flew away.

WESTERN AMBASSADOR. And what about the strawberries and plums?

EASTERN AMBASSADOR. And nuts?

OLD WOMAN. They're all way down under the snow.

COMMANDER OF THE ROYAL BODYGUARD. But at least the mushrooms are still there?

QUEEN. Yes, dried ones. (*Sternly.*) I see you're making fun of me.

OLD WOMAN. Heaven forbid, Your Majesty.

CHANCELLOR. These frauds should be handcuffed and jailed, Your Majesty. I saw at once that all they wanted was to wheedle a basket of gold out of us.

LADY IN WAITING. I too, Your Majesty, visualized from the start that these swindlers were cheating us. Who ever heard of such berries as waffles and beaks?

PROFESSOR. Whortleberries and bilberries, madam, are wild berries, which are found in forests, but of course in summer, not in winter. I pray Your Majesty won't be angry with me, but as I stated before neither berries, nor nuts, nor snowdrops can grow in our climate in the middle of winter.

QUEEN (*tearing off her corsage of snowdrops*). And what's this?

PROFESSOR (*his voice sinking*). Snowdrops.

OLD WOMAN AND HER DAUGHTER. Snowdrops, Your Majesty, real snowdrops fresh from the forest.

QUEEN (*sitting down on the throne and wrapping herself in her fur coat*). Well, then, if you don't tell me where you got them, I'll have your heads chopped off tomorrow. No, today. Right now. (*To the* PROFESSOR.) How do you say it? Don't put off till tomorrow——

PROFESSOR. What you can do today, Your Majesty.

QUEEN. Precisely. (*To the* OLD WOMAN *and her* DAUGHTER.) Well, I'm waiting for your answer. Only I want nothing but the truth. Or you'll find it most unpleasant. (The COMMANDER OF THE ROYAL BODY-GUARD *grasps the handle of his sword.*)

OLD WOMAN (*crying*). We don't know anything ourselves, Your Majesty.

DAUGHTER. We know nothing.

QUEEN. How can that be? You picked a whole basketful of snow-drops and you don't know where?

OLD WOMAN. We didn't pick them.

QUEEN. You didn't? Well, who did?

OLD WOMAN. My stepdaughter, Your Majesty. The wretch went to the forest for me and it was she who brought back the snowdrops.

QUEEN. So she went to the forest, and you went to the palace? Why didn't you bring her with you?

OLD WOMAN. She stayed at home, Your Majesty. Somebody had to look after the house.

QUEEN. Well, you could have looked after your house and sent the wretch here.

OLD WOMAN. It wouldn't have been so easy, Your Majesty. She's afraid to come near people, as if she were a little wild animal.

QUEEN. But I suppose your little wild animal can show us the road to the snowdrops?

OLD WOMAN. I'm sure she can do that. If she found the way once, she can find it again. Only I don't know if she'll want to.

QUEEN. How can she refuse, if I order her?

OLD WOMAN. She's very stubborn, Your Majesty.

QUEEN. So am I. We'll see who will outstubborn whom.

DAUGHTER. If she refuses, Your Majesty, order her head to be chopped off—that's all.

QUEEN. I know myself whose heads should be chopped off. (*Rises from the throne.*) Well, here's my decision. We're all going to the forest to pick snowdrops. You'll be given our fastest horses and, picking up your little wild animal, you'll catch up with us in the forest.

OLD WOMAN AND HER DAUGHTER (*bowing*). Yes, Your Majesty.

QUEEN. Wait. (*To the* COMMANDER OF THE ROYAL BODYGUARD.) Have two—no, four armed guards accompany them or these liars will slip away from us.

COMMANDER OF THE ROYAL BODYGUARD. Your will be done, Your Majesty. I'll teach them where dried mushrooms grow.

QUEEN. Excellent. Now let each one of us carry a basket. The Professor will have the biggest one. He must learn well how snowdrops grow in my kingdom in January.

CURTAIN

ACT IV

Scene 1

A forest. A round, ice-covered lake. In the center of the lake, a dark hole. All around are high snowdrifts. Two SQUIRRELS *appear on the branches of a pine and a fir tree.*

FIRST SQUIRREL. Hello, Squirrel.

SECOND SQUIRREL. Hello, Squirrel.

FIRST SQUIRREL. A happy New Year to you.

SECOND SQUIRREL. The same to you.

FIRST SQUIRREL. Here's a pine cone for you. Catch it. (*Throws one.*)

SECOND SQUIRREL. Here's a fir cone for you. (*Throws a fir cone.*)

FIRST SQUIRREL. Here's another one.

SECOND SQUIRREL. And another one for you.

RAVEN (*popping out above*). Croak! Croak! Hello, Squirrels.

FIRST SQUIRREL. Hello, Grandpa. A happy New Year to you.

SECOND SQUIRREL. A happy New Year to you, Grandpa. How are things with you?

RAVEN. As ever.

FIRST SQUIRREL. How many times have you celebrated the new year, Grandpa?

RAVEN. Hundred and forty.

SECOND SQUIRREL. My, my! You are an old raven, Grandpa.

RAVEN. My turn to die is long overdue, but death has forgotten me.

FIRST SQUIRREL. Is it true, Grandpa, that there's nothing in the world you don't know?

RAVEN. Yes, it's true.

SECOND SQUIRREL. Then tell us all you've seen.

RAVEN. That's too long a story.

FIRST SQUIRREL. Make it short.

RAVEN. Short? Croak!

SECOND SQUIRREL. No, longer than that.

RAVEN. Croak! Croak! Croak!

FIRST SQUIRREL. We don't understand your crow language.

RAVEN. That's a pity. You should study foreign languages, take lessons.

FIRST SQUIRREL. There are too many different people in our forest and everybody talks his own language.

SECOND SQUIRREL. Now, I can talk the hare language a little and I understand the wolves, but when it comes to bears and badgers I can't make out a single word.

RAVEN. You should try and learn. (*The* HARE *comes on with a leap.*)

FIRST SQUIRREL. Hello, docktail. A happy New Year to you.

SECOND SQUIRREL. And a merry one.

FIRST SQUIRREL. And best wishes on the new snow.

SECOND SQUIRREL. And on the new frost.

HARE. That's no frost. Why, I'm hot—the snow just melts under my paws. Look here, Squirrels, have you seen our Wolf?

FIRST SQUIRREL. What do you want the Wolf for?

SECOND SQUIRREL. Why are you looking for him?

HARE. I'm not looking for him. He's looking for me. I need a place to hide.

FIRST SQUIRREL. Climb up here, brother—hippity-hop, to the tippity-top! You'll be safe and sound when the Wolf comes around.

SECOND SQUIRREL. Come on, Hare, jump.

FIRST SQUIRREL. Jump up here. Jump up here.

HARE. You think it's funny. But the Wolf is out to get me. He's scouring the forest for me, he wants to eat me up.

FIRST SQUIRREL. That's bad, Hare. And you'd better make yourself scarce. I see the bushes moving—snow being knocked off them. Looks as if you're right about the Wolf. (*The* HARE *disappears. The* WOLF *comes out from behind a snowdrift.*)

WOLF. I feel he's here. This time that long-eared fool won't give me the slip—I'll get him. Squirrels, have you seen the Hare?

FIRST SQUIRREL. We certainly have. He has been looking for you everywhere, all over the forest, asking everybody about you: "Where's the Wolf? Where's the Wolf?"

WOLF. I'll show him where the Wolf is. Which way did he go?

FIRST SQUIRREL. That way.

WOLF. But why do his footprints go the other way?

SECOND SQUIRREL. They parted company—the footprints went this way and the Hare that way.

WOLF. Oh, you nutcracking rats, you tail twirlers! Just wait. I'll teach you to make fun of me.

RAVEN. Croak! Croak! Don't threaten, gray one. Better run away to save your skin.

WOLF. You won't scare me, old trickster. You've cheated me twice— I'm not likely to be taken in a third time.

RAVEN. Suit yourself. Only, soldiers are marching this way, with spades over their shoulders.

WOLF. Try that on somebody else. I'm staying right here to keep an eye out for the Hare.

RAVEN. There's a whole company of them.

WOLF. I'm not interested.

RAVEN. No, not a company—a whole regiment! (*The* WOLF *raises his head and sniffs the air.*) Well, who is speaking the truth? Do you believe me now?

WOLF. I believe my nose, not you. Raven, old friend, where can I hide myself?

RAVEN. Jump through that hole in the ice.

WOLF. I'll drown.

RAVEN. It'll serve you right. (*The* WOLF *crawls across the stage on his belly.*) Ah, you're frightened, old fellow? Now you're crawling on your belly?

WOLF. I'm not afraid of anybody, except men. No, not men, just their clubs. No, not clubs, rifles. (*The* WOLF *disappears. For a while the stage is quiet. Then footsteps and voices are heard. The* COMMANDER OF THE ROYAL BODYGUARD *rolls down the steep bank onto the ice of the lake. He is followed by the* PROFESSOR *descending in the same fashion.*)

PROFESSOR. Have you fallen?

COMMANDER OF THE ROYAL BODYGUARD. No, I just lay down for a rest. (*Rises, grunting, and rubs his knees.*) It's a long time since I've slid down a snowbank. Must be quite sixty years. Do you think this is a lake, my dear Professor?

PROFESSOR. There can be not the slightest doubt, this is some water basin. Most probably a lake.

COMMANDER OF THE ROYAL BODYGUARD. And a perfectly round one at that. Don't you think it is perfectly round?

PROFESSOR. No, it cannot be called perfectly round. It's really oval or, to be precise, elliptical.

COMMANDER OF THE ROYAL BODYGUARD. I don't know how perfect it is from the point of view of science but to the naked eye it's round like a plate. You know, I believe this is the very lake we're after. (*Shouts to the top.*) Hey, there. Tell Her Majesty that we've found a lake as round as a plate.

PROFESSOR (*shouting to the top*). An elliptical lake.

AN OFFICER OF THE ROYAL BODYGUARD (*from above*). What kind of lake? Epileptical?

PROFESSOR. Elliptical.

OFFICER. I'll try to tell Her Majesty.

COMMANDER OF THE ROYAL BODYGUARD. Report as I told you—round like a plate. Order the men to clear a passage down here at once. (SOLDIERS *carrying spades and brooms appear on the steep bank. They rapidly clear a passage down to the lake and spread a carpet runner over it. The* QUEEN, *followed by the* LADY IN WAITING, *the* AMBASSADORS, *and the other guests, makes her way down.*)

QUEEN (*to the* PROFESSOR). You told me that forests are inhabited by animals. But I don't see any animals here. Where are they? Show them to me.

PROFESSOR. I believe they are sleeping.

QUEEN. But it is still daylight. Do they go to sleep so early?

PROFESSOR. Many of them go to sleep as early as fall, Your Majesty, and stay asleep until the snow melts away.

QUEEN. There's so much snow here that it may never melt away. I never imagined snowdrifts could be so high. I like it. (*To the* LADY IN WAITING.) Do you?

LADY IN WAITING. I'm thrilled with our trip, Your Majesty.

QUEEN. Yet your nose has turned blue. You must go for a quick run on the ice. That'll warm you up. Run along. Run along.

LADY IN WAITING (*covering her nose with a muff*). With your permission, Your Majesty, I'll be delighted. (*Runs off awkwardly, slipping and losing her balance.*)

COMMANDER OF THE ROYAL BODYGUARD. Watch out! An ice hole!

LADY IN WAITING. What's an ice hole?

COMMANDER OF THE ROYAL BODYGUARD. Halt! I'll explain later! (*The* LADY IN WAITING *nearly falls into the hole but is caught in time by the* COMMANDER OF THE ROYAL BODYGUARD *and the* WESTERN AMBASSADOR.)

LADY IN WAITING. Oh, thank you! I nearly got drowned.

WESTERN AMBASSADOR. We'd have never permitted that to happen. Every one of us is ready to sacrifice his life for the sake of such a beautiful lady.

LADY IN WAITING. I'm sure of that. But why has this spot been left without ice? That's an unforgivable carelessness.

PROFESSOR. On the contrary, madam, I believe there was ice at least two feet thick there but it was deliberately removed.

LADY IN WAITING. By some criminals?

PROFESSOR. No, most probably by fishermen.

QUEEN (*clapping her hands*). How wonderful! Catch me a fish, quick, a live one!

COMMANDER OF THE ROYAL BODYGUARD. I'm sorry, Your Majesty, but I haven't a fishhook with me.

QUEEN. What a thoughtless man you are. Going to a lake and forgetting to take a fishhook along—it's incredible.

COMMANDER OF THE ROYAL BODYGUARD. Please forgive me, Your Majesty. In the future I solemnly swear I'll never go anywhere without a fishhook. Meanwhile, I should like to draw your gracious attention to the fact that the lake is round like a plate.

PROFESSOR. Elliptical.

COMMANDER OF THE ROYAL BODYGUARD. That's unimportant. The lake is frozen over and covered with snow, while high snowdrifts crowd its banks.

QUEEN. Well, and supposing all this is true?

COMMANDER OF THE ROYAL BODYGUARD. It means this must be the spot where the snowdrops grow.

QUEEN (*looking around*). Then go pick them quick.

COMMANDER OF THE ROYAL BODYGUARD. But they're not here, Your Majesty.

QUEEN. Look for them in the snow. They must have dropped there. That's why they're called snowdrops.

COMMANDER OF THE ROYAL BODYGUARD. Clear the snow from the bank. (SOLDIERS *go to work with spades and brooms. Everybody watches them with keen interest. Then the frost begins to take effect. The* QUEEN *and her suite shuffle their feet, turn up their collars, hide their faces in their furs, and rub their noses and cheeks. The* LADY IN WAITING *breathes into her muff. The* COMMANDER OF THE ROYAL BODYGUARD *slaps his arms together like a Russian coachman. The* PROFESSOR *blows on his cupped hands.*)

QUEEN (*impatiently*). Have you found a single snowdrop?

COMMANDER OF THE ROYAL BODYGUARD. Not yet, Your Majesty.

QUEEN. Let them dig faster. And bring me an extra fur coat.

COMMANDER OF THE ROYAL BODYGUARD. Dig faster!

LADY IN WAITING. Bring Her Majesty one more fur coat. And a fur cape for me too.

GUESTS (*one after another*). And for me. Please, one for me as well. (*The* SOLDIERS *wield their spades faster, making the snow fly in a thick shower. One of the* SOLDIERS *takes off first his cape, then his fur-trimmed jacket, and tosses them aside. Two others follow his example. Meanwhile, the* SERVANTS *bring fur coats and capes to the* QUEEN *and her retinue, who wrap themselves up in them.*)

QUEEN (*to the* PROFESSOR). I want you to explain this to me. Here

I've put on a second fur coat and I'm still cold. But these men have thrown off even their jackets.

PROFESSOR (*shivering*). Brrr — That's easy to understand, Your Majesty. Movement assists the circulation of the blood.

QUEEN. I don't understand a thing. Movement, circulation of the blood— You'd better call those soldiers. (*Two* SOLDIERS *come up; one, a middle-aged man, was seen in the first act; the other is quite young and beardless. The* YOUNG SOLDIER *hastily wipes his brow and draws himself up.*) Why did you wipe your forehead?

YOUNG SOLDIER. I beg to be forgiven, Your Majesty.

QUEEN. No, tell me why you did it.

YOUNG SOLDIER. Because of my foolishness, Your Majesty. Please not to be angry with me.

QUEEN. I'm not angry with you. Speak without fear. Why did you wipe your forehead?

YOUNG SOLDIER (*embarrassed*). I was sweating, Your Majesty.

QUEEN. Sweating? What does that mean?

ELDER SOLDIER. That's what we common folk say, Your Majesty. He means he felt hot.

QUEEN. Are you hot too?

ELDER SOLDIER. I should say I am.

QUEEN. Why are you?

ELDER SOLDIER. From using the spade, Your Majesty.

QUEEN. Give me a spade, quick. Give everybody a spade. (*Everybody begins to shovel snow. The* SOLDIERS *put their jackets on and stand some distance away watching the ladies and gentlemen. After a while, feeling the growing cold, they stamp their feet.*)

COMMANDER OF THE ROYAL BODYGUARD (*working with great energy —to the* LADY IN WAITING). Permit me to show you how to hold the spade. You shovel with it this way.

LADY IN WAITING. Thank you. It's a long time since I did any shoveling.

QUEEN (*leaning on the spade*). I didn't know you ever did any shoveling.

LADY IN WAITING. Oh, yes, Your Majesty. I used to have a sweet green little bucket and a shovel.

QUEEN. Why did you never show them to me?

LADY IN WAITING. I lost them in the park when I was three years old, Your Majesty.

QUEEN. When you were three years old? You? Ha! Ha! Ha! (*Resumes shoveling snow.*) But it does really make you feel warm. Isn't that true, Monsieur Ambassador?

WESTERN AMBASSADER. Oh, I've always loved sport, Your Majesty.

EASTERN AMBASSADOR. In my country this kind of sport is the occupation of slaves.

QUEEN. How interesting. Then they never feel cold?

EASTERN AMBASSADOR. Never, Your Majesty. How could they? Our climate is always hot.

QUEEN. And you have no snow?

EASTERN AMBASSADOR. None at all, Your Majesty.

QUEEN. Then why don't you shovel? You'll never have an occasion to do it at home. (*All shovel in silence. The* QUEEN *throws off her outer fur cape. The others follow suit. They continue shoveling.*) Oh, I've sweated! (*Flabbergasted, everybody stops shoveling.*) Did I say it wrong?

PROFESSOR. No, you said it right, Your Majesty, but if I may say so, the expression is used only by the common people.

QUEEN. Well, the Queen must know the language of her people. (*Throws her spade down.*) I'm bored with shoveling snow. (*Everybody sticks his spade in the snow. The* QUEEN *turns to the* COMMANDER OF THE ROYAL BODYGUARD.) Where are the snowdrops you promised me? Perhaps you expect me to dig up the whole forest?

COMMANDER OF THE ROYAL BODYGUARD. If it pleases Your Majesty.

QUEEN. It pleases me neither to dig nor to wait. What's happened to the women who were to lead the way for us?

ROYAL PROSECUTOR. I fear, Your Majesty, those two criminals have tricked the guards and escaped.

QUEEN (*to the* COMMANDER OF THE ROYAL BODYGUARD). You answer with your head for them, Commander. If they are not here in a minute— (*Sleigh bells tinkle. Horses neigh. A* COACHMAN *shouts:* "Whoa!" *Enter the* OLD WOMAN *and her* DAUGHTER, *followed by the* STEPDAUGHTER. GUARDS *walk on either side of them. When the* STEP- DAUGHTER *passes the* ELDER SOLDIER, *he gazes at her with surprise and salutes her. The* GIRL *nods to him.*)

COMMANDER OF THE ROYAL BODYGUARD. They're here, Your Majesty!

QUEEN. At long last!

OLD WOMAN. Here she is, my stepdaughter, Your Majesty. We've brought her as you commanded, Your Majesty.

QUEEN. So that's what the little forest animal looks like! Well, come closer to me, come up, don't be afraid.

STEPDAUGHTER. I'm not afraid.

QUEEN. I thought you were something like a bear but you turn out to be very beautiful. If you were garbed in fine dresses, you would look as well as I do, perhaps better. (*To the* CHANCELLOR.) What do you think of her?

CHANCELLOR. In the presence of my queen I see no one else.

QUEEN. Oh, I've forgotten you are short sighted. (*To the* PROFES- SOR.) And what have you to say?

PROFESSOR. I believe that a proper dress is an adornment to a woman. However, what this girl needs, it seems to me, is not adornments but a fur coat and a warm shawl.

QUEEN. This time you're right. Get her a fur coat and a warm shawl. (*The* STEPDAUGHTER *is dressed accordingly.*) Now one can hardly recognize you. Well, are you warm?

STEPDAUGHTER. I am, Your Majesty.

QUEEN. Tell me, did you pick the snowdrops for me?

STEPDAUGHTER. Yes, I did.

QUEEN. Then this very day you'll receive a basket of gold—a whole basketful, you understand? And if you want I'll also give you twelve silk and velvet dresses. Also satin shoes with silver heels and diamond buckles; also a bracelet for each arm and a ring for each finger. Do you want this?

STEPDAUGHTER. I thank you for your kindness. I'm glad my flowers pleased you. But there's just one thing: don't give me either dresses or bracelets or rings for each of my fingers. I don't want any of them.

QUEEN. What do you want?

STEPDAUGHTER. I want only one little ring.

QUEEN. What ring?

OLD WOMAN. Don't listen to her, Your Majesty.

DAUGHTER. She doesn't know what she's talking about.

STEPDAUGHTER. Oh, yes, I do. I had a little ring but you took it from me and don't want to give it back.

DAUGHTER. Did you see us take it?

STEPDAUGHTER. I didn't but I know you have it.

QUEEN (*to the* OLD WOMAN *and her* DAUGHTER). Hand me that ring, will you?

OLD WOMAN. We don't have it, Your Majesty.

DAUGHTER. Nobody ever saw us with it, Your Majesty.

QUEEN. They will now. Hand me the ring or you'll be sorry.

COMMANDER OF THE ROYAL BODYGUARD. Come on, be quick, you old witches. The Queen is getting angry. (*Glancing at the* QUEEN, *the* DAUGHTER *pulls the ring out of her pocket.*)

STEPDAUGHTER. I knew it.

OLD WOMAN. Oh, daughter dear! What made you hide somebody else's ring?

DAUGHTER. But you told me yourself to put it in my pocket if it didn't fit my finger. (*Everybody laughs.*)

QUEEN. This is a pretty ring. I don't think I have one as pretty myself. (*To the* STEPDAUGHTER.) Well, take it, if it's yours.

STEPDAUGHTER. Oh, thank you. I'm so glad, I can't find words to express myself. (*Stretches out her hand.*)

QUEEN. No, wait. I'll give you the ring, but first you must tell me where you found the snowdrops.

STEPDAUGHTER (*stepping back*). That I can't tell you.

QUEEN. You can't? Why not?

STEPDAUGHTER. I mustn't.

QUEEN. But don't you understand that I am the Queen and I want to pick snowdrops? They grow in my kingdom, in my forest, on my soil— (*Stamps her foot.*) And I still don't know where they grow. Now, come, tell me. You don't want to? Remember I can reward you but I can also execute you.

OLD WOMAN. Aren't you afraid of death, you wretched girl? Is it worth dying for the sake of snowdrops?

STEPDAUGHTER. You should have asked me that last night when you drove me out to pick snowdrops in a dark forest in a blizzard. You stayed at home while I was close to death.

QUEEN. Oh, I see! You must have got terribly frightened in the forest last night and are still afraid to visit the spot. You don't have to be afraid. My soldiers will clear the snow before us, and when it gets dark I'll order them to light the way with lamps and torches. We'll drive there in no time. It is faster to drive in a sleigh than walk on foot.

STEPDAUGHTER. I know that. Only you will never drive down the path that I trod on foot last night. I promised never to show that path to anybody and I won't.

QUEEN. To whom did you promise?

STEPDAUGHTER. I can't tell you.

CHANCELLOR. That's unheard of!

LADY IN WAITING. What impertinence!

ROYAL PROSECUTOR. An insult to Her Majesty!

OLD WOMAN. An insult it is. Just a sample of the insults *we* have to put up with!

QUEEN. Take away her fur coat and shawl.

DAUGHTER. Let her freeze.

OLD WOMAN. It serves her right. (SERVANTS *remove the* STEP-DAUGHTER's *fur coat and shawl, leaving her in her light dress and torn kerchief.*)

CHANCELLOR. Don't you think, Your Majesty, it's time to return to the palace?

COMMANDER OF THE ROYAL BODYGUARD. It'll soon be dark, Your Majesty, and it's getting colder and colder.

LADY IN WAITING. I fear you will catch a cold, Your Majesty. And so shall we. (*During this conversation the* ELDER SOLDIER *slips his own cape over the* STEPDAUGHTER's *shoulders, without being noticed by anybody.*)

QUEEN. No, we're going to pick snowdrops yet today. Let the cold get into her bones and she'll tell us where they grow. Well, feeling cold?

STEPDAUGHTER. No, Your Majesty.

QUEEN (*glancing at the* STEPDAUGHTER). Who threw a cape over her? Well? (*No answer.*) Apparently capes fall on her from heaven. (*Turns and notices the* ELDER SOLDIER.) Oh, I see. Come up here. Did you give her your cape?

ELDER SOLDIER. I did, Your Majesty.

QUEEN. How dared you?

ELDER SOLDIER. I felt hot again, sweaty, as we common people say, Your Majesty. And I didn't know where else to put my cape.

QUEEN. Look out you don't feel hotter still. (*To the* STEPDAUGHTER.) Give him back his cape at once and tell us where the snowdrops are. Are you going to? No? Perhaps you've forgotten about your ring? You'll never get it back. I'm going to toss it into the water, into that hole. You're sorry to lose it? So am I. But it can't be helped. Unless you speak. Well, then—one—two—three! (*Swings her arm and throws.*)

STEPDAUGHTER (*covering her face with her hands*). Oh, my little ring! (*Cries.*)

QUEEN. You thought I threw it? No, it's still here in my hand. Tell me where the snowdrops are and take your ring. We'll pick only one basketful and after that drive right back to the city. I'll have you wrapped in the warmest fur coat, seat you next to me in my sleigh, and drive you to my palace. Well, will you stop being obstinate? It's up to you—speak out, and you'll get the ring; keep your secret, and I'll throw it through the ice, to the very bottom of the lake. (*There is a pause.*) Well?

STEPDAUGHTER. Throw it.

QUEEN. Oh, so? All right. I'll throw the ring into the hole and I'll see that you follow it. Seize her! (*With a single movement throws the ring into the water.*)

STEPDAUGHTER (*darting forward, toward the hole*).
　　　　　　Roll on, my little ring,
　　　　　　Onto the porch of spring,
　　　　　　Into the summer hall,
　　　　　　Through the house of fall,
　　　　　　Over winter's carpet white
　　　　　　To the brothers' campfire bright!

QUEEN. That's that! What is she saying?(*A snowstorm begins. Flakes blow across the stage. The* QUEEN, *her retinue, the* OLD WOMAN *and her* DAUGHTER, *the* SOLDIERS, *and the* SERVANTS *try to cover their heads and faces from the biting wind. Through the noise of the storm,* JANUARY'S *tambourine,* FEBRUARY'S *horn,* MARCH'S *bells are heard. Together with the whirling snow vague white figures rush by. They may be the winds or they may be the winter months themselves. As they whirl, they carry the* STEPDAUGHTER *with them until she disappears.*)

QUEEN. Come here! Help! Quick! (*The wind spins her and everybody else on the stage. People fall, rise, grasp one another.*)

VOICE OF THE LADY IN WAITING. Hold me!

VOICE OF THE OLD WOMAN. Daughter dear, where are you?

VOICE OF THE DAUGHTER. I don't know myself. I'm lost!

VOICES. { Let's go home!
          Home!
          Get the horses!
          Where are the horses?
          Coachman! Coachman!

(*Crouching low to the ground, everybody grows silent. Through the noise of the wind, with increasing frequency, break the sounds of the* MARCH *bells and, later, of the* APRIL *pipes. The storm subsides. Sunshine returns. Birds chirp. Everybody raises his head and gazes about with surprise.*)

QUEEN. Spring has come.

PROFESSOR. It's impossible.

QUEEN. How do you mean "impossible" when leaves are budding on the trees?

WESTERN AMBASSADOR. So they are indeed. And what are the flowers?

QUEEN. Snowdrops! Everything has come out just as I wished. (*Runs up a hill which is covered with flowers.*) Wait. Where's that girl? (*To the* OLD WOMAN.) Where has your stepdaughter gone to?

OLD WOMAN. She's run away, the wretch!

ROYAL PROSECUTOR. Look for her!

QUEEN. I don't need her any more. I've found snowdrops myself. Just look what a lot of them! (*The ice on the lake is heard cracking.*)

COMMANDER OF THE ROYAL BODYGUARD. The ice is breaking.

LADY IN WAITING. I'm floating away!

OLD WOMAN. Help! Help!

DAUGHTER. We're drowning. (*The* QUEEN *claps her hands and laughs. The* COMMANDER OF THE ROYAL BODYGUARD *and his* SOLDIERS *help everybody reach the shore.*)

QUEEN. Come pick snowdrops, will you?

CHANCELLOR. I don't see them. Where are they, Your Majesty?

QUEEN. They've vanished.

COMMANDER OF THE ROYAL BODYGUARD. Great Scot! There are berries instead!

OLD WOMAN. Please look, Your Majesty—strawberries, bilberries, whortleberries—just as we told you!

LADY IN WAITING. Oh, those bills and waffles. How beautiful!

DAUGHTER. You see yourself we told the truth. (*The sunshine grows more and more blazing. The chirping of grasshoppers is heard. A cuckoo calls, bees buzz. Summer is in full swing.* JULY's *psaltery is heard in the distance.*)

COMMANDER OF THE ROYAL BODYGUARD (*gasping*). I can't breathe! It's too hot! (*Opens his fur coat.*)

QUEEN. What is it—summer?

PROFESSOR. That's impossible.

CHANCELLOR. Nevertheless, it is a fact. Real July weather.

WESTERN AMBASSADOR. It's as torrid as a desert.

EASTERN AMBASSADOR. No, it's cooler in our deserts. (*Everybody throws off his fur coat, fans himself with a handkerchief, sinks to the ground.*)

LADY IN WAITING. I think I have a sunstroke. Water! Water!

COMMANDER OF THE ROYAL BODYGUARD. Water for her ladyship. (*Thunder. Rain comes down in sheets. Leaves are blown from the trees. There is an instant autumn.*)

PROFESSOR. It rains!

ROYAL PROSECUTOR. Rains? It comes down in sheets!

A SOLDIER. Here's water for her ladyship.

LADY IN WAITING. I don't want water now. I'm drenched as it is.

A SOLDIER. That's true.

QUEEN. Bring me an umbrella.

COMMANDER OF THE ROYAL BODYGUARD. How can I get an umbrella, Your Majesty, when we left the palace in January, and now it must be— (*He looks around.*) October.

PROFESSOR. Impossible.

QUEEN (*wrathfully*). January, October! There are no months in my kingdom and never will be. I forbid them.

CHANCELLOR. As you wish, Your Majesty. (*It turns dark. A sudden hurricane sweeps the scene, bringing down trees and carrying away the fur coats and shawls that were thrown on the ground.*)

COMMANDER OF THE ROYAL BODYGUARD (*running after a fur coat*). Hold it! (*The wind blows out the* LADY IN WAITING'S *voluminous dress, and, barely touching the ground with her feet, she sails away after the leaves and coats.*)

LADY IN WAITING. Save me! I'm flying away! (*The darkness increases.*)

QUEEN (*her arms clasped around the trunk of a tree*). Back to the palace at once! Where are you all?

CHANCELLOR. We can't drive back, Your Majesty. We came here in sleighs and the snow has since been washed away.

COMMANDER OF THE ROYAL BODYGUARD. In such mud the only way to get home is on horseback.

ROYAL PROSECUTOR. That's an idea! (*Runs off. The* AMBASSADORS, *the* CHANCELLOR, *and the* COMMANDER OF THE ROYAL BODYGUARD *follow.*)

QUEEN. Where are you going? Stop! Stop, I tell you!

CHANCELLOR (*turning around and pressing his hands to his chest*). Don't be angry, Your Majesty. I have urgent state business to attend to. There are four proclamations and five decrees issued by Your Majesty to which I have to affix the seal. (*Runs off.*)

QUEEN. I'll issue the sixth decree ordering all of you to be executed.

WESTERN AMBASSADOR (*running*). Your Majesty will forgive me but I can be executed only by orders of my king.

EASTERN AMBASSADOR. And I only by orders of my sultan. (*Runs off.*)

VOICE OF THE ROYAL PROSECUTOR (*off stage*). Put me astride the horse. I don't know how to ride.

VOICE OF THE COMMANDER OF THE ROYAL BODYGUARD. Learn! (*There is a clatter of hooves. Only the* QUEEN, *the* PROFESSOR, *the* OLD WOMAN *and her* DAUGHTER, *and the* ELDER SOLDIER *remain on the stage. White flakes fly about.*)

QUEEN. Look—snow! Winter is on again.

PROFESSOR. That's very probable. After all, it's January.

QUEEN (*shivering*). Give me a fur coat. It's cold.

SOLDIER. I should say it is, Your Majesty. It's the worst thing to get wet first and frozen afterwards. Only, Your Majesty, the wind has blown all the fur coats away.

QUEEN. And what's that? Isn't that a fur coat?

SOLDIER. It is, Your Majesty. (*Walks up to the* OLD WOMAN *and her* DAUGHTER.) Well, give back the state's property.

OLD WOMAN. It was the state's before it became ours.

SOLDIER. Now it's the state's again. Well, let go, will you?

OLD WOMAN. I won't! (*The* DAUGHTER *and the* OLD WOMAN *hang onto the coat by its sleeves. The frozen sleeves break off with a cracking sound. The two women grab the sides of the coat but these break off too.*)

SOLDIER. What do you know? It cracked up as if it were made of glass. That's what I call a frost. (*Walks up to the* QUEEN.) Begging your forgiveness, Your Majesty, but there's no way of putting that coat together, much less wearing it. It's smashed to pieces.

PROFESSOR. This is the consequence of icification.

QUEEN. I'll soon become icified myself. Order the sleighs to be brought back. It's winter now, so we can drive in sleighs again.

PROFESSOR. That's perfectly correct, Your Majesty. In winter people ride in sleighs. (*The* SOLDIER *goes off.*)

OLD WOMAN. I told you not to go to the forest, Your Majesty.

DAUGHTER. She fancied snowdrops!

QUEEN. And you wanted gold! (*After a pause.*) But how dare you speak to me like that?

DAUGHTER. She's offended!

OLD WOMAN. We're not in the palace but in the forest, Your Majesty. (*The* SOLDIER *returns, drawing a sleigh.*)

SOLDIER. Here's the sleigh, Your Majesty. You can sit in it, if you wish, but there's nothing to pull it.

QUEEN. Where are the horses? Have they turned into ice or melted away?

SOLDIER. You may say they've melted away, Your Majesty. The gentlemen from your suite have galloped off on them.

QUEEN. I'll show those gentlemen what's what if I ever get back to the palace. But how am I to get there? (*To the* PROFESSOR.) Well, won't you tell me? You're supposed to know everything.

PROFESSOR. Unfortunately, far from everything, Your Majesty.

QUEEN. But we'll die here. I'm shivering and sore all over. Pretty soon I'll be so frozen I'll break to pieces like that coat. Oh, my ears and nose! My hands are frozen stiff.

SOLDIER. You ought to rub your ears and nose with snow, Your Majesty, or you'll be frostbitten indeed, touch wood.

QUEEN (*rubbing her ears and nose with snow*). Why on earth did I sign that idiotic decree?

DAUGHTER. Idiotic is the word for it. If you hadn't signed it, we'd be sitting at home by the fire now celebrating the New Year. Instead we're freezing to death here—no better than dogs.

QUEEN. Why did you pay any attention to such an idiotic decree? Fancied a sleigh ride with the Queen? (*Hops from one foot to the other.*) I can't bear it any longer. Oh, it's freezing! (*To the* PROFESSOR.) Think up something, can't you?

PROFESSOR (*breathing on his hands*). That's a difficult problem, Your Majesty. Now, if we could harness somebody to the sleigh—

QUEEN. Whom?

PROFESSOR. A horse, for example—or even a dozen dogs—

SOLDIER. Where will you get dogs in a forest? As the saying goes, a good master wouldn't drive his dog out in weather like this. (*The* OLD WOMAN *and her* DAUGHTER *sit down on a fallen tree.*)

OLD WOMAN. Oh, we'll never get out of here!

DAUGHTER. Oh, we're lost!

OLD WOMAN. Oh, my poor feet!

DAUGHTER. Oh, my poor hands!

SOLDIER. Shut up, you there! It's bad enough as it is.

OLD WOMAN. Why should we shut up? She brought us here. She's the cause of our freezing here.

DAUGHTER. She's the one—nobody else!

SOLDIER. Quiet! Somebody's coming.

QUEEN. That's for me.

OLD WOMAN. Huh! As if everybody thought only about her! (*Enter a tall man in a white fur coat. It is* JANUARY. *He looks around and knocks on the trunks with the air of a good manager. A* SQUIRREL *peeks out of a hollow; he shakes his finger at it, and it pops back. Noticing the uninvited visitors, he walks up to them.*)

JANUARY. What's brought you here, my friends?

QUEEN. We've come to pick snowdrops.

JANUARY. This is not the season for snowdrops.

PROFESSOR (*shivering*). Perfectly right.

RAVEN (*from his tree top*). Right!

QUEEN (*casting a frightened glance upward, then at* JANUARY). I realize myself we came here at the wrong time. Tell us how to get out.

JANUARY. The same way you came in.

SOLDIER. Pardon me, old man, but we drove here with horses and since then they've raced away without us. You seem to be a local man, isn't that right?

JANUARY. Local in winter, far distant in summer.

QUEEN. Do help us, please. I'll reward you royally. I can give you gold, silver—anything you want.

JANUARY. I don't need it. I have everything. I have more silver than you ever saw in your life. Look. (*He lifts his arm. The snow begins to glitter everywhere, sparkling with silver and diamonds.*) As for gifts, you'd better tell me what I can do for you. Tell me what you want for the New Year, what your wishes are.

QUEEN. All I want is to get back to the palace. Only we have nothing to pull our sleigh.

JANUARY. You'll have it. (*To the* PROFESSOR.) And what's your wish?

PROFESSOR. I should like everything to be back in its right place and time—winter in winter, summer in summer, and we in our homes.

JANUARY. I'll see to that. (*To the* SOLDIER.) And what do you want, Soldier?

SOLDIER. What do I need? To warm myself by a campfire, that's about all. It's blasted cold here.

JANUARY. You'll warm yourself. There's a fire near by.

DAUGHTER. As for us, give us a fur coat, Mother and me.

OLD WOMAN. Take it easy, girl. What's the hurry?

DAUGHTER. What's the good of waiting? Let's get a fur coat quick, right away—any fur coat, even dog fur.

JANUARY (*pulling two dog-fur coats from under his coat*). Hold them!

OLD WOMAN. Forgive me, sir, but we don't want these fur coats—she didn't mean what she said.

JANUARY. What was said was said. Put on the coats. Let them last you a lifetime.

OLD WOMAN (*holding a coat to her* DAUGHTER). You *are* a fool! If you wanted a fur coat, you might have asked for a sable.

DAUGHTER. You're a fool yourself. You should have told me that in time.

OLD WOMAN. And not only did you get yourself a dog-fur coat, you've forced one on me.

DAUGHTER. If you don't like it, give it to me, I'll be warmer with two. And you can freeze to death here under a bush—for all I care.

OLD WOMAN. Give it to you? Not on your life! (*The two put on their coats.*) So we had to go rushing off! To get what? A dog-fur coat!

DAUGHTER. Dog fur just suits you. You bark like a dog.

OLD WOMAN. You're a dog yourself! (*Gradually their voices turn into a bark and they themselves, with coats on, become dogs: the* OLD WOMAN *a smooth, black-haired dog with touches of gray; the* DAUGHTER *shaggy and red haired.*)

QUEEN. Oh, the dogs! Hold them! They'll bite us!

SOLDIER (*breaking off a branch*). Don't worry, Your Majesty. We have a saying—the dog fears a stick.

PROFESSOR. Properly speaking, dogs are excellent draft animals. The Eskimos use them for long journeys.

SOLDIER. You're right there. We can harness them to the sleigh— let them pull it. Pity there are only two of them. We need a dozen.

QUEEN. These two are worth any dozen. Harness them up quick! (*The* SOLDIER *harnesses the dogs. Everybody climbs into the sleigh.*)

JANUARY. Now you have a New Year's sleigh ride. Well, happy journey! Get going, Soldier—toward the little light. There's a campfire there. When you reach it, you'll be able to warm yourself.

CURTAIN

ACT IV

Scene 2

A clearing in the forest. Sitting around the campfire are the TWELVE MONTHS *and the* STEPDAUGHTER. *The* MONTHS *take turns throwing brushwood onto the fire.*

JANUARY.   Burn, campfire burn,
The winter night through.
Warm the finches and sparrows,
The roving wolf too.
Warm the ermine and fox
And the bear in his den,
Warm the owl in the tree
And the deer in the glen.

ALL.   Fire, burn high—
Flame, never die!

APRIL.   Burn, campfire, burn.
Warm the deep-buried roots,
Send the sap up the trunks
To the leaves and the shoots.
Let the gum in the pine
Fill the spring air with wine.

ALL. Fire, burn high—
Flame, never die!

JANUARY (*to the* STEPDAUGHTER). Well, dear guest, you too may throw in some brushwood. It'll make the fire burn brighter still.

STEPDAUGHTER (*throwing an armful into the fire*).
Fire, burn high—
Flame, never die!

JANUARY. Well said! Now it can't go out. You're hot, aren't you? Your cheeks are burning.

FEBRUARY. Nothing surprising, seeing she's come straight from the frost to such a fire. With us, both frost and fire are fierce, one hotter than the other. Not everybody can stand that.

STEPDAUGHTER. I don't mind. I rather like a blazing fire.

AUGUST. We know that. That's why we've let you sit by ours.

STEPDAUGHTER. Thank you. Twice you've saved my life.

JANUARY. The first time we felt sorry for you and allowed you to warm yourself. The second time you earned it.

OCTOBER. You kept your word and we've kept ours.

APRIL. Guess what I have in my hand.

STEPDAUGHTER. The ring!

APRIL. Right the first time. Take your ring. Wear it and you'll always have warmth and light, whether there's a winter frost, or a storm, or an autumn mist. Although they say April is a fickle month, the April sun, take it from me, will never deceive you.

STEPDAUGHTER. Ah, this lucky little ring of mine. It has come back to me after all. It was dear to me before, it'll be dearer still now. Only I'm afraid to return home with it—they may take it away from me again.

JANUARY. No, that won't happen again. There's nobody to take it away. You'll go back to your home and be mistress of the house yourself. Then we shall be your guests for a change.

MAY. We'll stay with you in turn. And each will bring his own gift.

SEPTEMBER. We months are rich folk. All you'll have to do is accept our gifts.

OCTOBER. In your garden you'll have such trees, such flowers, berries, and fruit as have never been seen in this world.

JANUARY. In the meantime, here is a coffer for you. It would hardly be right if we brothers sent you home empty handed.

STEPDAUGHTER. I can't find words to thank you.

FEBRUARY. You'd better open the coffer and see what's in it. We may not have put in things that you like.

APRIL. Here's the key. Open it. (STEPDAUGHTER *lifts the lid and examines the gifts. They include coats of sable, fox, and squirrel, a silver embroidered dress, a pair of silver shoes, and piles of other brightly colored dresses.*)

STEPDAUGHTER. Oh, I simply can't take my eyes off these things. I saw the Queen today, but even she didn't have such dresses or fur coats.

JANUARY. Well, why not try them on? (*The* MONTHS *surround the* STEPDAUGHTER. *When they step aside, she is seen wearing a new coat, a new dress, and new shoes.*)

APRIL. You do look beautiful! Both the dress and the coat suit you right down to the ground. So do the shoes.

FEBRUARY. It would be a pity, though, to tramp over the forest trails and through the brushwood. I see I'll have to give you a sleigh as well. (*Claps his hands.*) Ho, there, my forest folk! Bring me a bright new sleigh, with smooth silver runners and soft sable rugs! (*A number of forest animals—a* FOX, *a* HARE, *two* SQUIRRELS—*push forward a white sleigh with silver runners.*)

RAVEN (*from a tree*). A wonderful sleigh—wonderful runners!

JANUARY. You're right, old fellow, this is a fine sleigh. It's not every horse that you can harness to it.

MAY. Don't worry about horses. I'll give her horses to match the sleigh. My fiery steeds are shod with gold, their manes a-jingle with silver bells—they paw the earth and thunder rolls! (*The* HORSES *appear.*)

MARCH. What splendid horses! Whoa, there! They'll give you a fine drive but it won't be much fun without bells. Well, so be it—you'll have my bells. The more tinkle, the merrier the journey. (*The* MONTHS *surround the sleigh, harness the* HORSES, *put the coffer aboard. Meanwhile, the hoarse barking and growling of* DOGS *drift on from the distance.*)

VOICE OF THE SOLDIER. Come on! Come on! Get a move on, you dogs! And stop snarling at each other.

VOICE OF THE PROFESSOR. My, it's cold. And they're so slow!

VOICE OF THE QUEEN. Run them for all they're worth! (*Pitifully.*) I'm frozen though.

VOICE OF THE SOLDIER. They won't pull, the wretches!

STEPDAUGHTER. That's the Queen. Her teacher and the soldier are with her. I wonder where they got the dogs!

JANUARY. Have patience, you'll soon find out. Well, brothers, throw more brushwood into the fire. I promised this soldier to let him warm himself here.

STEPDAUGHTER. Yes, do let him, Grandpa. He helped me gather brushwood and gave me his cape when I was cold.

JANUARY. What do you say, brothers?

DECEMBER. If you promised, so be it.

OCTOBER. But the soldier is not alone.

MARCH (*peering through the branches*). That's true. With him are an old man, a girl, and two dogs.

STEPDAUGHTER. The old man is kind too—he got me a fur coat.

JANUARY. You're right, the old man means well, we can let him in. But how about the others? The girl seems to be spiteful.

STEPDAUGHTER. She certainly can be spiteful but by now her spite may have got frozen out of her. Do you hear her voice? It's quite pitiful!

JANUARY. Well, we'll see. But just so they don't find their way here again, we'll lay a trail for them where there was none before and will be none afterward. (*Strikes the ground with his staff. The trees move apart and the* QUEEN's *dog-driven sleigh comes into the clearing. The* DOGS *are still fighting, pulling the sleigh in opposite directions as the* SOLDIER *urges them on. In all their actions the two* DOGS *resemble the* OLD WOMAN *and her* DAUGHTER, *each of whom can be plainly recognized. The sleigh stops under the trees some distance from the campfire.*)

SOLDIER. Here's the campfire. The old man didn't fool me. Greetings to all this honest company. Allow me to warm myself.

JANUARY. Sit down and do so.

SOLDIER (*recognizing* JANUARY). Hello, master! You do have a merry blaze. But please permit me to take care of my passengers too. We soldiers have a rule—first find billets for your officers, then look after yourself.

JANUARY. Well, if you have such a rule, go ahead.

SOLDIER. Step this way, Your Majesty. (*To the* PROFESSOR.) This way, sir.

QUEEN. Oh, I can't move!

SOLDIER. That's all right, Your Majesty. You'll soon get warm. Now, let me set you on your feet. (*Lifts her out of the sleigh.*) And your teacher. (*Shouts to the* PROFESSOR.) Stretch your legs, sir. We're stopping for a rest. (*The* QUEEN *and the* PROFESSOR *walk hesitantly up to the campfire. The* DOGS, *tails between their legs, follow them.*)

STEPDAUGHTER (*to the* QUEEN *and the* PROFESSOR). Won't you come nearer? You'll get warmer that way. (*The* SOLDIER, *the* QUEEN, *and the* PROFESSOR *turn toward the* STEPDAUGHTER *and gaze at her with astonishment. The* DOGS *also notice her. Startled, they sit back on their haunches and begin to bark in turn, as if asking each other:* "Is that her?"—"Can it be?"—"Yes, it's her.")

QUEEN (*to the* PROFESSOR). Look, this is the same girl that found the snowdrops. But how gorgeously dressed she is now!

SOLDIER. No mistake about it, Your Majesty, that's her all right. (*To the* STEPDAUGHTER.) Good evening, ma'am. So we meet again— for the third time, I reckon. Only I can hardly recognize you. You look like a queen!

QUEEN (*her teeth chattering*). What are you saying?

SOLDIER. I beg your pardon, Your Majesty, that was just a manner of speaking. But you'd better warm yourself, Your Majesty, your teeth are chattering. As soon as we get a little warmer, we'll go on with your journey—slowly—clop—clop! (*Looking around, notices the white*

Horses *harnessed to the sleigh*.) Oh, these are brave horses! I haven't seen anything like them even in the royal stables. Whose are they?

JANUARY (*pointing at the* STEPDAUGHTER). There sits the owner.

SOLDIER. Permit me to congratulate you on the purchase, ma'am.

STEPDAUGHTER. It wasn't a purchase—it's a gift.

SOLDIER. All the better. The cheaper it's gotten, the dearer it'll sell. (*The* DOGS *dart at the* HORSES *and bark at them*.) Quiet, beasts! Back to where you were! Can you believe it! Hardly into your dogskin and already jumping at horses!

STEPDAUGHTER. They do sound angry when they bark—like quarreling, only you can't make out the words. I feel as though I've heard their barking before but I can't remember where.

JANUARY. Maybe you have heard it.

SOLDIER. Of course you have. Didn't they live in the same house with you?

STEPDAUGHTER. We had no dogs in our house.

SOLDIER. Take a good look—you may recognize them. (*The* DOGS *avert their heads from the* STEPDAUGHTER.)

STEPDAUGHTER (*throwing up her hands*). Oh, no! That's impossible!

SOLDIER. Possible or no, it's a fact! (*The red-pelted* DOG *comes up, whining, to the* STEPDAUGHTER *and fawns on her; the black* DOG *tries to lick her hand*.)

QUEEN. Look out, they'll bite you! (*The* DOGS *lie down, wag their tails, and roll on the ground*.)

STEPDAUGHTER. No, they seem to be getting more gentle. (*To the* MONTHS.) But surely they're not going to remain dogs the rest of their lives?

JANUARY. No, that's not necessary. Let them live with you for three years, guarding your house and garden. If by that time they learn to behave themselves, bring them here on New Year's Eve and I'll remove the dog pelts from them.

PROFESSOR. What if they don't mend their ways even in three years?

JANUARY. Then they can come back in six.

FEBRUARY. Or nine.

SOLDIER. Why, dogs don't live that long! Oh, aunties! It doesn't look like you'll ever wear kerchiefs over your heads again or walk on two legs! (*The* DOGS *jump at him, barking*.) There you are! (*Drives them off with a stick*.)

QUEEN. You won't mind, will you, if I bring my court dogs here too on New Year's Eve? My dogs are tame and gentle and can walk on their hind legs. Perhaps they will also turn into human beings?

JANUARY. No, not if they walk on their hind legs. As they have been dogs, so they will remain dogs. And now, my dear guests, it's time for me to attend to my business. Without me the frost doesn't crackle as it should in January, nor does the wind blow with the proper force, nor does the snow fall in the right direction. And it's time for you to begin your journey. The moon is high in the heavens and will light your way. Only you'll have to hurry up and move fast.

SOLDIER. We'd be glad to hurry up, Grandpa, but our shaggy horses bark more than they pull. With them we won't get home till next year. It would be different if we were given a lift with those white horses.

JANUARY. Well, ask the owner—perhaps she'll help you.

SOLDIER. Shall I ask her, Your Majesty?

QUEEN. No.

SOLDIER. Well, there's nothing to be done about it. Hey, you, my lop-eared steeds, get back into your harness! Whether we like it or not, we'll have to go for a spin with you. (*The* DOGS *nuzzle the* STEPDAUGHTER.)

PROFESSOR. Your Majesty.

QUEEN. Yes?

PROFESSOR. You know, Your Majesty, we're still a long distance from the palace, and the cold is fierce, a regular January cold, if I may say so. I'll never reach home and you'll freeze to death too without a fur coat.

SOLDIER. What do you say, Your Majesty?

DOGS. Ha-ooh?

QUEEN. How can I ask her for anything? I've never asked favors of anybody in my life. Suppose she answers "no"?

JANUARY. Who knows? She's just as likely to say "yes." Her sleigh is a big one, enough room in it for everybody.

QUEEN (*lowering her head*). It's not that.

JANUARY. What then?

QUEEN (*frowning*). Why, I've had her coat taken away from her, I wanted to drown her, I threw her ring into a hole in the ice. Besides, I can't ask, I wasn't taught to ask. I can only order. I'm a queen.

JANUARY. Oh, I see. We had no idea of that.

FEBRUARY. And who's that? Your teacher?

QUEEN. Yes.

FEBRUARY (*to the* PROFESSOR). How is it you didn't teach her such a simple thing? She knows how to order but not how to ask. Who ever heard of such a thing?

PROFESSOR. Her Majesty learned only what she wished to learn.

QUEEN. Well, if you want to know, I've learned a great deal today, more in a single day than I learned from you in three years. (*To the* STEPDAUGHTER.) Look here, my dear, give us a lift in your sleigh, please. I'll reward you royally.

STEPDAUGHTER. Thank you, Your Majesty, I have everything I need.

QUEEN. You see—she refuses. I said she would.

FEBRUARY. Apparently you don't ask in the right way.

QUEEN. How should I ask? (*To the* PROFESSOR.) Did I say it wrong?

PROFESSOR. No, Your Majesty, from the point of view of grammar, what you said was perfectly correct.

SOLDIER. Please forgive me, Your Majesty, I'm no scholar, I'm a soldier. I understand little about grammar. But allow me to instruct you this time.

QUEEN. Well, speak.

SOLDIER. If I were Your Majesty, I wouldn't promise her any more rewards—you promised plenty before—but I'd simply say to her: "Be so kind as to take me along with you." You see, you're not hiring a cab.

QUEEN. I think I see what you mean. (*To the* STEPDAUGHTER.) Please take us along with you. We're freezing.

STEPDAUGHTER. Of course I'll take you with me—gladly. I can even give you fur coats—all of you, your teacher and the soldier too. I have a lot of them in my coffer.

QUEEN. Thank you. For one fur coat I'll give you twelve—

PROFESSOR (*in an affrighted tone*). You're doing it again, Your Majesty!

QUEEN. I won't—I won't! (*The* STEPDAUGHTER *produces the coats. The* QUEEN *and the* PROFESSOR *put theirs on, but not the* SOLDIER.) Why aren't you putting yours on?

SOLDIER. I dare not, Your Majesty. The coat isn't according to the rules—of the prescribed cut.

QUEEN. Never mind that. Nothing we've done today has been according to the rules. Put it on.

SOLDIER (*obeying*). Allow me to sit on the coach box. Driving horses isn't like handling dogs—it's something I know more about.

JANUARY. Sit down, Soldier, drive your passengers. And mind you don't lose your cap on the way. Ours are fast horses, they overtake the minutes. Before you look back you'll be home.

STEPDAUGHTER (*from the sleigh*). Good-by, brother months. I'll never forget your New Year's campfire!

QUEEN. Neither shall I!

SOLDIER. Good-by, gentlemen! Best of luck to you!

SPRING AND SUMMER MONTHS. Pleasant journey!

WINTER MONTHS. Good sleighing! (*The sleigh drives away with the* DOGS *close behind it, barking.*)

STEPDAUGHTER (*looking back*). Good-by, April!

APRIL. Good-by, my dear! Expect me as your guest soon! (*The sleigh bells tinkle for some time before they finally die down. The dawn is breaking.*)

JANUARY.   Burn yourself out, campfire,
Turn into embers and die.
Drift from the logs, blue smoke—
Over the bushes float high.

Climb to the frozen treetops,
Curl away into the sky.

ALL THE MONTHS.   Burn yourself out, campfire,
Turn into embers and die.

APRIL.   The young moon is waning,
The stars fade one by one,
And from the gates of morning
Marches the flaming sun,
Leading in a new day.
Lo, the new year has begun!

ALL THE MONTHS.   Burn yourself out, campfire,
Turn into embers and die.

CURTAIN